From Citizens to Subjects

Pitt Series in Russian and East European Studies

Jonathan Harris, Editor

From Citizens to Subjects

CITY, STATE, & THE ENLIGHTENMENT IN POLAND, UKRAINE, AND BELARUS

Curtis G. Murphy

University of Pittsburgh Press

Published by the University of Pittsburgh Press, Pittsburgh, Pa., 15260

Manufactured in the United States of America
Printed on acid-free paper
10 9 8 7 6 5 4 3 2 1

Cataloging-in-Publication data is available from the Library of Congress

ISBN 13: 978-0-8229-6462-9

Cover art: Bernardo Bellotto (Canaletto), *Krasiński Square with the Palace of the Republic*, 1778
Cover design: Alex Wolfe

For Amanda, with love and gratitude

Contents

MAP 1. THE POLISH-LITHUANIAN COMMONWEALTH IN 1772

MAP 2. POST-PARTITION POLAND-LITHUANIA IN 1800

MAP 3. POLAND-LITHUANIA AFTER THE CONGRESS OF VIENNA IN 1815

Preface

LONG AGO, IN A high school European history class in rural Tennessee, I learned that there was once a country called Poland where, because of an inconvenient voting system known as the liberum veto, nothing could be accomplished. For this reason, the states neighboring this misguided land decided to divide the territory among themselves. We never heard about this country or its people again until the subject turned to the Second World War and the Holocaust. Later, in graduate school, I discovered that this "Poland" was in fact the Polish-Lithuanian Commonwealth, a complex, multi-ethnic, and confessionally pluralistic polity whose peoples came under the rule of empires professing to embody progress and civilization. I came to appreciate that the broad self-governing traditions and multi-religious coexistence of the Commonwealth had much more in common with contemporary liberal-democratic rhetoric in the United States and the European Union than did the rationalistic and colonial policies of the empires that subsequently carved up this country. The fact that most Anglophone historians, even experts on what was once called Eastern Europe, have labeled the former backward and the latter progressive seemed a great injustice as well as a lost opportunity to understand the whole picture of central and eastern Europe. Inspired by this conviction, I decided more than ten years ago to devote my graduate study to this region and to undertake the present project.

Since these initial impressions, I have become aware that many people have indeed written about the Commonwealth in English, though often indirectly in the realm of Jewish or Ukrainian studies. Moreover, a great deal of new work on the Commonwealth and its peoples has appeared in the last decade, some written by people who have become my friends and colleagues in the field; and congresses specifically devoted to Poland-Lithuania now take place with some regularity, attracting scholars not only from Poland, Ukraine, Lithuania, Belarus, and Russia but also from Britain, Germany, the United States, and Japan. The collapse of Communism and the expansion of the European Union have offered new opportunities to reexamine nineteenth- and twentieth-century narratives about progress and backwardness in Polish, Ukrainian, and Lithuanian historiography and have provided new perspectives to a generation of Anglophone historians for whom the division of Europe into western and eastern halves no longer forms the most salient fact of political geography.

Despite these promising developments, the territories of the former Commonwealth, like east central Europe as a whole, remain subject to orientalizing (and even auto-orientalizing) tropes and uninformed dismissals, particularly at the level of popular discourse. The tendency to conflate modern nation-states with premodern, multi-ethnic societies continues to fuel discussions about Poland's history of anarchy and feudal oppression and to encourage Poles to claim the Commonwealth's legacy of tolerance and participatory government as their own. At the same time, commentators unaware of premodern history frequently cite the region's "lack of democratic traditions" to explain contemporary political events. It is my conviction that European history in general requires a greater understanding of the territories of the former Commonwealth, not simply to correct erroneous stereotypes (often produced by imperial powers to justify their conquests) but also to reintroduce lapsed visions of liberty, self-government, and the political good. Once the rationalized unitary nation-state emerged as the only conceivable political model, alternative views of social and political organization fell into obscurity. Nineteenth-century historians developed narratives in praise of the "state-builders," wherein those monarchs like Louis XIV and Frederick the Great, who squeezed their populations in order to build palaces and wage more lethal wars, became agents of a progress, and this progress appeared to have arrived without any opportunity cost. Meanwhile, those peoples who checked regal ambitions (with the exception of the English) appeared backward and shortsighted. By overvaluing the rhetoric and perspective of the future great powers, whose dominance of Europe in prior periods was hardly foreordained, historians have omitted visions that are key to the larger picture of political change in Europe, and these neglected views may well serve as fruitful resources for contemporary political discussions. I hope that the present book may serve as a modest contribution to a larger corrective, which the history of east central Europe urgently requires.

This book would never have been conceived, must less written, without the advice, support, and constructive criticism of my dissertation advisor, Andrzej S. Kamiński, who first opened my eyes—with the help of certain voices from the past, including Jan Pasek and Bazyli Rudomicz—to the fascinating and multinational world of the former Polish-Lithuanian Commonwealth and its many peoples. As any one of his former students would attest, Andrzej has been an extraordinary advisor and friend, supportive but (like a good guild master) unwilling to accept any trace of intellectual laziness or shoddy craftsmanship. He has been an untiring advocate for this project since its inception in 2007, the result of casual conversation over excellent wine about citizenship and the Enlightenment. Although the book has taken its own twists and turns along the way, Andrzej has never ceased to render advice, support, and criticism even after I completed my dissertation and began to pursue my career. What follows are my own ideas, as developed through an encounter with the sources and the relevant literatures, as well as conversations with many specialists in the field, but if someone should observe that I am a product of the "Kamiński School," then I will consider this label a compliment of the highest order.

The research for this project took over two years, and led me to archives in Warsaw, Lublin, Kraków, and Kyiv, and I relied on several generous grants for support. The Fulbright-Hays Doctoral Dissertation Research Abroad Fellowship provided funds for a year of research in

Poland and Ukraine, while Łazarski University, which was then the home of the Institute for Civic Space and Public Policy, funded eight months of research in Warsaw. I also received funding from the Georgetown History Department, where I obtained my PhD, in the form of travel grants to conduct research and non-service fellowships for completing the writing of the initial dissertation. In 2015, the Polish History Museum provided funds for a summer research trip to Warsaw in order to collect materials that I had been unable to obtain for my dissertation. Finally, a Social Policy Grant from Nazarbayev University in Astana, Kazakhstan, my new academic home, has enabled me to cover part of the costs involved in the production of this book.

While conducting research in Poland and Ukraine, I relied on the assistance of a number of specialists from the region. I want to thank in particular Wojciech Fałkowski in Warsaw, Ryszard Szczygieł in Lublin, and Natalia Białouś in Kyiv for their time and advice, as well as the archivists of the Main Archive of Historical Records in Warsaw, the Central State Archives in Lublin, the Central State Historical Archives in Kyiv, and the Czartoryski Library in Kraków. I must also admit my debt of gratitude to Krzysztof Kossarzecki, my teacher of old Polish paleography, who helped me unlock many an obscure document. During the writing process I benefited from the enormously helpful advice of experts involved in the 2012 "Recovering Forgotten History" conference in Warsaw, sponsored by the Foundation for Civic Space and Public Policy. This yearly conference brings textbook and monograph authors to Warsaw for the purpose of broadening the inclusion of east central Europe in US and European history pedagogy beyond references to uprisings, the Holocaust, and anti-Semitism. I would like to thank the sponsors of the conference for supporting my trip to Warsaw, and I particularly wish to thank Marcin Wodziński and Krzysztof Łazarski for their comprehensive criticisms of my dissertation, which helped me produce this book.

At various times, many scholars read drafts or provided comments on parts of this work, and I wish in particular to thank Eugene Avrutin, Rachel Ball, Richard Butterwick, James Collins, John Corcoran, Catherine Evtuhov, David Frick, Karin Friedrich, Robert I. Frost, Gerald Mara, Cathleen McKenna, Stefan Rohdewald, Daniel Scarborough, Barbara Skinner, Theodore Weeks, and Jakub Wysmułek as well as the anonymous readers for their advice, which has helped me refine my argument and broaden the scope of this project. I also want to thank Peter Kracht at the University of Pittsburgh Press for his enthusiastic support of this book and advice along the way, as well as Bill Nelson for producing the maps. I also would like to mention the copyeditor at the University of Pittsburgh Press, Pippa Letsky, who in more ways than one has saved me (and this manuscript) from my own follies. Naturally, all mistakes and omissions are the result of my own negligence and should not reflect on any of the individuals listed above.

I also received support in other ways while writing this book. I want to thank my friends and colleagues Matteo Piccin and Maria Magdalena Przeciszewska, who have provided generous hospitality and succor ever since our first meeting in Warsaw's Main Archive of Historic Acts. Siobhan Doucette, Christopher Lash, Justyna Król, Barbara Pendzich, and especially Eulia Łazarska have provided help and support over the years in connection with all aspects of life and research in Poland. I would like to thank my parents, Charles and Kathie, and my in-laws, Albert and Mary Jo, who on numerous occasions and in diverse ways over the last ten years have made the research and writing of this book possible. Finally and most importantly, I would like to thank my wife, Amanda, who has supported this project in uncountable ways through love, copyediting of multiple drafts, and critical discussion, not to mention her willingness to live in Poland for several long stretches and to support our family while I completed the first draft of this manuscript. She, perhaps to her eternal regret, first suggested that I should learn Polish, and the fulfillment of this precondition allowed me the possibility of conceiving the project that now stands before you. I hope that the result will in some modest way repay her for the labor and trust that she provided during the long road that led to this book's completion.

A Note on Terms and Place Names

WHERE APPROPRIATE ENGLISH EQUIVALENTS exist, I have translated the names of the various offices and institutions encountered in this book. Thus, I use "palatinate" for *województwa* in the pre-partition period; "palatine" for *wojewoda*; "castle court" for *sąd gródzki* and "district" for the Polish *powiat* or Russian *uezd*. I use the term "province" as an equivalent for all nineteenth-century administrative divisions in both Russia and Poland, though I also make use of the Russian term *guberniia* when discussing matters of administration. In many cases, though, no English term fully captures the meaning of the Polish or Russian term, and I resort to the original language. Thus, for example, I use *starosta* (a castle steward with judicial and executive powers), and I employ the sometimes encountered Anglicism "starosty" to refer to the office of starosta (*starostwo*) with its concomitant responsibilities and benefits. Terms encountered for the first time will be rendered in italics.

As a result of the numerous border realignments that have defined the territories of the former Polish-Lithuanian Commonwealth, place names present a particular difficulty for the historian who does not wish to favor any particular nationality. In this work, I follow the practice of employing the version of the town's name recorded in the contemporary historical documents, meaning a preference largely for the Polish or German usage until Chapter 6, where the Russian form is generally employed. I make an exception only for cities with standard English equivalents such as Warsaw and Moscow. The Introduction and Conclusion employ contemporary names, while the footnotes indicate the name employed in the archive. Those towns referenced in this work, the names of which have varied over time, are listed in table 1 below.

TABLE 1. TOWN DESIGNATIONS EMPLOYED IN THIS BOOK

Eighteenth-Century Name	Nineteenth-Century Name	Present Name
Gdańsk/Danzig	Danzig	Gdańsk
Kamieniec-Podolski	Kamenets-Podol'skii	Kam'ianets-Podils'kyi
Kijów (palatinate)	Kiev	Kyiv
Krzemieniec	Kremenets	Kremenets'
Łuck	Lutsk	Luts'k
Lwów/Lemberg	Lemberg	L'viv
Mohyłów	Mogilev (Podol'skii)	Mohyliv-Podils'kyi
Nieśwież	Nesvizh	Niasvizh
Nowogródek	Novogrudok	Navahrudak
Ołyka	Olyka	Olyka
Poznań	Poznań /Posen	Poznań
Toruń/Thorn	Thorn	Toruń
Słuck	Slutsk	Slutsk
Wilno	Vil'na	Vilnius
Włodzimierz	Vladimir (Volynskii)	Volodymyr-Volyns'kyi
Zasław	Zaslavl'	Iziaslav
Żytomierz	Zhitomir	Zhytomyr

Common Abbreviations

AGAD	Archiwum Główne Akt Dawnych w Warszawie (The Main Archive of Historical Records in Warsaw)
AKP	Archiwum Królestwa Polskiego (AGAD)
AML	Akta miasta Lublina (Records of the town of Lublin after 1809 [APL])
AOZ	Akta Ordynacji Zamoyskiej (Records of the Zamoyski Entail [APL])
APL	Archiwum Państwowe w Lublinie (The State Archive in Lublin)
AR	Archiwum Radziwiłłów (The Radziwiłł family archive [AGAD])
ASK	Archiwum Skarbu Koronnego (The Crown Treasury archive [AGAD])
AZ	Archiwum Zamoyskich (The Zamoyski family archive [AGAD])
BC	Biblioteka Książąt Czartoryskich (The Library of the Czartoryski princely family, in Kraków)
DPKP	*Dziennik Praw Królestwa Polskiego* (The Legal Journal of the Kingdom of Poland, after 1815)

DPKW *Dziennik Praw Księstwa Warszawskiego* (The Legal Journal of the Duchy of Warsaw, 1807–1815)

KBO Księgi Komisji Boni Ordinis w Lublinie (Papers of the Good Order Commission in Lublin [APL])

KCW Księgi Komisji Cywilno-Wojskowych (Papers of the Civil-Military Commissions [APL])

KML Księgi miejskie Lublina (Records of the town of Lublin before 1809 [APL])

KRSW Komisja Rządowa Spraw Wewnętrznych (The Governing Commission of Internal Affairs, the authority in charge of towns from 1815 to 1867 [AGAD])

MDSC *Materiały do dziejów Sejmu Czteroletniego* (Documents on the History of the Four-Year Parliament)

ML Tak zwana Metryka Litewska (The So-Called Lithuanian Metrica [AGAD])

PC Permanent Council

PSZRI *Polnoe sobranie zakonov Rossiiskoi Imperii* (The Complete Collection of the Laws of the Russian Empire)

SGKP *Słownik geograficzny Królestwa Polskiego i innych krajów słowiańskich* (The Geographical Dictionary of the Kingdom of Poland and Other Slavic Countries)

TsDIAK Tsentral'nyi Derzhavnyi Istorychnyi Arkhiv Ukrainy m. Kyiv (The Central State Historical Archive in Kyiv, Ukraine)

VL *Volumina legum: Przedruk zbioru praw staraniem XX. Pijarów w Warszawie od roku 1732 do roku 1793, wydanego* (The Laws of the Polish-Lithuanian Commonwealth, published by the Piarist Order in Warsaw from 1732 to 1793)

From Citizens to Subjects

Introduction

Progress or Backwardness?

ENLIGHTENED CENTRALISM VERSUS CIVIC REPUBLICANISM IN THE FORMER POLISH-LITHUANIAN COMMONWEALTH

ON 27 MARCH 1971 Władysław Gomułka, former first secretary of the Polish People's Republic, fired off a lengthy letter to the Communist Central Committee, justifying the role of his government in the December 1970 strikes that preceded his dismissal. Gomułka argued that the violent protests of the Gdańsk shipyard workers, the prequel to the later Solidarity Movement, did not represent a response to rising prices, as the party subsequently determined, but flowed from "the worst historical traditions, deeply rooted in our society, and in the strong tendencies toward . . . unbridled anarchism, wild capriciousness, contempt for law and legality, [and] abandonment of any kind of accountability for our own country." He reminded the new party leadership, headed by Edward Gierek, that "the old, oligarchic Commonwealth lost its independence, ceased to exist, and was divided by neighboring countries due to the anarchy of the ruling Polish nobility," which "failed to keep up in development and fell behind, becoming weaker and weaker vis-à-vis its neighbors." In addition to his demands that the current leadership reverse course and return to his economic policies, Gomułka recommended that the Communist Party refocus its efforts on teaching history, asserting that, "if the young Baltic workers were taught the history of the partitions of Poland, they would not have set out on those December days down the road to anarchy; they would have understood where that road leads."[1]

Gomułka's history lesson may have served here to justify post-Stalinist repression, but the basic analysis reflected long-standing and broadly shared conventional wisdom about the Polish-Lithuanian Commonwealth, which was dismantled and ultimately abolished as a result of the partitions of 1772, 1793, and 1795. Even in the last decades of its existence, the Commonwealth served as a model of anarchic disorder and feudal underdevelopment for Enlightenment Europe, a cautionary tale about institutions and practices to eschew at all costs. In contrast to the centralized and bureaucratic states that dominated eighteenth-century European politics, the Commonwealth remained saddled with an "inconsistent, incoherent constitution," which inspired, in the words of John Lind, "a spirit of unsocial selfishness." Montesquieu and Voltaire found common ground in criticizing the Commonwealth for its poor institutional arrangements. For Voltaire, in particular, the Commonwealth embodied the backwardness and fanaticism of earlier epochs, and his epistles sharply contrasted the "anarchy" of the Poles during the Confederacy of Bar (1768–1772) with the beneficent and enlightened rule of his patron, Catherine the Great (r. 1762–1796).[2] The Commonwealth's German-speaking neighbors were even more contemptuous, coining the term *Polnische Wirtschaft* (Polish economy) as a shorthand for backwardness and describing the inhabitants in the language of eighteenth-century cultural imperialism as "Iroquois." The partitioning powers—Russia, Prussia, and Austria—made ample use of the Commonwealth's reputation as a backward and anarchic state to justify their first incursion into Polish territory in 1772, which the propaganda of the various rulers presented as a favor that would bestow order, security, and rational government upon the newly acquired territories.[3]

After the first partition, the Commonwealth served as a warning to all reformers about the costs of delaying political modernization.[4] The final two partitions, which occurred in response to the Commonwealth's last-ditch attempts at building a more centralized and potent state—a process that culminated in the Constitution of the Third of May 1791—served only to confirm the general consensus that a failure to appreciate the necessity of political modernization had doomed the country. Throughout the nineteenth century, the state historians of the partitioning powers persisted in justifying the continued occupation of the Commonwealth's lands in part with references to the Poles' anarchic nature, inability to govern, and failure to modernize. From this perspective, the destruction of the Commonwealth conferred a kind of progress, which translated into development and opportunity for these benighted regions. Russian elites, outraged by Alexander I's decision to grant a small piece of the former Commonwealth a constitution and civil rights in 1815, applauded Emperor Nicholas I's abrogation of the constitution after the crushing of the November Insurrection in 1830 as proof that Poles were incapable of understanding or maintaining a modern government. Echoes of the view that Russian rule brought progress and stability to the Commonwealth continue to appear in Russian history textbooks to the present day.[5]

Poles of all political orientations took the apparent lessons of the partitions to heart. Gomułka's letter recommended that the history curriculum in Polish educational institutions adopt more texts from the nineteenth-century Kraków School, represented by Michał Bobrzyński and Józef Szujski (conservatives who would likely have been horrified by the association), whose books placed culpability for the partitions squarely on the Commonwealth and its elite.[6] Despite Józef Piłsudski's federalist sensibilities, the model of the Commonwealth played only a negative role in the interwar Second Republic, while the postwar Polish People's Republic, purposefully drew upon negative images of the Commonwealth as a justification for promoting centralized and unitary government. The conviction that decentralization and local control played a role in the Commonwealth's destruction has endured into the post-Communist Third Republic, which has retained a powerful and bureaucratic central government under every ruling coalition. Neither the current Law and Justice Party (*Prawo i Sprawiedliwość* [PiS]) nor the liberal opposition have any sympathy for the Commonwealth's political structure. Opposition daily *Gazeta Wyborcza* routinely makes unflattering comparisons to so-called First Republic, while PiS leader Jarosław Kaczyński has often indicated his preference for centralized and unitary state, a structure in theory supported by Poles across the spectrum of political opinion.[7]

Underpinning this broadly shared negative attitude toward the Commonwealth lies the conviction that the so-called noble republic failed to develop into a modern state along with the other countries of Europe. In the sixteenth century, the Polish-Lithuanian Commonwealth resembled its European neighbors, all of which were characterized by diffused power structures, overlapping personal loyalties, and estate-based self-governments, but in subsequent centuries, as Claude Rulhière observed in his 1782 *History of the Anarchy in Poland*, Poland-Lithuania increasingly diverged from other members of the club: "The Poles admired none of the progress being made in public administration. Everywhere else the military arts were being perfected. . . . The collection and administration of taxation came to be regarded as an exact science, and skill in trade became a source of power. The Poles alone conserved all the old ways."[8] The concept of the state as a permanent institution standing above society only entered European thought at the end of the sixteenth century, and for most of the seventeenth century arguments for constructing a state rested primarily on claims about military contingency and the necessity of collecting taxes. In the eighteenth century, though, state-building merged with Enlightenment criticism of received tradition and irrationality to produce enlightened centralism, a new governing philosophy that aspired to introduce rationalization, professionalization, and standardization over the pluralistic and unwieldy array of local powers that still predominated in the European countryside. Enlightened officials viewed the state not only as a structure providing defense and justice but as an agent of reason, which would improve the well-being and productivity of their country's subjects. To this end, the state now aimed to acquire control over public health, sanitation, and urban planning as well as the finances of local governments.[9]

The chartered cities became particular objects of centralizing reforms as developments in science and technology brought issues of public health, sanitation, and urban planning to the attention of rulers. Further, as James Collins has emphasized, eighteenth-century centralism coincided with a "municipal revolution" in which cities received illumination, broad boulevards, as well as fire-fighting and waste-disposal infrastructure, reflecting the demands of an increasingly commercial and consumption-based society. City elites were not always willing to support these priorities without prodding from the central government.[10] In addition to cleaning the streets and preventing disease, government officials endeavored to direct the energies and resources of their populations toward greater economic productivity and entrepreneurship. Taking note of the economic and social transformations in The Netherlands, England, and parts of France, which Jan de Vries has dubbed "The Industrious Revolution," monarchs in central Europe, encouraged by the "Cameralist sciences," sought to promote entrepreneurial and labor-intensive behavior through police regulations and other policies of the "well-ordered police state." German Cameralism proposed that society should be ordered like a machine, in which each part played a role useful to the whole. Achieving this clockwork precision and implementing the numerous new regulations and policies of enlightened government required professionally trained administrators and civil servants who could advance the singular vision of the legislator over the competing and contradictory private interests of locally chosen magistrates. In propounding their arguments, rulers and their supporters drew upon legitimate grievances with the oligarchic and venal character of local elites, as well as the inconveniences of feudal inequality, the same resentments that propelled French Revolutionaries to dismantle the ancien régime.[11]

After the French Revolution, the centralized unitary state administered by appointed, trained experts became the only conceivable political model, while the subordination of formerly autonomous or semiautonomous cities into the hierarchical powers structure could be represented as progress and one of the presumed prerequisites for the modern state. Even in the late eighteenth century, thinkers such as Adam Smith had struggled to comprehend how the inefficiencies and divided sovereignties of medieval Europe could have been allowed to develop. In *The Wealth of Nations,* Smith concluded that only the weakness of medieval kings and their need for allies against the feudal lords had generated the conditions that enabled medieval plurality. Hegel saw the post-Napoleonic triumph of the unitary state as the essential condition for the full realization of human individuality. The feudal monarchies of the pre-Revolutionary period, he argued, lacked the prerequisite unity, "since functions were vested in particular corporations and communities and offices belonged to persons."[12] Several decades later, Max Weber also embraced the explanation of independent autonomous cities as a historical aberration that arose because of the weakness and backwardness of medieval rulers. Once rulers possessed a corpus of educated and informed administrators, he posited, urban autonomy became unnecessary. Liberals saw the destruction of the urban autonomy as a victory for liberty, since the collective ties woven by oligarchic elites, Jewish community leaders, and particularistic authorities imposed formal and informal restraints on individual autonomy. Even Otto Gierke, who celebrated the medieval commune, nonetheless argued that mass democracy had no connection with feudal liberties.[13] Further, the economic boom and rapid industrialization of the nineteenth century lent weight to Adam Smith's argument that unleashing the individual from guild restrictions, particularistic tolls, and price controls of medieval cities had benefited society as a whole.

This progressive view of history—the conviction that enlightened centralism and the eventual triumph of the unitary state were essential and necessary stepping stones on the road to the modern world—has remained an implicit assumption in conceptualizing Enlightenment Europe since the eighteenth century. Marc Raeff's *Well-Ordered Police State* offers a classic example of a historian presenting administrative and political change as necessary for economic and social progress, a conviction echoed in the many sympathetic portraits of Joseph II and Frederick the Great as progressive reformers.[14] For example, C. B. A. Behrens, Brian Downing, and Christopher Clark have praised Frederick the Great's assault on local privileges as good statesmanship, while concurrently criticizing those countries (Poland-Lithuania, in particular) that retained their complex system of localized privileges intact.[15] Martin van Creveld's synthesis of European state-building, now in its tenth edition, contains numerous cues to suggest that readers should sympathize with the monarchs battling to overcome the nobility, the clergy, and the feudal restrictions of the Holy Roman Empire. Economist S. R. Epstein has reaffirmed that industrialization required as a prerequisite the rise of the unitary state with the power to abolish particularistic privileges and complex webs of jurisdiction. According to this tradition, the costs of diminished city and local autonomy were more than repaid in the prosperity and development that ensued. More recently, Robert von Friedeburg has claimed that the rise of the state as a territorially defined "bearer of public order" based on law allowed the German states to integrate the claims of the Enlightenment and take the lead in areas such as infrastructure, old age pensions, and social security.[16] For both nineteenth-century and present-day adherents of the progressive tradition, then, the transition from the "anarchy" of the older, estate-based and pluralistic government to a unitary administration appears to represent a natural corollary to the progress of reason from the depths of medieval superstition and credulity, and countries that failed to make this transition—like the Commonwealth—were deservedly swept into the dustbin of history.

This transition, though, did not occur peacefully; the construction of an enlightened, centralized state demanded often violent confrontations between agents of the state and the privileged and self-governing corporate groups, local parliaments, and chartered towns that had enjoyed extensive political, judicial, and fiscal powers since the Middle Ages. Beginning in the seventeenth century, monarchs as diverse as Louis XIV, Charles II of England, and Frederick William of Prussia sought to wrest control over the appointments, responsibilities, and tax-collecting powers of local officials. While jurists and officials produced papers and memoranda that augmented the scope and purview of the central government, monarchs employed bribery, repression, and extortion to subordinate privileged elites and estates, facing down resistance and occasional revolts in the process.[17] The chartered towns and cities of Europe became major targets of these reform efforts because urban autonomy, particularistic privileges, and political prerogatives bordering on sovereignty most interfered with the central government's plans to rationalize and simplify government, as well as to promote uniformity in jurisprudence, law, and tax collection.[18]

In royalist propaganda and in the treatment of many sympathetic historians, those institutions and corporations that attempted to block or arrest the transition to the modern state frequently appear as backward, shortsighted, or wrongheaded. François Guizot, who provided perhaps the most unequivocal embodiment of this progressive interpretation of history in his *History of European Civilization*, summarized the conflict thus:

> There is something profoundly melancholy in viewing the loss of these ancient European liberties. . . . The patriots fought with passion and bemoaned with despair this revolution, which . . . they had a right to call

> despotism. . . . One can admire their courage and sympathize with their grief, but, at the same time, we have to understand that this was not only inevitable, but useful. The primitive system of Europe, the ancient feudal and municipal liberties had failed in the organization of society. . . . They could not produce either security or progress for society.[19]

Since citizens of the Commonwealth had more successfully defended their ancient feudal liberties than had others, progress demanded that the constitution of the country be dismantled from without. Indeed, as minister to King Louis-Philippe, Guizot vocally opposed French support for the Poles during the November Insurrection against Russia.[20] The view that the defenders of feudalism had to be supplanted continues to find favor among many historians of the Enlightenment. H. M. Scott, for example, in praising Joseph II's attempt to rationalize the Austrian monarchy even refers to the rights of the Hungarian estates to consent to taxation as a "ramshackle system of government." Echoing Weber's assertion about medieval communes, Friedeburg argues that the older associations of towns, knights, and princes never provided an alternative model of government to princely rule.[21]

This narrative of progress ignores the fact that city citizens and town residents possessed their own alternate conception of politics, which differed markedly in its assumptions, goals, and practices from the vision of enlightened centralism. Burghers and other urban groupings in the Commonwealth participated in a political culture informed by the ideas of civic republicanism, referred to by Quentin Skinner as the "neo-Roman theory of free states." Although characterized by a significant evolution over time, civic republicanism refers generally to a demand for self-government by the citizens of a city untouched by outside interference and dependent on the virtue of individual citizens to seek the common good.[22] As such, civic republicanism was both individualistic and collectivist, idealizing collective action and grounded in the corporate structures that characterized life in early modern Europe. Such collective action could only come about, though, because of the privileges that individuals enjoyed. Civic republicanism idealized Isaiah Berlin's "positive liberty," that is, the freedom to participate in government over the absence of coercion, and citizens presumed such freedom to derive from a specific constitutional arrangement rather than any notion of human rights. In the cities of the Commonwealth, civic republicanism depended less on the studied reading of classical authorities than the daily practice of politics in the sense described by Maurizio Viroli and Hannah Arendt.[23] It should be emphasized that civic republicanism presented an ideal (or a series of ideals) based on certain assumptions about human nature, but as an ideal and a worldview this conception presented city citizens with vocabularies, conceptual references, and predispositions that differed dramatically from those favored by enlightened reformers and statesmen.

The confrontation between enlightened officials and city elites pitted two contradictory and mutually incomprehensible political ideals against one another, but neither represented a neutral, dispassionate interpretation of reality. As Reinhart Koselleck argues, enlightened thinkers developed a progressive view of history for their own political ends, and their perspective emerged as the dominant discourse following the French Revolution. In other words, the most common interpretation of the eighteenth-century victory of enlightened statesmen was itself a polemical device used to undermine the position of city republicans no less than that of absolutist rulers.[24] In order to appreciate the motivations of local elites on their own terms, we must not judge them in terms of others' priorities. Instead we should follow Pierre Bourdieu and seek the habitus of city residents; that is we must endeavor to discover how seemingly irrational and backward reactions to well-intentioned policies flowed from a practical logic and a concrete awareness of a given community's interests and needs.[25] For example, enlightened thinkers emphasized material benefits and concrete objectives, and bureaucrats reacted with surprise and condescension when citizens united to prevent the paving of roads, the installation of sewer pipes, and the institution of measures designed to prolong life and improve health. Civic republicans, though, understood politics as persuasion and coequal decision-making. As Hannah Arendt affirms, the outcome of a given decision mattered far less than the ability of citizens to decide matters for themselves and preserve a constitution that guaranteed freedom.[26]

The residents of northern European cities may not have all read Machiavelli or Harrington, but this did not prevent city citizens from acting in accordance with civic republican assumptions or using a civic republican vocabulary. Heinz Schilling has argued that German cities demonstrated an implicit civic republican theory, shown in legal actions and pronouncements, and I propose that the same philosophy was present in the cities of Poland-Lithuania through the end of the eighteenth century. As Andrzej S. Kamiński has argued, the Commonwealth was a "civic space," where the well-known republicanism of the nobility influenced the behaviors and ideas of other, less politically enfranchised estates, including both the Christian burghers and the legally separate Jewish communities.[27] Proceeding from this framework, in this book I examine the clash of the two values systems—enlightened centralism and civic republicanism—in the Polish-Lithuanian Commonwealth from the eighteenth century to the late nineteenth century, by which point civic republicanism had been extinguished and the citizens of cities had become the subjects of centralized states. The Commonwealth was home to hundreds of towns with extensive privileges and rights, the majority of which—the private towns—were the property of individual nobles. Most cities in the Commonwealth were small and economically insignificant on the European scale; in the eighteenth century many burghers practiced agriculture, while much trade and handicraft production was the preserve of the disenfranchised Jewish population, which often rivaled the burghers in size and clout.[28] Nonetheless, even the smallest cities maintained an intricate web of privileges and rights based on the foundational German charter of Magdeburg Law, the defense of which continually reinforced the assumptions and mentalities expressed in republican literature.

Enlightened centralism came to the Commonwealth during the last decades of its existence, embraced by King Stanisław August Poniatowski (r. 1764–1796) and his coterie of Russian-backed reformers. The partitions only accelerated the process over the next century and under various regimes. Stanisław August and his allies sought to improve, stimulate, and revitalize the towns under his jurisdiction in accordance with the Enlightenment-era faith in the efficacy of centralizing and rationalizing policies.[29] Russian oversight narrowed the scope of the king's reform plans, and the royally controlled cities offered a space for experiments in enlightened government unlikely to provoke opposition from the ruling nobility. In addition, Polish cities were widely considered stagnant and underdeveloped, in need of revitalization and stimulus. Several laws passed in the first decades of the Commonwealth sought to transfer decision-making and economic power from city elites to Warsaw. The Constitution of the Third of May in 1791 culminated the process by offering greater civil rights to burghers while placing city governments under the control of new state agencies.[30] After the partitions, each of the absolutist powers pursued its own centralizing and rationalizing agendas in the territory, the most radical implemented by agents of Napoleon, who re-created a tiny Polish state in 1807, the Duchy of Warsaw, modeled on the structure of the French Empire. Polish officials in the Duchy attempted to tie all cities into a hierarchical system of supervision and control, including those that belonged to individual nobles, and Napoleon's system endured in its successor state, the Congress Kingdom of Poland, established by Tsar Alexander I in 1815.[31]

Including the Duchy as a separate entity, four different blueprints of centralization attempted to modernize and revitalize the cities of the former Commonwealth after the partitions brought an end to Stanisław August's own efforts. The study focuses specifically on the fate of those territories, which were transferred either to the Duchy (with a brief interlude in Austria) or the Russian Empire, respectively representing one of the most energetic and one of the most languid versions of enlightened centralization, though comparisons to the Prussian and Austrian partitions will also be made. Rulers in all four states promised rational, efficient government, improvements to urban space, economic development, and even changes in human behavior, but if one examines the concrete achievements of Enlightenment government in the lands of the former Polish-Lithuanian Commonwealth into the late nineteenth century, modernization and progress do not appear to enter the picture. Instead, we find that policies designed to bring order and simplicity provoked chaos and discord, in many cases adding additional layers of complexity and confusion. Rosters of salaried municipal officials as well as government-issued regulations multiplied, but old behaviors stubbornly persisted; the most prominent objects of government attention—the privately owned towns—stagnated and declined. Moreover, in straightening out the inefficiencies, overlapping jurisdictions, and disorderly chains of responsibility that characterized life for many citizens in the Polish-Lithuanian Commonwealth, enlightened centralism cordoned off the "civic space," which had encouraged many citizens to participate in self-government and attempt to influence their surroundings. In effect, I propose that Enlightenment government destroyed the remnants of medieval, positive liberty without offering much in compensation except for affirmations that this process constituted progress.[32]

Few readers in the English-speaking world are familiar with the Polish-Lithuanian Commonwealth except as an example of a country that failed to modernize. The story of centralizing and rationalizing reform in this part of east central Europe, however, suggests that the Commonwealth can yield an entirely different set of lessons to students of the Enlightenment and post-Enlightenment Europe. The reform experience in Poland-Lithuania argues against associating centralization and rationalization with progress and modernity and against inferring inevitability to the particular path of state-building upon which European rulers embarked. Fashionable ideas, unfounded assumptions, and unempirical convictions reflecting particular interests often played a decisive role in the plans and decrees of the enlightened absolutists, the French Revolutionaries, and the reformers surrounding Stanisław August and his successors. Like elites in developing countries seeking to "catch up," reformers in the Commonwealth consciously imported the models of centralization, rationalization, and universalization from the practices and theories of neighboring states with the aim of engineering modernization and economic growth in the face of external pressure. In the nineteenth century, policies of enlightened centralism represented a kind of colonial development that sought to improve the territory in question with policies modeled on the heartland. In each situation, the abstract models, including a priori assumptions about what a city should be, and the rational designs of legislators encountered unexpected resistance and failed to realize expectations, even after the benchmarks of a modern state—centralization, hierarchy, and repressive capacity—had already been achieved.

Historians have long accepted that many projects of Enlightenment-era rulers failed to achieve success, and even policies that eventually prevailed had to be scaled back or quietly abandoned upon first attempt. Neither Louis XV's battle with the guilds nor Catherine the Great's attempt to decree vibrant municipal societies from above achieved the effect intended.[33] In the last decade, though, an emerging historiography has begun to challenge not only the outcomes of enlightened projects but also the underlying assumptions and potential of the ideas themselves. Andre Wakefield's *Disordered Police State* argues that Cameralism, rather than contributing to modernization, served primarily as propaganda to disguise disorder, mismanagement, and irrationality behind a pretense of scientific government. Wakefield's study suggests that the depiction of Cameralism—a branch of enlightened centralism—as a stepping-stone to progress and modernity actually reflects an image consciously manufactured by eighteenth-century propagandists. In fact, as Iryna Vushko's *The Politics of Cultural Retreat* illustrates, enlightened plans such as the Habsburgs' intention to reorder Galicia into a model province while reforming both Polish and Jewish society failed precisely because of the internal contradictions of the absolutist-bureaucratic system. Hans-Jürgen Bömelburg's study of the Prussian partition, which formed the basis of a comparative piece on the colonial policies of the three partitioning powers from 1772 to 1795, correspondingly demonstrates how the administrative assumptions of the enlightened officials, rather than the backwardness of the locals, undermined each state's proclaimed policies of bestowing economic and material improvement on the new acquisitions. Glen Dynner's examination of alcohol regulations in nineteenth-century Poland further suggests that decades of social-engineering programs, in this case attempting to direct Jews away from the alcohol trade, failed to achieve any significant results.[34]

In the spirit of this emerging tradition I argue that, once untangled from the rhetoric of progress, modernity, and Enlightenment, the results of eighteenth- and nineteenth-century centralization in the cities of Poland-Lithuania achieved little beyond the transfer of political power and governmental control from several overlapping loci to one. There is no inherent reason to decorate this process with accolades of progress and modernity, nor to preclude the possibility of imagining alternative paths of development. A revaluation of enlightened centralism in the Commonwealth is particularly necessary, because since the partitions Poles have been perhaps the most ardent apostles of the progressive view of history that equates centralization with modernity. In 1790, the publicist of burgher origin Stanisław Staszic predicted that the future lay with absolutist monarchies, observing that the Commonwealth's neighbors more effectively encouraged their populations toward productive labor. After the partitions, many writers embraced the connection of centralization with progress and of local autonomy with backwardness.[35] Hugo Kołłątaj, a coauthor of the Constitution of the Third of May, welcomed Napoleon's creation of the tightly centralized and bureaucratic Duchy of Warsaw, which in his view eliminated the "spirit of provincialism" and "self-interest" of the old Commonwealth. Kołłątaj wrote approvingly of Napoleon's constitution, which introduced legal equality, uniformity, and centralized hierarchical control, as having surpassed the more democratic Constitution of the Third of May: "The Constitution of the Third of May was a great good, which we were able to achieve in that period when for the first time we dared to emancipate ourselves from eternal anarchy, but it cannot be compared with that, which the Great Napoleon has bestowed upon us."[36] Kołłątaj's contemporary Kajetan Koźmian, a memorialist who served in the government of Tsar Alexander's Congress Kingdom of Poland, even mused that Napoleon's strictly hierarchical and antidemocratic constitution better suited the Polish character and provided more effective checks against "our anarchic tendencies, our garrulousness, and our addiction to fractious quarreling with the government" than Alexander I's more liberal charter of 1815.[37]

For generations of Polish historians, these positions have become self-evident. Joachim Lelewel, the Polish Romantic historian who found much to praise in the values of community rule (*gminowładztwo*) in the old Commonwealth, remained a singular voice. More typically, the interwar successors to the Kraków School, such as Stanisław Kutrzeba and Władysław Konopczyński, reaffirmed the assessment of the Commonwealth's weakness as a mistake justly punished, with Konopczyński negatively contrasting Poland's decentralization to the effective taming of local institutions in other European countries.[38] Even the more optimistic "Warsaw School"—personified by Tadeusz Korzon, Władysław Smoleński, and in the twentieth century Józef Andrzej Gierowski—argued that the reforms of the Four-Year Parliament and the Constitution of the Third of May represented a rebirth in decline, which saved Polish culture from extinction under the partitioning powers. In other words the necessity of centralization, or its equation with modernity, has remained largely unquestioned.[39] Anglophone historians of the Commonwealth have agreed that the primary shortcoming of the country was its failure to develop an administrative capacity similar to that of the partitioning powers. Jerzy Lukowski's *Disorderly Liberty* offers the most recent iteration of this tendency in castigating the political culture of Commonwealth as hopelessly backward and unable to comprehend the necessity of wholesale reform.[40] As a result of this tradition, the term "progressive" has passed into Polish historiography as an analytical category, associated with the construction of modern state institutions and bureaucratic practices, and even Guizot's sympathy for those groups who resisted the state's encroachment on their powers and rights in the name of progress and centralization finds few sympathetic ears.[41]

Consistent with this view, Polish historians often describe the resistance of members of the nobility, burghers, and Jews to the reforms of Stanisław August as crankish, backward, and shortsighted. Voltaire's judgment of the Bar Confederates as "anarchists" and "fanatics," for example, has appeared in numerous accounts of the first partition, which often gloss over the legitimate grievances of the Confederacy.[42] With regard to urban reform, historians such Andrzej Zahorski and Aleksander Czaja attribute the shortcomings and failures of central policies in the Stanislavian era to the backwardness of the country rather than to any deficiency in the reforms themselves.[43] Far less attention has been paid to the perspectives and motivations of urban residents themselves. Writers from Tadeusz Korzon to Krystyna Zienkowska have emphasized the civil rights granted to burghers by the reforms of 1791, neglecting to discuss the accompanying imposition of administrative supervision and central control. Only one, relatively obscure historian of Lublin, Józef Kermisz, observed this connection.[44] Although nationalist sentiments may have permitted a more critical analysis of reforms implemented by Russian, Austrian, and Prussian authorities (Russian historians have, by comparison, evaluated their own country's urban reforms much more critically), the reforms of Napoleon in the Duchy of Warsaw often receive approbation as "progressive" and "modern," despite the disenfranchisement of urban citizens and official abrogation of the Jewish population's civil liberties under Napoleon.[45]

Cities in the Polish-Lithuanian Commonwealth have the reputation of weakness, insignificance, and subservience to the ruling nobility, a judgment summed up in Rousseau's famous statement that "the Polish nation is made up of three orders: the nobles, who count for everything; the middle-class, who count for nothing; and the peasants, who count for less than nothing."[46] Excluded from national politics at the end of the fifteenth century, burghers appear in most treatments as living isolated in their towns, having been sidelined by their more economically effective Jewish rivals and made subservient to the customs and manners of the nobility. In particular, studies of political conceptions and behaviors have typically focused on the ruling nobility (*szlachta*), also known as "the political nation," who dominated the institutions of national and local government, using their powers to monopolize international trade and oppress the towns.[47] Why should we care about the ideas and conceptions of the downtrodden and isolated burghers? Indeed, the *absence* of burghers from the national political stage and the unwillingness of urban residents to challenge the nobility, as representatives of the Third Estate did in France, has served for historians, particularly in the Communist period, as yet another indicator of the country's backwardness.[48] Historians of Polish Jews such as Gershon Hundert have even used the "powerlessness" of the burghers as one explanation for the relative success and prosperity of Jewish communities within the towns. As Hundert notes, in contradistinction to Christian burghers, Jews benefited from national and international networks, as well as countrywide institutions such as the Council of Four Lands.[49]

In fact, the burghers, the Jews, and other residents of both private and royal Polish towns still enjoyed extensive privileges and rights into the eighteenth century while cities in contemporary France and Prussia answered to centrally appointed officials. Centuries of self-government with republican institutions produced a civic republican culture of rights and assumptions about civic space that manifested itself in the everyday language of lawsuits, petitions, and in 1789 the written polemics sponsored by a collective protest movement of townspeople, which brought hundreds of city representatives to lobby the parliament in Warsaw. The rights of burghers and Jewish communities existed more in theory than in practice in the eighteenth century, and town residents faced extensive restrictions on their political activity by nobles, royal officials, and their own magistrates, but the language and assumptions of civic republicanism endured into the nineteenth century. More to the point, historians have often mistaken rhetoric for reality in attributing weakness and oppression to town residents, who adroitly manipulated their legal and political prerogatives to resist external burdens and taxes—in many cases by overstating their inferior position to authorities and adjudicators. The narrative of the oppression of the weak by the strong, a convenient justification for centralization, further overstates the authority and abilities of the so-called oppressors, either royal officials or private town owners, who required cooperation and alliances with local authorities to enact any change. One could argue in fact that the ideal of the medieval urban republic stayed alive much longer in the Commonwealth (as well as in the German states) than in its Italian homeland, and echoes of civic activity persisted in the western borderlands of the Russian Empire until the middle of the nineteenth century.

Attempts to reform the urban landscape of the former Commonwealth have received periodic treatment in Polish historiography, but their implementation at the local level, the responses of the urban residents, and the government's subsequent policy adjustments have largely escaped attention. A focus on the plans and designs of the central government has tended to draw attention away from the fact that the burghers, Jews, and nobles who inhabited the Commonwealth's towns carried their own "unenlightened" political assumptions and preferences, which influenced responses to reform legislation.[50] City citizens were not simply reacting to reforms from ignorance but, rather, articulated concrete preferences based on their a priori expectations about the purpose and goals of politics. Jewish communities acted likewise, despite their formal exclusion from the urban power structure in most cities. Moreover, various central governments modified their regulations and plans in response to actions on the ground, so a genuine understanding of the efficacy of enlightened reform requires an investigation of the dialogue of reform, response, and counterresponse from the era of the Commonwealth and beyond the partitions, when many of the same policies reappeared with increased vigor and scope.

With a few exceptions, the partitions have often been treated as an inviolable threshold in Polish historiography, but the destruction of the Commonwealth offers a unique opportunity to test the consequences of multiple policies on the same subjects, as well as to observe continuities in assumptions and plans across time and place.[51] Following this dialogue of central-to-local negotiation over more than a century of transformation requires a combination of macro policy studies and detailed explorations of individual cases. Legislative acts, minutes and reports of central government bodies, and the statistical information collected by state agents provide the general picture for this book, while micro studies of the municipal records, protests, and petitions of over twenty towns in the period offer an opportunity to examine specific consequences at a local level.[52] Eschewing the capitals in favor of the "typical," small-to-medium sized town (under ten thousand people in the eighteenth century, with most under five thousand), this book is focused principally on royal and private cities from three regions: the Lublin province of contemporary southeastern Poland, which includes the cities of Lublin, Chełm, and Zamość as well as a number of smaller settlements, and the Volhynia and Podolia provinces of contemporary western Ukraine, including cities such as Luts'k (Łuck), Kamianets'-Podils'kyi (Kamieniec Podolski), Kremenets (Krzemieniec), and Dubno. In addition, Niasvizh (Nieśwież) and Slutsk (Słuck), capitals of the extraordinary wealthy and influential Radziwiłł family in present-day Belarus, will also feature prominently.

Examining both royal and private towns creates a useful control group, since private towns remained excluded from most state-led reforms until the nineteenth century. They also serve as the best illustration of the limitations of imagination imposed by the unitary and rationalistic assumptions of absolutist rulers. Private towns were characterized by a combination of public and private property, shared sovereignty, and a web of privileges and commitments that defied all attempts at classification according to the prevailing categories of unitary sovereignty and absolute property rights. The geographic region chosen further offers the possibility of comparing the experience of burghers, Jews, and other town residents across four distinct regimes, excluding only the Prussian partition. The Lublin region fell to Austria in 1795, only to join Napoleon's Duchy of Warsaw in 1809. In 1815 Napoleon's Duchy became Tsar Alexander I's Congress Kingdom of Poland, a state that continued to follow the Napoleonic legal code and bureaucratic model throughout the nineteenth century. The Ukrainian and Belarusian territories, by contrast, fell under direct Russian control between 1793 and 1795, becoming part of the provincial structure of the Russian Empire.

In chapter 1 I illustrate the diverse and pluralistic urban model that persisted in the Commonwealth until 1764, focusing on the many inhabitants of the towns and the historical circumstances that led to Stanisław

August's ascension. As detailed in chapter 2, the reforms of the cities began in earnest after the first partition in 1772, when the Department of Police in the Permanent Council obtained legal authority over urban revenue and finances, and the new regime employed its limited powers to take control over magistracy spending and tax collection. In addition, Good Order Commissions descended on the principal cities and proceeded to rewrite urban constitutions, adjudicate property disputes, and rationalize budgetary procedures. As a result of the inherited assumptions of the Enlightenment, resistance and opposition to these well-meaning and beneficial reforms could only be labeled by reference to such shibboleths as the "legacy of inveterate disorder" and the "ignorance and simplicity of the people." The resistance was, however, significant and the reforms ultimately served as a catalyst for a countrywide burgher-rights movement, the subject of chapter 3.

As recounted in chapter 3, cities were far from unitary institutions but, rather, constellations of estates characterized by overlapping jurisdictions and mutually exclusive privileges. Urban residents of every estate nonetheless acted in accordance with a preexisting civic republican ideology that contravened the basic premises of the burghers' enlightened allies who supported urban reform during the Four-Year Parliament. What appeared to enlightened reformers as a messy, tangled system of incessant conflict and discord in fact concealed a system that continually readjusted the balance of power to prevent any group—burghers, Jewish communities, or noble officials—from completely dominating any city and successfully oppressing the "weak." The same could be said with regard to the relationship of private town owners and their citizens, the subject of chapter 4. Private cities remained largely unaffected by centralizing reforms, and owners continued to offer generous privileges and exemptions so as to encourage settlement. As an investigation of the Zamoyski and Radziwiłł properties reveals, attempts by owners to implement Enlightenment-inspired projects on their properties fared little better than reforms in the royal towns because of a combination of intransigence, inertia, and the impracticability of the measures themselves.

As the second partition overturned the reforms of the Third of May Constitution in the Commonwealth, French revolutionaries were pushing the principles of sovereignty, rationality, and uniformity to their logical conclusion. The abolition of privileges, the reorganization of France into uniform departments, and the centralization of the Jacobin Terror achieved the dreams of monarchs across Europe. Napoleon's code consolidated most of these achievements and the Grande Armée exported unitary, rational government to every corner of Europe, including the territories of the former Commonwealth.[53] As discussed in chapter 5, Napoleon's system tightly controlled the appointment and authority of urban magistrates, and all decisions required written permission from superiors. At the same time, the orderly flow of information, budgets, and reports from the provinces to the capitals masked a fundamentally chaotic reality. Napoleonic officials struggled to subordinate the private towns into the state hierarchy while simultaneously maintaining respect for the private property of the owners as mandated by the Napoleonic Code. The hierarchic system established by Napoleon endured in Alexander I's Congress Kingdom, despite the liberal constitution promulgated by the new ruler. So, too, did the conflicts between state officials, private town owners, and burghers. From the perspective of urban autonomy, the November Insurrection of 1830 and the subsequent revocation of the Polish constitution only served to entrench the system, which puttered along under increased bureaucratic inertia and dysfunction until the Insurrection of 1863 inspired a new reorganization as well as a full-scale Russification campaign.

In western Ukraine and Belarus, as recorded in chapter 6, Russian administrators also struggled to incorporate the private towns into the hierarchical system, but the Russian state proper possessed a much smaller administrative presence than the Congress Kingdom, as well as much more limited ambitions. In fact, many private towns continued to operate largely without regard to the regulations of the state, which tolerated autonomy for landowners in exchange for professions of loyalty. Royal towns subject to Catherine's Charter to the Towns found their options and control much more strictly circumscribed, while Russian officials increasingly described urban underdevelopment as a function of the region's ethnic composition, in particular the large Polish and Jewish populations, the presence of which served as a pretext for denying the full range of self-governing prerogatives promised by the Charter in the Ukrainian towns. As a result, full administrative integration never occurred, and the western provinces remained distinct from the

Russian core provinces even after the 1870 urban reorganization. Separate laws and administrative procedures also characterized urban life in Prussian Poznania and Austrian Galicia, where private towns, restrictions on Jewish populations, and administrative peculiarities persisted after 1848, while central officials undermined the autonomy of local self-government throughout the nineteenth century.

As subjects of foreign powers, Poles, Jews, and Ukrainians encountered unique challenges, but as members of centralized and hierarchical states urban residents in the cities of the former Commonwealth experienced the common European tide of Enlightenment and Napoleonic centralization. By the middle of the nineteenth century, urban autonomy, the Jewish kahal, particularistic privileges, guild restrictions, and other trappings of the medieval city republic had been abolished across Europe. Mid-nineteenth-century residents of Lublin, Zamość, Luts'k, and Dubno had more neighbors and different rulers than their predecessors in 1764, but this fact alone lends no credence to the conviction that this process represented progress, modernization, or liberalization. In some cases, conditions had improved and residents enjoyed greater equality with their neighbors, but in many respects the possibilities, economic rights, and protections had decidedly worsened. Centralization shifted power away from often corrupt and oligarchical local elites, who were at least subject to the influence of "tumults" and other informal pressures, to an often corrupt and capriciously legalistic bureaucracy, which faced much less pressure. Moreover, as Marcin Wodziński argues, the ambitious and enlightened goals of reformers in the eighteenth century dissipated in the nineteenth into minimalist concerns for order and security, with little regard for the economic and material welfare of town residents.[54] Tellingly, the Russian governor of Podolia province submitted a report in 1834 on town finances to his superior, the governor-general, in which he promised to send a separate dispatch on town cleanliness and construction, since no space on the prefabricated government form was allotted for this topic.[55]

Further, centralization in both the Kingdom of Poland and Russia proper conspicuously failed to unleash economic growth or the entrepreneurial spirit. The state waged a continuous campaign against urban alcohol production as a source of drunkenness and indolence, for example, but alcohol sales continued to generate the lion's share of municipal revenues and personal incomes throughout the nineteenth century. The Congress Kingdom's Minister of Finance tacitly admitted the absolutist state's inability to spur economically productive activity in 1822 when he wrote, "Unfortunately, the situation of the government in a country undeveloped as ours is that the government must take the initiative in everything and in every field."[56] Most demonstrably, centralization destroyed the conditions that allowed private towns the possibility of prospering. Napoleonic administrators and their Russian successors devoted enormous energy and resources to improving the lives of private town residents and protecting burghers from their owners, but the result removed all possible incentives that had once motivated owners to invest in their properties and offer concessions to residents. Private towns in both the Congress Kingdom and the western provinces declined relative to state-controlled towns, and most were converted into villages in an 1870 reform. The Enlightenment state and its officials, particularly in the Congress Kingdom of Poland, also proved much more unfriendly to Jewish populations, who could no longer count on the protection and alliances afforded under conditions of multiple and overlapping sources of power. In some ways, the inequalities, particularisms, and conflicting jurisdictions of the old regime provided more security and opportunity than the post-Enlightenment state.

One may object that this contention proceeds from an examination of territories annexed by the Russian Empire, among the most economically underdeveloped regimes in nineteenth-century Europe. Different conclusions might have resulted had the focus concentrated more on Prussian-occupied Poland, which enjoyed much greater economic prosperity even under conditions of bureaucratic oversight and Germanification. Indeed, the tightly centralized Duchy and its successor scored some notable economic achievements in the constitutional period prior to 1830, and as a result the Congress Kingdom remained the most industrially advanced region of the Russian Empire throughout the nineteenth century. Moreover, by focusing on the Russian Empire into the third quarter of the nineteenth century, I do not consider developments of mass democracy, parliamentary representation, and local self-government that reached Prussian Poland, Galicia, and even the Russian Empire. The appellation of progress and modernity might seem much more fitting in 1906, when residents of the former Commonwealth could elect parliamentary representatives, and many enjoyed institutions of local self-government. Finally, one could contend that, where I speak of the problems, shortcomings, and failures of centralization, I really refer to the misfortunes of the partitions themselves. The lands of partitioned Poland became the periphery, the frontier territory of three regimes, and economic and social development naturally took a backseat to security, control, and state-building in the core. Following the residents of the former Commonwealth, therefore, simply confirms the unhappy fate of people who allow their state to fall prey to outside powers.

In fact, though, the Congress Kingdom of Poland possessed one of the most liberal constitutions of the era (if frequently violated in practice) from 1815 to 1830, and therefore this study does examine enlightened centralism within the context of a liberal parliamentary democracy. As will be evident, the existence of parliamentary institutions and an expanded suffrage offered only a putative political power to individuals in the face of hypercentralized bureaucratic structure. France, the original model of the Congress Kingdom, failed to overcome the contradictions between centralism and liberal democracy for the eighty-year period between the Jacobins' destruction of "federalism" and the birth of the Third Republic. Tocqueville could justly argue that the centralization of the state into the prefectural system meant that every French revolution in the nineteenth century had attempted to "graft the head of liberty onto a servile body."[57] Even in Britain, the birthplace of liberalism, the political structure differed not so dramatically from the Congress Kingdom, at least according to J. Toulmin Smith's 1851 polemic, *Local Self-Government and Centralisation*. Smith argued that Britain's national parliament and free press masked a despotic system of centralized control that was appropriating the functions of local government and the Common Law by "pretenses of the public good, sympathy for the poor, care for the public health, regard for economy, and so forth."[58] In this sense, the Russian state in the apogee of autocracy under Nicholas I represents only centralism in a period where local control, autonomy, and particularism had receded but liberalism and industrialization had yet to triumph. The Russian example highlights the fact that the methods, practices, and assumptions of enlightened centralism do not necessarily produce economic growth, liberal conditions, modernity, or progress. In fact, enlightened centralism could and did lead to languid, paralytic provincialism, in which the state can succeed only in blocking initiative.

A more serious objection is that this study shows disproportionate sympathy for the city residents without just consideration of the genuine good-faith efforts of Enlightenment-era thinkers and officials to solve real, pressing infrastructural and hygienic problems, which plagued the cities of Poland-Lithuania with particular acuteness. Like enlightened officials, I too prefer clean paved streets, the sanitary disposal of waste, and fireproof buildings to the alternative that existed across eighteenth-century Europe, but the concerns of this book are not the intentions of officials, only the outcomes of their policies. The crucial question remains as to whether the means proposed by enlightened officials from multiple regimes to solve the undeniable problems of urban life in Poland-Lithuania justified the self-congratulatory narrative created by the partitioning powers and the self-critical story told by generations of Poles. I argue simply that it did not, and if I show particular sympathy for the perspective of anti-Enlightenment burghers, kahal elders, and nobles, I do so only because the continued hegemony of the Enlightenment narrative of progress, which has achieved the status of "common sense" in both popular and academic discourse, has so long dismissed the mentality of the townspeople as anachronistic and backward. I feel that a corrective is necessary and that the mentality of civic republicanism in the Commonwealth's towns deserves its proper hearing in order for historians to evaluate both the significance of the eighteenth-century transformation and the costs of modernity.

1

We Built This City on Magdeburg Law

CITIES AND CITIZENS IN THE POLISH-LITHUANIAN COMMONWEALTH BEFORE THE FIRST PARTITION

AT EIGHT IN THE morning on 2 December 1789, delegates from 141 royal cities across the Commonwealth convened in the Warsaw town hall. Dressed in the black gowns of magistracy officers and led by the Warsaw mayor Jan Dekert, the delegates crammed into fifty horse-drawn carriages and proceeded down the narrow crowded streets of Warsaw's medieval center toward the royal castle. At the castle, the "Black Procession" gathered in an audience hall, where the city representatives waited patiently for one hour, after which King Stanisław August appeared and received a petition expressing the burghers' demands for greater civil and political rights. Having delivered their petition and kissed the monarch's hand, the burghers departed to present a second copy to Stanisław Małachowski, the marshal of the parliament.[1] This relatively innocuous event, the first collective action by the urban estate in the history of the country, aroused fear and panic among members of the nobility. In France the urban poor had already taken the Bastille and murdered the royal governor. The burghers themselves appreciated the parallel: a few days after the Black Procession, when a prominent nobleman wished to appropriate the theater seat of Dekert's wife, she warned, "Remember what is happening in Paris."[2]

In reality, though, the burghers' demands had little in common with the complaints of the French Third Estate, whose urban ringleaders advocated a complete dismantling of the ancien régime. The burghers wanted to expand their existing rights within the framework of the Commonwealth and to empower urban magistracies to have more control over town residents—including Jews, nobles, and clerical orders—who had largely exempted themselves from city jurisdiction. Moreover, in contrast to the violence and mutiny that characterized the French Revolution from the beginning, the Polish-Lithuanian burghers stressed their nonviolent, peaceful intentions. When Stansiław August communicated to Dekert that the contents of the petition sounded too radical for the ears of the noble parliamentarians, the mayor ordered the document redacted. Beyond publishing numerous pamphlets and lobbying privately with officials, the city representatives remained passive in their role and largely dependent on allies within the parliament. Most delegates returned home the following month.[3]

The French monarchy and the Polish-Lithuanian Commonwealth were both "feudal" regimes, with overlapping jurisdictions, confusing and contradictory legal systems, seigneurial privileges, and estate-based rights, yet the urban citizens in France led the charge to overturn the system while the burghers to the east mounted a peaceful action to preserve and expand their position. Part of the explanation for this divergence appears in the writings of William Coxe, who visited the Commonwealth in the late eighteenth century, recording mostly unfavorable impressions. About Polish and Lithuanian cities, though, he noted: "The burghers, however, still enjoy a considerable portion of freedom, and possess several immunities: they elect their own burgomaster and council, regulate their interior police, and have their own criminal courts of justice, which decide without appeal . . . when defendant, [a burgher] must be cited before the magistrates of his own town, from which an appeal lies only to the king in the assessorial tribunal. To this exemption from the jurisdiction of the nobles, though only in one species of causes, the burghers owe the degree of independence which they retain."[4] In contrast, French cities had long ago lost most of their autonomy to royally appointed intendants, venal mayors, and centralized regulations. Perhaps, as Tocqueville once asserted, aspiring oligarchs in France felt the inequalities, inefficiencies, and injustices of society more acutely, given the absence of even the illusion of local control.[5] In contrast, city citizens in Poland-Lithuania had numerous grievances and suffered many injustices, but the protections and self-governing rights of the cities, if only on paper, continued to bind burghers to the Commonwealth's system even after the Warsaw government began its own experiments in enlightened reforms in the last quarter of the eighteenth century.

In the early nineteenth century, the economist Wawrzyniec Surowiecki published a book entitled *On the Decline of Cities and Industry in Poland*, which traced the ultimate cause of economic ruin in the country to the introduction of a separate legal status for the burghers, most of whom had originally emigrated from the German lands. Previously, Surowiecki claimed, there had been no status distinctions or separate laws in Poland, and the introduction of estate divisions cursed the country with the iniquities of "German feudalism."[6] Few burghers in the eighteenth century would have accepted this analysis, and the petitions and polemics connected with the Black Procession repeatedly invoke the rights, privileges, and prerogatives of the urban estate as the foundation of the prosperity and happiness of prior epochs. For burghers, the cornerstone of their liberties rested on Magdeburg Law, a medieval charter of urban organization introduced into most Polish, Lithuanian, and Ruthenian cities during the Middle Ages. As one eighteenth-century pamphlet published by the Warsaw magistracy expressed it: "German law introduced a *free* and *feudal* government on the model of the German Reich . . . [creating] free and republican [cities]."[7] The term "Magdeburg Law" became shorthand for the entirety of a city's accumulated privileges and concessions, and the date of this royal charter entered into each city's collective memory as the beginning of freedom, even when reality did not correspond to the promises of the charter.

The protections of Magdeburg Law, though, competed with the privileges of the nobility, the rights of royal officeholders, and the exemptions granted to Jewish communities and religious orders. In fact, every city formed a constellation of overlapping and competing authorities; political powers and rights often accrued through the negotiation of competing claims. Magistracy oligarchs, urban citizens, Jewish residents, and even the inhabitants of privately owned towns all enjoyed some measure of autonomy and self-government. Not every member of every estate shared an equal voice nor were privileges and rights always respected, but Magdeburg Law formed the boundaries of a "civic space," where citizens could maneuver to influence their surroundings through collective action. Even the most oligarchic magistracies or despotic royal official had to consider the demands of citizens of all confessions, while the complex constellation of laws, offices, and jurisdictions, far from heightening urban violence, actually facilitated neighborly interaction and served to ameliorate conflict between theoretically antagonistic groups. As David Frick and Yvonne Kleinmann have recently explored, both royal towns such as Wilno and private towns like Rzeszów developed modi vivendi, in which Christians and Jews could share rooms, guild positions, and tax-collecting obligations while bringing disputes to one another's courts.[8]

Enlightened officials saw only disorder and irrationality in the messy web of corporations, institutions, and legal practices that characterized each city, but as Edward Muir has shown, such imprecisions and tangled hierarchies offered a means for each group to preserve and defend its rights through "continuous litigation," meaning the exploitation of imprecise and competing jurisdictions to protect and advance one's prerogatives at every available judicial instance.[9] Burghers did not go to law light-mindedly, but in defense of the civic republican concepts articulated by Heinz Schilling, which city citizens shared with their Jewish and noble neighbors. Such convictions included the demand that all members of the community share in its burdens and have some voice in the political process, regardless of the presumption that elites should have official positions of power.[10] In the pluralistic Commonwealth, conflict arose precisely over the boundaries of each groups' competing claims within individual cities, such as the question of whether disenfranchised Jewish residents should pay taxes to the city treasury. Unequal distributions of power and shifting conditions meant that no conflict was ever conclusively resolved, but even the weakest believed that the system would ultimately respect their rights, a fact evinced by their legalistic actions and pronouncements. In petitions, protests, and legal challenges, members of the urban estates continued to draw upon the vocabulary and assumptions of civic republicanism, even as the political and urban elites elsewhere increasingly embraced an alternative, "enlightened" vision of state and society. In this later outlook, the existence of intermediary institutions such as Magdeburg Law cities appeared anachronistic and detrimental to the country.

To understand why Polish and Lithuanian burghers continued to revere their prerogatives in the face of new ideological and political currents, it is necessary to place the history of cities in the Commonwealth within the broader story of urban life and changing conceptions about the state in European thought. From the emergence of de facto independent urban republics in medieval Italy, the concept of a walled city republic moved to the northern European lands, where territorial sovereigns delegated rights and privileges to their own urban "republics." Rulers permitted the establishment of independent urban communities so as to weaken the power of the feudal lords and augment the exchequer, which benefited from the commerce, currency circulation, and tax revenue enabled by cities. City republics and chartered towns throughout Europe were characterized by particularity, plurality, and idiosyncrasy; institutions, customs, practices, and laws varied wildly among cities, even within a single polity and often within an individual city. Broadly speaking, chartered towns enjoyed the right to elect town councils and judges, which claimed extensive authority over local taxation, legislation, defense, and justice. Charters of liberties granted to cities transformed servile people in a position of feudal dependence vis-à-vis local lords into free citizens, with individual property rights and liberties. In addition, monarchs frequently granted permission for residents to hold markets and fairs, collect tolls and fees, and enjoy exemptions from royal exactions.[11]

Only cities in the Ottoman Empire and Muscovy remained outside of this general pattern and subject to princely control. In medieval Muscovy, towns were not juridical units but collections of communities (*obshchiny*), each with specific rights derived from their duties and obligations toward the state. In this respect, town residents differed from peasant villagers only in the type and variety of state impositions demanded of them. The main population of the town, the *posadnye liudi*, paid direct taxes to the government in exchange for their right to share the communal grant of the *posad* (the area within the town walls). Other inhabitants of towns, such as government servitors, soldiers, monks, and wealthy merchants received exemption from town obligations, as they performed different types of service for the tsar. This connection between service and status stood in stark contrast with the situation in Europe, where enrollment in a given city's *Album Civile* conferred civic equality with all other members of the burgher community, regardless of one's profession.[12]

In the Renaissance chartered, self-governing urban communities existed across Europe, and their extensive legislative, judicial, executive, and commercial powers created the impression of de facto independence. Machiavelli claimed, for example, that the free cities of Germany feared neither the emperor nor any other territorial lord. His contemporary Guicciardini observed that Antwerp, despite answering to the margrave of Brabrant "governs and rules herself almost in the way of a free city and republic."[13] This independence inspired city elites across Europe to identify with the civic republican tradition emerging in Italy and Flanders. In the early seventeenth century, the Dutch jurist Johannes Althusius argued that cities were associations that preceded the larger polity. Urban communities, he claimed, formed the original contracting parties by whose consent the commonwealth came into being, and therefore, cities could decide among themselves to dissolve the union into its constituent parts. The Warsaw burghers adopted this posture in 1789, writing that Magdeburg Law "created republics, and these republics combined created the Commonwealth."[14] Urban elites could thus claim to be representatives of the "republic," which only by chance or convenience formed part of a larger polity. In this conception, undue royal interference represented a kind of foreign oppression. At a minimum, elites viewed their privileges and commercial concessions as a kind of private property, the removal of which would constitute unjust taxation.[15]

Cities and towns in the medieval Polish kingdom conformed to the general European pattern of urban autonomy and self-government, notwithstanding regional peculiarities. King Kazimierz the Great (r. 1333–1370) authorized the burghers in his principal cities, including Kraków, Lwów, and Płock, to govern and judge themselves according to the model of urban self-government employed in the Saxon city of Magdeburg. By offering these privileges Kazimierz hoped to attract settlers with specialized knowledge, capital, and commercial connections to populate his thinly peopled and undermonetized territories. Since most of the original urban dwellers of the Polish Crown were German-speaking, the king's city charters offered burghers both exemption from the feudal jurisdiction of Poland's great lords and a familiar model of urban government. In the original model of Magdeburg Law, the king appointed an official, the *wójt* (German, *vogt*, Latin, *advocatus*), as an intermediary between royal power and the urban community, and the citizens of the city elected a city council, as well as aldermen to assist the wójt in performing his judicial functions. Elections were held each year, and every three months one member of the city council would assume the duties of mayor (*burmistrz*). In addition, Magdeburg Law granted individual freedom to burghers, including the right to buy, sell, and bequeath real property in the town, to move residences at will, as well as to engage in any number of commercial activities, including the production and sale of alcohol. In exchange for these privileges, towns funneled money to the king via rents and other direct taxes, as well as indirect taxes on markets, mills, and taverns.[16]

In accordance with medieval political theory, the primary business of urban government involved order and justice, and municipal councils in the larger cities gradually appropriated civil and appellate jurisdiction from the wójt. The city council also enjoyed the legislative authority to make laws in the name of the king as well as the right to build walls and maintain militias for defense.[17] In order to accomplish these tasks, the council required funds, and an important pillar of urban self-government became the right to collect and dispose of revenues without interference. Magdeburg Law allowed the town council to raise funds through direct levies on all urban residents in times of urgent need, while individual royal privileges granted revenue from specified tolls, levies, and in some cases, peasant villages. Beyond extraordinary expenses for constructions and repair, city magistracies required little regular revenue since town officials served pro bono, a practice consistent with the Aristotelian view (transmitted via civic republicanism) that political officials should remain independent from outside influence. In reality, though, transaction fees, fines, and "gifts" for services—including judicial verdicts—did supply certain honoraria to councilors.[18]

Urban republics in every European country usually devolved into closed or semi-closed oligarchies, headed by merchant patriciates who appropriated the republic rhetoric of liberty and self-government to defend their privileges and powers against royal encroachment and popular resentment. One should note, though, that republican theory even in its most articulate and sophisticated iterations, operated on the presumption of elite rule, a conceit easily justified by reference to Aristotle.[19] Polish cities proved no exception to the general rule; the largest cities came to be dominated by powerful families who monopolized the city councils. The city fathers of Kraków, Lublin, and Lwów, for example, purchased the office of wójt from the king, thereby removing the main source of royal interference and enhancing the political role of the council, entrance to which was increasingly restricted.[20] Nonetheless, neither royal power nor popular participation disappeared completely. In the first place, the merchant-dominated city councils had to contend with the continuously expanding constellation of artisanal guilds, which allowed some disenfranchised burghers a forum for vocalizing their interests. Further, the king's interest in retaining influence in the cities presented disaffected citizens with a channel for challenging the urban oligarchy through litigation and appeals to mediation. Among other consequences, the continuous integration of monarchs in urban affairs facilitated the spread of Polish as the common language of city business. In contrast to the situation in Hungary and Bohemia, the descendants of the original German settlers in Poland had largely abandoned German by the fifteenth century.[21]

The small landlocked Kingdom of Poland gradually expanded over the course of the fourteenth and fifteenth centuries, largely as the result of a dynastic union concluded between the Polish Crown and the enormous patrimony of the Lithuanian grand dukes in 1385. Having spread out from present-day Lithuania to conquer the western half of Rus' from the Mongols, the Lithuanian rulers presided over an enormous, sparsely populated territory consisting mostly of Ruthenian-speaking Orthodox peasants previously under the control of Rurik's remaining princely descendants. Grand Duke Jogaila embraced Catholicism, married Poland's female "king," Jadwiga d'Anjou, and ascended to the Polish throne as the first monarch of the Jagiellonian dynasty. Beginning with this personal union, Polish laws and practices began to penetrate into the Grand Duchy, including the use of Magdeburg Law as a model of urban government. The union produced a powerful and expansive polity, which subdued the Teutonic Knights and acquired the Prussian cities of Danzig and Thorn, but Jogaila and his descendants had to secure the support of the Polish nobility for their military endeavors and regal prerogatives through concessions of political liberties and rights. By 1505 the Polish nobility, the *szlachta,* had acquired a habeas corpus grant, legislative powers, and authority over taxation; nobles now pressed the last Jagiellons for a full union with Lithuania, partly out of suspicion of the rulers' more absolutist prerogatives in the Grand Duchy.[22]

The legal union of the two countries, achieved in 1569, created the Polish-Lithuanian Commonwealth, the largest country in Europe, which now possessed a common monarch, parliament, and system of local government but separate treasuries, armies, and ministries. The union also increased the influence of the wealthy Lithuanian princes, whose enormous latifundia dwarfed the estates of the more middling Polish nobility, by granting them an equal role in the common parliament. Moreover, as part of the campaign to cajole the Lithuanians into embracing the union, King Sigismund August transferred all of Lithuania's Ukrainian territories to the Polish Crown. Poland now bordered Muscovy directly and included territories once integral to Kievan Rus', including Kijów (Kyiv), Bracław, and Volhynia.[23] After Sigismund August's death in 1572, the Jagiellonian dynasty expired, and the Commonwealth's noble citizens decided to cement their gains by instituting a fully elective monarchy, in which kings had no right to influence the choice of their successor. According to the so-called Henrican Articles, signed by Henri de Valois upon his election as king in 1573, elections for future monarchs could only take place following the death of the reigning king, an innovation designed to maintain the status quo of republican freedom against the "absolutist" designs of any subsequent king. Future monarchs were also required upon election to recognize a bill of rights enshrining the powers of parliament as well as the political and religious liberties of the nobility. While ceding substantial power to the nobility, Polish monarchs retained their role as overlords of the cities, including the right to grant privileges and exemptions to individual towns. In fact, royal power over the cities increased in the late sixteenth century with the creation of the Assessor Court as an ultimate instance appellate court for burghers under the authority of the king.[24]

In the fifteenth century, representatives from the largest cities had participated in royal elections, signed treaties, and elected deputies to the parliament. Formally, large commercial centers such as Kraków, Poznań, and Lwów (not to mention the cities of royal Prussia) continued to enjoy this prerogative as corporate entities (such an ennobled city was equivalent, effectively, to a single noble) after the inauguration of the elective monarchy. Nonetheless, cities as a whole lost representation and legislative power after the 1400s, with individual towns increasingly relegated to the role of lobbyists at dietines and parliaments. The burgher publicist and Warsaw lawyer Michał Świniarski claimed in 1789 that, "although the law of 1589 confirmed all urban privileges, the cities' participation in the parliaments dwindled through no fault of their own."[25] In fact, individual cities voluntarily declined invitations to participate in sixteenth-century national parliaments, preferring to deal with the king one-on-one rather than submit their business to a fractious and potentially hostile parliament. As Karin Friedrich has shown, the estates in Royal Prussia evinced the same attitude, and the Union of Lublin compelled the Prussians against their will to send representatives to the national parliament rather than negotiate with the king via their own, regional estates. The magistracy of Kraków continued this approach in 1789, when the city submitted its own petition to the king and parliament, refusing to participate in the Black Procession. In retrospect, the cities' preference for the king proved detrimental, as parliament ultimately obtained the right to authorize new taxes for all subjects of the Commonwealth, leaving burghers to accept the consequences.[26]

The burgher publicists Adam Mędrzecki and Fredryck Barssa opined that "the expiration of Jagiellonian dynasty inaugurated an era of neglecting the cities and ignoring their privileges," and burghers in the eighteenth century could certainly look back to the Jagiellonian Renaissance with nostalgia.[27] In the sixteenth century, relative peace and prosperity reigned; as a result of the booming overseas grain trade, even inland towns such as Lublin and Lwów blossomed into major commercial and artistic centers. Taxation skimmed from trade, artisanal production, and peasant exchange allowed for the construction of churches, townhouses, and even sewer canals. According to Bogucka and Samsonowicz, 30 percent of buildings in 1600 Kraków had running water, and water pipes existed in sixty other cities. Cities not only had money to spend, but—importantly for later Enlightenment thinkers—magistracy chancelleries kept orderly records of revenue and expenditures.[28] Even after the nobility gained the upper hand in 1572, urban prosperity continued to increase until the mid-seventeenth century, when the declining European grain trade and the outbreak of sustained internal warfare combined to reduce the material and economic position of the cities.

The Zaporozhian Cossack uprising led by Bohdan Khmelnyt'skyi in 1648 plunged the Commonwealth into chaos, providing a pretext for invasions from Muscovy, Sweden, and Transylvania. Although the forces of the Commonwealth proved resilient enough to recover and recapture most of the territory by 1660, the combined incursions left a trail of destruction, depopulation, and economic ruination, particularly in the cities, which had suffered repeated besiegement, destruction, foreign occupation, and exaction.[29] In the wake of this devastation, mutual suspicion between monarchs and parliamentary republicans wrecked any hope of compromise in the interests of strengthening the country. By 1652 opposition to the king's plan to elect a successor while still alive had crystallized around the right of liberum veto, which allowed any one deputy's objection over any piece of legislation or procedural matter to wreck all the achievements of the parliament. In this period, internal discord meant that the parliament, which typically convened only once every two years, failed to raise sufficient funds to defend the country, despite, as Robert Frost argues, the continuing effectiveness of the Polish cavalry on the battlefield.[30] The disparity of forces between the Commonwealth and its neighbors revealed itself during the Great Northern War, when Poland and Lithuania unwillingly played the role of battlefield between soldiers of Poland's Saxon King, August II Russia's Peter the Great (r. 1696–1725), and Sweden's Charles XII. Once again, military occupation, disease, and exaction decimated the urban population of the Commonwealth, and the economic recovery under August III (r. 1733–1763) was marred by complete political stagnation at the top, wherein not a single parliament after 1736 was completed successfully.[31]

As war and economic stagnation undermined the position of towns within the Commonwealth other, more creeping changes—which had been taking place even before the sixteenth century—altered the dynamic of power in the cities. In particular, urban citizens and magistracies increasingly had to contend with new and more formidable powers within town walls. Royal officials known as starostas, whose power and prerogatives expanded during this period, offered alternative loci of political authority, while legal enclaves inside and outside the city walls reduced the magistracy's writ and tax base. Jewish communities brought economic competition, as well as their own set of privileges and exemptions, often forming their own, rival cities. Meanwhile, an ever greater number of Christian burghers and Jewish communities were relocating to privately owned towns, which were exempt from royal jurisdiction. The new dynamic of powers within the cities challenged the authority and unity of city government, but greater particularism and plurality did not lead the cities to ruin, as was long claimed. In fact, plurality helped revitalize certain urban centers by offering greater economic opportunities and legal possibilities for defending life, liberty, and property. On the other hand, the increasingly complex constellation of overlapping rival jurisdictions would bedevil the reform efforts of enlightened officials, who proceeded from assumptions about city organization based on foreign models of rationality and good order.

STAROSTAS

Originally created as castle stewards, the starostas administered a collection of royal lands surrounding the castle adjacent to a walled city. So-called judicial starostas mixed executive functions, including responsibility for implementing court verdicts and maintaining public order, with judicial duties. As the principal judge in the castle courts (*sądy grodzkie*), judicial starostas exercised jurisdiction over nobles and noble-owned properties, including those within city walls. Other starostas, called nonjudicial, merely managed royal lands; such a position served as a reward granted by the king, the so-called *panis bene merentium* (bread of the well-deserved). Distributing these lucrative offices offered the elective kings a patronage opportunity to engineer coalitions of supporters, and beneficiaries naturally expected to reap the maximum reward from their spoils. Both starosta types received the lifelong usufruct of the royal lands over which they presided, and this revenue included rents and produce from peasant villages as well as monopoly rights over extramural alcohol production, mills, and bridge tolls. In addition starostas collected rents and dues from urban properties in the smaller, less wealthy cities. Consistent with medieval practice across Europe, the starosta's position lasted for life, though in extraordinary circumstances the monarch could deprive someone of the office.[32]

Both nonjudicial and judicial starostas enjoyed pecuniary and judicial privileges within the small towns in their jurisdiction, and sixteenth-century monarchs sought to use these officials as agents of oversight in the cities. Starostas were charged with ensuring the implementation of laws within cities, as well as auditing accounts in municipal registers. In many cases starostas acquired political prerogatives such as the right to name certain members of the city council.[33] In 1562 King Sigismund August had attempted to regulate the duties and responsibilities of each starosta position, in part by establishing the *kwarta*, a sum starostas were required to pay from their earnings (one-fourth of their income after expenses) to support the military. Although starostas originally paid other revenues to the royal fisc, in time the *kwarta* became the only duty of all starostas vis-à-vis the treasury. Both types of starosta positions became lucrative prospects, particularly as the judicial starostas could subcontract away all of their judicial and executive functions to subordinates. Sigismund August's reform had also tried to ensure clarity in the distribution of urban revenue between the starostas and the magistracies, as well as the two groups' respective political prerogatives. Periodically, parliament would authorize a lustration audit (*lustracja*) of each city, during which time officials deputized by parliament examined privileges, recorded complaints, and sorted out the often contradictory and frequently nonextant privileges. The determinations of the lustration officials established precedent for starostas and magistracies to claim particular privileges and exemptions in future lawsuits.[34]

Unfortunately, as a result of parliamentary paralysis and internal warfare, no lustration audit took place between 1665 and 1765, during which time starostas appropriated more and more of the revenues of the magistracy, in particular the peasant villages and extramural monopolies possessed by the town. In many cases, it should be noted, cities lost revenues when city councilors alienated pecuniary rights to starostas for immediate gain, either to cover extraordinary financial outlays (necessitated by military occupation, for example), to settle debts, or to provide illicit compensation to individual councilors. Starostas and magistracies could litigate disputes about privileges and rights before the Assessor Court, but the written privileges frequently perished in the numerous urban conflagrations of the seventeenth century, while enforcement of decisions proved difficult since the starostas and the city magistracies were themselves the officers in charge of implementing court verdicts. For example, a privilege from King August II granted full autonomy to the Lublin magistracy on parity with Kraków in 1703, but the starosta of Lublin continued to select two of the quarterly mayors of the city each year, a practice that stretched back to the city's founding.[35] Smaller cities often rested in a more dependent position. In some small towns in the Lublin and Volhynia regions, starostas illegally acquired the office of wójt from the magistracy and even demanded corvée labor from the burghers as part of their "compensation package." Burghers were not passive victims, it should be noted, but frequently opposed the starosta's actions, in petitions, at law, and in the street, which occasionally led to confrontations between townspeople and the starosta's soldiers.[36]

JEWISH COMMUNITIES

Another change in the urban landscape was the increasing prominence of Jewish communities in the Commonwealth's towns. Jews had been settling in the Commonwealth's lands since the thirteenth century, but immigration and a natural increase in population that outpaced Christian reproduction combined to make Jewish communities a significant presence in most towns by the sixteenth century. Polish monarchs, ever hopeful of attracting currency to the kingdom, offered charters of privileges and protections to Jewish communities, usually authorizing self-government and exemption from municipal jurisdiction. Jewish communities also received privileges specifying the trades in which they could engage, typically a much broader array of commercial occupations than in western Europe. Jews in all parts of the Ashkenazi world, in places as diverse as Alsace, Bohemia, and Transylvania, had developed institutions of communal government, but nowhere did Jewish communities dispose of such political prerogatives as in the Commonwealth. Jewish communities in each Polish town administered their affairs through the auspices of the kahal, an elected board of secular elders (*parnassim*) that in many respects paralleled the functions—and the oligarchic character—of the town magistracy. The kahal collected taxes, hired the local rabbi, and supervised the rabbinical courts, among other functions. Since Jews were not usually permitted to participate in the urban guild structure, community elders also formulated compacts and agreements with the burghers, which further detailed the Jews' permitted trades, residential restrictions, and responsibilities vis-à-vis the town treasury.[37]

Christians resented the presence of Jews as commercial competitors, and the magistracies sought to prevent sales of Christian property to Jews, since such transactions further expanded the authority of the kahal at the expense of the magistracy's direct jurisdiction. In larger towns such as Kraków, Warsaw, Lublin, and Poznań, the magistracy obtained and enforced the royal privilege of *De non tolerandis Judaeis*, which allowed municipal authorities to exclude Jews from residing within the intramural city. In these cases Jews tended to congregate in the suburbs, creating their own rival towns outside the city walls. Kazimierz near Kraków is the most famous such example, though many such "sister-towns" existed, ostensibly run by a Christian magistracy but in reality home to the region's Jews. In Lublin, the area outside the walls came to be called "Jewish town," which comprised over half the population of Lublin by the eighteenth century.[38] In smaller towns the Jewish community often lived in a separate quarter or street, and agreements with the magistracy (frequently violated) specified how many houses the Jewish community could rent or own. Originally, the palatine (*wojewóda*) served as the protector of the Jewish community's privileges and arbitrator for Jewish-Christian quarrels, but after the seventeenth century, the starosta became the natural superior of Jewish communities within royal towns. Eventually starostas replaced the palatine as the legal authority over the kahal and adjudicator of interfaith disputes. In larger cities such as Wilno (Vilnius), Jews were compelled to bring lawsuits against Christians before the Christian magistracy's bench and vice versa.[39]

For a variety of reasons, including broader economic ties, and as Adam Teller argues, the creation of "ethnic-controlled economies" in certain town industries such as alcohol-distribution, Jewish communities weathered the seventeenth-century storm better than Christians did and came to dominate the economies of many towns.[40] Acknowledging the Jewish communities' economic potential and tax-paying capacity, monarchs renewed and expanded the commercial and residential privileges for Jews. For example, in the 1670s, King Jan Sobieski (r. 1674–1696) promulgated a series of privileges to the Jewish communities of Chełm, Chęciny, and Kazimierz Dolny, hoping to attract Jewish settlement for the purpose of urban revitalization. These privileges equated Jews with Christian citizens in terms of commercial liberties while requiring that the Jewish communities submit to all municipal exactions. The kahal of Chęciny referenced these privileges in a 1777 petition to the central government, which stated that the Jews in the city not only paid all urban taxes but even recorded property transactions between Jews in the municipal record book, suggesting a greater degree of integration than elsewhere.[41] Despite this parity, or perhaps because of it, tensions could always erupt with Christian burghers, who were defined by a different set of privileges and thus constituted a rival estate. Burghers complained that starostas shielded the Jewish community from city taxes and other burdens, or that Jews had settled outside their designated quarter or houses. These grievances periodically led to violence, persecution, and the notorious blood-libel accusations, in which evidence obtained under torture justified grisly death sentences at the hands of the magistracy. Although traumatic, violence remained an extraordinary event, and many of the ritual murder accusations that led to death sentences were in fact sponsored and overseen by members of the clerical estate.[42]

JURYDYKAS

A further transformation in the urban landscape after 1572 appeared with the proliferation of *jurydykas*, particularly in larger towns. Jurydykas ("jurisdictions") were legal enclaves ranging in size from a single house to a microtown on municipal property. Property belonging to nobles and religious orders had gained exemption from municipal jurisdiction in the sixteenth century, placing residents under the authority of the starosta rather than the magistracy. Most towns had a few houses belonging to either the starosta, a noble, or a benefice, but in larger towns such as Lublin and Włodzimerz (Volodymyr-Volyns'kyi), nobles established their own townships on extramural, urban real estate. Residents in these jurydykas benefited from the commerce, which the principal town enabled, but could eschew paying town taxes or exactions. Like Kazimierz near Kraków, Podzamcze ("Under the castle") in Lublin started life as a jurydyka, which the starosta established in order to host the Jewish population barred from settling in the city proper. Forming part of the extramural city's so-called Jewish Town, Podzamcze gained urban status in 1566 as the result of a royal charter that legally transformed Lublin into two separate and equally sized jurisdictions.[43] Magistracy officials resented jurydykas enormously and successfully lobbied parliaments in 1656, 1659, and 1764 to liquidate all jurydykas, but without effect. Throughout the seventeenth and eighteenth centuries, jurydykas in fact expanded and acquired additional urban property from burghers, which diminished the power and tax base of the magistracy. Municipal prohibitions on selling land to nonburghers proved ineffective.[44] At the same time, jurydykas brought competition to the cities in the form of producers who were not subject to the restrictions of the main town's guild structure.

PRIVATE TOWNS

From the beginning of autonomous urban corporations in Poland, not all towns were directly subordinate to the king; many cities belonged to individual nobles and the great lords, whom the Polish monarchs had inherited in the process of unifying the medieval kingdom. Like rulers elsewhere in northern Europe—including Ireland, Scotland, Norway, Bohemia, Silesia, and Hungary—Polish monarchs desired more urban settlements than they could afford. By allowing noble lords to erect towns on private property, monarchs could increase the circulation of coin and expand the tax base at minimal cost while creating a market for previously cash-poor peasants to convert their grain into currency.[45] For their part, lords benefited from monopolies, tolls, and rents on their properties, which were paid by the burgher settlers as well as their peasant exchange partners. With few outlets for capital outside of land, private towns also offered an investment opportunity with potential long-term gains for the noble lords.[46] A sixteenth-century economics handbook by Anzelm Gostomski advised entrepreneurial nobles to invest in towns, highlighting the large potential profits from mills, market fees, tariffs, and alcohol. Gostomski stipulated only that the owner must strictly supervise toll collectors and prevent residents from consuming flour or beer external to the owner's monopoly production. Whether as the result of Gostomski's advice or not, private towns expanded rapidly after the sixteenth century, far outpacing the construction of new royal towns. Many new settlements appeared in the Grand Duchy and Polish Ukraine for the benefit of the wealthy and powerful Ruthenian and Lithuanian princes.[47]

Since burgher settlers were scarce commodities and prospective town owners found themselves in direct competition for residents with already existing cities both at home and abroad, nobles had to offer not only commercial privileges but the personal freedom, self-government, and autonomy that burghers enjoyed elsewhere. In the interest of competition, Polish town owners petitioned the king for charters of Magdeburg Law as well as royal privileges permitting markets and fairs for their towns. Magdeburg Law guaranteed that burghers settling in private, Polish towns (unlike their counterparts in countries such as Ireland and Scotland) enjoyed rights of property inheritance and transferability, as well self-government and personal freedom. In theory, these freedoms included the right to move at will, though owners occasionally imposed financial costs on those who vacated their property.[48] As a result, private towns existed in a hybrid status between royal authority and particularistic jurisdiction, especially after a series of parliamentary acts in the middle of the sixteenth century granted greater autonomy to noble town owners at the expense of royal supervision. Owners who wished to preserve their profits accepted that urban self-government served as one of the attractions to potential residents. Moreover, the competition among owners for commercially minded settlers meant that potential town founders faced market pressures to keep direct taxes and rents comparatively low. The benefits enjoyed by private town burghers rested not on magnaminity but on the rational economic calculation of profit-maximizing owners.[49]

From the seventeenth century, private towns increasingly attracted Jewish settlers, who came to comprise the overwhelming majority of the population in many such cities. Private towns, according to Gerson Hundert, were less residentially segregated than royal towns, and Jews were often allowed to enter Christian guilds. After 1539 private town owners enjoyed exclusive jurisdiction over their Jewish residents, and many nobles offered generous privileges that were unavailable in royal towns. In effect, most private cities developed parallel governing structures, in which the magistracy administered the Christian burghers while the kahal controlled Jewish life with the owner serving as mediator. Some private towns in the Lublin region pushed integration further, allowing the kahal to select one of the four mayors each year or at least to take part in magistracy elections as informal observers.[50] Moreover, as Moshe Rosman and Adam Teller have shown, powerful owners of private towns could shelter Jews from violence and exploitation more effectively than could the king and his starostas. Whatever their personal prejudices, owners of private towns evidently saw Jewish communities as economically useful and frequently leased to individual Jews monopoly rights connected with alcohol production (which in private towns, with some exceptions, belonged exclusively to the lord) and mill-grinding.[51] In many of these towns, the future shtetls of nineteenth-century myth, the Christian magistracy held sway over a tiny fragment of the population, but the majority of the inhabitants answered to the kahal and the owner. In the eighteenth century, Jewish families in Międzybórz—the birthplace of Hasidism—occupied most of the wealthy and prestigious stone houses on the market square. The Besht's hometown was hardly an exception, a fact that may explain Malby's pronunciation that the "Jews are the real masters of Poland," though violence and accusations of blood libel nonetheless could occur in both private and royal towns.[52]

FROM PUBLIC GOOD TO PARASITE

Despite the significant challenges faced by magistracies and other urban groupings resulting from the destruction and depopulation of the Northern Wars, cities continued to solve material and political problems with their own resources, while the addition of new groups and jurisdictions as well as the proliferation of private towns brought new economic opportunities and facilitated the slow recovery that began after the conclusion of peace in 1717. Even in wartime conditions, city governments undertook significant new construction and repair, while both royal and private city magistracies issued good order regulations for the purpose of improving health, sanitation, and trade.[53] Jewish communities revived trade, often serving as essential suppliers and dealers for Christian artisans, whose trades would have withered without such intermediaries. Moreover, scholars are more and more questioning the linguistic separateness and mutual hostility of Christians and Jews. David Frick and Adam Teller have shown that Jews in Wilno and Lublin made frequent recourse to gentile courts, even in cases between Jews that should have been subject to rabbinical jurisdiction. The frequent renegotiation of burden-sharing compacts between Christians and Jews also testify to a kind of interaction in which violence was the exception.[54] Meanwhile, the continual founding of private towns by up-and-coming nobles such as Stanisław Szczuka, as well as the need to recruit new settlers, meant that there were always lords willing to offer attractive conditions and undertake enormous investments in order to lure burghers and Jews to new vistas. Among the conditions offered were creative power-sharing arrangements between Christians and Jews, which required the two groups to cooperate in order for the town to function.[55]

Not anarchy (as later claimed) but the presence of a *limited* royal authority fostered the conditions of republican government in the Commonwealth's cities. Until the mid-eighteenth century, the Commonwealth elites continued to accept diversity, plurality, and particularism as the norm. Jan Sobieski and August II, monarchs known for their efforts to increase royal power at the expense of parliament, followed the tradition of granting individual privileges to specific burghers, jurydykas, Jewish communities, and private town owners, while addressing conflicts and violence with ad hoc and issue-specific commissions. Indeed, despite complaints by historians such as Jerzy Lukowski regarding the lack of centralized oversight in the Commonwealth, the monarchy continued to intervene and reorganize urban government throughout the seventeenth century. Royal power proved particularly significant in checking the oligarchic tendencies of magistracy elites. Citizens dissatisfied with their urban government's distribution of funds or execution of justice could appeal for higher protection, in some cases staging violent protests against their leaders. The king, as dominus directus of the city, would then dispatch a royal commission to facilitate an agreement between the magistracy and the citizenry, as happened for Lublin in 1691. Such solutions did not involve rewriting the urban constitution but, following the same logic of royal elections, served to reset the balance of power between competing forces. Monarchs also intervened in other ways, whether establishing a paving commission for Warsaw in both 1693 and 1742, and ordering the city council of Lwów to admit Orthodox members in 1745. Congenially disobedient starostas could lose their positions, while kings remained able to reward or punish city elites; Kraków and Poznań lost the right to elect their city councilors in the seventeenth century for rebellion, a right that Kraków subsequently regained.[56] Elsewhere in Europe, however, newer, "modern" political conceptions were already remaking the relationship between the center and the cities, though these ideas only found a receptive audience in the Commonwealth toward the mid-eighteenth century.

If city republics and chartered towns appeared natural and necessary to Renaissance statesmen and thinkers, the eighteenth-century consensus viewed city liberties as pernicious and anachronistic. Since at least the thirteenth century, royal officials had complained about the dangers of city autonomy to both rulers and the burghers themselves.[57] After the Renaissance, rulers and their publicists moved more forcefully to limit if not abolish the urban corporation for the purpose of expanding the prerogatives and tax-collecting attributes of the central government. Bodin's concept of sovereignty, developed in tandem with the emerging theory of the state served as one of the first pillars of the assault. As Heinz Schilling argues, city governments had no adequate theoretical concepts, with which to counter claims of royal sovereignty, since municipal privileges indisputably originated from the king. Despite the theoretical dissonance, monarchs nonetheless had to accept city autonomy until central institutions developed adequate resources to overpower their urban subjects.[58] In this environment, Althusius's vision of the city community as the primary contacting party to the larger polity found few admirers, even among thinkers such as Jean Domat, who referred to urban corporations as a "public good of the Kingdom." Domat affirmed that only the sovereign monarch could authorize the creation or dissolution of city communities, while the rights of city communities to levy taxes or alter statutes required permission from the king. He further listed among the functions of city governments "obedience to the orders of the prince; execution of the orders directed to them, as also of the orders of the courts of justice."[59] Domat's theory elided with the practice of his patron, Louis XIV, whose policies aimed to subordinate the cities for the purpose of extracting greater state revenue but not to eliminate corporations altogether.[60]

While Domat defended the monarch's ultimate authority over urban communes, other writers were already questioning the right of independent cities to exist at all. The fathers of the philosophy of individual liberalism began to see the existence of urban autonomy, subordinate or not, as detrimental to the state's prerogatives. Hobbes provided the most succinct exposition of this new outlook in the *Leviathan*: "Another infirmity of a commonwealth is the immoderate greatness of a town . . . as also the great number of corporations, which are as it were many lesser commonwealths in the bowels of a greater, like worms in the entrails of a natural man."[61] As Hobbes understood, even Domat's "obedient" corporations posed problems for any state aiming for coordinated universal policies rather than particularistic solutions. In the eighteenth century, enlightened statesmen proposed that the newly developed police sciences, commonly known as "good police," would increase prosperity, promote economic growth, and foster the common good. Scientific advancements offered elites in the capitals a bird's-eye view of the state, making good police regulations the responsibility of the center and transforming the function of local magistrates from government into implementation. For such purposes, the nonprofessional local elites who dominated the cities seemed increasingly ill-suited, affected as they were, in the words of Cameralist writer Johann von Justi, by "side issues, emotions, and narrow interests."[62] Physiocratic and Cameralist writers, specialists in "good police," both agreed that a corpus of scientifically trained, professional administrators could perform the duties of urban magistrates with greater rationality and consistency, and the central government would devise fairer and more productive economic policies to replace the plethora of guild restrictions, commercial concessions, and economic prerogatives so jealously guarded by the urban elites. Physiocrats like Turgot fought to eliminate guilds and urban privileges in France, while the creation of institutions like the Kriegs-und-Domänenkammer in Prussia and the Kreisämter in Austria placed urban authorities in a chain of accountability leading to the throne.[63]

From subordination of urban communities and elimination of privileges developed the idea that standards should be universal and applicable to all parts of the kingdom, regardless of tradition and local peculiarities. Justus Möser may have celebrated particularism and diversity as defenses against despotism in his *History of Osnabruck*, but Voltaire's complaints about the inconveniences of particularistic powers and jurisdictions found support among reform-minded monarchs and the literati.[64] Elite society in the eighteenth century, with its increasingly commercial orientation, found the internal tariffs, bridge tolls, mandatory storage fees, and price controls increasingly cumbersome and irrational. Again, peculiarities and local privileges may have irked consumers and businessmen, but urban elites staunchly defended their city prerogatives, tolls, and commercial rights as a patrimony and the private property of their estate. Private town lords and magistracies had been tinkering with good order regulations for decades, but state officials now sought to override traditional prerogatives with uniform standards, applicable to all provinces. Weights and measures, building codes, sanitary regulations, and police policies connected with good order became instruments for subordinating local elites, as failure to comply could be grounds for revoking privileges or appointing officials to monitor the local elites.[65] Enlightened centralism as a package of policies enacted in the name of rationality, uniformity, and material improvement appealed to central European monarchs such as Maria Theresa and Frederick the Great, but perhaps the best expression of this drive can be found in Russia.

Facing the urgent necessity to raise funds and marshal resources in his war with Charles XII, Peter the Great had attempted to plant wealth-generating towns in Russia based on his observations in Holland. Peter experimented with urban self-government as a means of unleashing the country's economic potential, but the state always viewed elected mayors and town councils as government servants; urban officers even received positions in Peter's new table of ranks.[66] Catherine the Great's 1775 provincial reform and the 1785 Charter to the Towns attempted to further Peter's administrative changes by transforming the towns into financially independent corporations, which would serve as loci for provincial control. The reforms applied the model of St. Petersburg to the entire empire, granting a governing structure designed for the wealthy capital to provincial hamlets, for the state often had to designate peasant villages as "cities" in order to have enough centers of provincial control. In practice, Catherine's reforms strictly circumscribed the competency of town governments by placing most responsibilities in the hands of appointed governors, treasury chambers, and boards of social welfare. Combining political devolution with Enlightenment-era hostility to self-government and autonomy, Catherine's reforms failed to spur the creation of a strong urban stratum outside the wealthy capitals and a few provincial centers, but her precise and unitary directives appeared in Enlightenment eyes as models of rationality, uniformity, and symmetry.[67]

Enlightened centralism as practiced in other European countries began to appear much more attractive to some members of the Commonwealth's elite during the politically stagnant reign of August III. With each passing year, Poland-Lithuania's republican constitution, dysfunctional parliament, and tiny army appeared more vulnerable in comparison to the neighboring absolutist states with their swelling bureaucracies and armies. Moreover, the peace of August III's reign had not brought a wholesale revival of trade, as long durée structural factors reduced the profitability of the Polish grain trade and the importance of the Commonwealth's cities in international commerce. Frederick the Great's punitive tolls and policy of flooding the Commonwealth with debased coinage further undermined the economic outlook of the country and contributed to urban stagnation.[68] In this context, reformists began demanding not only parliamentary reform but the establishment of a more powerful and far-reaching executive apparatus. Crucially, urban improvement served as a major argument in pamphlets advancing justifications for building a more vigorous government. More cautious critics of the liberum veto, such as Stanisław Leszczyński and Stanisław Poniatowski the Elder, shared the conviction of wholesale reformers like Stanisław Konarski, who penned a four-volume defense of majority rule in parliament, that proper government attention (*opieka*) could overcome the structural difficulties faced by the Commonwealth's cities and inaugurate a new era of prosperity after decades of ruination and disorder. Even the future king, Stanisław Poniatowski the Younger, included urban reform in his pamphlets on improving the Commonwealth, which he composed for the future Catherine the Great during their courtship.[69]

Poniatowski's reformist dreams mirrored the secret plans of his powerful Czartoryski cousins whose political faction, the "Family," intended to impose a wholesale reform of the Commonwealth based upon English parliamentary practice and Cameralist social engineering. The Czartoryskis had approached Catherine upon her ascension to the Russian throne in 1762, seeking support for a coup d'état against August III in favor of Adam Kazimierz Czartoryski. In preparation, the Family composed a blueprint, which envisioned a more powerful central government responsible to a plurality-based parliament, whose decrees would be enacted by professionally trained officials. Like Joseph II and other proponents of enlightened centralism, many members of the reform party also envisioned that a more powerful state would guarantee greater civil rights for burghers and other disenfranchised groups.[70] Although Catherine decided not to support the coup, August's death in 1763 opened an opportunity for the Russian empress to gain greater influence in the Commonwealth. Catherine immediately communicated her support for Poniatowski, who was poor, dependent, and still devoted to her, unlike his wealthy and influential cousin Czartoryski. Poniatowski was a dark horse candidate, but the opposition failed to produce a credible alternative, and Catherine's support for Poniatowski was patently obvious. Russian soldiers did not appear in large numbers, but the nobles who convened in Warsaw to elect a new king sufficiently appreciated the costs of displeasing the empress. Stanisław Poniatowski the Younger was unanimously elected in 1764; as a sign of his reformist intentions, the new king took the name Stanisław August upon his coronation.[71]

Stanisław August's ascension brought to Warsaw a number of enlightened and reform-minded politicians, and the new king, supported initially by the Czartoryskis and other members of the Family, enjoyed a limited space to pursue reforms in the first two years of his reign. Catherine intended to modernize the Commonwealth just enough to convert the country into a viable satellite of Russia, and she acquiesced to a series of confederated—and thus plurality-governed—parliaments, which authorized legislation designed to improve and rationalize the treasury, military, and judiciary. The Czartoryskis also succeeded in significantly curtailing the liberum veto before the Russian ambassador took notice.[72] Deputies to the first successful parliaments in a generation also supported urban reform based on Enlightenment principles. The convocation parliament abolished all jurydykas, answering decades of petitions from the urban estate, though the law soon lapsed into irrelevance. A bill in 1766, "The City of Wilno," brought the Commonwealth squarely into the vanguard of contemporary economic thought in dictating (again, without effect) that all guilds should be abolished. Signaling that Polish elites no longer conceived of Jewish communities as economically beneficial, the same two parliaments abolished the Council of Four Lands, the "national" Jewish parliament, and required Jewish communities to renegotiate their privileges and rights with their city magistracies.[73]

The 1767–1768 parliament, the last to meet before the first partition, promised to rescue the royal cities of the Commonwealth from exploitation and mismanagement through the creation of Good Order Commissions (*komisje boni ordinis*), though these bodies would only appear in earnest after the partition. Since reformers shared the conviction that urban decay had partially resulted from the poor choices of the urban elite, the same legislation required the starostas to audit each city's financial records every year, a rule long practiced in private towns by officials of the owner. Further, burghers were now instructed to appeal cases to the starosta's castle court before turning to the Assessor Court, which faced an enormous backlog.[74] Significantly, none of these early reform attempts targeted the private towns, which would remain largely exempt from government intervention until the end of the century. Unfortunately for the reform party, the extraordinary parliament called in 1767 served primarily as a test for Catherine's power in the Commonwealth. The empress's push to have the liberum veto enshrined as a "Cardinal Law" guaranteed by foreign powers, as well as a disingenuous campaign in defense of religious dissidents promoted by Catherine and Frederick the Great provoked resistance, backlash, and ultimately a rebellion known as the Confederacy of Bar.[75]

The Confederacy, supported by prominent nobles such as Karol Stanisław Radziwiłł, fought simultaneously against the king's supporters and Russian soldiers. For four years the Commonwealth descended into civil war, and cities experienced a new round of occupation, devastation, and forced exactions from rival armies. When Austrian troops marched into the Commonwealth, supposedly to contain an outbreak of disease, Catherine and Frederick determined that all three countries could benefit themselves territorially at Poland's expense. Once an agreement had been reached between St. Petersburg, Vienna, and Berlin, the Commonwealth had no realistic means of resisting. Stanisław August dutifully summoned a parliament in 1773, which lasted until 1775 and legalized the territorial transfers. The Commonwealth ceded the future provinces of West Prussia (minus Danzig and Thorn) to Frederick the Great; East Galicia, including Lwów, Zamość and the Wieliczka salt mines, to Austria; and eastern Belarus to Russia. As a partial bone to reformers, the partitioning powers allowed certain centralizing reforms, including a Commission of National Education to manage the schools of the newly defunct Jesuit Order.[76]

More significantly, the partition parliament authorized the creation of the Commonwealth's first executive administration, the Permanent Council. Partially a rational centralized administration desired by enlightened statesmen and partially a leash on the king, whom St. Petersburg now viewed as overly ambitious, the Permanent Council consisted of thirty-six senators and deputies, with the king relegated to the role of a chairman with two votes. The Permanent Council issued administrative decisions and regulations in pleno, but the day-to-day business fell to its five conciliar departments: Justice, Treasury, War, Foreign Affairs, and Police. Each of these departments consisted of between four and eight members of the council, along with the analogous minister.[77] The Crown Marshall, Stanisław Lubomirski, became the minister responsible for the Department of Police (*Departament Policji*). Consistent with the eighteenth-century understanding of the term "police," this new department's portfolio encompassed internal affairs, public order, and economic improvement. In practice the presidency of the biweekly meetings rotated among the regular members, who included supporters of the king as well as members of the opposition. Regardless of affiliation, the department's members all subscribed to the idea that central power could more rationally and efficiently direct the resources of the country, making towns, burghers, and royal officials more "useful."[78]

The Commonwealth now had the trappings of a rudimentary state structure, as well as a sufficient pool of officials committed to imposing a program of rational reform, at least with regard to royal cities. Educated elites in Poland-Lithuania enjoyed a plethora of foreign models from which to draw reform plans, and the cities, which had been newly depredated and ruined by the civil war of 1768–1772, seemed desperately in need of revival and stimulus. Officials in Warsaw, though, had so thoroughly embraced the assumptions of enlightened centralism as to forget that civic republican values still dominated the city councils and jurisdictions. In fact, the distance between the assumptions of the Permanent Council and city hall were broader than elsewhere. Although Prussia, Austria, and France had gradually whittled away at the prerogatives of urban corporations since the seventeenth century, the Commonwealth's elites and their successors would confront royal towns, which had developed in the direction of greater particularism, autonomy, and complexity since the Renaissance.

2

If Only Our Commission Had More Power

ENLIGHTENED CENTRALISM AND THE ROYAL CITIES AFTER THE FIRST PARTITION

FROM APRIL 1777 A steady stream of petitions, complaints, and manifestos began flooding into the Kraśinski Palace, the Warsaw headquarters of the Department of Police.[1] Burghers, starostas, and Jewish communities presented often wildly contradictory versions of confrontations arising from a recent legislation on urban alcohol production, while Good Order Commissions requested guidance and assistance in overcoming resistance to new taxes and regulations. Officials in Warsaw had not anticipated that such fierce resistance or discord could arise as a result of rational policies, which were designed to bring order, cleanliness, attractiveness, and good management to urban society. As a result government agents attributed all shortcomings to the backward and anarchic character of urban society as well as to the insufficiency of the center's coercive force. Tomasz Ostowski, acting chairman of the Department of Police, summarized the center's attitude in his 1778 report to the parliament: "In each step taken toward establishing good order, the Department has encountered enormous resistance, resulting partially from the novelty of things, partially from the inveterate disorder [of the towns], partially from the inadequacy of the law, and the power granted to [the Department]."[2] In biannual reports, memoranda, and legislative projects between 1778 and 1788 (after which the parliament abolished the Department of Police), government officials continuously sounded the theme of well-intentioned and reasonable reforms floundering because of administrative deficiencies and irrational resistance. Consistent with the ideology of enlightened reformers, few observers questioned the assumptions and values coded into the reforms or investigated the reasons that locals might have resisted or sabotaged the new provisions.

In Polish historiography the desperate financial and material conditions of the towns fully justified measures such as the Good Order Commissions, institutions lauded for attempting to reorganize and rationalize city governments, despite facing resistance and alleged incomprehension from local elites.[3] Aleksander Czaja's study of the Permanent Council concludes that the institution failed to "subordinate the cities to state control," and magistracies and starostas "demonstrated undisguised disobedience" to the central government's regulations. Jerzy Lukowski notes that an effective local administration only appeared with the creation of Civil-Military Commissions in 1788, while Andrzej Zahorski and Krystyna Zienkowska follow the assertion of Korzon that only the reforms of 1791, including the "Law on Free Cities" and the Constitution of the Third of May, promised an effective administration for implementing rational reforms.[4] Although varying in emphasis, all these interpretations coincide in identifying with the perspective of the state officials, whose monopoly of reason and rationality remains unquestioned. Extrapolating from this logic leads to the same conclusions reached by government officials at the time: the absence of a more centralized, efficient, and coercive administrative machine like that of the partitioning powers represented the only impediment to engineering economic, demographic, and financial improvement in the Commonwealth's cities.

The overlapping evaluations of eighteenth-century officials and contemporary historians, in Poland and elsewhere, have reduced the values and priorities of the burghers, Jews, and other local actors to backwardness and obstinacy. This narrow categorization dismisses the political actions of the urban inhabitants who resisted and thwarted enlightened reforms based on sober calculations arising out of a specific set of values that prioritized civic republican decision-making over material improvement mandated from above. Moreover, a focus on the limitations of the central government omits the reality that enlightened centralism was itself constructed from a pool of assumptions and beliefs about human nature and ideal government that were no more "rational" or "reasonable" than the mentality of the townspeople.[5] Lacking a hierarchical administrative machine, government officials in the Commonwealth nonetheless adopted the expectations and procedures of enlightened centralism and rational-bureaucratic formalism as practiced in the absolutist monarchies. Bureaucrats presumed that legislative authority and hierarchical superiority would automatically translate into the obedient implementation of all commands by officials accustomed to centuries of wide latitude in managing local affairs. Operating on a priori assumptions about the proper purpose, function, and appearance of a city, the central government failed to consider the variegated nature of Polish cities and the divergent constellations of privileges and rights. As a result, attempts to enact universalizing regulations and rules patently produced distinct and often contradictory results in each city.

Two policies in particular substantially affected urban life for royal towns in the period prior to the Four-Year Parliament (*Sejm Czteroletni*, 1788–1791): the institution of Good Order Commissions for the principal cities and a government-supervised alcohol monopoly instituted in all but the largest towns. Both measures sought to improve and rationalize government and finances as well as to augment and expand revenue streams in the royal towns, with the ultimate goal of improving municipal infrastructure, cleanliness, and attractiveness. The reforms included a certain degree of social engineering designed to encourage burghers and Jews to fulfill particular economic roles. Specifically, the laws intended to remove Jews from alcohol production, as Enlightenment-era political theory regarded this economic activity—the predominant industrial activity of the Commonwealth—as pernicious and parasitic, particularly in the hands of Jewish tavern-keepers and alcohol producers.[6] More rational and tightly supervised urban governments, in which townsmen pursued the most useful ends, would improve the financial, fiscal, and demographic position of the country in general.

As soon became evident, the reformers underestimated the urban estates' attachment to their rights, self-governing powers, and prerogatives, conceived collectively as a kind of private property. Defending their collective property of privileges proved considerably more important for starostas, magistracies, burghers, kahals, and jurydykas than enjoying the material and financial benefits promised by Warsaw. The reforms fanned the flames of inter-estate rivalry, becoming a weapon in the continuous negotiation of power and authority between urban groups, which cooperated with or resisted the new restrictions and regulations depending on the particular advantages offered. The alcohol-production (*propinacja*) law pitted urban estates against one another (and against the central government) in a zero-sum competition for control of a monopoly lease, the right to which significantly overshadowed any possible gains from the revenue generated. Meanwhile, the Good Order Commissions tussled with recalcitrant magistracies and burghers who valued the commissions' contribution to struggles with other estates but simultaneously sought to escape their accompanying regulations.

In attempting to re-create and understand the dialogue between the towns and the burgeoning state in this period of centralizing reform, I combine a macro analysis of urban petitions and central government responses connected with the alcohol monopoly law (1777–1788) with a micro study of the papers of the Lublin Good Order Commission in the years of its activity. For the propinacja law, the focus is particularly on the 135 petitions written in the first two years of the reform (1777 and 1778) as well as letters from a select group of cities from the entire period of the reform to 1788.[7] Comparing the department's activities with the Lublin Good Order Commission, one of the most active and well-documented of these commissions, offers an opportunity to observe parallels in the actions and assumptions of enlightened officials both in the center and in situ. Moreover, the two groups, despite their formal separateness, frequently collaborated, as the Good Order Commissions received funding from the alcohol monopoly and assumed the task of implementing the department's regulations.

As evident from the numerous petitions, complaints, and memoranda produced in this period, agents of the central government and the urban estates existed in two disparate mental worlds, and interaction often faltered in mutual miscommunication and incomprehension. Adding to the confusion, all the urban estates carefully appropriated the government's language of "order," "economic improvement," and "beautification" as a rhetorical strategy to further their particular ends, confirming officials in their conviction that sound, beneficent policies were failing because of the "ignorance" and "rapacity" of elected magistrates, as well as the legacy of "anarchy" and "disorder." Faced with poor results to salutary policies, as well as limited information about local conditions, officials could only conclude that rational improvement required greater coercive power as well as a well-oiled bureaucratic chain reaching down to the lowest level of government. These conclusions would inform subsequent reform efforts, including the major urban legislation of 1791. Reformers, though, frequently conflated "good order" with aesthetic appearance, favoring beautification and grandiose building projects as solutions to acute and intractable economic problems, and few questioned whether these priorities served the best interest of the town residents.

THE IMPORTANCE OF BEING ORDERED

The reform party associated with King Stanisław August, and even many of the monarch's opponents, had largely embraced the Enlightenment-era and Cameralist faith in the efficacy of universal solutions, central control, hierarchical organization and oversight as means of social and political improvement. The Commonwealth's royal towns, in particular, seemed ideal candidates for development projects. Everyone agreed that urban centers—not individually, but as a whole—were in a state of collapse and poverty, having never recovered from the wars of the seventeenth century. Even before the destructive civil war that preceded the first partition, foreigners' accounts, polemics, and town petitions invoked the image of "ruined," "filthy," and "neglected" towns in need of stimulus (*dźwignięcie*).[8] Lublin, once a major center of commerce and one of the largest cities in the Commonwealth, appears in multiple mid-eighteenth-century accounts as a dilapidated open sewer, lacking trade, illumination, and police. In the majority of royal towns, most numbering under one thousand people, many burghers practiced subsistence agriculture, differing from the surrounding peasants only by their title, while such commerce as existed was the preserve of Jews, whom enlightened officials regarded as parasitic and certainly not suitable replacements for a Christian *Bürgertum*. Those who did practice some industry usually brewed beer and distilled alcohol, and the result was that towns not only generated little industry or commerce but, in the mind of reformers, fostered a culture of drunkenness and negligence among the surrounding peasantry.[9]

Despite the economic and social costs of the many wars, the most recent being the Confederacy of Bar, reformers blamed the poor condition and economic stagnation of towns on ineffective and inept local governments. Town magistracies, in the center's view, failed to collect enough revenue or to budget properly for expenses. Moreover, reformers alleged that city councilors, who received no official compensation, had alienated property and revenue sources to outsiders for immediate personal gains, which erased the generous endowments granted by the Piast and Jagiellonian monarchs. Upon arriving in Lublin in 1780, the Good Order Commission under Chairman Kajetan Hryniewiecki ordered a thorough audit of the city's revenue sources. The chairman was indignant to discover that, "due to their fossilized anarchy prior to the arrival of the commission," the magistrates in the city council had signed away most of the town's revenue sources and properties, including the city gate, which certain Jews (who were legally barred from residing within the city walls) had converted into shops. Moreover, of the forty sources of revenue granted to the city magistracy by royal privileges dating back to Kazimierz the Great, Lublin only benefited fully from ten, partially from another six, and had completely lost or neglected the remaining twenty-four, netting a meager annual revenue of 4,444 zlotys, which did not even cover the 5,502 zlotys of planned expenses. For comparison, the forthcoming tax on alcohol would net between 9,000 and 10,000 zlotys per annum for the city treasury.[10]

Furthermore, poor record keeping and accounting meant that the remaining funds were often plundered or squandered on fruitless lawsuits. As evidence, reform-minded leaders pointed to crumbling walls, abandoned or demolished town halls, vacant lots, and badly maintained roads.[11] Burghers felt the imperative to defend their privileges against encroachment by starostas and jurydykas at law, which along with war costs strained municipal finances, but enlightened officials saw the problem as one of improper budgeting and supervision. As Hryniewiecki recounted in a 1782 letter to the king, his commission aimed to impress upon the Lublin citizens that "they cannot be happy without government, and they cannot be governed without orderly financial records."[12] Fear about the reliability of both city magistrates and starostas motivated reformers to tie all revenue-generating reforms to a bureaucratic chain of command. In the words of Bazyli Walicki, a member of the Permanent Council, new sources of urban income such as the alcohol monopoly needed to be "protected" from the rapaciousness of local officials.[13]

Finally, the widespread production of alcoholic beverages, a privilege granted to individuals as part of the Magdeburg Law, siphoned energy and resources away from more socially beneficial pursuits, while the concentration of alcohol stills in mostly wooden houses with straw roofs occasioned numerous urban conflagrations. As Chairman Ostrowski wrote in 1778: "[The revenue from alcohol production], which thus far has contributed only to drunkenness, and has been the reason that burghers have ceased to be burghers, i.e. merchants and artisans, could [if appropriated by the government] return them to the past, to their estate, and make them useful to the whole country in general."[14] From the burghers' perspective, the right of propinacja was an important social and economic prerogative, one of the privileges (and often the only one) that differentiated town citizens from the enserfed peasantry. As a defender of burgher prerogatives, Crown Chancellor Andrzej Młodziejowski, explained in 1777, propinacja also offered economic security "to every burgher in town . . . [so that] each could have a way to make a living,"[15] Just as nobles increasingly turned their rye and wheat into vodka, as the overseas grain trade slowed in the seventeenth century, burghers in royal towns frequently relied on propinacja to supplement their income. Starostas also enjoyed propinacja rights on the territories subordinate to them (including, in some cases, on intermural real estate) and frequently leased this right to Jews. In addition, residents of jurydykas also distilled and sold alcohol beverages under the protection of their patron and in defiance of the magistracy's writ.[16]

Reformers objected not only to the proliferation of alcohol production but also to the prominence of Jewish communities in urban propinacja. Many alleged that Jewish alcohol production added to the drunkenness and immiseration of both the peasantry and the burghers. Separating

Jews from alcohol production became an element of a general Enlightenment project to make Jews "useful," possibly by encouraging Jewish communities to take up agricultural pursuits. As one anonymous publicist wrote in 1774: "Towns are made up for the most part of Jews, an idle community, for whom the only worthy industry is to separate the peasant from the fruit of his labor. . . . One has to devise means in order to make Jews more useful to the country. The easiest method would be to oblige them to send their children to spin flax and wool or perform similar tasks."[17]

At the same time, the Commonwealth's coffers were dependent on the keg tax (*czopowe*), an excise levied on the production and sale of alcohol. Although the government collected this income irregularly, usually in time of war, the keg tax became a constant levy after 1761. From 1776 to 1788 the keg tax from the towns was the third largest source of revenue for the Commonwealth, behind the hearth tax (*podymny*) paid by all peasants and burghers and the starostas' *kwarta*.[18] The dilemma for government reformers, therefore, was to encourage burghers to take up more diverse trades, and preserve the Commonwealth's meager income intact.

Reforms enacted between 1768 and 1776 endeavored to correct these problems by introducing a more rational, supervised urban administration, controlling the expenditures of urban government, and regulating the production of alcohol in a manner beneficial to the cities and the whole country. The creation of Good Order Commissions in 1768 aimed to tackle a number of these issues through bodies of noblemen charged with auditing the funding in cities "in conjunction with the appropriate local authorities" and determining whether urban institutions were functioning properly. Prior to the first partition only a Warsaw commission came into existence, but after 1778 many more appeared, in part because the prerogative to charter these commissions remained solely in the king's hands and not subject to the Permanent Council.[19] Between 1778 and 1788, Stanisław August authorized more than a dozen such commissions for towns including Kraków, Poznań, Wschowa, Lublin, Sandomierz, Wilno, Brześć-Litewski, and Łuck, though the commissions varied in their accomplishments and some never actually convened. To prevent turf battles, starostas received a seat on the commissions, though not a deciding voice. The commissions had broad leeway to reshape towns according to their exclusively noble members' own convictions, though many of their decisions drew word for word from the lengthy regulations published by the Poznań Good Order Commission in 1778.[20]

The creation of the Department of Police within the Permanent Council added a further element of central oversight. In its first two years of existence, the Permanent Council lacked clear jurisdiction and functioned poorly, though the debates and proposals of the members offer an informative glimpse of the priorities and aspirations of the first state administration in the Commonwealth. In particular, the minutes reveal the dominance of Enlightenment-era political theory, including a broadly shared enthusiasm for centralized standards and uniform policies, as well as a strong familiarity with contemporary debates and practices across Europe. Within months of the Permanent Council's creation, the future chancellor Antoni Okęcki had proposed a measure that would have required all beggars to carry attestations and wear external markings that would be identical across the Commonwealth. Other members debated the introduction of standardized weights and measures in the cities as well as the wholesale abolition of guilds (authorized by the 1766 law) across the Commonwealth, though none of these projects was enacted.[21]

Frustrated with the council's limitations, in 1776 Stanisław August obtained permission from Otto von Stackelberg, the new Russian ambassador, to confederate the parliament for the purpose to expanding the reforms. Stackelberg, with the aid of Russian military power, ensured that the dietines returned compliant deputies to the parliament, which authorized further clarifications and additional powers to the Permanent Council. After a contentious debate, in which representatives of the government assured the opposition that neither the Department of Police nor the Good Order Commissions would interfere in private towns or replace the position of starosta, the parliament authorized a series of new powers for the central government, including the right to expend town incomes for "the most useful police regulations."[22] In addition, the parliament passed a wholesale and substantial propinacja reform, titled "A Regulation for Nowy Korczyn and Other Royal Towns in the Crown." Under the pretext of the numerous fires caused by private stills, the statute forbade individual distilling by burghers and Jews in the royal towns of the Polish Crown (the Grand Duchy of Lithuania was excluded). Christian townsmen and the starosta would now have to compete at a public auction for a one- or three-year monopoly alcohol contract, the proceeds for which would be earmarked for the town's use and beautification. No auction would be valid without an attestation by the starosta, who was also entitled to participate. Jews were officially deprived from propinacja "under any pretext."[23]

Even after the authorization of the propinacja legislation, a contentious debate raged in the Permanent Council at the beginning of 1777 over whether the central government could really deprive hundreds, if not thousands, of burghers and Jews of their principal incomes in the name of urban improvement. Młodziejowski protested that the law did not annul the burghers' individual *ius propinandi*. Given the importance of alcohol production for many burghers' livelihoods Młodziejowski argued that the propinacja law intended to auction off town taverns. Acting chairman Bazyli Walicki, on the other hand, pressed for the broadest possible interpretation of the law. He inserted a provision in a draft proclamation announcing the new rules that, "the revenue [from propinacja] is reserved for the general use of the town by law, and it may not be touched without the approval of the Department of Police."[24] The formula became embedded in the final decree, promulgated by the "King with the approval of the Permanent Council" in March 1777, mandating that all towns in the Polish Crown hold auctions no later than April of the same year, with the money reserved for state-approved projects. The decree allowed starostas to bid for the contract but stipulated that a burgher would win in the event of an equal bid. The amount collected from the keg tax would provide the threshold for the absolute minimum bid. Further, the Permanent Council required that any potential monopolist must provide evidence of sufficient collateral in the event of default.[25]

Taken together, the reforms of 1768–1776 proposed to reorganize significantly urban government and society in the name of the entire country's economic development. The new regulations largely left the urban power structure intact, and in fact the skeletal administration in Warsaw would require cooperation and assistance from local officials at every stage. Reformers openly doubted the reliability of magistracies and starostas, but a lack of funding and personnel required using the material at hand. Moreover, the Permanent Council could not challenge the position of the starostas, as the most prominent members of the government were themselves starostas, and the kings' ability to distribute these offices had remained one of their main sources of power and influence until 1775.[26] Despite the universality of the regulations, further, the Good Order Commissions appeared on an ad hoc basis, beginning with the principal town of each palatine, and the work of each commission varied enormously. Finally, the private towns and royal cities in Lithuania were completely excluded from the propinacja law. A more far-reaching reform in 1776 had annulled Magdeburg Law in the Grand Duchy for all but the eleven largest cities, placing the Treasury Commission in direct control of the former cities' finances. This extreme measure followed the same logic as the propinacja law and provided a warning for recalcitrant magistracies; the law stated that "[Magdeburg Law has] not achieved [its] intended effect, since the inhabitants continue ignorantly to practice agriculture, having not been encouraged to become merchants, traders, or artisans."[27]

ALCOHOL, A BURIED TREASURE

The propinacja reform reached the towns in 1777, a few years before most Good Order Commissions arrived, though the two measures eventually overlapped. From 1777 to 1778, propinacja took up most of the Department of Police's energies, and members devoted untold hours to resolving the many unanticipated disputes that erupted between urban residents over the right to the monopoly. A complaint written in May 1777 from the magistracy of Tuszyn, a town in the Sieradź palatinate of Great Poland, provides an archetypical illustration of the conflicts encountered:

> Following the orderly conclusion of the auction according to the decree of His Majesty and the Permanent Council, the city of Tuszyn awarded the propinacja contract to the Honorable Kostrzewski, the city scribe and a lawful resident [*dobrze osiadłemu*], who offered a sum equal to that of the starosta. . . . However, Prince Czetwertyński, the starosta, ordered his people to seal off the brewery and the beer from the contractor, and has forbidden burghers the right of propinacja since his acquisition of the sta-

rosta office, allowing Jews to distill on city property in violation of the most recent parliament's law.[28]

The starosta responded that the burghers failed to make a public announcement of the auction, as required by law, "and conspiring among themselves in a disorderly manner with a view of only their private economic interests," granted the contract to someone without sufficient collateral for only seven hundred zlotys, when the starosta assured the department that the town's propinacja could raise eight thousand. Moreover, the starosta denied authorizing the sealing of any brewery.[29] In this instance, the department sided with Kostrzewski, noting that the contract included the signature of one of the starosta's authorized representatives, but we can already see the basic disconnect. Members of the Department of Police remained largely indifferent about the identity of the auction's winner. As the purpose of the law was to generate money for local improvement, the government primarily desired that the auctions conclude as speedily as possible.

On the other hand, burghers, starostas, and Jewish communities had a variety of economic and political motives to win the propinacja contract for one of their own at all costs, if not to sabotage the introduction of the reform altogether. In fact, many petitions in early 1777 requested exemption from some provisions, drawing on the ambiguity of terms

TABLE 2. PETITIONS REVIEWED BY THE DEPARTMENT OF POLICE, 1777–1778

TYPE OF CASE	NUMBER	PERCENTAGE
Requests for exemption from the law	13	9
Challenges to the auction or to the monopoly contract	76	56
Complaints from contract holders and other grievances	21	16
Requests to expend the propinacja fund	25	19

within the legislation as well as within the Polish-Lithuanian legal tradition in general (see table 2). In the first place, the law excluded large cities (*miasta*), defined by the government as cities in the highest taxation bracket. Historically, however, the term *miasta* could refer to the palatinate capitals or other cities of onetime economic importance, a fact that inspired numerous petitions for exemption from relatively minor towns.[30] Lublin successfully evaded the law, as did other cities, including Kamieniec Podolski, Piotrków, Poznań, Kraków, and Warsaw. In its place, the Permanent Council established an excise tax (the "half-keg tax") on individual distillers for the benefit of the city coffers, subject to the same restrictions as the propinacja law. Ironically, this "exemption" solved the monetary problem but proved much more popular; many burghers lobbied for a similar exemption for their own cities.[31] Jewish communities also lobbied to escape the outright ban on distilling, and despite the "under no pretext" clause in the legislation, many succeeded. The kahals of Chełm, Chęciny, and Kazimierz Dolny could all produce privileges equating Jewish residents to burghers, a possession that apparently trumped the 1776 restrictions. Notably, these concessions did not mean a return to the status quo ante, as victory merely meant the right for one of their members to potentially win the contract, not a return to the previous individual freedom of profession.[32]

When exemptions from the legislation could not be obtained, starostas, burghers, and Jewish communities advocated their legal claim to the monopoly contract. For starostas the motivation for winning the propinacja auction rested on purely economic calculations: combining the burghers' propinacja with their own would create an almost complete alcohol monopoly on their territory. As revealed by burgher and starosta petitions, starostas employed a number of strategies to secure the contract or at least prevent the burgher contingent from obtaining it. In the first place, the starosta could simply refuse to appear at the auction, a move that automatically invalidated the process according to the 1777 regulations. Conversely, if the starosta chose to compete and lost, he or she could complain to the government that the burghers had colluded to conduct a secret, unsupervised auction.[33] Some starostas accused town councils of awarding the contract to a burgher despite a higher bid by themselves. Others alleged that towns had declared a winner in violation of specific regulations mandating a minimum bid and the possession of sufficient collateral. Finally, starostas could exploit their prerogative to name town officials, which usually included the right to select one of the four quarterly mayors each year. Using this leverage starostas could pressure town magistrates into providing written support for their position, and many cases adjudicated by the department include separate letters from the mayor in support of the starosta.[34]

For burghers, competing in the auction could be advantageous in completely nonmonetary ways. In many cases, towns had a legal right to practice propinacja, but for one reason or another (typically because of conflict with the starosta over the nature of those rights), the burghers had ceased to enjoy their prerogative to produce and sell alcohol. By alerting the department of their desire to hold an auction, such towns could obtain an official government decision mandating a propinacja auction, which had the effect of the center's confirming the burghers' right to produce alcohol. Starostas in such cases would protest that burghers had no such rights or, in any case, had long since ceased to exercise them, but the department always favored the towns when documentary proof was available. Townsmen in Urzędów and Krzemieniec obtained such favorable resolutions, a result enhancing their prerogatives vis-à-vis the starosta. Turning to the department in this manner proved a roundabout way of obtaining additional royal privileges regardless of the financial benefits of the law.[35]

Burghers consistently fought to ensure that the monopoly contract would be awarded to a member of their estate, a fact that appears puzzling for several reasons. First, no matter who obtained the contract, the money produced would end up in the same treasury with the same restrictions. Second, even if a burgher did outbid his rivals, not all townsmen would necessarily benefit. The winner could just as easily employ outsiders or Jewish intermediaries to conduct his distilling operations, and many town citizens would remain without their previous income from alcohol.[36] Nonetheless, in case after case, burghers demonstrated extraordinary estate solidarity and closed ranks to ensure that the monopoly contract would remain in burgher hands. For example, when mayors chose to side with the starosta, town citizens would compose separate petitions to the Department of Police to dispute their magistrates' testimony. When the starosta complained that the winner did not have enough collateral to support the amount pledged, the towns consistently replied with a sworn attestation that the community would collectively pledge its property to support their fellow burgher's contract.[37] In 1778 two towns admitted to the department that, in an effort to prevent the starosta from obtaining the contract, the winner had bid an amount that could not possibly be collected. In both cases, the town communities had knowingly pledged their collective property in support of this unrealistic bid.[38]

Perhaps the best example of the burghers' mentality and self-conception with regard to propinacja can be found in a series of petitions from the townsmen of Łęczyca. In July 1777 the townsmen and the Jewish community separately requested exemption from the law. In the burghers' petition, the authors noted that the town had only been classified as "small" due to fires and military extractions. The Łęczyca petition requested exemption from the law on the basis of its ancient privileges. The petition continued that, if the department were to reject its request, the town would pay 913 zlotys toward the propinacja fund in lieu of an auction. The Department of Police rejected both of these proposals. Two weeks later, the department received a letter from the marshal of the Łęczyca palatinate dietine requesting "in the name of the entire citizenry of Łęczyca palatinate" that the town remain exempt from the propinacja law "and in full possession of the rights of a capital town."[39] As the marshal made evident, the town had turned to the dietine for support after receiving the first rejection, since noble assemblies traditionally brought the requests of local towns to the national parliament. The bureaucratic formalism of the department, however, took no interest in noble patronage and rejected the second petition. The Jewish community in Łęczyca displayed a similar tenacity, sending three separate requests for exemption, all of which were denied.[40]

Even after losing their bid for exemption, the townsmen of Łęczyca refused to cede their collective right to propinacja. Following the loss of the 1779 propinacja auction to the starosta, Senator Walerian Łuszczewski, the magistracy simply refused to sign his contract. After the latter complained to the Department of Police, the burghers replied: "The town wishes to keep this auctioned propinacja for itself, and to this end, requests that the contract for the propinacja monopoly be given to the Honorable Hawrocki, the mayor and a respected citizen."[41] The department sided with the starosta, but Łuszczewski subsequently protested that the Łęczyca townsmen continued to import and sell spirits in violation of the law. In response to both complaints, the department informed Łuszczewski that he, as starosta, was responsible for enforcing the law.[42] This exchange illustrates two of the principal problems with this reform: the central government underestimated the burghers' attachment to their propinacja rights and overestimated the willingness and ability of starostas to serve as subordinate agents of central power. Łuszczewski, who was not only starosta but a senator and therefore a member of the wealthy elite, could not enforce his will even in one of the smallest provincial capitals in the Commonwealth.[43]

The struggle of townspeople across the Commonwealth to retain propinacja in burgher hands reflects the strength of their collective attachment to this right, regardless of the law's aims or the department's goals. If a burgher received the contract, then, in appearance at least, the town had preserved its privileges intact. On the other hand, if the starosta successfully outbid the burghers, then the town had effectively forfeited its rights and therefore lost a piece of the burghers' collective identity. For this reason, the burghers of Dubienka in the palatine of Bełz refused the starosta's offer of one thousand zlotys per annum if the citizens would renounce their right to propinacja. The burghers in this case did not dispute the starosta's assertion that none of them had exercised this right in decades.[44] Jewish communities also banded together to lobby for exemption from the law. Again, winning such dispensation created a possibility that could benefit only one member of the community, but the kahal always supported these efforts, as well as individual Jewish claims to the contract. The idea that alcohol production was an individual right and the prerogative of an estate was not unique to the Commonwealth's townsmen. The Russian Empire's Zaporozhian Cossacks listed propinacja as one of their fundamental rights in a 1764 petition to Empress Catherine II, and this prerogative remained one of the few "ancient liberties" of the host, which tsars through Nicholas I (r. 1825–1855) respected.[45]

Complaints and countercomplaints from burghers, Jews, and starostas wrecked the department's time line, and many towns remained in violation of the law for the first two years of its existence. In general, the Department of Police had three options for resolving cases: It could award the contract to one of the parties; order a new auction, or a first one, if none had yet been completed; or tell the petitioning parties to settle their disputes in court, that is, to take their dispute to the Chancellor's Assessor Court. Warsaw typically sided with the party that produced the most thorough documentation to prove their claim, and officials attempted to appear neutral, justifying decisions with references to laws and decrees.[46] The department was particularly inflexible with regard to the regulation stipulating that the minimum bid had to exceed the city's annual keg-tax payment. Burghers or starostas who accused their rivals of winning the contact on a lower bid almost automatically achieved their goal of having the auction annulled. Bidders, justifiably, claimed that they could never make a profit after paying such a sum to the town coffers. In response, the department explained that any town that did not receive its minimum bid would be financially disadvantaged vis-à-vis others. Nonetheless, consistent with Crozier's analysis of bureaucratic functioning, officials periodically bent or even violated their own precedents to remind subordinates of the chain of command.[47]

TABLE 3. ADMINISTRATIVE DECISIONS OF THE DEPARTMENT OF POLICE, 1777–1778

DECISION	NUMBER	PERCENTAGE
Town magistracy ordered to hold an immediate, first auction	15	20
Auction invalidated and a new auction ordered	28	37
Contract upheld for a burgher	18	24
Contract upheld for a starosta	9	12
Contract upheld for a member of the Jewish community	1	1
Petitioners told to resolve their dispute in court	5	6

The majority of petitions resulted in a decision that an auction should take place in the near future, resulting in further delays and problems (see table 3). The Department of Police issued this verdict any time one of the petitioners could claim that a rival had failed to observe one of the eight regulations enumerated in the March 1777 decree. This rubric also encompasses cases in which no auction had yet occurred.[48] Towns quickly learned that stalling had potential benefits. In Włodzimierz, for example, burghers justified repeated delays with the claim that the illegal distilling by the starosta and jurydykas had discouraged potential bidders. Reminding the department of the magistracy and the starosta's repeated, yet unsuccessful, requests for a Good Order Commission, the town government claimed that it could not possibly fulfill its obligation until a commission convened in the city. Since the town had no contract by March 1778, the Department of Police was compelled to issue a face-saving ruling, allowing individuals to continue private distilling so long as they paid taxes to the state-controlled propinacja fund.[49] Not surprisingly, burghers preferred this "temporary" compromise, which the department reluctantly applied in other towns that had successfully postponed their auction through 1778. In future years, the department withheld this option, and even Włodzimierz eventually submitted to a propinacja monopoly.[50]

For members of the Department of Police, the sheer number of disputes and the general lack of respect for its regulations simply reflected the "inveterate disorder" and "disobedience" of the towns. The town magistracies' inability to follow rules ostensibly designed for their own benefit reinforced the belief that town poverty was the result of local leaders' negligence and corruption. Hence the metaphor expressed by Ostrowski in the department's first biannual report: "The Commonwealth has a significant funding source under the supreme authority of Your Royal Highness, hidden in the towns, and laying like buried treasure. In the last two years, the Department of Police has begun to dig it up, to exhume the propinacja fund, which can be used for the beautification and improvement of the towns."[51] The government had to uncover this money because of the burghers' presumed "simplicity," a label that acting chairman Adam Szydłowski employed in 1782 to explain the townsmen's indifference toward efficiently exploiting their resources. He noted that the propinacja income was the one certain source of funding for towns, others being "questionable, lost, or neglected."[52] Notably, the department felt no more secure dealing with the starostas. When the department did reach a decision with regard to a disputed auction, the winner was twice as likely to represent the burgher party as the starosta (see table 3). This seems to suggest that the government found individual town communities no less reliable than their starosta supervisors.[53]

GOOD ORDER COMES TO TOWN

Many of the petitions to the Department of Police requested that the government dispatch Good Order Commissions, justifying delays and violations with regard to the general disorder. The magistracy of Włodzimierz's petitions for a Good Order Commission—supported enthusiastically by the starosta, incidentally—only stands out for its lack of success. For unclear reasons no commission ever convened even for the palatinate capital of Łuck.[54] By the early 1780s many such commissions were active in the major cities, and word spread that town governments were regaining lands, toll rights, and rents thanks to the work of the commissions, which enjoyed broad judicial authority. In particular, commissions devoted enormous time and effort to settling revenue disputes between magistracies and starostas as well as jurisdictional quarrels between city governments, kahals, religious orders, and jurydykas. Burghers particularly appreciated the fact that commissions often defended and enforced *De non tolerandis Judaeis* restrictions. In fact, many commissioners, including Hryniewiecki in Lublin, openly subscribed to the Enlightenment-era anti-Jewish convictions about the supposedly pernicious role of Jewish competition in the cities and upheld residential segregation as a manifestation of "good order."[55] Commissioners served pro bono, though the commissions required the services of a secretary, surveyor, and other ancillary employees, and the propinacja or half-keg tax provided a convenient source of revenue for this purpose.[56]

The Good Order Commission for Lublin received a charter in 1780, and the commissioners remained a visible presence in the city throughout the decade, notwithstanding circuit tours of other cities in the palatinate.[57] Under Hryniewiecki's guidance, the commission was particularly active, and the department allowed the commissioners broad leeway to utilize the half-keg tax, which in Lublin produced significant revenues. Like the Department of Police, Hryniewiecki emphasized the future benefits of his rationally conceived measures, and his letters reveal a degree of shock and frustration at the resistance and discord that accompanied the commission's reforms. The commissioners lost no time in auditing the magistracy's funding sources, as well as conducting a survey of the properties in the city and the suburbs. Hryniewiecki described the previously prosperous city as dirty, decaying, and poorly managed. Short-term gains had trumped long-term planning, as evidenced by the fact that the magistracy had even sold thoroughfare space as commercial real estate, making the city streets so narrow that "a single carriage can hardly pass through [the roads]."[58] To prevent future decisions of this nature, Hryniwiecki, following the model of the Poznań Good Order Commission, proposed a more rational organization of city government than the model of quarterly rotating mayors established by Magdeburg Law. Instead of "unqualified," nonprofessional officers serving without compensation, and presumably enriching themselves through fees from the sale of properties and transactions, in 1782 the commission established an elected city president and vice president with one-year terms. The president would be in charge of the overall administration and the town courts, while the vice president would take responsibility for sanitation, fire prevention, construction, and "police." Not content with these broad categories, the Good Order Commission drafted a comprehensive list of detailed regulations in 1784 for the new magistrates to enforce.[59]

According to the new rules, magistracy officials, in particular the vice president, would now supervise the construction of sewer canals for removing waste, while enforcing restrictions against throwing rotten food, feces, broken glass, spoiled beer, or house water into the street. In accordance with the Enlightenment emphasis on specificity and comprehensiveness, the Good Order Commission endeavored to plan for all eventualities, as illustrated by the following regulation:

> If an animal corpse is found in front of someone's property, the owner of that property or the person living there should immediately investigate and determine who dragged or threw the corpse. Having established the

> culprit, the discoverer should report that person to the sanitation inspector or the town prosecutor. If, however, the owner of this animal corpse is not found, then the executioner [*mistrz*] should be called immediately to remove it. If a foul stench from the corpse arises due to the discoverer's neglect to inform the executioner . . . that person will have to pay the said executioner double for the removal of the animal corpse.[60]

The Good Order Commission further forbade the release of galloping horses, rabid dogs, or pigs into town streets, presumably a commonsense measure. To combat fire, the commission ordered an end to the construction of wooden houses within town walls, as well as the practice of storing vodka and oil within these domiciles. Lublin and all its jurydykas were required to hire night watchmen. To round out these measures, the commission forbade betting games in public places and stipulated that anyone who wanted to display monkeys, dogs, or bears or to put on a comedy show in town must obtain permission from the magistracy.[61] Evidently, the new vice president would have his hands full.

Envisioning that the new magistracy authorities would became professional officials, the Good Order Commission determined to pay councilors and mayors regular salaries based upon a rationalized budget for computing revenue and expenditure. Lublin's revenue stream prior to the 1780s could not possibly provide for a salaried government as the magistracy funded itself via indirect taxes, fees, and rents from peasant villages, an amount that barely served to cover the costs of the service staff.[62] Until additional revenue sources could be unlocked, the commission was compelled to impose direct taxation on the city's merchants and artisans to the tune of five thousand zlotys—more than the city received from all its other revenue sources combined. The twenty-five merchant guilds, comprising some two hundred members, carried the bulk of this new tax, paying three thousand zlotys, while the forty-three artisan guilds contributed the remainder. For capital improvement projects, the commission could draw on the half-keg tax, instituted in lieu of the propinacja monopoly, which netted over nine thousand zlotys per annum. Hryniwiecki imposed further taxes so as to create a dedicated treasury for paving the streets and a fund to mitigate the costs of billeting soldiers, both costing a further three thousand zlotys.[63] All these revenues, as well as further monies unlocked in the course of the com-

TABLE 4. ORDINARY BUDGET FOR LUBLIN (1783), COMPOSED BY THE GOOD ORDER COMMISSION (KBO), NOT INCLUDING THE SEPARATE HALF-KEG, PAVING, AND BILLETING TREASURIES

Revenue	Zlotys	Expenditure	Zlotys	Debts	Zlotys
I. Historical revenue		Town president, vice president, 2 secretaries, and 1 archivist	2,000	Remnant owed to the surveyor hired by the KBO	1,548
Interest from a 15,000 zloty deposit	900				
Bridge toll	1,260	Treasurer, quarter-master, prosecutor	600	To the same, for ell measurement (79 cm)	540
Rents from Ponikwoda village	460	Archive copyists	900	Remnant owed the KBO secretary	2,340
Fees from city scales, approximately	100	Bookbinder for repairing town records	600	Remnant owed the KBO prosecutor	200
Tax on petty sellers and hawkers	100	Assistant prosecutor	100	Debt owed to Pacewicz by order of the KBO	2,240
Rents from bakers; irregular tolls for market sellers and bridge tolls for Jews	400	2 beadles and 4 guards	936	Owed to Konopka by order of the same	1,400
		Equipment and clothing for beadles and guards	700	Owed to Zielenewska by order of the same	1,000
Sum	3,420 (sic)	Maintaining bridges, roads, the well, and well-keeper (approx.)	800	Debt of Borakowski owed to Krebs by order of the same	500
II. Revenue created by the KBO					
Levy on merchants (Jan. 1782 to Jan. 1783)	2,736	Carting off filth and cleaning city streets	200	Sum of expenses plus debts	21,276

Levy on artisanal guilds	2,111	Executioner	72	Desired revenue for covering expenses	5,600
III. Conditional Income		Trumpeter	300		
Promised by merchants and distillers if the Jews are expelled from the suburbs	1,500	Choirmaster of the Collegiate Church	300		
		Extraordinary expenses, such as chancellery for economic matters; postal paper; fodder; representatives in Warsaw; hearth tax; fire regulations, etc.	4,000		
A levy on French and Hungarian wine could more or less import	6,000				
Sum Total	15,767	Sum Total	11,508		

Source: AGAD, ML IX.105, 90–92.

mission's judicial activities would make their way into rational financial records, which the commission now required the magistracy to compose.

In reality, the fiscal policies of the Good Order Commission produced a fair share of disorder, even within the seemingly rational budgetary policy. The records compiled by Hryniewiecki's commissioners indicated that the new system often overestimated the capacity of the town's potential, failed to account for extraordinary expenses, and even employed disingenuous accounting practices to plug the holes. The budgets themselves contained a number of suspicious items (see table 4). For example, from 1782 through 1787, one line of revenue includes a contribution of 1,500 zlotys from merchants and distillers on the condition that Jews be expelled from suburbs. Since Jews comprised half of the town's population of 8,500 in 1787, and by law they resided in the extramural suburbs, dubbed the "Jewish Town," this provision assumed a wholesale forced emigration that was patently beyond the commission's abilities (and would have represented an economic and demographic catastrophe for Lublin). Another line in the 1783 budget, included as part of the revenue total, indicated that a tax on Hungarian wine "could produce," six thousand zlotys for the town, though Hryniewiecki admitted that he had no success in collecting these monies. For this reason, the projected revenue for 1783 appeared much higher than any subsequent year.[64] Notably, without these two items, the budget for the 1780s would not balance.

In addition to financial chicaneries, the commission faced the more serious problem of collecting the funds inscribed into the record books. In the first year of the Good Order Commission's levy on merchants and artisans, the Departments of Police, War, and Justice in the Permanent Council held a joint conference in response to pleas by Hryniewiecki for military assistance in collecting the new taxes, a sign that all was not going according to plan. The conference concluded that the Good Order Commission should rely on local authorities, meaning the magistracy and the starosta, to enforce its decisions. Although the commission managed to collect much, though not all, the money desired, in 1783 Hryniewiecki again appealed to the Department of Police for military personnel to assist with extracting the levy. This time the department, which possessed few options itself, suggested that Lublin employ its own city militia. The reliability of the magistracy as agents of the commission was hardly exemplary, as evidenced by a 1785 letter to King Stanisław August, in which Hryniewiecki expressed gratitude for a recent royal list to the magistracy requiring officials to render assistance in collecting these taxes and punishing "disobedience."[65]

Meanwhile, the merchants themselves collectively composed a complaint to Crown Chancellor Młodziejowski in 1783 requesting that the chancellor annul the taxes, "which are mostly paid by the merchants." The petitioners noted that the new taxes "have profited the Commission secretary by 300 zlotys," while the remainder has merely settled "a few debts."[66] The merchants continued by pleading with the chancellor that, if the taxes imposed for 1783 were collected, then they at least be cancelled after 1784. The chancellor does not seem to have responded, but after four years of diminishing returns for the taxes, the commission finally relented. Having repaired the municipal gate with the half-keg tax funds, the commission now leased six shops to merchants, which provided funds to cover the salaries. The commission also experienced passive resistance and evasion with regard to the paving and billeting treasuries. In a 1783 letter to Subchancellor Jacek Małachowski, Hryniewiecki requested additional money for paving from the Permanent Council's extraordinary fund, noting that the town had only collected three thousand out of its four thousand zloty target, and this only with great difficulty.[67] The Permanent Council supported the request for one year, but the commission continued to face difficulties in collecting funds, particularly from the fifteen-odd extramural jurydykas, whose residents refused to fund the treasuries and declined to pay the half-keg tax. In addition, the tax farmer, who leased the right to collect the half-keg tax, repeatedly pleaded with both Hryniewiecki and the Permanent Council about his inability to collect the tax from brewers and distillers, a fact that he claimed threatened him with bankruptcy.[68]

Hryniewiecki, in line with officials in the Department of Police, attributed resistance and undercollection to "disobedience," "disorder," and long-standing "anarchy," which the commission could not overcome because of its limited enforcement abilities. As Hryniewiecki observed to the king in 1785, "[the town citizens] see that the commission has the power to order but no power to compel obedience."[69] Perhaps no story better illustrates the obstacles faced by the Good Order Commission in imposing order and obedience than the commission's long-running confrontation with Lublin's executioner, a dispute revealed in a brief filed by the Good Order Commission's prosecutor in October 1789: "The local executioner is paid by the town, has a free apartment, and collects incidental benefits. However, he refuses to execute criminals . . . without a separate payment. Since the prosecutor, not having money for this additional expense, has to bring greater harm to society by letting these criminals free, the court orders the wójt's office to force the executioner to carry out [the court's] orders without any extra compensation. Further, when assisting with executions, the wójt's office should not claim any special compensation for itself."[70] Prior to the appearance of salaries, municipal officials collected gifts and rewards for performing their functions, either in adjudicating disputes, authorizing transactions, or executing criminals. The meager salary allotted to the executioner by the Good Order Commission—seventy-two zlotys in comparison to the mayor's two thousand—hardly provided a sufficient inducement to break with the tradition of special compensation (for such a sum one could rent a single room in a townhouse or buy ten barrels of beer), particularly given the unpleasant nature of the job and the low probability of finding a replacement. The commissioners imagined that a rationalized budget would automatically convert officers of the magistracy into obedient state servants, and the executioner's intransigent demand for a traditional "head premium" placed Hryniewiecki in a quandary. Conceding to the executioner would set a bad precedent and undermine the already shaky foundations of the municipal budget, but the commission's rules, as well as general law and order, would collapse while the "power of the sword" remained on strike. In the end, the commission caved and ordered a new round of taxes in August 1790, justified in part by the need to raise funds to compensate the executioner and combat rising public disorder.[71]

At least the Lublin Good Order Commission could dispose of the half-keg propinacja tax, which not only compensated its employees but provided a significant sum for capital improvement projects. The propinacja funds proved to be the only major source of revenue upon which the commission could reliably depend, and the Department of Police allowed Hryniewiecki and his commissioners a wide latitude in disposing of these funds. Guided by Hryniewiecki, Lublin employed its alcohol-tax funds to repair the two city gates, the city bridge, and the town hall, edifices that remain to this day. These projects eventually brought revenue in the form of real estate leases, but implementing these repairs required the commission to overrule prior decisions of the magistracy. For example, the magistracy had previously resolved to dismantle the Kraków Gate and recycle its bricks; Hryniewiecki overruled this decision in favor of saving the gate, a fact that threatened the city with legal action from those who had obtained a contract for the demolition work. Other cities could not even imagine such problems. The Good Order Commission in Żytomierz, capital of Kijów palatinate, had no propinacja fund because of ongoing litigation between the magistracy and the starosta. In order to repair the town hall, the commission was compelled to float a thirty-thousand-zloty loan on behalf of the magistracy, an endeavor that the Department of Police approved despite its general antidebt policy.[72]

SPENDING THE BURIED TREASURE

The dependence of the Good Order Commissions on the alcohol-tax funds opened a new front in the second major conflict of the propinacja law: the battle between magistracies and the Department of Police over who controlled the new revenues. In 1777 the department had issued detailed regulations forbidding town governments from expending the funds until Warsaw received a formal petition from the magistracy with a cost justification, including a complete report of that town's sources of revenue, debts, and ordinary expenditures, as well as an attestation from the starosta (or Good Order Commission) confirming the necessity of the proposed project.[73] As had become apparent by the mid-1780s, however, city magistracies chafed under these restrictions, and the presence of a Good Order Commission offered an inviting pretext for magistracy officials to request funds for their own use. In 1784 the department issued new regulations seeking to forestall this "abuse": "Examples of arbitrariness and profligacy are multiplying in the expenditure of town revenues. . . . The largest number of towns violating the regulation against disbursing the propinacja fund without permission typically conceal their actions as expenses for supporting Good Order Commissions."[74] As a solution, the king and the Permanent Council pledged to find funding for the commissions independent of the propinacja fund. Meanwhile, the commissioners themselves, in conjunction with the starostas, were to submit requests for using this funding for any additional expenses, bypassing the input of the magistracies entirely.[75]

As this conflict reveals, the propinacja reform did provide a convenient excuse for town governments to raise revenue without incurring local opposition, and funds began filling city coffers after 1778. As the propinacja monopoly increasingly became the norm, reviewing requests to allocate the new funding superseded adjudicating contract disputes as the dominant occupation of the department. The petitions highlight a second disconnect between the assumptions and priorities of the center and the townsmen. Town magistracies, accustomed to wide discretion in spending matters, presumed that the money in the propinacja coffers belonged to their town. The department, meanwhile, viewed this revenue as a state fund under its protection. This divergence created a game in which town leaders played dumb, ignored rules, and exaggerated expenses in order to obtain permission to employ the maximum amount of money, often on priorities to which the department would not have consented. For its part, the government tried to approve the minimum amount necessary for completing a particular project, maintaining vigilance against "misuse" and "theft" whenever possible.

From the outset the department sought to emphasize its undisputed control over the town's propinacja funds by amending or modifying spending requests. Since towns continued to view the money as theirs, magistracies frequently presented nonspecific requests to "spend the fund" or to use "the previous year's intake," enumerating a list of projects to which the money would be applied. In order to impress upon the towns that, on the contrary, the money belonged to the state, the Department of Police consistently approved only half the amount requested, regardless of the petitioners' goals or the available money.[76] Even when the towns requested an explicit amount, the department chose to make a demonstration of its authority by approving half the proposed sum. In fact, the department authorized half the amount requested in twenty out of the twenty-one petitions submitted in 1777–1778.[77] Beyond demanding that towns implement their chosen projects with only half the funding, the department often added further demands such as requiring the purchase of firefighting tools, to demonstrate the center's superior position. This entire process, in the words of the department's 1788 report, was to prevent the towns from allocating this funding "on froth" (*na pienią*) or "arbitrarily" (*domyślenie*), that is, on projects not prioritized by the central government.[78]

Town governments responded to the department's paternalism with a number of counterploys. Since the department would approve only half the amount requested, towns would propose more than required or compose multiple requests. If the starosta or Good Order Commission supported the town, then the department had little choice but to approve the petition.[79] Notably, starostas consistently backed the requests of the towns, despite their recent and bitter conflicts over propinacja contracts. In my view, this was largely because the rivalry between starostas and towns was primarily an economic and political contest, and not the manifestation of some type of class or estate hostility. For example, the town of Warka had witnessed an especially acrimonious battle for the contract. After the dispute concluded, however, the burghers not only obtained money for repairing their town hall with the assistance of the starosta but requested that the latter even oversee the construction.[80]

Other, more peripheral towns simply ignored the department's writ, holding the propinacja auction legally but expending the funds, in the words of the central government, "according to their own caprice" (*własnym domyślem*). Audits conducted by the department in Chełm and Piotrków in the 1780s, for example, indicated that both towns had failed to request permission for using the fund. In the case of Chełm, both the magistracy and the kahal cooperated to use the fund in a lawsuit against the starosta without reference to higher authority.[81] Lacking a corpus of on-the-ground agents beyond the Good Order Commissions, the government often had to believe reports received or had to hope, in the absence of reports, that regulations were being observed. As Chairman Mniszech wondered rhetorically in 1786, "are the propinacja sums recorded in our registers actually located in the town treasuries? Have the sums approved for the various town needs been faithfully and effectively used?"[82] Standardization offered one potential solution. In 1786 the department hired an architect to design a generalized town hall plan for which the construction costs would be known in advance, thus preventing town magistracies from inflating their spending requests. In his report to parliament, Mniszech noted that the architect had created two plans, one wooden and one of stone, to accommodate various town budgets. Evidently, the government intended to enforce this plan, for when Łęczyca requested permission to use its funds to build a new town hall in 1787, the department required that the town employ the standardized design.[83]

Slowly, the Department of Police began building a professional corpus of inspectors who, backed by military force, could impose regulations on disobedient towns. In 1787 one of these inspectors arrived in the troublesome town of Łęczyca and subsequently reorganized all the city's revenue sources into a rationalized budget based on leasing revenues to tax farmers. In 1788 the department indicated to parliament that its officials had conducted similar inspections in thirty-five towns.[84] In 1788 a delegate from the department arrived in the town of Solec with a military contingent to compel the town council to obey the department's regulations. Solec had failed to present a report on its use of the propinacja fund for the law's entire eleven-year existence. According to the delegate, the town had expended the entire fund on court cases, and "it wasted the remainder on disorder." In its final report, the Department of Police complained that it had employed military power to subdue only four such towns.[85] Inspections and military "corrections" could at best provide only temporary solutions, as the commissioners were only too aware. The Good Order Commission in the town of Piortków, for example, complained to the Department of Police in 1784 that, having returned from a circuit tour, the commissioners discovered that all fire and financial regulations had been abandoned soon after the commission left town.[86]

PROGRESS ONLY FOR THE OBEDIENT

In 1788 the Department of Police authored what, in retrospect, would become the last biannual report of the agency's existence. Shortly thereafter, the parliament decreed the abolition of the Permanent Council, which was widely viewed as a tool of Russian domination and executive overreach. The Department of Police disappeared, bringing an end to central oversight over the propinacja revenues (but not the municipal alcohol taxes, which magistracies continued to collect into the nineteenth century), while the new Civil-Military Commissions soon appeared in the principal cities of the Commonwealth. A new epoch of reform would soon begin, and authors of subsequent legislation had plenty of opportunity to digest the apparent lessons of this first experiment in urban improvement, as officials in the Department of Police and the Good Order Commissions had broadcast the perceived shortcomings of the 1768 and 1776 laws in biannual reports, newspaper articles, and memoranda to the king and the now defunct Permanent Council.[87]

Chairman Szydłowski summarized the dominant perspective that insufficient power doomed otherwise praiseworthy measures in his 1782 report: "In 1776 the Commonwealth indeed broadened the power of our department . . . but since no power of enforcement was given, the department's authority over the towns has been limited to those that wish to be obedient."[88] Hryniewiecki sounded a similar theme is his 1782 letter to Stanisław August, writing that the Lublin Good Order Commission "would happily and swiftly bring order, cleanliness and, eventually, attractiveness to the royal town of Lublin, if only the town were subordinate to [it] exclusively."[89] Uncertain obedience characterized all the agents upon whom the department and the Good Order Commissions relied, including both the starostas and magistracies, neither of whom fulfilled regulations or followed procedures. As the auction disputes evinced, local officials spent more time quarreling and litigating among themselves than implementing the reforms intended to improve their communities.

Meager means and personnel also limited the geographic range of the measures, with obedience and compliance markedly lacking in the Ukrainian provinces of the Crown. In his 1778 report Ostrowski observed that the propinacja fund had unearthed tens of thousands of zlotys in income, but he noted, "this fund would be even more significant had several towns, particularly Ukrainian, been obedient to the regulations of this law."[90] A 1779 decree intended to clarify the auctioning procedure further complained that a significant number of towns "specifically in Kiev, Volhynia, Podolia, and Bracław palatinates" had not sent reports regarding their auctions, and thereby "prejudice the revenues, which have been placed under the Department of Police's supervision."[91] Szydłowski wrote that "the Lithuanian and Ukrainian towns could say that they have no Department of Police," attributing this problem to the fact that the Ukrainian cities, "having been settled largely by Jews and Cossacks, are without law, without offices, and without privileges . . . [and] hardly know that they are royal towns."[92] Indeed, between 1777 and 1788, only five royal towns out of fifty-one in the four palatinates of Ukraine appear to have corresponded with the department. Moreover, fewer Good Order Commissions convened in Ukraine, despite summons from the king and repeated requests from town citizens and starostas.[93]

Officials in the Department of Police could imagine only one possible solution to these limitations: the expansion of a permanent executive power to coerce magistracies, kahals, and other locals into implementing the laws designed for their improvement. In 1782 Szydłowski proposed a royal decree to compel the town councils to auction not only propinacja but all town revenue sources, such as bridge tolls, market fees, and rent payments from peasant villages belonging to the towns. As with propinacja, expenditure of these revenues would require the

Department of Police's authorization. Town auditors did impose this solution in Łęczyca in 1787, and this model became the norm in Napoleonic Poland. To oversee this process Szydłowski unsuccessfully proposed that the parliament create centrally controlled *intendants* (*intendentów*) to make circuit inspections and ensure that government decrees were faithfully executed. These *intendants,* like members of the Good Order Commissions after 1784, would receive direct compensation from the propinacja fund.[94] Later reports dropped the French term but not the proposal to give the department direct supervisory power over a more subordinate and rationally conceived hierarchy of officials. The Department of Police's final report to parliament in 1788 called for the establishment of fifteen police commissars for the Polish Crown "to assist" the starostas in overseeing and regulating towns, with funding supplied once again from the propinacja treasuries.[95]

In all the hand-wringing about deficiencies in the coercive apparatus, the officials in the Permanent Council never seem to have questioned the assumptions and theories informing the plans. Placing culpability for urban blight on the drunkenness of the burghers, the incompetency of the town magistracies, and the disingenuousness of the Jews, Warsaw bureaucrats ignored the long-term and external causes of the cities' decay and stagnation. Both the Department of Police and the Good Order Commissions favored beautification and hierarchy as a solution to problems caused by the Commonwealth's precarious international position. When offered a chance, burghers lost no time in criticizing the government's solutions. As the 1789 burgher petition records, "Freedom and law will much more enrich free people engaged in trade and industry than the sprinkling of millions on the aid and beautification of cities."[96] Stanisław Staszic, a publicist of burgher origin who generally favored a strong centralized state, also argued against the philosophy of the reforms: "Whoever thinks that external order, the speckling of paint on homes, and removing waste from cities will introduce trade and wealth into the country has no knowledge of our economic needs."[97] In terms of material and social achievements, the reforms after the first partition did fail to match expectations, but one success does emerge. Magistracies and kahals learned to expect regular decrees and ordinances from the center, orientating their actions toward higher authorities and anticipating disciplinary action. None of the reforms on their own altered the republican culture of the cities, but elites succeeded in constructing a foundation of state consciousness, upon which the more far-reaching reforms of the Four-Year Parliament would build.

3

Weaponizing Good Order

URBAN POLITICS AND CIVIC REPUBLICANISM IN THE ERA OF CONSTITUTIONAL REFORM AND PARTITION, 1788–1809

"THE CITY AUTHORITIES AND jurydykas do not obey the [Assessor Court] decrees and constantly oppose the starosta; moreover, the burghers continually summon the starosta to court, which not only compels him to undertake unnecessary expenses, but deprives the burghers of the means to pay rents due to the starosty."[1] So reads one line of Prince Janusz Sanguszko's petition, which lustration auditors recorded during their visit to Krzemieniec on 17 July 1789. Sanguszko, who also held the position of wójt, communicated through his administrator that none of the urban residents paid their ground rents to the castle, while those living in the jurydykas refused to perform their labor duties (*szarwarki*), despite both provisions having been mandated by recent Assessor Court decrees. In a detailed response, the burghers charged the starosta with demanding rents from tax-exempt buildings, preventing burghers "with his soldiers and boyars" from constructing new buildings on formerly Jewish possessions that had been awarded to the city by the Assessor Court, and forbidding city authorities from enforcing verdicts in cases between Christians and Jews. The city magistracy further charged the kahal of Krzemieniec with refusing to quarter soldiers, perform *szarwarki*, or pay property taxes to the cities, using the protection of the starosta to violate an agreement concluded by the city and the kahal in 1786. Not to be outdone, the Jewish community recorded its own complaint in which the kahal elders alleged that the burghers were preventing Jews from rebuilding their houses following a citywide fire, while compelling the dispossessed owners to pay ground rents. The starosta, the kahal claimed, provided no protection against the daily violence and oppression of the burghers, who routinely confiscated Jewish goods, illegally summoned Jews to burgher courts for the purpose of levying spurious fines, and contrary to what the burghers asserted, forced the majority of billeting duty on Jewish homes.[2]

Lustration officials collected similar acrimonious complaints and mutually contradictory petitions in town after town, which officials in Warsaw viewed as further evidence that despite the best efforts of the Good Order Commissions and the Department of Police the royal towns of the Commonwealth not only remained disobedient but suffered from internal discord and chaos. How could cities pave roads, construct infrastructure, or develop policies for economic growth if all parties were locked in continuous litigation and intractable power struggles? In the lands partitioned in 1772, the new authorities had moved quickly to replace this perceived morass with their vision of good order; all three states deposed starostas from their offices and sought to replace the tangled web of jurisdictions and immunities with rationally conceived and hierarchically structured municipal governments. In an effort to prevent the transmission of old habits, the Austrian and Prussian regimes even imported nonnative officials to staff virtually all levels of administration.[3] Enlighteners observing the pace of reforms in the Commonwealth had reached similar conclusions about the solution to intercity conflict by the time that what would later become the Four-Year Parliament convened in 1788. Hugo Kołłątaj and Stanisław Staszic, champions of greater civil rights for the burghers, attributed urban discord to a weak central government, and both advocated a more muscular and rationally designed state as means of ensuring the success of urban improvement projects.[4]

The Four-Year Parliament enacted many of these proposals, and legislation from 1788 through the collapse of the Commonwealth in 1795 strengthened the role of the state within the cities while aiming at greater uniformity and rationality. Taking advantage of Russia's momentary preoccupation with an Ottoman war as well as the disingenuous support proclaimed by Prussia's new king, Friedrich Wilhelm II (r. 1786–1797), the parliament confederated in 1788, and the deputies embarked upon a program of wholesale reform. Within months, the parliament had abolished the Permanent Council, promulgated the creation of a hundred-thousand-man army, and delegated a commission to design a new constitution for the country. In a change from previous practice, laws authorized by the parliament after 1788 became valid immediately, rather than at the end of the session. Deputies authorized the first lustration audit of the Crown lands and starosties since 1765, and lustration committees began work the following year. In 1789 the parliament further established Civil-Military Commissions in every palatinate to oversee the recruitment, billeting, and transfer of soldiers, and these bodies continued and expanded the activities of the Good Order Commissions. Most crucially, the urban reform law entitled "Our Free Royal Cities"—passed two weeks before the Constitution of the Third of May on 19 April 1791—strengthened the magistracies' control over all urban space, excluding the starostas from any oversight and placing Jewish communities under city authority. In June 1791 the parliament created a new centralized Police Commission with extensive new powers over the cities.[5] Even the 1793 parliament, which overturned the Constitution of the Third of May under pressure from Russian-backed magnates, retained centralized police institutions, a testament to the widespread acceptance of Enlightenment solutions for the reform of cities even among the most zealous defenders of the unreformed Commonwealth.[6]

In Polish historiography the urban reform law has long featured as a "progressive" measure that portended a more just and inclusive society. Significantly, the urban reform laws seemed to fulfill desires expressed by the burghers themselves. Recall that, during the Black Procession in 1789, the collected towns of the Commonwealth led by the Warsaw magistracy appealed to parliament for greater civil rights, including the protection of *neminem captivabimus* (akin to habeas corpus) and the right to purchase landed estates. Burghers in their petition submitted to the king further requested the right to serve the country in the officer corps, the ecclesiastical hierarchy, the central government, and even the legislature, employing Enlightenment language about public utility and the common good. The burghers' agreement to unite recorded, for example, that "the public interest should henceforth be the interest of all towns, both Polish and Lithuanian" while the petition opined that "true liberty, freedom, and individual security requires that no one levies any burdens or obligations on a person without his knowledge and consent."[7] Thanks to the lobbying of influential supporters, including the king himself, members of the burgher estate received virtually all their desiderata save the right to participate in the legislature. City magistracies obtained complete jurisdiction over all groupings within urban space, including Jews, jurydykas, and noble property owners. Nobles now had to submit to city jurisdiction and citizenship, while starostas lost all political prerogatives within the towns.[8] The gains appeared so significant that townspeople across the country publicly feted the new law, and magistracy elections for 1792 opened with expressions of gratitude to the king and the parliament, while burghers such as the famous cobbler Jan Kliński fought arduously to defend the Commonwealth both in the war with Russia in 1792 and in the Kościuszko Uprising of 1794.[9]

On the other hand, not every member of the urban community benefited. "The Polish burghers were just as conservative as the majority of the nobility," wrote Arthur Eisenbach, noting that the townspeople in 1789 primarily aimed to enhance their own privileges and exemptions, including the wholesale exclusion of the Jews from urban citizenship.[10] In fact, the Jewish communities of the Polish Crown lands had submitted their own petition in 1789, entitled "A Humble Request," which also borrowed from the lofty language of Enlightenment universalism to advance arguments for eliminating barriers to trade and residency for Jewish urban citizens. Officials across the Commonwealth frequently propounded that the common good should transcend religious differences, and the "Humble Request" directly appealed to this sentiment. Declaring the willingness of the Jewish community to pay significant taxes, the request concluded, "We want for this country to become our Fatherland, which would grant us the freedom to secure a livelihood and the strength to pay taxes."[11] Unfortunately, despite the comparatively large amount of time devoted to debating the Jewish Question, the Four-Year Parliament failed to authorize any reform altering the social or political restrictions on Jews in the Commonwealth. Indeed, by granting the requests of the Christian townspeople, the parliament ipso facto removed some of the protections and securities previously enjoyed by urban Jews, who along with other losers in the 1791 settlement—the jurydykas and starostas—mobilized to stymie and frustrate the new constitutional order.[12]

As with similar attempts to rationalize urban space in the partitioned lands, the reforms of the Four-Year Parliament underestimated the complexity of urban politics in the Commonwealth, which involved perpetual negation among a constellation of corporate structures, each with its own accumulation of privileges and duties. Players included not only the burgher magistracy and the Jewish kahal but also organized assemblies of urban citizens, residents of jurydyka enclaves, starostas, monasteries, and royal institutions such as the Assessor Court. Privileges and exemptions existed on paper and in the imagination of each authority, and many a group's rights contravened or impinged upon another estate's autonomy or exemptions, necessitating continuous litigation and petition writing to all authorities who might provide assistance. Paradoxically, complaints such as those recorded in Krzemieniec belied a functioning balance of power, in which no authority dominated and no group lacked options for redressing grievances. In fact, multiple power centers and authorities created space for aggrieved citizens to seek succor under the law, while shifting loyalties among the groupings undermined the control of any one player. For example, although starostas have frequently played the role of oppressors and villains in Polish historiography, these officials also sheltered malcontents and minorities, notably the Jewish community, from persecution by magistracy officials.[13]

Interventions meant to create good order and benefit the urban citizens instead sowed discord by scrambling the balance of power among estates, each of which appropriated new centrally mandated duties and burdens as weapons to further their gains or arrest the loss of power. Rather than overseeing the enactment of good order regulations, administrators on the Civil-Military Commissions, the Police Commission, and even post-partition authorities found themselves drawn further into seemingly intractable conflicts among groups. The rational-bureaucratic assumptions and one-size-fits-all mentality of the reform legislation bore a significant share of the responsibility for the continuing discord, as did the tendency of enlightened officials to attribute the qualities of fiscal profligacy, ignorance, and insubordination to all urban groupings. On first reading, the priorities of the Warsaw legislators and the burgher-rights movement appeared to elide, but in fact the two sides approached the problem of urban reform from two entirely different perspectives, a fact that common goals and the mutual employment of Enlightenment rhetoric served to mask. All urban estates, despite their mutual hostility and apparent unhappiness remained committed to a republican vision of self-government, whereas enlightened officials both in the late Commonwealth and in the partitioning powers viewed cities as a component of the state's administrative structure. In practice, each state was prepared to allow a certain degree of self-administration, but only according to an abstract blueprint without reference to local peculiarities. As a result of this disconnect, conflicts among local players over the boundaries and limitations of these reforms continued to bedevil urban politics from 1791 through the final partition of the Commonwealth.[14]

The reforms of the Four-Year Parliament and beyond generated a new wave of pleas, protests, and proposals, from the refined, flowery propaganda pieces sponsored by the Warsaw magistracy to the complaints prepared in regional city councils in anticipation of lustration officials. A broad comparison of the often mutually contradictory petitions and depositions from the Lublin, Chełm, and Right-Bank Ukraine regions in this period highlights the common political values, assumptions, and aspirations shared by seemingly antithetical estates, with differences based more on "whom" than on "what." The urban estates all possessed privileges that granted autonomy from external interference as well as jurisdictional powers, if only over their own members. In quotidian legal and extralegal encounters, Jewish communities, jurydykas, and town magistracies all sought to maximize their autonomy from the legal jurisdiction and the burden-imposing powers of outsiders. For their part, starostas and magistracies fought to extend both their jurisdiction and their authority to impose taxes and other burdens over the maximum possible number of subjects. As revealed by the complaints, recorded by assiduous officials, the anxieties of urban life could make individuals appear petty, vindictive, and insular. Starostas and other noble officers protested about not receiving sinecure revenues. Burghers complained of Jews violating residential restrictions, though the burghers themselves had enabled such violations by selling the property in the first place. Jurydyka magistracies resisted demands to contribute taxes and services to the main town while benefiting from its existence. Even Jewish elders complained of legal taxes and burdens as violations of their privileges and exemptions.

At the same time, if one considers the perspective of each petitioner, such selfishness and jealousy becomes resilience and tenacity in the face of continuous challenges to that petitioner's status and existence. From this view, the loss of any one prerogative could become the first step on the slippery slope to subjugation and servility. Like their ostensible opponents, the so-called conservative nobility, urban estates subscribed to the civic republican conviction that freedom represented a specific institutional arrangement rather than an inherent human right. For this reason, the totality of privileges served as the bulwark against tyranny and servitude, and each group imagined this accumulation of particularistic rights as the indivisible private property of the estate.[15] The magistracy of Kraków provided a key to this mentality, when in 1789 the city fathers sought to block a proposed propinacja reform, which unlike the 1776 measure would have affected the large cities equally. The magistracy inveighed that "the property of the city is just as sacred as that of those granted legislative powers [that is, the nobility]," pondering: "What will be sacred, if a citizen sees no security for himself in the book of law, when the legislation of the Commonwealth can disappear with each new impulse? What foreigner would dare abandon his home and the graves of his ancestors to settle in Poland when privileges granting freedoms, which have been secure for several centuries, can so easily be destroyed?"[16] Such innovations formed a major justification for the burghers' appeal to participate in parliament; not the desire to create laws but, rather, to prevent deleterious changes. In this respect, the view of the burghers mirrored the ideas of the seventeenth-century republican Andrzej Maksymilian Fredro, who penned a defense of the liberum veto as a bulwark against "harmful novelties."[17]

In pursuing these broadly similar goals in petitions and legalistic challenges, the various estates employed rhetorical strategies designed to win sympathy from outsiders and potential allies, a fact that obscured the power dynamics on the ground. At the local level, estates facing challenges to their autonomy framed their complaints as oppression and a violation of their contract with the monarch and parliament, while polemics at the national level transformed the issue of maintaining and honoring privileges into a matter of public utility. Countering the "privilege defenders," starostas and magistracies appealed for assistance to actualize their presumed legal rights, invoking the language of law and order, which converted oppression into enforcing the law. Starostas and magistracies also deployed the new vocabulary of enlightened reform, expressing their desire to contribute to the broadly circulated goals of "good order," economic revitalization, and implementation of the laws, goals that were thwarted by the resistance of the "privilege defenders." For example, one anonymous noble suggested that blame for the frequent legal battles between starostas and burghers should fall on the latter's reflexive legalism, caused by too many lawyers "encouraging [their fellow burghers] to legal battles."[18] Both "law enforcers" and "privilege defenders" played the victim and accused their opponents of violence. The contrasting petitions suggest that such claims, though real enough in a society with a "continual background static of violence," contained a hyperbolic and rhetorical character reminiscent of the Notary's complaints on behalf of his "wounded" masons in Aleksander Fredro's play "The Revenge."[19] Taking such grievances at face value has led to an overemphasis on the subjugation and helplessness of urban actors, who usually proved more resourceful and indomitable than their missives conveyed.

Into this mixture of enlightened and republican posturing burghers poured vitriolic Judeophobic rhetoric, which appears to support the common claim that ethnoreligious hostility and specifically the desire to eliminate Jewish competition fueled and sustained the Black Procession.[20] On a day-to-day basis, however, burgher grievances against Jewish communities and other "foreigners" had little to do with religious, ethnic, or class animosity but, instead, involved a competition for resources and authority between legally distinct groups in a dynamic of shifting power relations. The rhetoric of religious antipathy frequently accompanied these disputes in petitions and polemics but as a justification or a calculated appeal for sympathy directed toward higher authorities. In practice, magistracies had to accept the kahal's presence within the estate constellation, and most burgher complaints express a desire not to eliminate Jews from the cities but to make Jewish communities pay more taxes, perform more burdens, and quarter more soldiers, whether equitably or not. Other authorities shared similar jurisdictional concerns, and even the kahals worked and petitioned to prevent outside powers from exercising authority over internal Jewish disputes.[21] No less than burghers or jurydyka residents, Jewish communities vigorously defended their autonomy, employing strategies such as lawsuits, petitions, and temporary alliances with other urban estates. In this sense the Jewish communities, despite suffering from numerous social and legal debilitations, nonetheless constituted a kind of estate, and the actions of individual Jews and kahal elders suggest a broad acceptance of the civic republican mentality. In fact, magistracy-Jewish interaction resembled the relationship of starostas to magistracies and magistracies to jurydykas.

Reading petition after petition of invective and claims of oppression, one instinctively sympathizes with the perspective of the enlightened reformers, who sought ways to end the apparent quagmire. The means adopted, though, invariably provoked further conflict, as officials in both the Commonwealth and the partitioning powers overestimated the potential of rational ex novo solutions to erase accumulated habits and practices. "Privilege defenders" continued to drag their feet in implementing external decrees, just as "law enforcers" still hid unwillingness to take action behind claims of disobedience. Moreover, the polemics and petitions of urban groupings, full of demands for change and references to the common good, disguise the degree to which most estates remained anchored in the system and basically satisfied with the framework of urban self-government. What emerges from the mutually recriminatory petitions between, in turn, magistracies and starostas, Christians and Jews, and cities and jurydykas is a common respect for the law, the particularistic order, and the authority of institutions such as the Assessor Court. Conflict tended to revolve more around competing interpretations or glosses of judicial verdicts, which always contained enough ambiguity for offended parties to litigate another day, and a far greater number of battles took place in front of judges than on the streets. From the perspective of the center, this meant the frivolous expenditure of millions on legal costs, but the system served the interests of local parties, who preserved the authority to defend themselves and play a role in local politics. Starostas, burghers, Jews, and jurydyka residents repeatedly affirmed a desire to enhance prerogatives and rights vis-à-vis others, not to eliminate their own autonomy and local control.

THE STAROSTA IS SEEKING TO EXTEND ABSOLUTE POWER OVER THE BURGHERS

Detailed evidence of interurban conflict appeared in large measure during the 1789 lustration, the first audit authorized by parliament since the passage of the 1768 and 1776 reforms. Word of the lustration officials' arrival must have spread well in advance, since each urban community in every city greeted the auditors with carefully composed petitions and lists of grievances. Łuck, the capital of Volhynia palatinate, provided a particularly detailed set of petitions, including responses and counteraccusations, which suggest that locals had eagerly anticipated the lustration officials' appearance. A faction of burghers led by the former mayor, Paweł Dastkiewicz, made the first move, directing a series of allegations against Franciszek Moszyński, the wójt. As in Krzemieniec, the position of wójt (in theory the top position in the town but usually an official presiding over small claims and criminal courts) had passed into possession of the starosta, in this case Prince Józef Czartoryski, who had named Moszyński to the job. Beginning with the standard complaints about the starosta's control of the propinacja monopoly, Dastkiewicz accused Moszyński of seeking to "extend absolute power over the burghers." The wójt had "abrogated magistracy courts, maintaining only [his own] courts with compliant individuals." Much of Dastkiewicz's ire focused on his fellow burghers, however, among whom "a few individuals, less concerned about the whole" had allegedly conspired with the starosta to elect stooges to the city council. In colorful language containing notes of classical republican discourse on the importance of virtue, Dastkiewicz narrated the alleged betrayal: "At the election of this year, some men who have no property, others, illiterate and caring nothing about the law, others noted for their inability to satisfy their greed, still others drowned in whispered improprieties (like a corn cockle among choice wheat causes bad growth), all exempting themselves from society, the unity of government, the whole, and the law that restores and maintains the city, connived with the well-born Moszyński under the armed guard of the starosta's soldiers and elected six officials for city posts."[22] These starosta-approved councilors, Dastkiewicz claimed, had permitted the wójt to dispense justice with chosen individuals. Reminiscent of the Krzemieniec kahal's claim about the magistracy's improper jurisdiction, the Łuck petition recorded that "through fabricated cases and improper prosecution, [Moszyński] has deprived many burghers of their property, sent them to ruin, and ordered them imprisoned like criminals." In support of this petition, Dastkiewicz appended the signatures of twenty-five burghers, fifteen of whom claimed to have occupied some role in the town's government.[23]

Moszyński, Czartoryski, and the new mayor, Jan Chromowicz, each issued counterpetitions justifying their actions and leveling character assassination charges at Dastkiewicz to suggest that his virtuous concern for unity disguised crass pecuniary interests. The first two petitions emphasized the starosta's patronage of the town, including his past expenditure of one hundred thousand zlotys, an enormous sum, to litigate on behalf of the town. Moreover, the starosta had appointed Moszyński at the request of the burghers themselves, who wished to have an outside voice to settle the internal disputes that had rocked the city since Dastkiewicz's election. In Chromowicz's version, Dastkiewicz's election as mayor had been the fraudulent work of a small minority, imposed violently on the rest of the city. As mayor, the counterpetitions alleged, Dastkiewicz had pilfered city resources and floated loans for himself using city credit. As evidence of Dastkiewicz's lawless corruption, the three petitions asserted that the former mayor's son-in-law had punched someone in the face without facing prosecution. Czartoryski attributed Dastkiewicz's actions to a desire to protect his alcohol business from concession fees owed to the starosta in accordance with the latter's royal prerogatives. As for the twenty-five cosigners, Chromowicz and his supporters insisted that none of them had ever held any positions in the magistracy, though Chromowicz's own petition contained the signatures of only six illiterate burghers.[24]

Remarkably, even the issue of sending delegates to Warsaw for the Black Procession became an object of Łuck's internal disputes. Chromowicz alleged that, no longer in office, Dastkiewicz continued to sign documents and appropriate mail, including a letter from Warsaw mayor Jan Dekert requesting delegates for the unified burgher assembly. The lustration officials even recorded a response by Dastkiewicz to the counterpetition, in which the former mayor responded that the letter from Dekert had been addressed to the entire city, not the magistracy. The ex-mayor intimated that Moszyński and Chromowicz would have suppressed the letter out of spite toward the burgher estate. The lustration officials concluded their report with the understated remark that, "from the above complaints, one can conclude that there are quarrels and disagreements about the condition of the city."[25] In particular, the officials could not resolve the contradiction that both Dastkiewicz and Chromowicz claimed to be victims, accusing the other of violence and illegality.

Historians have tended to take the complaints of burghers about starosta oppression at face value, particularly since such testimony confirms a narrative about the oppression of the weak by the strong. Dastkiewicz's struggle, at first glance, appears to support a historiographic commonplace that the burghers in the small towns of the Commonwealth groaned under the oppression of the starosta. According to Władysław Ćwik, for example, the 1768 law mandating that magistracies present their financial records to the starosta and submit to the starosta's intermediary appellate jurisdiction merely legalized the starosta's domination over the burghers.[26] Starostas in most small towns already exercised some control over the magistracy in appointing or nominating mayors, and control over the office of wójt, as in Łuck, Krzemieniec, Urzędów, and other cities, brought a means of interfering in the town's judicial infrastructure. Moreover, petitions from burghers after 1768 appear to corroborate the assertion that these measures effectively enshrined the de facto rule of the starostas. Several small towns submitted complaints echoing Dastkiewicz's petition about the starosta's interference in the legal system, unjust tax collection, and oppression of the burghers. Apparently, starostas themselves presumed that their political authority had increased. One starosta, answering the complaint that he had illegally suspended the town's courts and fired the elected wójt, replied nakedly that this official was a "drunkard who continually caused conflict in the town" and, moreover, that "no burgher in the town is competent to serve as a judge."[27]

Nonetheless, we should examine these accusations carefully, particularly since every group in the Commonwealth produced them. In case after case, groups adopted an offensive strategy to shield themselves from accusations of wrongdoing, depicting one group's legitimate enforcement of the rules as oppression, violence, and depravity or recasting the failure to remit lawful dues as the imposition of illegal burdens. Holders of sinecures become victims of "disobedience" and "injustice" when subordinates refused to remit payment, and legitimate attempts to collect community taxes could be cast as illegal interference in a separate group's internal affairs. We cannot necessarily determine the exact course of events on the ground, but it seems clear that no community accepted oppression passively or submitted to external authority without resistance. Even members of the privileged nobility voiced complaints about the injustices suffered from burghers. An anonymous pamphlet, *A Reply from the Nobility to Cities Requesting Ownership of Landed Estates*, wrote of the "injuries and persecutions" inflicted upon the Warsaw nobility "by the burghers and their courts."[28]

Moreover, there is ample evidence to suggest that, even in the post-1768 conditions, starostas could no more impose absolute domination over town residents than could magistracies exercise complete control over Jewish communities. The conflict in Łuck between the starosta-supported magistracy and its opponents finds parallels in other towns where burghers frustrated the policies of royal officials and reported their dissent to the central government.[29] In fact, starostas from some of the Commonwealth's least populous, poorest, and presumably most vulnerable towns complained about "disobedience" and their inability to "bring order" or "enforce the laws." Petitions about the 1776 propinacja law often included unrelated grievances, as petitioners exploited the opportunity of communicating with higher authorities to vent their frustrations. Several starostas asserted that burghers had refused to appeal to their intermediary court or follow other measures of the 1768 law. Others accused the townsmen of failing to recognize the officials legally appointed by the starosta, such as the mayor and wójt. The starosta of the tiny town of Tuszyn, Prince Czetwertyński, wrote that "these rebellious [burghers] dared even to beat up the starosta's men, refused help to the starosta's peasants during a fire, and illegally excluded the [starosta-appointed] wójt from city council meetings."[30] In other words, the estate structure of the town limited the starosta's potential to impose absolute control because of the plurality and diffusion of legal and personal power—attributes of the urban constitution that the reform legislation of 1768 had failed to overcome. More to the point, one should remember the degree to which phrases such as "disobedience" and "oppression" served as useful pretexts to escape unwanted burdens assigned by the center, as when officials requested statistical information or the fulfillment of regulations.[31]

Posing the conflict as one between rapacious starostas and victimized burghers further ignores the fact that city citizens were not a homogenous group but were divided into parties for whom the starosta often served as a convenient ally. A number of antiburgher polemicists during the Four-Year Parliament such as Jacek Jezierski, accused Dekert and his supporters of seeking to enhance the tyranny of the magistracies over the common citizens, and starostas often characterized themselves as checks on the magistracy's oppression. The starosta of Kazimierz Dolny complained to lustration officials in 1789 that "the burghers in this city, in their disorder, have never presented accounts of receipts and expenses . . . and, as a result, the powerful oppress the poor."[32] The Chełm magistracy accused the starosta of "exploiting the illiterate burghers," by deceiving them into signing protests against the city government. The starosta responded that the magistracy "autocratically" ruled over the "illiterate burghers," recording transactions to suit the elite rather than the contracting parties and auctioning city land for pennies to benefit the oligarchs on the city council.[33] Divisions within and without the city offered the starosta the possibility to expand political authority, but this seems a far cry from absolute power. Rather, the "illiterate burghers" or common citizens formed an object of contention between the magistracy and the starosta and became a player in urban politics in their own right. The common citizenry could and did sue the magistracy before the Assessor Court, and potential appeals to the starosta by privilege-defending citizens placed further pressure on the magistracy to court public opinion.

The appearance of Civil-Military Commissions in every palatinate after 1789 opened a new forum to which magistracies, citizens, and starostas could direct their complaints. Parliament had decreed the creation of these institutions so as to supervise the conscription, payment, and quartering of the soldiers in the massively expanded army, duties that included the enforcement of a new system of internal passports to prevent desertion.[34] Billeting soldiers had always been a burden in a country lacking any system of barracks, but the sheer volume of new soldiers taxed the resources of the city authorities, even if the recruiting reality failed to match the parliament's ambitions.[35] Town magistracies as well as jurydykas and kahal authorities were required to staff checkpoints and register visitors. The commissions also supported the newly activist government's efforts to "see" the population by requiring all communal authorities to record births, deaths, and marriages, an innovation for many communities, which subsequent governments still struggled to enforce even a half century later. The commissions further continued the "good order" duties bequeathed by the previous reform bodies, issuing regulations on such matters as road repair, sanitation improvement, and the implementation of uniform weights and measures.[36]

Locals, though, viewed the commissions primarily as new judicial instances in which to practice their "continuous litigation" and thus avoid the expenses and delays of hearings at the Assessor Court. In settling scores with their rivals, urban groupings found it convenient to describe their privilege-defending complaints in the language of good order and rationality. For example, a nobleman, Wilczkiewicz, brought the magistracy of Żytomierz before the Civil-Military Commission in 1791 for negligence in repairing town roads. Wilczkiewicz claimed that, as he was riding through the city with the personal effects of a local military commander, his three-horse carriage overturned after hitting a giant pothole, which caused the valuables in his care to fall into the mud. Many of the artifacts, including a Turkish pistol, were lost, and he complained to the Civil-Military Commission that "all these damages resulted from the disorder of the town." Even after the empowerment of the starosta's courts, nobles complained, the burghers evaded lawsuits by relying on the protection of the Assessor Court, and Wilczkiewicz's suit showed the opportunity offered nonburghers to challenge magistracies. For its part, the magistracy retorted with the familiar excuse of the "law-enforcer," namely, the city had ordered the citizenry to repair and shore up roads in front of their homes, but "no one obeys."[37]

Other nobles also saw the commissions as allies against the apparently rapacious burghers. According to a petition from 1790, the city of Urzędów had inundated a local noble's stables with military horses, which remained on his land long after the commission had ordered their removal.[38] The common citizenry also found the new institutions a convenient ally in holding the magistracy to account. Krzysztof Korn, a citizen of Lublin and future mayor, made a similar accusation as Wilczkiewicz against the magistracy for negligence in repairing roads. The city in this case justified its failure to act by pointing to empty coffers, suggesting that the battle may have involved an internal dispute about the allocation of urban resources.[39] Starostas were also quick to approach the new bodies with their complaints. In March 1790 the starosta of Chełm wrote to the Civil-Military Commission complaining that the magistracy's beadle had "quartered soldiers in the starosta's village of Obłonie, collected forage from the peasants, and ordered each peasant to remit oats. He even told the soldiers that the peasants were rich and can afford to pay."[40] Reading such complaints, one emerges with the impression that the magistracies, not the nobles or starostas, were the chief oppressors of the innocent.

Not only were the Civil-Military Commissions impelled to resolve local grievances about the balance of power, but the commissions themselves became objects of complaint. After the creation of the Police Commission in 1791, the Lublin magistracy wrote to Warsaw that "the beadle of the Civil-Military Commission, accompanied by his retinue, placed innocent artisans under arrest, invaded the homes of magistracy officials, and has worked such unpleasantness on peaceful people that many artisanal workers have begun to leave the city."[41] Instead of introducing good order or providing effective local government, as asserted by Lukowski, the commissions found themselves pulled into urban politics, becoming another power center to which citizens and authorities could appeal as a convenient privilege defender, and against which legalistic maneuvers might be made when commissioners became burdensome "law enforcers."[42] As a result, the Civil-Military Commissions had less resources available to enforce their good order regulations against the expected passive resistance of the locals. Repeated promulgation and posting of the same rules testifies to this problem. For example, the Lublin commission reissued its good order rules in May 1791 with the preface, "Experience teaches that the more often one reads, the easier and more powerfully that work impresses itself in the memory," expressing regret that decrees, "which have already been issued several times," so quickly lost their force.[43]

The seemingly endless political and legal conflicts in urban society also caught the attention of government officials and parliamentarians, who increasingly demanded a more rational organization in order to facilitate good order and improvement measures. The topic of starosta-magistracy discord had appeared during parliamentary debate even during the 1770s. One proposal, later embraced by Staszic in his *Warnings for Poland,* consisted of simply selling the starosties to the occupants outright, converting royal towns into private property on the theory that starostas would thereafter have an incentive to protect and care for their cities as did private town lords.[44] Officials closer to the government, on the other hand, approached the problem of urban politics as an issue of insufficient central supervision and direction. In its final (1788) report to parliament, the Department of Police had claimed that the "mutual antagonism" between starostas and magistracies had frequently convinced locals to request that the department send its own employees to intervene, requesting more police commissioners for this purpose.[45] Hugo Kołłątaj also saw the problem of inter-estate rivalry in a weak central government, which lacked "sufficient executive power and jurisdiction to compel via judicial verdict or punish the disobedient." In classical liberal fashion, Kołłątaj advanced the abolition of particularistic privileges as a means of bringing harmony to the cities. Kołłątaj's anonymous letters called for abolishing Magdeburg Law in favor of a common law code for all citizens, "since civil law should not consider a person's status, but interest."[46] Supervising the entire edifice, Kołłątaj envisioned a centralized police commission with more powers than the defunct Department of Police, "which would have a view of the entire economy and . . . under the rule of [executives who] have the power of compulsion, would be able to implement its praiseworthy regulations."[47]

Magistracies across the Commonwealth concurred that city government lacked sufficient power to implement good order regulations, but the polemics of 1789 demanded that decision-making authority remain within the cities. As expressed by the polemics financed by the Warsaw magistracy, burghers and city authorities wanted from Warsaw not a supervisory structure but allies to help them as equal partners defend imagined and extinguished privileges against rival estates. No one called for the elimination of Magdeburg Law, and in fact much of the publicists' ire focused not on local rivalries but on the efforts of the state since 1764 to improve and benefit the urban estate. The Warsaw magistracy led the campaign to deflect enlightened officials' claims of urban discord and misgovernance against the center. As a 1778 petition to the Department of Police expressed the issue, urban disorder reflected the inability of the center to provide stability for the country: "Due to wars, fires, and pestilence, the city has frequently been forced to indebt itself in order to ransom its citizens' lives and property. You cannot, therefore, accuse the city of neglecting its funds, when it has so frequently been forced to endure revolutions. . . . Let the magistracy only be granted assistance in ruling over its citizens, as the law requires, and the city will undoubtedly take its place among the ranks of well-ordered cities."[48] Michał Świniarski further alleged that the new efforts to shore up municipal finances represented an unjust intrusion into local matters. Countering the accusation that the cities were misappropriating their limited funds on litigation, Świniarski observed that royal charters already provided monies to the towns for the purpose of maintaining order, "and if these are not sufficient, the magistracy has the right to impose additional taxes on all the town citizens, which all, without exclusion, are obligated to pay."[49]

In 1789 a joint petition from the Lithuanian cities developed a similar theme that discord was not a function of local self-government but, rather, the inability of local government to function properly. Lithuania had seen all but eleven of its largest cities lose Magdeburg Law rights in 1776, and the petition specifically countered official rhetoric about the benefits of central control: "Everyone complains that the Lithuanian cities are in the worst disorder of all, but who today would banish an owner [*gospodarz*] in order to make an orderly house? Similarly, why would you banish the master [*gospodarz*] of the city, the magistracy, if you want an orderly city?" Instead of order, the 1776 reform had created judicial chaos, as the frequent absence of the starosta, now charged with adjudicating all city disputes, rendered justice among the burghers virtually nonexistent.[50] City elites demanded a return to the unrestricted powers of magistracies from the imagined past, but the Black Procession learned to advocate for its cause in the Enlightenment language of good order, economic improvement, and the common good. As the petition of the Black Procession recorded: "the rights and privileges [of the urban estate] once effectively supported the power and adornment of the country. . . . Since the neglect of those rights and the abasement of our estate, Poland has excelled only in disasters, the heaviest blows of which have fallen upon us."[51] Further, the rights and freedoms of the urban estate were "so intimately bound with the ancient happiness of Poland that the former and the latter have languished and expired as one." Even Dastkiewicz made such a connection between privilege and prosperity when he mocked Józef Czartoryski's professed concern and patronage of Łuck as subterfuge: "The urban government was good before the starosta appointed a wójt, for then each received justice from the magistracy and the city contributed one hundred thousand zlotys to the treasury every year."[52]

The common demand for civil rights, advanced by both burgers and their enlightened patrons, served to mask the larger divide between republican preferences and enlightened aims. Parliamentarians ultimately accepted the request for civil rights, but legislators also intended to institute orderly self-administration in the cities, in which locals could choose those officials who fulfilled central decrees. For this reason, the urban reform law Our Free Royal Cities granting burghers civil rights also subordinated the "internal order and revenues" of cities to the Police Commission of Both Nations, established by law two months later. Together with the Constitution of the Third of May, these measures transformed the relationship of the cities to the central government, which now possessed the attributes of a state. The king, created as a hereditary monarch, presided over a council of ministers (*straż praw*), which included Crown Marshal Jerzy Mniszech as Minister of Police. The Police Commission of Both Nations included six plenipotentiaries from the cities in its fifteen-member composition and, in theory, supervised the Civil-Military Commissions, creating a hierarchical structure of accountability from the magistracies to the king. Our Free Royal Cities abolished all jurydykas and enclaves, granting magistracies jurisdiction over every inhabitant, including the Jewish population.[53]

The Constitution of the Third of May and its attendant legislation enjoyed a short life, as a few disgruntled nobles appealed to Catherine the Great for support against the new order and the empress found the request a welcome pretext for intervention. The malcontents proclaimed a confederation at Targowica, and the influx of Russian soldiers convinced the king that joining the confederation was the only means of saving the constitution. Instead, the new "disorders" allowed Russia and Prussia to demand additional territories from the country. A kangaroo parliament summoned to Grodno in 1793 legitimized the new annexations, and the deputies overturned the Constitution of the Third of May. Although many of the reforms were abolished, the legislation on cities survived the culling. In fact, the only significant change in urban matters involved the division of the Police Commission into two parts, one for the Crown and one for Lithuania, a concession to the Targowica republicans' federalist sensibilities. The Grodno constitution turned out to be the last legislation of the Polish-Lithuanian Commonwealth, for the ink had barely dried before an insurrection led by Tadeusz Kościuszko provided the occasion for the partitioning powers to end the existence of the Commonwealth altogether, eradicating the country completely in 1795.[54]

The brief duration of the constitutional reforms complicates any effort to discuss their place in the history of Enlightenment reform, but certain features are suggestive. In the first place, the magistracies lost significant autonomy, as evidenced by the correspondence between the cities and the Police Commission after 1791. Town magistrates suddenly appeared hesitant to undertake any decision or at least to present themselves as subservient. The magistracy of Lublin reported in 1792 that it would not allocate money or fix the price of victuals without the commission's acquiescence. The town of Warka was more obsequious, writing in 1791, that "The town never [takes] the least step without the knowledge and permission of the [Police] Commission."[55] In part, this solicitousness continued the traditional posture of the "law enforcers," who could now disguise their inaction as waiting for approval rather than local disobedience, but magistracies may have also experienced a honeymoon period connected with the new legislation, which did grant significant civil rights for burghers. Among those rights, burghers gained a voice on the very body in charge of enforcing usefulness in all the towns collectively. For example, the burgher publicist Adam Mędrzecki became a member of the Police Commission.[56]

On the other hand, the new legislation did not resolve conflicts between the starosta and the magistracy, despite the limitation of the former's authority. In fact, the legislation's division of cities into circuits for administrative and judicial purposes opened a new field for starostas and magistracies to contest ownership of urban property. For example, the city of Wschowa in Great Poland sought to prevent certain jurydykas from remaining under the jurisdiction of the starosta, without which "an orderly organization for the city cannot happen, and our city faces ruin."[57] Legalistic disputes about the title to certain revenues also continued, as evidenced by a declaration from Łuck that the city's resources were so meager because of an ongoing lawsuit in the Assessor Court with Czartoryski that the magistracy could not afford the stamped paper upon which to record petitions.[58] The town of Smotryca in Podolia even claimed that the starosta continued to "tyrannize both Christians and Jews" by sending Cossacks into the city to execute his own justice without regard to the new law.[59] Such conflicts would continue, even as the country ceased to exist.

THE MAGISTRACY, IN ITS EVER-INCREASING EFFORT TO OPPRESS THE JEWS

"Differences in ceremony and religion cannot exclude anyone from striving for the public good," proclaimed the Civil-Military Commission for Kijów palatinate in an effort to encourage rabbis to present statistical information to central authorities, but the presence in almost every town of a Jewish community with its own set of rights and privileges created a much more complicated, triangular dynamic that facilitated both rivalries and alliances and further muddled efforts at enlightenment reform.[60] In theory, the starosta held ultimate jurisdiction over the Jewish community and could adjudicate Jewish-Christian quarrels, and there had long existed a precedent for the Jewish community to seek protection from the starosta, as the one official in town who had the power and political interest to keep the magistracy in check.[61] Starostas, much like private town lords, often employed individual Jews as leaseholders, and this marriage of convenience encouraged these officials to ally with the kahal when it came under pressure from the magistracy. The precise legal and economic relationship between the magistracy and the kahal varied in each city on the basis of traditions, written agreements, and particularistic royal privileges. In 1768 the parliament approved legislation that required Jewish communities to negotiate agreements with magistracies detailing the terms of the Jews' residency rights. Although this law seems to have languished in most cities, its mere existence strengthened the need for an alliance with the starosta to defend the kahal's judicial and pecuniary autonomy. Magistracies, for their part, always eyed the possibility of extending judicial powers over the Jewish community, if for no other reason than the prospect of increasing the court fees paid by litigants to individual judges.[62] Conflicts between Christians and Jews, however, largely concerned secular issues, such as negotiating the limits of privileges and rights. Both sides appealed to law and legality, defending privilege and autonomy and, in doing so, demonstrated their mutual immersion in a rights-based republican culture.

Until the last decade historians have tended to claim that the burghers' attitudes toward Jews were driven by prejudice and religious antipathy.[63] The polemics financed by the Warsaw magistracy provide plenty of evidence to confirm this interpretation. In *On the Founding Principles of Cities*, Świniarski presented standard anti-Jewish propaganda, arguing that "Jews use not only their earnings, but also contract loans to destroy the burghers, selling their goods for nothing, which wins them the support of the public and the protection of creditors." Świniarski even proposed forced resettlement as a solution: "Spain buys people in Africa at great cost to mine its gold in America. Poland has gold growing on the ground (since we obtain Dutch gold for our wheat), and farming is nothing like being buried alive in a mine. And we cannot impel the Jews to take up farming? I say 'impel' because this nation has no point of honor, no love for the country, or any other motive, which would encourage this pursuit."[64] One should not take Świniarski's proposal as a reflection of the attitudes of all burghers in the Commonwealth, since the pamphlet reflected first and foremost the position of his employers, the Warsaw magistracy. Warsaw possessed one of the most extreme restrictions on Jewish residency and commercial activity in the Commonwealth, but there was an exemption on these measures during a parliamentary session. Since the Four-Year Parliament had opted to remain sitting long after the typical six-week expiration date, Warsaw burghers had been exposed to Jewish competition for much longer than usual, and the polemical campaign aimed first and foremost to cancel this exemption.[65] In smaller towns, on the other hand, burghers depended much more on Jewish goods and services, and grievances had little to do with religious, ethnic, or class animosity. Instead, petitions reveal a more secular competition for resources and authority between legally distinct groups in a dynamic of shifting power relations. Christian burghers may have sincerely desired to expel Jews from the towns, but this rhetoric nonetheless distorts the actual motivations and limitations that informed inter-estate negotiation on a day-to-day basis.

Many burgher complaints about Jews in fact reflected the power struggle between the starosta and the magistracy, in which jurisdiction over the kahal served as a point of contention between political rivals. For example, in a petition to the Civil-Military commission, the starosta of the Chełm land (*ziemia chełmska*, a part of the old Ruthenian palatinate) protested the magistracy's attempt to exercise improper authority over the city's Jews. "Recognizing the magistracy as oppressive toward the Jews," the starosta reported, the Assessor Court had already awarded the Jews the right of judgment by a rabbi and the kahal, with appeal to the starosta alone. Józef Boguchwalski, the former wójt and delegate to Warsaw, countered that the court had actually placed the Jews within Chełm under the authority of the town council, "except for cases between Jews concerning their religion, which belong to the authority of the Jewish court." Admitting that the Jews "do not wish to abandon the starosta," Boguchwalski considered the starosta's apparent protection of this community as a pretext for "placing both the Catholics and the Jews of the town under his usurped authority."[66] As Gershon Hundert and Anna Michałowska-Mycielska have both observed, Jewish law made no distinction between religious and secular matters, and Jewish elders vehemently (if not always effectively) discouraged appeals to non-Jewish courts. The debate, on the surface, appeared theoretical, but in reality the question of jurisdiction more properly referred to the authority to command and impose burdens. In this case, the commission sided with the city and pronounced an injunction against the starosta's issuing of decrees to the Jewish community, "which has tended to cause only disorder and confusion." Jews and Christians meanwhile were ordered to settle internal matters for themselves with appeal to the Civil-Military Commission.[67]

Legal disputes between Christians and Jews frequently arose from the common burgher belief that the starosta sheltered the Jewish community from paying taxes, performing burdens, or honoring restrictions. Dastkiewicz's complaint offers an exemplary statement of the starosta's presumed protection: "The Jews perform all manner of handicrafts, maintain all the distilleries, and practice trade, while not needing to pay guild or city taxes. . . . Jews and Karaites exempt themselves [from the burdens caused by] soldiers passing through or lodging in the town by giving extensive gifts to the starosta, freeing themselves from maintaining even the starosta's soldiers, who are pushed onto the burghers."[68] As a result of this protection and oppression, Dastkiewicz claimed, the Jews had elbowed Christians out of the prime real estate: "The Jews have occupied all the houses on market square, and having households everywhere in the town, they have worked out an agreement for city property: they do not allow Catholics to buy property from Jews, but themselves seek to buy up property from Catholics."[69] The starosta Czartoryski denied offering any special favoritism to the Jews and observed that the Jews were saddled with their own taxes (which accrued to the starosta, of course). Taking a liberal economic position that no magistracy would support, Czartoryski boasted that the competition between Jews and Christians benefited consumers, "as no city in the region has meat as cheap as Łuck." Czartoryski suggested that the lustration itself would show whether the burdens and taxes of the town were divided equitably.[70]

Violations of residential restrictions presented a common leitmotif of burgher petitions, though these "illegalities" could only come about through the decision of individual burghers to sell their property to Jewish families. The authority of the magistracy rested, in part, on its ability to uphold the privileges of the burgher estate, which often included restrictions on Jewish commercial activity and residency rights. From the perspective of the magistracy, each property transferred to an individual Jew necessarily became unmoored from the magistracy's financial and judicial control, no matter how integrated a given Jewish community might have been. Like Dastkiewicz, burghers from various small towns blamed the Jews' ability to violate the law not on their own economic failings but on the protection and complicity of the starosta. In effect, burghers employed the image of illegal possession of homes by the Jewish community as a means of attacking the starosta's "oppression." One town asserted that the law provided for the Jewish population to occupy only two houses, yet due to the starosta's protection, the community had nonetheless appropriated all trade and business in the town. Starostas regularly denied showing any special favoritism or authorizing exemptions for the Jewish communities, but complaints from burghers in petition after petition mirror Dastkiewicz's assertion to the contrary.[71]

If an element of ethnoreligious hatred can be discerned in these remarks, there is also a component of the "privilege-defending" mentality. For each community, privileges once added became an indivisible component of the estate's "private property," and this included privileges that excluded or discriminated against others. Referring to the perceived loss of privileges in the eighteenth century, Świniarski lectured in his 1789 pamphlet that, "No one explained the reason for taking our property, which has been secured by privilege, and burghers expected that they would not lose this right without summons, convocation, or decree."[72] Heinz Schilling has argued that German burghers lacked an adequate natural-rights vocabulary to combat the claims of the territorial state over urban government, but Polish and Lithuanian cities retained their autonomy long enough for Świniarski to buttress his civic republican claims about privileges as private property with eighteenth-century political theory, writing "the entirety of privileges, secured by laws and sealed by public trust, were conditions as fundamental for burghers as natural law."[73] In both the civic republican and natural law versions, then, the occupation of houses by the Jews in a greater number than privileges allowed signified to the zero-sum mind of estate politics the diminution of the burghers' rights and privileges, even if, as some Jewish communities asserted in their petitions, the Jews paid the same taxes as the Christian citizens. This privilege-defending mentality transcended the narrow world of the Christian burghers. On at least one occasion, a Jewish community joined forces with a Christian magistracy to protest the unjust intrusion of a third group, the Tatars, into the urban economy.[74]

Resentments about the violation of property restrictions spilled into conflicts about billeting and quartering soldiers, and the arrival of Civil-Military Commissions created a new institution for local parties to weaponize in their intercity disputes. The commissions in fact added grist to the mill, since expanded billeting duties, as well as uncompensated labor as gatekeepers, passport inspectors, and night watchmen had to be allocated among the various urban communities.[75] The question immediately arose as to how each town should divide these new burdens between the burghers, Jews, and jurydykas. Burghers and Jews had differing conceptions about how a just solution to the problem would look, but neither side shied away from pressing for maximum deference to privileges and compacts, turning the Commonwealth's military-building effort into another arena for local politics. Complaints from many towns alleged that the Jewish communities received protection from billeting burdens through their relationship with the starosta, though litigation before the Civil-Military Commission suggest that Christian magistracies sought to transfer this burden to Jewish families as much as possible.

For example, in May 1790, the Civil-Military Commission of Lublin palatinate heard a contract dispute between the Lublin magistracy and kahal about the terms of quartering. According to the suit, the Jewish community had promised the previous spring to contribute one thousand zlotys per annum to the town treasury in lieu of billeting their allotment of seventy soldiers. Unhappily, Lublin received 233 more soldiers than anticipated, and in response the magistracy allocated the majority of the surplus, 170 recruits, to the extramural "Jewish Town." The commission found the magistracy in violation of the agreement and decreed immediate new accommodation for 92 of the soldiers housed in Jewish homes. A second hearing in October 1791, however, revealed that Lublin's magistracy had thus far failed to comply, and the commission ordered the prompt transfer of soldiers from the "Jewish Town" under penalty of legal prosecution against the town magistrates. In another instance, the kahal of one small town complained that the magistracy was pressing the Jews into manning the passport checkpoints in equal proportion with the Christians, disregarding the fact that the town possessed only 47 Jewish homes in comparison to 352 Christian domiciles.[76]

Officials in Warsaw appreciated that conflicts between Jews and Christians complicated the work of the Civil-Military Commissions, and most educated citizens of the Commonwealth viewed Jewish commerce as harmful to the livelihood of Christian burghers, who were supposed to be fulfilling commercial and productive functions. A few writers during the Four-Year Parliament suggested political emancipation as a solution, but more often enlightened officials viewed the solution in assimilatory measures along with continued political and economic restrictions (which would theoretically subside following the achievement for total assimilation, however measured). In his *Political Law of the Polish Nation*, Kołłątaj proposed an assimilationist solution of using legislation to compel Jewish residents to dress and speak as Poles while restricting Jewish communal autonomy. This pamphlet called for abolishing all kahals in the country, which he viewed as states within the state, and delegating their tax-collecting functions to the Treasury Commission. A single Jewish court for the entire palatinate would adjudicate religious matters, while verdicts would require the assent of a Civil-Military Commission, which he envisioned as a permanent element of local government. Rabbis would be strictly forbidden from pronouncing a verdict of *cherem* on members of the community, and Jews would lose all alcohol-production privileges. In essence, Kołłątaj's plan for the Jewish community mirrored the reality for the majority of Lithuanian cities after 1776, when legislation placed urban economic matters under the Treasury Commission and delegated city justice to the starostas.[77]

In the "Humble Request," the representatives of the Jewish communities in the Polish Crown sought no less than the burghers to defend communal autonomy and refute the assertion that greater state control and restriction would benefit the country. Like the town magistracies, Jewish communities aimed to expand their already existing privileges within the general framework of the estate system, which they wanted to preserve. Using arguments of economic utility, the request countered accusations against the Jews for impoverishing the burghers, arguing that blame should rightly go to the "eternal misfortunes and revolutions of the country, and particularly to the Swedes."[78] Further, the petition observed that the residential restrictions in many towns brought no economic benefits, as evidenced by the fact that many of the poorest cities had the most stringent regulations on Jewish settlement. In making these arguments, the petition made the same connection as the burghers between the accumulated privileges of a particular group and national prosperity. The petition argued that expanded economic and residential liberties would allow Jewish communities with international connections to facilitate the export of homemade products and transfer hard currency back to the Commonwealth. In return for a just allocation of taxes, the Jews promised to enrich the country, and the model held up as exemplary by the petition was not Joseph II's *Toleranzpatent* or similar proposals circulating in Warsaw but the privileges of Chełm, Chęciny, and Kazimierz Dolny, where the Jews enjoyed "citizenship and [commercial] freedom equal to burghers."[79]

Parliament was debating separate legislation on the status of the Jews in line with Kołłątaj's assimilationist proposals as Russian troops crossed the border in 1792, so the Four-Year Parliament never addressed the status of the Jewish population, who now found themselves under hostile authorities. A petition in 1792 complained that, "the Constitution of the Third of May has guaranteed freedom, life, property, and public peace to each resident of the Commonwealth, [leaving] the Jews as the most unhappy of all, having been placed under the power and authority of the city magistracies, the result of which is the cruelest revenge and persecution."[80] Jews proved no less resilient than Christian burghers in seeking allies and addressing complaints to protect their own prerogatives against outside powers, and the reforms of 1791 were by no means the final word. Magistracies continued to complain to the Police Commission about the "disobedience" of Jews in the face of magistracy decrees, particularly with regard to providing the statistical information that cities had to collect.[81] Jewish communities also turned to all available authorities for redress against the magistracy's claims of power, as the ongoing dispute in Krzemieniec reveals. In January 1794 the kahal authored a petition to the Police Commission, claiming that, "the magistracy of Krzemieniec, in its ever-increasing effort to oppress the Jews . . . has forbidden the collection or payment of [kahal-levied taxes], claiming that such matters belong to its jurisdiction."[82] Here, the kahal was behaving much like the magistracy in the face of starosta demands for rent. The kahal's right to collect internal taxes, a prerogative backed by royal privileges, potentially compromised the individual Jewish members' ability to remit city taxes, at least in the eyes of the magistracy. In protesting the magistracy's actions, that kahal was both protecting its law-enforcing powers and defending its sacrosanct privileges like any republican institution.

The kahal further alleged that the burghers continued to use violence to enforce the latter's interpretation of the 1786 decree limiting the number of Jewish possessions on the market square. In one violent altercation, a burgher had assaulted a Jewish woman who was trying to guard her property. Significantly, the Jewish complaint did not challenge the validity of the Assessor Court's decision or the lustration audit upon which the judges had grounded their decision; instead the kahal attacked the burghers for violating the Jews' legal right to the forty permitted houses. In its March response, the Police Commission admitted that the legal situation for Jews remained unclear and, in the meantime, ordered the Jewish community to seek justice in the starosta's court, with an exception only for issues of immobile property. In effect, the Police Commission admitted that the starosta remained the only recourse for Jews in the face of intensified persecution.[83] Indicative of the privilege-defending mentality of both sides, the Russian occupation of the country in 1794 only changed the addressee to whom the parties appealed. In September 1794, the kahal addressed its complaints to the Russian General Ivashkevich, already the commander of the local garrison. The most significant consequence of the Commonwealth's collapse to the parties in Krzemieniec was apparently the associated inconvenience for litigation. The kahal noted that a hearing between the Jews and the Christians had been expected this year, "but the well-known revolution in the country has forced the Jews to delay a final settlement with the burghers."[84]

The magistracy, represented by Mayor Teodor Kwiatkowski, responded in kind by directing its own countercomplaints in early 1795 to Russian General Feodor Buxhoewden, then the highest authority in the former Commonwealth. Kwiatkowski justified the violent altercation as the enforcement of municipal regulations and complained about the interference of the starosta, who was still shielding the Jewish community from fulfilling their financial and billeting obligations. As the magistracy explained, Krzemieniec alone had to bear all the billeting duties of the district, which entailed feeding, housing, and satisfying the requisition demands of ninety soldiers daily, yet the starosta protected the Jewish community from providing "taxes, quarters, carts, fodder, or night watchmen; and the burghers do not collect a single grosz from the Jews." General Buxhoewden issued two resolutions, one empowering the local district court (*sąd ziemski*) to adjudicate the matter and the other demanding that all parties submit to the district court until a new judicial system could be established.[85] Common to both the kahal and the magistracy was the misplaced expectation that Russian authorities would honor and enforce all their rights and privileges, as well as the seemingly sacrosanct decisions of the now defunct Assessor Court. As participants in a republican culture, neither side could imagine an alternative outcome, just as the Targowica republicans naïvely believed that Catherine's support did not portend the end of their way of life.[86]

DESPITE THE LAW, WHICH EXPLICITLY ABOLISHES ALL JURYDYKAS WITHOUT EXCEPTION

The secular origin of Christian-Jewish rivalry, as in the magistracies' resentment of "illegal" Jewish property ownership appears more visible if viewed in comparison to the relationship of magistracies to jurydykas and other competitors. These minitowns or enclaves, exempt from the magistracy on the basis of noble or clerical privilege, expanded the same way as did Jewish communities: individual burghers sold real estate to nobles and clerics who could claim exemption from the magistracy for their property on the basis of their legal status. Complicating matters, jurydykas often attracted Jews, particularly in larger cities, which enforced *De non tolderandis Judeais*, though many jurydykas had mixed populations.[87] Protests against jurydykas echo protests against Jewish real estate purchases in several important respects. In both cases, magistracies complained about the violation of the law and the infringement upon their tax base, and petitions from magistracies employ similar language, using terms such as "swallowed up" or "encumbered" to describe the effect of the Jewish presence or the jurydykas on the town. The town of Włodzimierz, for example, complained that it was so encumbered by jurydykas that even the town hall had passed into clerical hands.[88]

Jurydykas differed from Jewish communities in that the former could be exempt from the starosta's jurisdiction, offering a point of common interest for starostas and magistracies that allowed the two sides to cooperate, if only briefly. Both magistracies and starostas resented jurydykas as islands exempt from taxation and jurisdiction. In 1765, long before Dastkiewicz's confrontation with Moszyński, the previous starosta of Łuck, Stanisław Czartoryski, had complained to lustration officials about the local monasteries, which "having removed themselves from both the starosta's and the town's jurisdiction, distill spirits illegally and pay no taxes either to the starosta or the town coffers."[89] Almost twenty years later, Józef Czartoryski wrote in 1784 to the central government protesting that, as a result of the proliferation of jurydykas in Łuck, only 20 percent of the town was under his authority.[90] In fact, magistracies and starostas resented any remotely autonomous institution that could evade taxation and commercial control. Świniarski, who as a Warsaw burgher did not have to contend with a starosta, wrote that the two greatest hindrances to urban growth were "foreign merchants and Jews." Similarly, a petition from Kamieniec Podolski protested against the soldiers of the local garrison, who "receiving a salary, nonetheless distill spirits, carry out trade, make crafts, and engage in peddling, stealing the last piece of bread [from the burghers]."[91]

As with other simmering disputes, the presence of the Civil-Military Commissions offered magistracies an opportunity to confront the secular and ecclesiastical jurydykas. The commissions announced in their proclamations the intention to distribute burdens equally among all residents of the region without regard to status. For magistracies, such rhetoric offered a welcome pretext to protest against the negligence of jurydykas in fulfilling billeting and labor duties. The commissioners ordered Podzamcze and other enclaves to repair roads, provide night watchmen, and inspect passports under penalty of fine, and the same was true across the Commonwealth. Repeated warnings, reprimands, and fines from the commission suggest that bringing the jurydykas to heel proved particularly difficult, but their actions offered succor for the long-standing resentment of city magistrates. Magistracies also turned to the commissions' courts to prosecute grievances against jurydykas, including monasteries. The magistracy of Lublin initiated a process against the Sisters of Mercy nunnery for blocking up a sewer canal flowing out from the city with rubbish. The sisters responded that the city had thrown refuse into their nunnery, and the magistracy's canal pumped dirty water directly into their homes.[92]

The urban reform law in theory ended the problem of magistracy-jurydyka rivalry by folding the latter into the jurisdiction of the former, but as with Christian-Jewish tension, problems with jurydykas continued beyond the partitions. In fact, jurydykas remained part of quaternary constellation that still included starostas, magistracies, and Jews.[93] Starostas and magistracies continued to quarrel over whether a given territory would join the truncated starosty or form part of a circuit within the cities. In Krzemieniec, the magistracy alleged that the starosta had extended his jurisdiction to the Jews and Christians in the former Jesuit jurydyka "for his own profit" and "despite the law, which explicitly abolishes all jurydykas without exception."[94] More controversial was the case of Podzamcze, a jurydyka near Lublin with a royal foundation charter dating from 1566. According to the jurydyka's petition, the Assessor Court had upheld the "city's" separateness in 1614, which the Department of Police had confirmed as recently as 1780. In January 1794, Marcin Klemenc, the wójt of Podzamcze wrote to the Police Commission to protest the Lublin magistracy's assault on its privileges. Noting that his enclave hosted "both Christians and Jews," Klemenc observed that Podzamcze possessed a foundation charter approved by the king dating to the sixteenth century. The Lublin magistracy countered that the 1793 parliament had abolished all separate jurisdictions within a city, which was considered "one entity from the first house in the center to the last in the suburbs." In this case, the magistracy blamed the starosta for protecting Podzamcze, and he confirmed the burghers' suspicions by writing a letter in support of Podzamcze's autonomy. The Police Commission, however, ultimately ruled to absorb the enclave into Lublin's magistracy, a victory for the city but perhaps not so much for the residents of Podzamcze or the "Jewish Town" of Lublin in general.[95]

A BRIEF EXAMINATION HAS REVEALED GREAT DISORDER

Following the final partition of the Polish-Lithuanian Commonwealth, the occupying powers moved to integrate the new territories into their prefabricated administrative molds, much as each had done in 1772. While Prussia imported not only institutions but also officials to staff the towns, Austria and Russia allowed a limited degree of local self-administration (see chapter 6 for the Russian case). Lublin and Chełm formed part of Austria only from 1795 to 1809, and in many ways Austrian rule presented a fitting epilogue to the Constitution of the Third of May as Habsburg officials proceeded from many of the same assumptions. Austrians followed a hierarchical and rationally divided administrative structure designed to prevent the entanglements and disputes that had characterized urban life in the Commonwealth. The province of Galicia—headquartered in Lemberg (L'viv) and administered without exception by a nonlocal until the mid-nineteenth century—was subdivided into districts, each with an administrative office (*Kreisamt*) with the responsibilities of the old Civil-Military Commissions and Police Commission. As in 1772, Austrians abolished all starosties and distributed the rural lands to loyal servitors, while cities became unitary administrative units with complete jurisdiction over former jurydykas and Jewish residents. As after 1791, city magistracies now fulfilled functions dictated by regional and central authorities, though the number of rules increased substantially in the spirit of Josephinism, and magistrates now had the obligation to enforce rules covering the gamut from bread ingredients to makeup quality.[96]

Smaller towns retained elective elements in Galicia, but only for the purpose of fulfilling local self-administration at minimal cost to the state. On the one hand, magistracies now disposed of much greater authority to levy burdens and fines. The Lublin magistracy punished apparently disobedient citizens, including members of the Jewish community, with fines and prison terms without regard to the starosta's protection.[97] On the other hand, the absence of privilege defenders meant that magistracies could not appeal to the time-tested recourse of the unwilling law enforcer in the Commonwealth: the inability to compel obedience. District circulars frequently scolded the magistracies of Lublin and Chełm for negligence, disorder, and poor administration of finances. As in the Prussian and Russian partitions, magistracies proved much less effective than administrators anticipated in collecting new taxes for the state or in following procedures. A typical circular observed that "a brief examination has revealed great disorder in both municipal and kahal revenue records."[98]Administrators worried about the lack of "qualified" officials to serve governmental posts in cities with long histories of self-rule, and Vienna also blamed town authorities for the fact that the population of Lublin had shrunk by two thousand people between 1797 and 1807.[99]

In 1805 the perceived inability of urban magistracies to stem disorder and compel obedience became the pretext to abolish self-administration in all cities, replacing the "arbitrary" selection of officials with central appointments of professional civil servants. Even this solution, however, proved no cure for disorder, and Austrian ambitions to turn Galicia into a model well-ordered province gradually subsided over the course of the nineteenth century. As the privilege defenders and law enforcers ceased to play a role in the administration of towns, the abuses of local administration—from scribes overcharging petitioners to bakers circumventing price tables—became the state's responsibility. As Iryna Vushko argues, the Habsburgs not only failed to refashion the province but in fact presided over the decline of living standards in Galicia.[100] In the hierarchical administrative structure staffed by itinerant bureaucrats, a system the Commonwealth was on its way to establishing in its final decades, there was no starosta to provide a counterbalance to the magistracy and no jurydyka in which to escape the restrictions or decrees of the main town.

In his *Discourses on Livy*, Machiavelli proposed that the struggle of orders in Republican Rome, far from weakening the constitution, was in fact responsible for the liberties enjoyed by citizens, since neither patricians nor plebeians could secure dominance.[101] Similarly, the apparent disorder of urban life before the 1790s meant that no one group could completely oppress another; estate divisions and overlapping jurisdictions checked the ambitions and aspirations of each group, in a way that a centralized hierarchy would not. Even after 1768 the starostas did not completely dominate the magistracies, nor did the magistracies cement their power over the Jewish communities after 1791, in part because the "privilege defenders" found allies among the rival "law enforcers." The most vulnerable of the urban estates, the Jewish community, gained some security and recourse from this complexity, and kahal elders showed themselves to be model republicans as they vied with rival authorities to exploit the overlapping jurisdictions and multiple power centers in order to evade restrictions and burdensome obligations. Republican politics may not have been the most efficient way of building roads or enforcing hygienic measures, but the overlapping space between mutually recriminating complaints showed a common culture of civic activism. For the partitioning powers, like the Four-Year Parliament, this anti-hierarchical civic activism could only appear as a symptom of decay and anarchy, which a further expansion of enlightened centralism would cure.

4

Enlightened Profit-Seeking

THE PRIVATE TOWNS OF THE ZAMOYSKI AND RADZIWIŁŁ ESTATES IN THE EIGHTEENTH CENTURY

NO TWO INDIVIDUALS BETTER exemplified the contrasting currents of the Commonwealth's final decades than Andrzej Zamoyski and Karol Stanisław Radziwiłł. The former, a onetime member of the Czartoryski party, represented a model enlightened statesman, imbued with optimistic rationalism and reformist zeal. After a brief service as chancellor, Zamoyski devoted several years in the 1770s to compiling a law code designed to improve the status of the peasantry and townspeople, which the parliament summarily rejected in 1780. A wealthy landowner and, eventually, inheritor of the family's entail, Zamoyski received notoriety for commuting his peasant's labor dues to cash payments.[1] Prince Radziwiłł, by contrast, has long served as a stereotypical, hyperbolic personification of "Sarmatian" backwardness and degeneracy. Violent-tempered, rude, and poorly educated, Karol Stanisław owned the largest fortune in the country, derived from a collection of estates, which together dwarfed most territorial states of the Holy Roman Empire. Having wasted much of his youth in idle, drunken splendor, Karol Stanisław was twice exiled from the country for opposing the king and the Russian empress. He spent his final decades vegetating on his

Belarusian estates, drilling his private army, and hosting lavish, ornate banquets, for which his immense income proved insufficient.[2] If Radziwiłł and Zamoyski differed wildly in their temperaments and political convictions, both nobles shared a common identity as owners of massive landholdings and numerous chartered towns and cities, including the splendid residential capitals of Nieśwież and Zamość.

Exempt from virtually every one of King Stanisław August's eighteenth-century urban reforms, private towns experienced an alternative Enlightenment. These entities constituted almost 65 percent of all towns in the Commonwealth after the first partition, a number that increased toward 90 percent as one moved east into the Ukrainian and Belarusian regions (see table 5). Further, almost 60 percent of urban residents in the late eighteenth century, as measured in hearth-tax records, resided in private towns. Such towns spanned the gamut from tiny agricultural settlements that were barely distinguishable from villages to large, fortified, and economically diverse commercial centers, which attracted merchants and artisans from across Eurasia. In the Chełm land, in Volhynia, in Podolia, and in the Nowogródek palatinate in Belarus, private towns overshadowed the royal capital, often by a significant margin.[3] Although politically isolated, no private town was immune from the currents of Enlightenment reform, in part because of the Commonwealth's porous and shrinking borders and in part because the owners themselves perceived the need to implement changes on their properties in accordance with the spirit of the times. The Prussian embargo, the flood of debased currency, the Russian invasions, and the changing

TABLE 5. POPULATION FIGURES FOR PRIVATE TOWNS IN THE LATE EIGHTEENTH CENTURY

Town Type	No. in the Crown	No. in Lithuania	Total	Urban Population by Hearth[1]
Royal	224	151	375 (26%)	58,360 (34%)
Clerical	78	67	145 (10%)	11,203 (10%)
Private	603	329	932 (64%)	100,469 (59%)

Source: BC 1093 (Population of Poland and the Reasons for Its Decline, 1777), 589–626; Rostworowski, "Miast i mieszczanie," 141–42.

1. Includes the Polish Crown only.

overseas grain trade conspired to render private towns less economically significant in the eighteenth century. Many owners reached for the remedies of enlightened centralism favored by the king. Transforming the behaviors and attitudes of private town burghers and Jews, though, proved no less complex than reforming the royal cities.

Private towns have traditionally appeared in historiography as examples of the nobility's excessive power and an unfortunate symptom of the central government's weakness. This is a judgment summarized in Kołłątaj's *Political Law of the Polish Nation*. Declaring that "private towns are not free," Kołłątaj elaborated that liberty for burghers required owners to abdicate political and judicial control in favor of the state.[4] As a result of their separation from royal oversight, private towns fit well into the narrative of the oppression of the weak by the strong, similar to the arguments about starostas and magistracies. Private town owners may have granted privileges and rights to residents, but in the words of Gershon Hundert, "municipal autonomy was a fiction."[5] Moreover, the dependence of residents on the whims of the great lords meant that burghers and Christians had no power to resist ever-increasing tolls, fees, and rents, which formed the basis of the owner's revenue. Rack-renting private town owners could squeeze money out of helpless burghers, much as the lords raised dues and labor obligations on the peasantry. For Tomasz Opas, a preeminent historian of private towns, the most obvious symptom of the lord's excessive power was the inability of most private town burghers to appeal cases to the royal Assessor Court. Andrzej Zamoyski was famous for having made an exception for a few of his own private towns, but for the rest the lord remained the final authority and appellate judge. Based on this dependence, Opas described the eventual abolition of private towns in the nineteenth century as an "emancipation" comparable to the ending of serfdom.[6]

More recently, historians such as Moshe Rosman, Irena Grochowska, and Adam Teller have challenged the indigent owner stereotype by emphasizing the enormous undertaking involved in managing large estates with private towns. Grochowska's study of Stanisław Szczuka and his town of Szczuczyn, founded at the end of the seventeenth century, presents a picture of the lord's continuous involvement in improving the town, attracting residents, managing crises such as fires, and resolving disputes between the citizenry and the magistracy.[7] Despite the costs and difficulties involved, nobles continued to construct new towns throughout the eighteenth century, and these settlements found willing immigrants. In fact, the governments of Stanisław August and, later, Joseph II complained that Polish nobles had erected too many towns too close to one another, oversaturating the market and taking resources from royal towns.[8] In most respects, Polish nobles behaved similarly to their counterparts in Hungary, Ireland, and Scotland, where recent studies have also revealed a more complex and nuanced relationship between owners and residents because of a combination of economic and political forces. Lindsay Proudfoot's analysis of private towns in Ireland, for example, argues that the wealthy and powerful duke of Devonshire was unable to exercise significant influence in his towns using either the carrot or the stick.[9]

Until recently, Anglophone studies of private towns in the Polish-Lithuanian Commonwealth have largely been confined to the field of Jewish studies, and for good reason: private towns often boasted large and vibrant Jewish communities. Lords viewed Jews as reliable administrators and leaseholders, and privileges granted to Jewish communities in private towns often included a significantly greater package of rights and immunities than could be found in royal cities. In many cases Jews outnumbered Christians, whose magistracy controlled a tiny segment of the population, while the kahal disposed of far greater revenue than the official city government. Owners, as Yvonne Kleinmann argues using the case of the Lubomirski family's Rzeszów, sought to maintain a legal balance between Christians and Jews and avoid the impression of favoring either group. As Adam Kaźmierczyk has shown, private town owners integrated Jews into their administrative and legal systems, which usually resulted in greater Jewish-Christian interaction at the commercial and judicial level. In one case, for example, the city magistracy adjudicated an internal Jewish dispute regarding the validity of an election to the kahal, an unthinkable occurrence in most royal towns. Using the example of the Radziwiłł family's Żółkiew, Stefan Gąsiorowski has confirmed the enormous premium that owners placed on Jewish-Christian cooperation, which often translated into joint tax-collecting and spending ventures, as well as commercial enterprises.[10]

No study on private towns, though, has attempted to understand the

TABLE 6. THE LARGEST TEN CITIES IN THE POLISH CROWN AFTER WARSAW, 1777

City Name	Town Type	Palatinate	Hearths	Approx. Pop.
Warsaw	Royal	Mazovia (Great Poland)	11,622	64,000
Kraków	Royal	Kraków (Little Poland)	4,004	23,591
Lublin	Royal	Lublin (Little Poland)	1,829	8,550
Ostrzezów	Royal	Wieluń Land (Great Poland)	1,651	9,000
Poznań	Royal	Poznań (Great Poland)	1,514	8,300
Leszno	Private	Poznań (Great Poland)	1,446	7,900
Mohylów	Private	Podolia (Ukraine)	1,167	6,400
Dubno	Private	Volhynia (Ukraine)	1,127	6,200
Szarogród	Private	Podolia (Ukraine)	1,124	6,200
Rawicz	Private	Poznań (Great Poland)	1,041	5,700
Wschowa	Royal	Poznań (Great Poland)	1,035	5,700

Source: BC 1093, 589–626; Kleczyński, "Spis ludności."

interlocking relationship binding Christians, Jews, the owner's bureaucracy, and the royal government into a coherent system of mutual dependence and benefit. The Polish-Lithuanian Commonwealth created a unique "incubator" (to borrow Mack Walker's term) for private towns, which combined a privilege-granting monarchy, a weak central power, and a high demand for commercial settlers.[11] The country was just unified and homogeneous enough that private town owners had to compete with one another to attract and retain burghers, a fact that required the lords to promise generous benefits, including low taxes and significant autonomy, to Christian and Jewish communities. As a result of these opportunities, many private towns prospered and developed markets and fairs that attracted international merchants. Not all private towns became success stories—most, in fact, remained small, semi-agricultural settlements—but the Commonwealth's incubator did offer the potential for auspicious private towns to develop into viable commercial centers that rivaled the most prosperous royal towns. Five of the ten largest towns within the Polish Crown's 1772 borders (at which point Zamość had been incorporated into Austria) belonged to private lords (see table 6).

Private towns in the Commonwealth offer one of the strongest counterarguments to Max Weber's claim that medieval and early modern rulers tolerated self-government simply because they lacked the trained officials to manage the localities themselves.[12] Private town owners employed legions of administrators, including surveyors, economic managers, tax collectors, bailiffs, judges, and governors, but owners explicitly renounced interference in the internal affairs of the magistracies and the kahals. Such commitments were often respected in the breach, but offers of generous self-government, low taxes, and protection against external aggression formed major components of the lords' public relations campaign to attract and retain settlers in a country with a shortage of qualified artisans and merchants. The first step in luring settlers involved securing a grant of Magdeburg Law for the city from the king, as this charter guaranteed self-government, individual freedom of movement, and transferable property rights. Lords delegated such powers because royal cities and the towns of competing owners offered the same provisions, and not because of any limitation of resources. In fact, owners often had to sweeten the deal by promising additional perks to prospective residents, including expanded commercial opportunities and decreased prohibitions for Jewish communities. In some private towns, Jewish communities gained access to the guild structure and even to the magistracy. Owners relied upon a basic level of Jewish-Christian cooperation for the city to function, pushing the two parties to work together when disputes emerged.[13] Even when an owner chose to intrude into the public sphere reserved for citizens, he or she often struggled to achieve aims at variance with the interests and predilections of town residents.

The residential capitals of the Zamoyski, Radziwiłł, and other families served as symbols of power and splendor, and lords accumulated social capital from their elegantly decorated cities, but private towns served above all as revenue-generating investments. Karol Stanisław Radziwiłł's town of Słuck, in fact, bypassed his residence of Nieśwież as the most populous and important city in the region.[14] In a cash-strapped country, towns created markets for peasants to convert grain into coin, which lords could then collect through alcohol sales, mill fees, and tolls on merchants arriving for market and fair days. Crucially, though, residents of private towns paid few, if any, direct taxes to the lord. Again, the scarcity of commercial people in the Commonwealth created a seller's market for settlers, who often received tax exemptions and privileges that were unthinkable for the owner's serfs. Rack-renting owners could and did attempt to squeeze more revenue from burghers, particularly in the eighteenth century, but as Ber Birkenthal reminded the new owner of Bolechów in 1765, the residents could respond to excessive taxes by leaving for a different city where the lord offered more favorable terms.[15] In fact, the stereotype of the indigent, avaricious owner better reflects the post-partition reality, when the absolutist states deprived owners of political, paternalistic, and privilege-granting powers, leaving immediate profit as the only benefit of owning a private town.

In the late eighteenth century, private towns faced significant pressures as a result of Russian integration in the Commonwealth and the subsequent first partition. Internal family dynamics also strained the finances of both the Radziwiłł and the Zamoyski families. Karol Stanisław had to abandon his so-called principalities of Nieśwież, Słuck, and Ołyka in Belarus and Ukraine after unsuccessfully agitating against Stanisław Poniatowski's election, and his return in 1767 proved short-lived, leading to a renewed exile from 1769 to 1778 following his support for the Confederacy of the Bar. During his absence, the prince depended on the cooperation and support of his administrators, while Russian troops stood garrisoned in his cities. The massive debts incurred abroad clouded Radziwiłł's return to the country, and the prince's death in 1790 plunged the family into crisis, as quarrels arose over the management of the estates during the fourteen-year minority of Dominik, Karol Stanisław's nephew and heir to the entire fortune. Dominik's minority also coincided with the final two partitions of Poland, which awarded most of the family holdings to the Russian Empire.[16]

Andrzej Zamoyski faced his own difficulties, beginning with his role as an assistant to his profligate brother, Jan Jakub, in managing the Zamoyski entail, located in the Lublin province of contemporary Poland. As de facto owner after 1777, Zamoyski inherited the troubles caused by the first partition of Poland in 1772, which divided the entail almost exactly in half. Zamość and the town of Tomaszów fell under Austrian rule, while smaller cities such as Kraśnik and Szczebrzeszyn remained in the Commonwealth. After intense lobbying, Zamoyski finally obtained a patent in 1786 from Joseph II, allowing the entail to preserve its customs exemptions and operate as a single economic and juridical unit, a state within two states. The Austrians initially allowed Jan Jakub and Andrzej Zamoyski significant latitude in managing their towns and lands, but the centralizing and unifying tendencies of the Habsburg monarchy could not leave these territories wholly to the management of their owner. In order to maintain a vestige of his previous role, Zamoyski had to serve as a spokesman for Habsburg interests, while implementing imperial regulations and decrees.[17]

The partitions and occupations saddled the two families with expenses arising in part from ruined and desolated cities, and each turned to Enlightenment-inspired good order regulations with a view toward revitalizing his property. These efforts, despite the considerable power of the two actors, achieved only limited success and seem to reflect the growing powerlessness of the owners in the face of external pressures. In some ways, the Zamoyski and Radziwiłł family estates present atypical examples of the relationship between private towns and their owners. As two of the four families in the entire Commonwealth with the parliamentary-conferred right of entail, the families could preserve their fortunes in a manner denied to other nobles, who were subject to the common law of partible inheritance.[18] As a result, the two families never ceased to play a role in the country's politics from their rise to prominence in the sixteenth century to the collapse of the Commonwealth, and both expended considerable sums on fortifying and embellishing their capitals. At the same time, the enormous properties of each family included a wide range of town types, including many medium-sized and agricultural towns of peripheral interest to the owner. Moreover, the two families faced the same economic and political challenges as all Polish-Lithuanian lords, while their private town reforms fared no better than those of much less powerful owners.[19] In a sense, examining the private towns of the Zamoyskis and Radziwiłłs offers an opportunity to take the full measure of the private experience, viewing not only the typical but also the extraordinary possibilities created by the uniquely devolved system of the Commonwealth.

THE PRINCE'S PERSONAL PROTECTION

Next to the Jagiellonian dynasty and its descendants, the Radziwiłłs constituted the most important family in the Grand Duchy of Lithuania, which until the Union of Lublin had included the Ukrainian palatinates of Volhynia, Kijów, and Bracław. In 1586 three Radziwiłł brothers, recently made princes of the Holy Roman Empire, received parliamentary approval to entail their properties, which became the "principalities" of Ołyka, Nieśwież and Kłeck. The fortunes of the family waxed and waned over the next centuries, but in the eighteenth century Michał Kazimierz managed to acquire title to all three entails and the bulk of the family fortune passed to his son Karol Stanisław in 1762.[20] From the beginning, the Radziwiłłs had sought to crown their prominence by building elegant capitals. To this end, Mikołaj Krzysztof Radziwiłł, owner of Nieśwież, petitioned King Stefan Bathory for a grant of Magdeburg Law and commercial protections for burgher settlers. The king acquiesced in December 1586 with a charter of Magdeburg Law for Nieśwież "on the model of Wilno," as well as concessions for markets and fairs and immunities from internal tariffs for the burghers. The king also granted Radziwiłł the right to hear appeals from the burghers in the city, which, from Bodin's point of view, would represent a concession of sovereignty to a private individual. At the same time, the exchange demonstrated the significant power of the king; without the charter of Magdeburg Law, the prince would have had difficulty attracting settlers. For this reason, Mikołaj Krzysztof's correspondence in this matter with the under chancellor of Lithuania betrayed a certain anxiety about securing this privilege, repeatedly mentioning Magdeburg Law and market concessions as the most important privileges to seek from the king.[21]

The prince's concern reflected the reality that even an immensely wealthy and powerful lord required the king's charters as part of his public relations campaign to attract commercial settlers to populate a private town and generate revenue for the treasury. Magdeburg Law offered potential settlers assurances of individual freedom and property ownership as well as autonomy in matters of jurisprudence and local administration. For the burghers, this meant a model of self-government that was reminiscent of the royal towns in the fifteenth century;

instead of the king selecting a wójt to serve as a royal representative, judge, and first officer of the magistracy, the prince confirmed the citizens' choice for this official, who then presided over the elections of the city council.[22] A starosta, again modeled on the royal pattern, supervised the entire "principality," including the town and the surrounding villages, serving as appellate judge for nonburghers. City magistracies in private towns fulfilled an important judicial and administrative role in the complex organization of the principality, which included economic stewards, leasers, nobles, surveyors, and secretaries, and the Radziwiłłs demanded respect for the town governments as one of many institutions with a dedicated role to play. In 1657, Michał Kazimierz Radziwiłł (grandfather of his eighteenth-century namesake) complained that certain people were exempting themselves from the magistracy's jurisdiction and taking litigation directly to the starosta; he ordered subsequent violators imprisoned for disregarding city privileges.[23]

The Radziwiłłs employed the municipal freedoms and rights of Magdeburg Law as components of a recruiting drive to attract more settlers, who could contribute goods and taxes to the principality. In 1724 Michał Kazimierz Radziwiłł sent word to burghers throughout the Grand Duchy of Lithuania, declaring that "we will never violate the freedoms of Nieśwież or disturb the free settlement of citizens." He offered to endow any burghers from Minsk or other nearby cities with similar freedoms, should they settle in his city, emphasizing that the new residents would retain their right to leave at any time.[24] In 1747 the prince also instructed his starosta to respect the internal autonomy of the burghers: "If a burgher should have court business with another burgher, this does not belong to the Lord Starosta's competency and it should never be judged by the Lord Starosta, but in the town hall according to Magdeburg Law, from which appeal belongs exclusively to me."[25] In addition to judicial autonomy, the Radziwiłłs also reserved taxes and tolls for the city treasury, effectively forgoing revenue for the sake of maintaining a magistracy. Rents from urban and rural property (a kind of property tax, in effect) accumulated to the town treasury under the jurisdiction of the magistracy, and the municipal coffers also received revenue from merchant stalls and market tolls.[26] Judicial and financial independence, far from being an inconvenience necessitated by limited resources, provided the family with tools to attract people to the cities.

At the beginning of the eighteenth century, the magistracy of Nieśwież collected approximately five hundred zlotys per annum, a sum which had risen to around one thousand by the 1770s.[27] Such sums, while hardly enormous, compared favorably with other royal towns on a per hearth basis. While Nieśwież disposed of around 2.6 zlotys per household, Lublin boasted 2.4 prior to the arrival of the Good Order Commission. As in royal cities, municipal funds primarily compensated service staff, including the secretary, executioner, city soldiers, and a schoolteacher.[28] The Radziwiłłs made provisions to protect the revenue for the city by ensuring that all urban residents paid city taxes. A privilege from 1647, for example, stipulated that Jews buying urban property from Christians were subject to the same city taxes and obligations (including service as night watchmen and repair duty) as Christian citizens. Moreover, the owners forbade burghers to sell their property to nobles and members of the clergy, who could exploit their privileged positions to obtain exemptions from city taxes. As late as June 1791 the family's caretaker administration reminded the citizens of Słuck and their wójt to transfer property only to fellow burghers, warning that "many local nobles are seeking to buy urban property under various pretexts."[29]

As in other cities, the Jewish kahal operated as a parallel structure of self-government, with its own revenue and legal competency, although Jewish residents of Nieśwież were "citizens" of the city to a much greater degree than in royal towns, and they regarded themselves as such in their petitions to the family. The magistracy also received competency to adjudicate quarrels between Christians and Jews, when the former were defendants. As plaintiff, a Christian burgher had to summon a Jewish defendant to the starosta's castle court, which provided some measure of protection against spurious charges. Unlike some other private town owners, the Razdiwiłłs did not accord Jews any political function in Nieśwież, though practice did not always follow prescription. In 1688, Katarzyna Radziwiłłowa, observing that "great disorder has arisen due to the Nieśwież Jews penetrating into city government and prying into business, which does not belong to them," ordered that Jews not be allowed to participate in the magistracy "in the least matters" or even attend city council meetings. She further stipulated that Jews should not serve as tax collectors for the magistracy or work the toll booths at the city gates, an indication that the parallel worlds had become a little too intertwined for the family's taste. This was not a principle universally held across the Radziwiłł estates, for the kahal sent delegates to magistracy elections in Żółkiew, where Jews also participated in tax collecting jointly with Christians.[30]

Self-government remained more than a fiction, but there were limits to the burghers' autonomy. In the first place, the owner played an active role in the management of the estates and towns, as attested by the voluminous correspondence between the princes and their starostas, wójts, magistracies, economic stewards, and sundry employees. Despite his reputation for indolence, Karol Stanisław Radziwiłł followed in the steps of his predecessors in issuing regulations, resolving conflicts, and planning the development of his territories, even during his long absence in exile. Radziwiłł was particularly vigilant in terms of preserving his own prerogatives and rights. For example, the owner's control over the wójt served as the lynchpin of influence in the city. In 1772 Karol Stanisław informed the magistracy of Ołyka of his choice of wójt, explaining that his absence from the country prevented a normal review of the candidates presented by the citizens.[31] Seven years later, the prince berated the citizens of Ołyka for allowing the same wójt to retire and holding a new election without seeking the lord's permission. Radziwiłł invalidated the election and ordered the emeritus wójt to return to work until a proper election could be organized.[32]

Magistrates referred complex criminal investigations to the owner, particularly when the death penalty could be involved. In one instance, the city council of Ołyka requested Michał Kazimierz Radziwiłł's decision when the burghers discovered that a married citizen had retained a second wife and child back in his home province of Mazovia.[33] The prince ordered the man returned to his old family (with no indication as to how to resolve the status of the second wife and child). In other cases, the owner instructed the magistracy to investigate crimes committed by local peasants. In all Magdeburg Law cities, the salaried city executioner served as chief inquisitor, and torture remained an accepted means of interrogation, though the practice was officially forbidden in royal cities after 1775. In theory a sadistic lord could exploit this power, since common law required three separate inquisitions (that is, torture sessions) before an accused person could be declared innocent. In the few instances between 1762 and 1786 when Karol Stanisław ordered the magistracy to investigate a particular crime, the prince made no overt indication of the desired outcome. Although the subtext would have been obvious, for example, when Radziwiłł instructed the Nieśwież magistracy in 1781 to conduct "a most exact inquisition" with regard to a captured villager accused of arson and theft of the prince's silver, the prince nonetheless reminded the councilors to follow the procedures dictated by Magdeburg Law, with the possibility of appeal reserved for the owner. In fact, private towns could be less brutal than comparative royal towns; ritual murder accusations on private property against Jewish communities were more likely—with some exceptions—to end in a fine levied on the kahal rather than a grisly execution.[34]

The magistracy and the wójt also corresponded with the owner on matters of urban planning, repair, and investment. The owner took a particular interest in the upkeep of revenue-generating capital such as the mill as well as the defensive walls and the town hall.[35] For residents of the Radziwiłł family's three capital cities, the owner's interference and oversight translated into greater investment and endowment for the city, which served as a showpiece of the prince's wealth and power; commensurately, burghers profited as producers and suppliers for the princely court. The owner paid far less attention to smaller towns, such as Dawydgródek, Mir, and Sławatycz, which resulted in greater autonomy but less support. A capital city, though, required protection and adornment, both in material and socioeconomic terms. Like many private towns, Nieśwież served as a fortress to protect the family, and the impressive defenses played a role in attracting residents. In fact, both locals and foreigners acknowledged the superior material quality of private town fortifications over the defenses of royal towns.[36] Nieśwież further boasted a parochial school, a Jesuit college, and a hospital, funded by a dedicated tax revenue established by the family in the sixteenth century. Inventories from the early eighteenth century indicate that the Radziwiłłs made sure the town hall remained in good condition, as a symbol of wealth and power.[37] The city served as a site for festivities, parties, and princely entrances; in such instances, city magistrates assisted the prince's official staff with decorating and provisioning the city. As an indication of the tenor of these spectacles, Karol Stanisław reproached one of his subordinates in 1780 for gathering only two dancing bears for an upcoming princely *joyeuse entrée* into the city; Radziwiłł demanded a minimum of eight bears for all future events.[38]

If, in practice, self-government in Radziwiłł's private towns fell short of the autonomy promised, the family offered other inducements to both Christian and Jewish settlers. Consistent with the personal rule of the prince, Radziwiłł offered to employ the family's personal fortune, influence, and private army to shelter residents from competition, excessive burdens, and other demands of outsiders, a practice known as *protekcja*. Rosman has described protekcja as one of the services that powerful families provided to their Jewish settlers, but the Radziwiłł family explicitly extended this offer to all residents, as Michał Radziwiłł informed his Nieśwież starosta in 1747: "The Lord Starosta will provide every kind of protekcja, both to the Christian burghers and the Jews living in my towns, being aware of the debts, which they have in outside towns. If they themselves owe money, the Lord Starosta should ensure that they punctually pay and remit in order to maintain the best credit."[39] The service of protekcja, even in its more paternalistic forms, further bolstered the Radziwiłł family's campaign to populate their towns. In 1771 Karol Stanisław Radziwiłł ordered the magistracy of Żółkiew to post an announcement at all markets and fairs, advertising that new settlers would receive freedom from any taxes, while those returning would obtain "Land allotments, as well as any help with construction, support for their needs, and, especially, strong protekcja from the starosta and myself." A further instruction later that year reminded the starosta that Christians and Jews, especially the leaseholders, should particularly be given protekcja, "So that they are not harmed by anyone, despite reason or justice." In other words, outsiders could not privately execute judicial verdicts on the prince's citizens (as famously described in Mickiewicz's *Pan Tadeusz*) without appeal to the family.[40]

The family took the service of protekcja seriously, as did most private town lords, a circumstance indicated by the Lithuanian cities' petition to parliament in 1789, in which the royal towns complained that the lordly protection undermined the magistracy's powers and encouraged emigration to private towns. The correspondence of the Christian and Jewish citizens of Nieśwież, Ołyka, and Słuck with the Radziwiłłs reveals how protekcja required the family to respond regularly to petitions and to resolve claims of abuse.[41] In fact, the prince's burghers primarily requested protekcja from Radziwiłł's own employees and delegates, from the starosta down to the magistracy. A complaint by the Christian butchers' guild in 1748 that the principality's officials had failed to pay for the meat at the funeral of Michał's mother was met with a reply ordering the starosta to investigate.[42] When the Ołyka magistracy complained in 1751 of the unjust and illegal dues collected by the leaseholder on beehives, the owner responded that the practice would be forbidden. Other petitions contain no answers, as when the Ołyla kahal complained of the governor's "harsh and merciless" collection of taxes in 1771, but the prince's unbroken stream of privileges and instructions suggests that problems reached the lord, even in exile.[43]

In other instances, citizens requested protection from elemental disasters and military occupations. As the majority of buildings in each town were constructed from wood, a conflagration could erase an entire community within hours. Fires razed Nieśwież in 1758 and Ołyka in 1773, in the latter case destroying homes, stalls, and the synagogue. Radziwiłł, as owner, was expected to provide loans to rebuild his towns, and residents requested tax relief during the rebuilding process.[44] Russian soldiers, who were garrisoned in Radziwiłł's towns more or less continuously from the election of Stanisław August to the prince's second return in 1778, served as another scourge for city residents. The occupation began with a military incursion into the town, which destroyed lives and property; city citizens then had to billet, feed, and provision the foreign soldiers. In response to complaints directed toward the prince in 1779 that the citizens of Nieśwież had borne billeting duties for fourteen years without relief, Radziwiłł instructed a commissar to compile a list of material damages caused by the occupation, with records of commensurate monetary value for potential compensation. The citizens of Ołyka also requested protection, "as others nearby have" from the garrison's demands.[45]

The costs of maintaining and overseeing private towns consumed far more revenue than the owners obtained from the meager taxes paid directly by citizens, who remitted rent and property taxes to the town treasury, not the owner's coffers. Jewish citizens paid a capitation tax, and the owners had tried to institute a similar levy on the Christian burghers in the seventeenth century, but a privilege from 1654 freed burghers from this burden in perpetuity. A later inventory declared that, "by the privileges of the prince, no other duties or taxes shall be made or given until the expiration of [the town's] freedoms," a promise the family would come to regret in a later epoch.[46] Jewish butchers, as in other cities, also paid a tax on kosher meat, and residents of the extramural suburbs had to render produce in kind or labor services for use of rural plots, but all these fees totaled between 900 and 1,300 zlotys per annum from the city throughout the seventeenth and eighteenth centuries. In comparison, the entire revenue for the principality of Nieśwież in 1673 was 335,000 zlotys.[47] The real money came from indirect levies, including the alcohol monopoly, mills fees, and market tolls, which the owner bundled into a "general lease," farmed out to an individual or group of individuals on a semiannual basis. The leaseholders, always Jewish merchants with only one exception, collected tolls, oversaw alcohol production, and maintained the mills with the assistance of the prince's armed guards. In the 1770s, when the prince collected around 1,300 zlotys from the city of Nieśwież every year, the general lease on tolls, mill fees, and alcohol concessions netted 35,000 zlotys per annum. Ołyka's lease raised even more, over 54,000 zlotys per year.[48]

As explicitly stated in the general leaseholder's contract, the owner strictly enforced his monopoly on mills and spirits, with an exemption in the latter case only for weddings and baptisms. Notably, the monopoly on alcohol meant, in practice, an excise tax on distillers and brewers, as well as a tariff on imported wine, rather than some kind of centralized control. The prince's burghers, just as in royal towns under the propinacja law, made a living from alcohol; the citizens of Ołyka even believed themselves to have a privilege of brewing and distilling from one of the prince's ancestors, a conviction expressed in petitions in both the eighteenth and nineteenth centuries. The prince had to investigate such statements carefully, since one could never be sure what previous generations had promised, and each new prince had approved all past privileges in toto.[49] In other words, the burghers of Radziwiłł's estates hardly groaned under feudal oppression. More importantly, the residents of the principalities as a whole (and even beyond) contributed to the owner's revenue; the burghers did not so much profit the owners as facilitate their acquisition of currency. In fact, Radziwiłł's burghers paid less in taxes than most royal townspeople.

ZAMOYSKI, INC., AN ORDERLY CORPORATION

Jan Zamoyski (1542–1605) rose from middling nobleman to a wealthy landowner and influential politician, serving kings Stefan Bathory and Sigismund III as both chancellor and grand hetman. Capping his extraordinary career, Zamoyski obtained an entail from the parliament in 1589, for which the newly chartered city of Zamość would serve as residential capital. The founder specifically intended Zamość to serve as a showpiece of his rising authority, and he hired an Italian architect, Bernardo Morando, to design the layout and fortifications of the city in accordance with Renaissance notions of geometry and symmetry. Zamoyski took an active interest in the appearance of the town hall and the main homes on the market square; he also granted privileges and protections to encourage Jews, Armenians, and Greeks to settle in the city. In an act unmatched by other private town owners, Zamoyski obtained a papal charter to establish a university modeled on the Kraków Academy (now Jagiellonian University), which became the second school of higher learning in the entire Commonwealth that was not administered by a religious order. Zamoyski's patronage and personal interest allowed his capital to flourish beyond all other private towns. In the seventeenth century, tax assessors ranked Zamość among the first cities of the Commonwealth in terms of wealth and population, and the city's fortifications proved almost alone in withstanding the Swedish army during the Deluge.[50]

Zamoyski proved equally nonconformist when establishing institutions to manage his properties and cities. Rather than the personal paternalistic rule of the Radziwiłł princes, Zamoyski instituted a structure more analogous to a modern corporation with interlocking councils and well-defined jurisdictions, which removed the day-to-day administration from the owner's purview. At the apex, the Economic Council oversaw routine operations, composed precise budgets for each fiscal year, leased out monopoly rights, and supervised the collection of rents and tolls.[51] The chairman of the Economic Council, the burgrave, served as the liaison between the owner and the burghers of the entail. Appointed by Zamoyski, the burgrave periodically conducted inspection tours of all the towns, in which he reviewed finances, issued instructions from the owner, and presided over town elections. In addition, the burgrave also served as the chief justice on the Zamoyski tribunal, the highest court of appeals for the entail's burghers. Burghers from across the property elected judges to serve on the tribunal, and cities contributed funding for the secretarial staff. As in the Radziwiłł estates, the Zamoyski administrative structure coexisted with a system of self-government and communal autonomy that served as a component of the overall management of the estates as well as an inducement to attract commercial settlers to the towns of the entail.[52]

Bazyli Rudomicz was a seventeenth-century burgher, academy professor, city councilor, and judge on the tribunal whose diary presents a detailed portrait of the interactions between the citizens, the magistracy, and the lord during the Swedish wars and the crisis provoked by the childless owner's death. In 1665 the late owner's sister, Gryzelda Wiśniowiecka claimed possession of Zamość, and she fought a pitched battle both militarily and in front of the Crown Tribunal against the legal heir of the entail, Zdzisław Zamoyski, who was supported by the ascendant Sobieski family. A formidable presence, Wiśniowiecka dominated the town and at one point threatened to expel Rudomicz on suspicion of covertly supporting Zdzisław. At the same time the city's administrative organs appeared to operate without interference from the owner. Rudomicz himself represented a "privilege defender" par excellence when it came to upholding the prerogatives of the academy as well as his personal immunities. Rudomicz further presented magistracy elections as being free from the owner's pressure and depicted himself campaigning to support his preferred candidates, while the city council debated and approved economic and good order measures. On one occasion, the mayor, upon learning of being left out of the loop by the city council, thundered improbably, that "next to God, he was the most important person in the city."[53] Although exaggerated, this statement does suggest the important role delegated to city councilors and the significance of city elections in legitimizing the owner's power. When citizens neglected their civic duties, as when the residents of Kraśnik stopped holding annual elections in the 1760s, the owner's representatives issued reproaches and orders to follow tradition.[54]

As already indicated by Rudomicz's diary, the Zamoyskis also allocated funds for the towns of the entail to run magistracies with some discretion. As in the Radziwiłł estates, a certain hierarchy distinguished the well-funded capital from other cities. Rents from commercial space in the town hall, as well as a lease on the city brewery, funded magistracy business in Zamość, netting 4,405 zlotys for the town (19.6 zlotys per hearth at the time) at the end of the seventeenth century. As opposed to real estate taxes, the Zamoyski town citizens paid personal taxes in which the magistracy divided the lump sum required among the households, in theory taking wealth and means into account. Smaller towns, such as Kraśnik and Tomaszów, relied more heavily on these direct taxes to fund municipal governments. In fact, Burgrave Antoni Kochowski reprimanded the citizens of Kraśnik in 1775 for failing to exercise their legal right to lease the town hall and the sellers' stalls on the market square.[55] Unlike Zamość, the operational budget of a small town like Kraśnik was extremely small, since 45–65 percent of the total revenue raised was employed to meet the community's tax obligations to the Commonwealth government. The remnant, as in Nieśwież, compensated the support staff of the magistracy and financed minor repairs.[56] After 1772 other cities in the Zamoyski entail had to pay Austrian taxes, since the first partition had split the entire entail into two. The entail remained a single juridical unit, with a common economic council, tribunal, and burgrave functioning on both halves, but the obligations of the individual towns changed. Tomaszów, which stood in the Austrian corridor, had to pay for a number of officials and chancellery expenses mandated by Vienna, just like cities under the jurisdiction of the Good Order Commissions.[57]

The budgets for the entail administration in the eighteenth century showed that the Zamoyski capital continued to receive substantial support from the owners. For example, the largest line item on the budget for Zamość was equipping and compensating the garrison that defended the town. In the late eighteenth century, this provision absorbed 4–6 percent of the entail's total revenue. In addition, Zamoyski paid the operating costs of the town hall and supported a veritable army of carpenters, stonemasons, painters, and blacksmiths for maintaining the castle, the town, and the properties of his entail.[58] For the fiscal year of 1773–1774, the Zamoyski "corporation" reinvested 22 percent of the 62,862 zlotys received from Zamość in tolls, fees, and leases on repairs and maintenance in the town as well as provisions for the family residence. Subsequent years did not see such generous spending, but expenditures on Zamość continued to consume a large share of the entail's budget.[59] With regard to other towns of the entail, the Zamoyski family was significantly less generous. Kraśnik appeared in the expense column of the entail budget only once between 1767 and 1782. Tomaszów occurred twice, once in 1782 when the Zamoyskis funded an administrative building for the Austrian authorities and again with reference to a tiny expenditure for repairing the town's brewery.[60]

Zamoyski's formal bureaucratic structure, along with the sundry requirements of Austrian authorities, worked against the use of protekcja as a specific tool of recruitment or policy. Injured burghers and even peasants could appeal to the tribunal for justice, and even the highest officials in the administration of the entail took their grievances to this forum.[61] Some burghers did present supplications, which the administration duly recorded in a dedicated register of petitions and responses, but the records indicate that the owner's personal intervention was a rare occurrence. In one notable response Andrzej Zamoyski supported the request of a Kraśnik burgher for material support and financial aid in establishing a brazier workshop in 1773, but otherwise the tribunal seems to have functioned in lieu of the owner's informal role.[62]

As in the Radziwiłł estates, the Zamoyskis employed the magistracy and wójt to handle judicial matters for the local peasants. Rudomicz recorded one instance in which Gryzelda Wiśniowiecka instructed the magistracy to investigate a peasant woman accused of stealing the host (a witchcraft accusation, in essence). The court tortured the accused woman three times, as was standard practice, but she refused to recant, so the wójt declared her innocent and punished the accusers.[63] Although an extraordinary story, the incident does corroborate the assertion that private town owners were most concerned with the maintenance of order and peace, delegating relative latitude to the magistracy in this field. In the Zamoyski entail, Jews also took their complaints against Christians to the magistracy, but Christians had to prosecute Jews before the kahal, a legal situation much more congenial to interethnic equality and similar to the situation described by David Frick in Wilno. Such arrangements had little connection to the owner's attitude toward the Jewish population. The Zamoyskis, like the Radziwiłłs, considered Jews economically essential to their towns—but also pernicious. As their instructions attest, the Zamoyskis retained this view well into the nineteenth century, holding that a given city's Jewish population should live separately from the Christians and eschew residences on the showpiece market square.[64]

Like Radziwiłł's towns, Zamość and the other towns of the entail served as centers for the owner to gather indirect taxes rather than sources of revenue in their own right. In 1629, out of a total revenue of 104,507 zlotys for the entail, the entire contribution of Zamość was 77 zlotys, paid by the butchers' guild to the owner. Rents and citizens fees had risen to 2,000 zlotys by 1685, though this figure still only comprised 1 percent of the total. As in the Radziwiłł territories, the Jewish population paid a special capitation tax netting an additional 3,000 zlotys, and town citizens across the entail also collected money for a dedicated fund called the "gunpowder tax," which supported the defensive garrison in the capital. The 3,648 zlotys required for this expenditure added 700 zlotys to the obligation of the Zamość citizens, with the rest spread out among other towns; Tomaszów and Kraśnik paid 440 and 220 zlotys respectively.[65] As in other private towns, the most significant revenue came from the mills, market tolls, and particularly, the alcohol monopoly. In 1659, for example, when the town produced 216 zlotys for the family, the mill brought in 12,000.[66] As the eighteenth century progressed, propinacja increasingly balanced the entail's budget. Zamoyski's propinacja income from Zamość alone in the fiscal year 1771 was 18,201 zlotys, rising in 1774 to 51,988. In the same year, alcohol sales furnished 6 percent of the entire entail's revenue, that is, 82,515 out of 1,303,606 zlotys, which was a small but vital sum that, unlike agricultural produce, did not have to be exchanged for currency.[67] Again, private cities generated wealth not so much from the residents as by the function of allowing the owner to monetize and tax the produce of the peasants.

GOOD ORDER AS PROFIT MAXIMIZATION

The examples of Zamość and Nieśwież may have inspired Adam Bukar, a parliamentary deputy from Kijów palatinate, to propose that the government sell all royal lands and cities to nobles, who would in theory manage the properties better than the starostas and offer protekcja to their new subjects.[68] Of the ten largest towns within the 1772 borders of the Polish Crown, five belonged to private individuals (see table 6), but not every private town laid golden eggs for the owner. The overwhelming majority, including many of the towns owned by the Radziwiłłs and Zamoyskis, remained small, largely agricultural settlements with limited commercial value. Such disappointing towns posed a challenge for their owners, particularly when the privileges of previous owners had already abolished most of the rents and dues that residents paid. The economic and political realities of the Commonwealth in the late eighteenth century undermined the value of even the wealthiest private towns, which forced owners to experiment with new methods to revive their towns, many of which drew from the currents of enlightened centralism. While the Zamoyskis echoed many of the policies of the Good Order Commissions in trying to reform their cities on the cheap, Karol Stanisław Radziwiłł tinkered with traditional good order measures but largely maintained the status quo.

To a large degree, good order regulations in private towns were models rather than borrowings. When the reformers in Stanisław August's circle and the Permanent Council discussed urban reform, many of the ideas proposed alluded directly to good order and cleanliness regulations that nobles had been promulgating in private towns for over a century. Rudomicz recorded a number of good order measures, some initiated by the owner and others voted in by the citizens, including urban planning and fire-prevention measures. In the seventeenth century, the Radziwiłł family also tied various urban privileges to instructions about construction, repair, and cleanliness.[69] The chronicles of Andrzej Komoniecki, the wójt of Żywiec, also mention regulations from 1700, which resemble urban reforms undertaken by King Stanisław August in the royal towns; Franciszek Wielopolski, the owner of Żywiec, instructed burghers to present their accounts to the property administrator and to utilize urban revenues for repair and maintenance. Fire-prevention regulations imposed by the Good Order Commission of Lublin, for example, appear in Radziwiłł's 1747 instructions and the budgets for Tomaszów and Kraśnik in the 1760s, years before the commissions began operating outside of Warsaw.[70]

In general, however, the instructions of town owners prior to the

Enlightenment reflect the humanistic preference for general ethical pronouncements, which entrust the details to local authorities. Michał Radziwiłł's 1747 instructions to the Nieśwież starosta, for example, emphasized the importance of creating an inviting and secure atmosphere for merchants. Referring to upkeep and repair, the owner instructed the starosta to ensure that the magistracy took action, but he emphasized that the magistracy itself should manage urban property. Karol Radziwiłł repeated these general guidelines to his Żółkiew starosta in 1771.[71] References to tradition and established practice, combined with a strain of suspicion toward novelty, fill much of the correspondence between owners and burghers prior to the final third of the eighteenth century. The instructions on behalf of the minor Klemens Zamoyski (d. 1767) to Tomaszów in 1762 most succinctly illustrate this mentality: "[My] instructions will not describe the customs of this town as they are quite extensively recorded in the election record books, and further it is better to observe old customs and ensure they are implemented than to forget newly written ones."[72] Many of Zamoyski's subsequent points, including injunctions such as the requirement to hang a crucifix in the courtroom as a reminder of the magistrates' oaths, reiterate points from Bartołemej Groicki's sixteenth-century manual on Magdeburg Law. Karol Radziwiłł also emphasized tradition, requiring his newly appointed starostas of Żółkiew and Nieśwież to fulfill the instructions of his father and ancestors.[73] This was not merely laziness but a reflection of the anxieties and concerns of the urban population, for whom—as for citizens of royal cities—innovation implied a potential loss of liberties and freedoms. In 1751, when the citizens of Ołyka petitioned the prince for the resolution of certain difficulties, the letter began with an expression of gratitude "to God and the prince" that the most recent instructions had not "established or conceived" any novelties.[74]

External circumstances, though, required owners to experiment with novelties both out of necessity and conviction. In the Zamoyski entail, the influence of Austrian administration over half the territory played an obvious role, but Andrzej Zamoyski also self-identified as a child of the Enlightenment. Running the entail unofficially after 1767 in the stead of his ill and profligate elder brother, Andrzej assumed the task of negotiating with the Habsburgs for confirmation of the family's rights. After 1778 Andrzej enjoyed sole ownership of the entail as well as the title of count, but Joseph II pointedly dragged his feet in confirming the property's customs privileges until 1786. The Habsburgs also subjected the newly created count to the petty humiliations of Austrian bureaucratic formalism. When Zamoyski wrote to Vienna in protest the treatment of his residents, the Austrian chancellor advised him to address his concerns to the *Kreisamt* captain or the governor of Galicia.[75]

The Austrian authorities did allow Zamoyski to retain a certain degree of control in his towns. In 1774 Galicia governor Heinrich von Auersperg wrote to Zamoyski (in Latin) with assurances that the local administration would consider municipal elections in Zamość a private matter, so long as the newly elected councilors took an oath to the empress and her coemperor. As the price for this privilege, Zamoyski had to serve as the spokesman for Austrian interests in his towns. For example, Zamoyski's economic and political instructions to Tomaszów after 1772 increasingly refer to Austrian priorities, such as implementing imperial decrees, following Austrian judicial procedure, and apprehending deserters from the army. These instructions came in addition to orders and regulations delivered to city magistracies by the *Kreisamt*.[76] Zamoyski's limited autonomy in Zamość did not last long, as the impressive fortifications and dedicated revenue streams of the city attracted the interest of Austrian authorities, who designated the city for government "care"—meaning, in particular, the reorganization of the city government along more hierarchical principles.[77] A measure of the new relationship appears in an exchange between the citizens of Zamość and Andrzej Zamoyski in 1783. The Zamość citizens complained that the new Austrian government had appropriated city funds earmarked for the education of poor children and requested the owner's intervention and assistance with raising funds for repair. In response Zamoyski blamed the citizens for wasting money and failing to follow proper regulations; on the matter of intercession, Zamoyski admitted that his power to help the burghers was now limited, but he added somewhat unconvincingly that, "The owner will not forget to provide help and assistance to his burghers."[78]

The economic disruptions caused by the partitions, as well as the costs of implementing Austrian regulations, threatened Zamoyski's bottom line, serving to further highlight the fact that most of the entail's towns were underperforming expectations. In the spirit of enlightened centralism, the Zamoyskis sought to use police regulations to correct the townspeople's behavior and improve their economic potential on the cheap. In fact, the Zamoyskis had been moving in this direction since the 1760s. Instructions from Burgrave Franciszek Dzierżanowski to the small towns of the entail, for example, show an increased concern that burghers perform specific commercial functions, a situation that would require a higher level of education. In 1768 Dzierżanowski read the owner's instructions at the annual election in Kraśnik, which included the following command: "In practically all the towns of the Zamoyski entail, the burghers have sold all their houses to the Jews and have become suburbanites, and further they do not teach their sons skills, or if their sons do receive education, they do not apply themselves to commerce and trade . . . and burghers, having rights from the kings and the owners in hand and not being aware of them, and not having houses in the town, should not be honored with such rights or called burghers, but serfs more apt to perform corvée labor." Having thus berated the residents, Dzierżanowski instructed the town citizens to hire a schoolteacher, for "if children become educated, then . . . this knowledge will be available for good and in the future will contribute to the happiness of the town." The burgrave concluded with promises that the burghers' actions in the sphere of education would win the approbation of the owner and improve the financial situation of the town; they should not "regret the expense" for either a school teacher or other functionaries, such as a tax collector and secretary.[79]

As evinced by the tone of Dzierżanowski's instructions, the Zamoyskis intended the town citizens to carry the costs of the improvement in addition to rents, tolls, and monopoly restrictions. A similar approach characterized efforts to improve urban space in the small towns. In 1762 the burgrave asked the magistracy of Tomaszów to repair the town jail; in 1767, Dzierżanowski pleaded with the town to erect a safe building to house the town's records, noting that many poorer towns in the entail had found the means to construct such a depository.[80] Dzierżanowski similarly beseeched the residents of Kraśnik in 1768 to repair one of the rooms in the main gate tower to house council meetings and store records. The burgrave explained that the magistracy should comport itself in a manner befitting an official institution and stop holding official meetings in the town tavern, "because neither courts nor councils should take place where people drink, eat, and prepare food, while visitors continuously come and go."[81] Zamoyski required the burghers of Zamość in 1783 to draft the suburban residents for labor duties such as repairing roads and bridges. In addition, he ordered the town council to forbid the construction of wooden buildings within the town.[82]

A similar calculus applied when Andrzej Zamoyski acted to rationalize the urban administrations of the entail in line with the regulations of the Good Order Commissions, which the onetime chancellor had sponsored and patronized.[83] After 1772 the entail's burgraves began emphasizing the necessity both of keeping precise records and of having multiple officials sign off on all expenses. In 1775 Burgrave Antoni Kochowski explained to the newly elected magistracy of Kraśnik that keeping records of spending decisions, which both the mayor and the treasurer had to authorize, would create greater trust within the community. He emphasized that the council should thus not regret the money needed for the extra paper and copying work.[84] In 1778 the burgrave informed the Kraśnik magistracy that officials such as clerks, tax collectors, town servants, and school directors would receive annual salaries. The town would now have to expend significant sums on previously pro bono officials. In addition, the administration of the entail compiled a table of administrative fees for the town officials to follow, which included surcharges for recording official protests and decrees, making transactions, and hearing complaints. Under Austrian pressure, Zamoyski also turned the mayor and the wójt of Tomaszów into salaried officials in 1771, anticipating changes that the Good Order Commission would introduce to Lublin and other royal towns in the 1780s.[85]

As the Good Order Commissions and the Department of Police also discovered, translating commands and regulations into concrete changes proved difficult without constant oversight, nagging, and threats. Zamoyski's regulations collided against inertia, disobedience, and the unwillingness of burghers to subsidize the cost of the owner's reforms. In 1772 the burgrave again reminded the citizens of Kraśnik to send their children to school. In 1786 the same official reprimanded the town because only five children were attending the school, which, in addition, was still not properly heated. Moreover, the schoolteacher was owed substantial back pay.[86] The Civil-Military Commissions struggled with similar disobedience with regard to the equally novel passport regime, responsibility for which theoretically fell on private town citizens no less than on their royal counterparts. The commission cited the magistracy of Kraśnik once for failing to post checkpoints and, again, for granting a passport to a runaway serf, offenses that each carried a two-hundred-zloty fine. Other private towns in the region received penalties for failing to repair roads, using nonstandard measures, and auctioning passports for sale to the highest bidder. In a moment of particular cultural illiteracy, the commission fined the kahal of Wieniawa for delaying to register the passport of an individual who had arrived on a Saturday.[87]

After 1795 the entire entail, along with the Lublin and Chełm regions, fell to Austrian control. The new administration inspired and cajoled landowners to undertake their own regulations and decrees, which mimicked the spirit of the Zamoyski regulations. For example, in 1790 the Sanguszko family instructed the town of Firlej to keep separate books for different kinds of business—judicial, financial, and commercial.[88] The owners of Modliborzyce and Żółkiewka instructed their burghers to incur no expenses without the joint approval of the mayor and treasurer. By 1800 the owner of Żółkiewka had added a provision that only he could approve new expenses. As with the Radziwiłłs and Zamoyskis, owners encountered difficulties in translating regulations into practice. In Żółkiewka in 1798 the owner was still nagging the burghers to record their finances properly, while in the same year Janusz Sanguszko complained that the burgers of Lubartów had refused to accept his legally appointed wójt.[89] On the other hand, the same owners allowed their towns to continue holding elections even after the Austrians annulled magistracy elections for royal towns in 1805. Despite the increased restrictions, private towns were the only institutions from the Austrian partition to enter the Napoleonic Duchy of Warsaw in 1809 with an uninterrupted tradition of self-government.[90]

Karol Stanisław Radziwiłł also confronted the problem of unproductive and economically underperforming cities (issues exacerbated by his long and costly exile) as well as the damages inflicted upon his estates by Russian soldiers. The prince returned in 1778 to discover his capital full of empty homes, disorderly shops, and neglected infrastructure, a scene repeated across the towns of the principalities.[91] Moreover, while the owner was away, the leasers and administrators played. Throughout Radziwiłł's absence, the wójt of Nieśwież, Jerzy Paszkowski, had plied the prince with obsequious assurances and reminders of his faithful service, but the wójt's death in 1779 unleashed a flood of complaints. Citizens and the magistracy criticized the late Paszkowski to the commissars whom Radziwiłł had delegated to investigate city disorders. The citizens accused Paszkowski of raising property tax rates for the purpose of paving the main streets, at the same time as he demanded that citizens perform the labor without compensation. For its part, the magistracy claimed that Paszkowski had exempted himself from the Commonwealth's hearth tax, leaving the rest of the city to make up the difference. Further, Paszkowski had taken city land for his own use, failed to present accounts during elections, and even refused to pay the city secretary his salary one year in retaliation for a supposed debt.[92]

To regain control of the situation Karol Stanisław issued his own good order and police regulations. His chancellery produced decrees, confirmations, and orders on a daily basis, but in contrast to the Zamoyskis, he showed much less enthusiasm for enlightened rationalism. In 1776, while Radziwiłł remained in exile, the prince's administration delivered a decree to the principality of Nieśwież that included instructions for fire prevention, new construction, and education. Every city in the principality had to send two pupils to Nieśwież, where they would study civil law in preparation for service in the magistracies. Radziwiłł ordered the town governments, not the parents, to bear the cost of 150 zlotys per student. The magistracy of Nieśwież, at least, fulfilled the order, as the petition of the town citizens to the commission in 1779 included the complaint that citizens had to pay this extra education tax.[93] Upon his return to the country Radziwiłł also issued "good order" instructions to his cities on a monthly basis, most of which were modeled on decrees dating to the seventeenth century. In 1781 he ordered the citizens of Nieśwież to build merchant stalls out of brick instead of wood. Radziwiłł commanded the magistracy to read this announcement aloud to the accompaniment of drums. Another order reminded citizens to ensure that chimneys in the town be constructed of brick and roofs not made of straw.[94]

Karol Stanisław's good order regulations aimed above all to beautify and adorn his capital according to his own particular aesthetic, even at the expense of economic productivity. Like the Zamoyskis, the prince disliked the fact that members of the Jewish community occupied the most prestigious houses on the main streets and the market square. As in other estates, the prince contracted most of his leases and tolls to Jewish intermediaries, but Radziwiłł still expected each community to remain in its proper place. In November 1779, Karol Stanisław ordered the deputy starosta to expel all Jews living outside their quarter "in order to return the city to its former beauty," as well as to investigate how such violations occurred in the first place. Radziwiłł complained of the starosta's negligence in this matter, but the deputy starosta fared little better; the order to expel the Jews from the market was repeated in 1782.[95] Some Jewish families were relocated, and the prince granted the now vacant lots to favorites, but the process failed to achieve the prince's intention. In 1806 Dominik Radziwiłł's surveyor again reprimanded the citizens for allowing Jews to occupy prime real estate in the city. Radziwiłł's ethnic urban planning proved not only impossible to implement but also fiscally counterproductive. In attempting to fill vacant lots in the market square with residents, the prince often granted the property to servants and favorites, whom he freed from the city's tax obligations. The 1779 complaint observed that the exemptions enjoyed by officials like Paszkowski narrowed the tax base and undermined municipal finances.[96]

Unlike the Zamoyskis, Karol Stanisław issued no precise regulations with regard to the city magistracies' day-to-day functions, and the internal struggles of the family after the prince's death left little time for novelty. In 1790 Maciej Radziwiłł wrote to Mayor Karol Klawzowski with an order to maintain continuity in urban government and finance, above all to ensure the continued flow of revenue from the estates to the owner. Maciej further had to contend with the fallout from the Targowica Confederacy, which led to a renewed Russian occupation of Nieśwież and Słuck. In October 1792 Maciej wrote to Colonel Lipiakin, commandant of Nieśwież, asking the Russian officer to respect the jurisdiction of the starosta and the magistracy; the prince also requested that the colonel investigate accusations of property damage levied by the burghers, reminding the official of Maciej's own obligation to protect the property for the minor Dominik. He also ordered the starosta of Słuck to examine similar complaints.[97] While dealing with Russian penetration into the Commonwealth, Maciej continued to issue good order regulations to the cities in his principalities. For example, he instructed the wójt and kahal of Słuck to cooperate in repairing bridges and embankments in the city.[98]

In 1793 the Targowica Confederacy dispossessed Maciej and granted stewardship of the family fortune to Michał Hieronim Radziwiłł, a client of Catherine the Great. An absentee landlord who managed Dominik's Belarusian and Ukrainian territories from his hereditary property in Prussian Poland, Michał Hieronim faced the task of accommodating the management of the family towns and villages to Russian rule, which brought new taxes, recruiting obligations, and regulations. Among other changes Radziwiłł replaced the starostas—a term too closely associated with the old Commonwealth—with commissars, who served as intermediaries between the Russian government and the cities.[99] The commissars had much less leeway to offer protekcja, a reality indicated by an early nineteenth-century petition "for the lord's serious reflection and consideration" from the Jewish citizens of Nieśwież. In spite of Karol Stanisław's illogically discriminatory policies, the petition still expressed nostalgia for the old order: "And what most greatly pains and hurts us is that we have not the least protekcja, due to which we have already come to a state of affairs, in which only those who live here do not harm us. When we had a starosta, then we had someone to whom we could appeal in our troubles; someone who would stand up for us, but now we have no protector. Thus, we beg that we could have some kind of protekcja from his lordship."[100] Upon obtaining his majority in 1804, Dominik would briefly attempt to return to the paternalistic rule of his uncle, but the interests of the Russian state would negate his ability to offer the kind of protections and privileges that served to attract settlers under the Commonwealth.

Private town owners in the Commonwealth sought, above all, to maximize the return on their investments, though considerations of prestige and political theater shaped decisions with regard to the family capitals. In a cash-strapped country with limited avenues for profitable investment, towns facilitated the circulation of coin and assisted landlords in the management of large territorial estates. City citizens collectively became, at least in theory, the owner's golden-egg-laying geese, serving to convert grain and other agricultural products into currency, which could then provide taxes, tolls, and fees. Scarcity made both Christian and Jewish burghers valuable, creating conditions in which owners competed with one another for citizens by offering commercial, political, and fiscal privileges. When Stanisław August visited Nieśwież in 1784, in a ceremonious speech the mayor boasted of the city's privileges and liberties, and though the entire event was staged with the acquiescence of Karol Stanisław there was more than a kernel of truth to his remarks. As can be seen from the conditions the same owners set for their peasants, these concessions were not out of magnanimity but stemmed from economic interest.[101]

Such a system could only function in the decentralized Commonwealth, which kept the owners loosely bound to one another under a common umbrella of legal tradition and political space, but which allowed owners wide latitude to design their own recruiting techniques. The paternalistic Radziwiłłs and the corporate Zamoyskis both offered burgher settlers distinct packages that partially depended on the city of choice. For greater paternalistic protection, but less autonomy, settle in Nieśwież; head to Zamość for regularized administration; for less oversight and external support choose Ołyka or Kraśnik. City citizens could make this choice, since the king's charter of Magdeburg Law guaranteed individual freedom, and owners understood that impingements on this right (which did happen) could threaten future business; hence Michał Kazimierz Radziwiłł's insistence that settlers would be free to leave at any moment. Royal charters and concessions bound each private city to the Commonwealth, but the king's weakness meant plurality and particularism. Private towns would not have achieved such prominence in either a stronger state or the absence of one. Many of the principalities of the Holy Roman Empire could have existed within any one of Radziwiłł's estates, but the rulers of territorial states in the Reich increasingly claimed complete sovereignty and thus the right to rule over cities as royal, thus state, towns.[102]

The enormous authority granted to private town owners in the Commonwealth did not always translate into power, as evidenced by the reactions to their eighteenth-century reforms. Zamoyski and Radziwiłł both confronted a landscape in which global economic and political factors—including the flood of debased currency, the diminishment of the Vistula grain trade, and the gradual dismantling of the Commonwealth—conspired to undermine the value of private towns. Applying Enlightenment-inspired remedies to a greater or lesser degree, owners encountered passive resistance and disobedience from magistracies and starostas, upon whom the power of the lord rested. Zamoyski found only begrudging cooperation with his educational policies, the implementation of which demanded the kind of supervision and control the owner was not prepared to grant. Radziwiłł tried to expel the Jews from the center of his capital residence, but his own dependence on Jewish leaseholders and the economic realities of the town largely invalidated his plans.

Much more difficult to evade were the regulations and restrictions of the absolutist successors to the Commonwealth, whose paid civil servants and agents of enforcement felt less compunction about negotiating with the residents or listening to the owners. The uniformity of the post-partition states negated the ability of owners to offer competitive benefits or princely privileges. The only benefit of owning a private town became immediate monetary gain, as the ability to attract future settlers became severely curtailed. As a result, the stereotype of the oppressive rack-renting town owner, though not without application to the Commonwealth era, became more appropriate after the partitions.

5

The Apogee of Enlightened Centralism

TOWN AND STATE IN THE NAPOLEONIC AND POST-NAPOLEONIC PERIOD

NAPOLEON'S CRUSHING DEFEAT OF the Prussian army in 1806 overturned the partition settlement and offered citizens of the former Commonwealth an unexpected second chance at state-building. Having aided Napoleon's forces with regular soldiers and partisans, the Poles reaped their reward in the 1807 Treaty of Tilsit, which authorized the creation of a Polish state out of Prussia's share of the second and third partition. The Duchy of Warsaw, as the new state was called, expanded to include much of Austrian Galicia following another spectacular victory by the French emperor in 1809. As with all his satellites and protectorates Napoleon imposed French laws and political structures on his Polish wards. In the Duchy, "Poles" served as ministers, prefects, subprefects, and mayors; Poles implemented the *Code Napoléon*; Poles guarded the border and served in the army; and Polish administrators disposed of a hierarchical administrative machine that, many hoped, would overcome the failings and injustices of the old Commonwealth.[1] As before, the economic, social, and material improvement of the cities took a prominent place in the plans and proposals of the new governing elite. The Napoleonic system and the Polish character of the Duchy survived the fall of its original benefactor, as well as the November Insurrection of 1830, granting a generation of Enlightenment-inspired reformers an unprecedented opportunity to realize the aspirations of the Department of Police, the Good Order Commissions, and the urban reform law of 1791. Now, however, no official could complain that the state lacked coercive power or sufficient hierarchical control.

"Two centuries ago, our cities prospered," wrote Maciej Jabłonowski, prefect of the Lublin department, but "Polish laws, which benefitted only the ruling classes [*klassie warujące* (*sic*)], caused the collapse of cities." The prefect asserted in his 1812 report to the minister of Internal Affairs that the new Polish state would ensure equality under the law and protection of each urban settlement from the rapacity of the nobility.[2] Not content with equality and justice, enlightened reformers of the partition generation hoped the new state's curation and energetic government would transform the urban landscape by directing citizens to greater productivity and unleashing the economic potential of urban society. Cities would become thriving commercial and industrial centers under the adroit management of a well-oiled machine of state ready and able to prevent disorders and improprieties from arising. Faith in the progressive power of state administration, a conviction held by French officials under Napoleon as well as Josephinist bureaucrats in Austria, achieved special power among post-partition Poles seeking to explain and escape their lamentable position.[3] The new system would be the antithesis of the "German feudalism" that doomed the Commonwealth, but state care required the abrogation of the burghers' own particularistic privileges and rights. As Ignacy Stawiarski wrote in an 1807 pamphlet, "It would be futile to reestablish [the cities'] individual privileges, the fruit of feudalism and misrule."[4]

In Polish historiography up to the present, the creation of the Duchy of Warsaw appears as a pivotal moment, in which Poles finally gained a "modern, progressive" administration and developed a proper understanding of governance—in short, a period of progress and development that endured through the constitutional period of the Congress Kingdom of Poland (1815–1832). Such an arrangement might have produced a prosperous society had the November Insurrection of 1830 not led to a quarter century of repression and reaction on the part of Russian authorities.[5] In fairness, the Napoleonic system produced some remarkable economic changes, despite difficult external circumstances such as multiple wars, military exactions, and occupations, but the system of enlightened centralism was already falling far short of its promise even a decade prior to the insurrection.

The hierarchical layers of oversight and supervision proved insufficient for correcting the "disorder" and malfeasance in the cities, despite an orderly chain of command and the power to discipline state officials at all levels, in part because agents of state based their policies on abstract models of urban life that in no way corresponded to the actual demographic, political, or economic reality of the former Commonwealth. This abstraction, derived from French and English reality, assumed that cities should be adorned with magnificent public buildings, that burghers should pursue trades and crafts unrelated to alcohol production, and that Jews should have a minimal role in urban life. Unfortunately, the state had to employ most available resources for the professional salaried bureaucracy, much vaunted as an agent of change, but the costs necessitated a desperate search for revenue streams. In order to pay the salaried officials who would transform society, the state found itself dependent on revenue from alcohol production, which enlightened reformers had long held responsible for the country's underdevelopment. Meanwhile, despite the view of Napoleonic officials that the large unassimilated Jewish populations constituted a symptom of disorder, the essential roles of Jews in the economy of most small towns meant that the government remained dependent on revenue from this population for fiscal survival. The resulting contradictory policies toward the Jewish population neither encouraged assimilation nor altered the prominence of alcohol or Jewish middlemen in the urban economy. In the end, social engineering failed because discipline and exhortation by highly vigilant administrators became the state's only tools, as the system denied any role to local initiative and lacked the ability to inspire productive, forward-thinking behavior.

Nowhere did enlightened vision and disorderly reality collide more conspicuously than in the state's policies toward private towns, an undertaking that consumed enormous effort and energy on the part of government officials and administrators. The nature of private towns—which had divided property rights, local self-government, and obligations to both the owner and the state—defied the neat and orderly political conceptions of Napoleonic legislators and officials. On the one hand, the Napoleonic state anchored its legitimacy on a professed respect for liberal property rights, enshrined in the Code Napoléon's abolition of all feudal tenures and use rights. Officials could not simply appropriate private towns from their owners without violating both the legal basis of society and their own liberal conceptions about the appropriate role of the state. On the other hand, the Duchy and its successors presumed that urban settlements should inherently be subordinate to and dependent upon the central government. In reconciling these two impulses, Napoleonic legislators and administrators actively sought to separate town governments from their owners' influence, favoring complete central control over any settlement, which they could remotely classify as urban. As one result of this policy, the state definitively severed the equilibrium of power and economic interest that had allied private town citizens with their noble town owners under the Commonwealth. Unable to tolerate the judicial, political, and paternalistic power of nobles or the wide autonomy of their towns, the state abolished the owners' power to offer competitive benefits as well as the townsmen's tradition of self-rule, often in the name of benefiting the residents of these towns themselves.

The Napoleonic state's activist efforts to improve and uplift the social position of private town burghers produced the opposite effect, and the waning of enlightenment enthusiasm and reformist vigor after the 1820s relegated these settlements to an unfortunate status quo of continued dependence without protection. In the same way, efforts to transform cities into enclaves of well-ordered commerce collided against the contradictory headwinds of enlightened vision and immediate fiscal need. As in Austria and Prussia, the central government vastly overestimated the ability of a rational blueprint to erase long-standing traditions of resistance and community organization. Confronted with continued disorder and the inability of repression to shorten the gap between vision and reality, state officials blamed the human material available and pressed for ever more layers of oversight and accountability, the presence of which succeeded primarily in draining municipal coffers. In the period after 1832, the state retreated from the most ambitious goals of social transformation, just as Austrian officials gradually resigned themselves to the Polish domination of Galicia and the tenacity of traditional Jewish society. In this period, which Marcin Wodziński and others call the "post-Enlightenment," officials referenced Enlightenment-era rhetoric in pronouncements and professed allegiance to the goals of good order and social change, but they quietly allowed legalism and bureaucratic infighting to excuse dysfunction and impotence until a second Polish revolution in 1863 ushered in a new era of Russification and rapid social change, signified by an urban reorganization decreed in 1867.[6]

Despite modifications, the powers, underlying assumptions, and convictions of state officials present a significant continuity from 1807 to 1867, allowing for an investigation of policies, concrete aims, and achievements of enlightened government in a period when the state faced no organized opposition. The Lublin province, a poor region predominantly settled with private towns and theoretically most in need of state "care" serves as the principal case study. A brief survey of the three periods in question—the Duchy of Warsaw (1809–1815), the Congress Kingdom of Poland (1815–1832), and the post-Insurrection Period (1832–1867)—precedes an examination of three areas that best illustrate the inability of enlightened centralism at its apogee to realize the dreams of eighteenth-century reformers: managing the bureaucratic hierarchy, rationalizing urban finance, and improving the plight of private towns. No exhaustive study of any individual town can be attempted; rather, the sections focus on examples most illustrative of the means by which the contradictions between vision and reality hampered the achievement of each regime's goals.

REGIME CHANGES, 1807–1832

For the western and southwestern regions of the former Commonwealth, incorporation into the Duchy of Warsaw meant a second regime change in the space of fifteen years. The Treaty of Tilsit obliged Prussian king Friedrich Wilhelm III (r. 1797–1840) to cede the regions of Poznań, Warsaw, and Thorn to the Duchy of Warsaw, and the Duchy expanded in 1809 to embrace Austrian Galicia, including Lublin, Chełm, and Zamość along with the entire Zamoyski entail (Lemberg [Lwów] remained in the Austrian empire).[7] Nominally, the Saxon king, Friedrich August III, ruled the Duchy of Warsaw, though Napoleon dictated the constitution. French soldiers also resided in many of the towns, and

Napoleonic institutions, including the Code Napoléon, became the standard. Napoleon's hierarchical system stretched from the king down to village mayoralties. The king nominated all prefects, subprefects, and mayors at his pleasure, meaning citizens had no opportunity to present possible candidates. Appointed administrators supervised the towns' budgets, announced government instructions, and fulfilled orders and regulations.[8] This system did allow for limited, largely symbolic civic participation, operating within strict confines. Nobles and, for the first time, burghers could elect deputies to a largely ceremonial parliament, but the law specifically rejected any association with *szlachta* democracy, warning that "[At these assemblies] there will be neither place for agitation of any nature nor voting on petitions or suggestions."[9]

The Constitution of the Duchy represented the epitome of eighteenth-century liberal thinking, which promoted individual freedom from the tyranny and abuse of local government. In place of nonprofessional oligarchs, trained and salaried administrators fulfilling precisely defined functions would manage city affairs under the supervision of regional and national superiors. Among other effects, Napoleon's new structure required exponential growth of officialdom at all levels, even in comparison with the relatively built-up bureaucracies of Prussia and Austria. The principle of employing salaried officials, appointed from above, held for private cities as well. State officials sought, wherever possible, to grant "independent" administrations to even the smallest of settlements, meaning governments accountable not to the owner but to the prefect.[10] Many genuinely welcomed the new order, which promised to sweep away the provincialism, petty tyranny, and conflation of private and public goods that had characterized the old order. Stanisław Węgrzecki, the mayor of Warsaw, celebrated the subordination of local government and transformation of officials into cogs in the great machine of state since this system promised greater equality for all. He wrote that, under the Napoleonic regime, "prefects, subprefects, municipal presidents, mayors and wójts . . . do not judge, nor do they do anything with their heads; they simply carry out the unequivocal regulations handed down to them, which even those governing must obey."[11] In the vision of reformists and government servants such as Joachim Owidzki and Hugo Kołłątaj, professional, specialized training would develop a cohort of disinterested state workers who could enact the enlightened projects of the government. Hierarchical supervision, stretching down to mayors and city councilors, would coordinate the efforts of these officials while ensuring that government servants did not misappropriate or waste scarce resources "arbitrarily."[12]

Not everyone agreed with this analysis, and the hierarchical state encountered opposition from both noble republicans and formerly self-governing towns, in part because officials often failed to appreciate the radicalness of these changes at the local level and the dissatisfaction provoked by the abolition of all vestiges of self-government.[13] In a telling letter to the Ministry of Internal Affairs from 1811, the citizenry of Solec in the Radom department, "who have always elected the magistracy themselves," expressed their community's frustration at this new powerlessness. Denouncing the fact that a certain Józef Kozarski "has been named mayor of the town, against all law and reason, in spite of the fact that he was not presented by the town, has never served the town, is unqualified, and cannot be trusted since he does not possess any collateral with which to hold him accountable." In response, the ministry informed the citizens that, "since the change of government and introduction of a new constitution, the prerogative of cities to present candidates for city office has ceased." Further, the king had personally selected Kozarski, the ministry continued, meaning that this official could not be removed without evidence of incompetence. In such a case, the community could complain to the subprefect.[14] One could doubt the utility of this avenue, as well as the respect and legitimacy enjoyed by these officials, since the citizens of Zamość did write numerous complaints against their magistracy, whose members remained in power for several years and referred to accusations against them in an 1816 letter as symptoms of the "city residents' antipathy and disobedience vis-à-vis their superiors."[15]

Napoleon also left the Duchy an unfortunate legacy in his equivocal policy with regard to the Jewish population. The constitution promulgated by Napoleon did not recognize differences in religion, but following an anti-Jewish turn in Napoleon's own policies at home, Friedrich August "temporarily" deprived the Duchy's Jewish residents of voting rights, civil service opportunities, and civic rights in the cities. Moreover, the state continued to enforce and even expand *De non tolerandis Judeais*, requiring Jews (about 28 percent of the urban population) to live in the extramural suburbs of the principal cities, an area now called the *rewir*. Officials in the Duchy also began a policy of making inconsistent exceptions to the rules for the wealthiest and most assimilated. In many ways these policies combined both the anti-Jewish sentiments of Christian burghers with Enlightenment attacks on unassimilated Jews as economic parasites and roadblocks to social progress.[16] Plans to deprive Jews of a role in alcohol production, an aim of the government since the 1776 propinacja reform, continued to occupy the attention of the highest levels of state, as did proposals to resettle Jews on agricultural land as farmers. Further, Polish officials equated illegal or quasilegal Jewish settlement outside the *rewir* with urban "disorder" comparable to unpaved, waste-covered streets and vacant lots.[17]

The Duchy had little time either to enact its reform legislation or observe the fruits of its policies since the majority of existence was spent on a war footing, feeding French soldiers and raising an army for Napoleon's 1812 campaign to Moscow. As Napoleon retreated from his failed expedition, which had included the participation of ninety thousand Poles (almost one-sixth of the entire army), Russian soldiers crossed into the Duchy. Instead of punishing the Poles and absorbing their Duchy into Russia as many expected, Emperor Alexander I announced his intention to continue the existence of the Duchy as a constitutional state under Russian protection. Alexander had expressed sympathy for liberal institutions early in his reign, and his close advisor Prince Adam Czartoryski had long advocated for the tsar to correct the injustices of the partitions. By playing the liberal card and announcing plans to create a separate Polish state, Alexander successfully countered Prussian and Austrian claims to the same territory. As a result of Alexander's successful diplomacy, the Congress of Vienna accepted the "Congress Kingdom of Poland," which encompassed a truncated Duchy of Warsaw, minus Poznań, Thorn, and Kraków. In 1815 Alexander promulgated the Polish constitution, which granted a bicameral legislature elected by both nobles and burghers along with civil liberties such as freedom of the press, speech, and religion. In an act unimaginable to previous Russian tsars, Alexander even swore on the Gospels to uphold and guard this new constitution.[18]

As subsequent events proved, Alexander's vision of parliamentary government bore little resemblance to the British constitutional monarchy. Alexander wished the agencies and branches of government to cooperate for the common good, and the emperor had no taste for parliamentary infighting or the concept of "His Majesty's most loyal opposition."[19] Moreover, Alexander and his viceroy in the kingdom, General Józef Zajączek, held most of the levers of power in comparison to the parliament. Konstantin Pavlovich, the emperor's younger brother, became the chief of the Kingdom's military, while Nikolai Novosil'tsev, a trusted advisor to the emperor, gained informal access to the bureaucratic machinery.[20] The state had little difficulty undermining electoral opposition, as the Kingdom retained the centralized administrative structure bequeathed by Napoleon, and administrative decisions modified or curtailed the liberal freedoms promised in the constitution. Even elections to the parliament took place in assemblies, over which officials appointed by the central government presided. Nonetheless, the Congress Kingdom enjoyed one of the most liberal constitutions in Europe, less restrictive than Louis XVIII's *Chartre*. In this respect, the Congress Kingdom offers a useful example of enlightened centralism in the conditions of liberal democracy.[21]

The Congress Kingdom replaced individual officials with collegial boards, but the principle of tight supervision and oversight remained. The Ministry of Internal Affairs became the Governing Commission for Internal Affairs and Police (KRSW), headed by a minister chairman, which, despite modifications in labeling, would remain on top of the hierarchy until 1867.[22] At the provincial level, departmental prefects handed the baton to provincial commissions, which supervised circuit commissars, city inspectors, municipal magistracies, and village mayoralties. Cities in the Congress Kingdom received a new organizational structure in 1818, but fundamentally the Napoleonic system continued unchanged. Provincial "citizen councils," consisting of elected notables, offered a bone to local government, but their powers remained purely advisory—they could advocate for local needs to state officials without any expectation of success.[23] The Congress Kingdom also inherited the Enlightenment identification of professional administration and supervision with progress, in part because most Duchy officials remained in government service after 1815. As Tadeusz Mostowski, chairman of the KRSW, intimated in 1818, provincial and local governments could not achieve effective results without the coordination of the central state.[24]

In most respects the goals and presumptions of state officials continued unchanged after 1815. Enthusiasm for using state power to revitalize and improve the cities remained high, as testified by reminiscences of officials such as the chairman of Lublin's provincial commission, Ignacy Lubowiecki. As before, state officials endeavored to balance the incompatible demands of "liberating" private towns from their lords while respecting the owners' property rights.[25] The Congress Kingdom's Jewish policy also continued the Duchy's provisions; the 1825 Civic Code confirmed the "temporary" restrictions of 1808. Further efforts were undertaken to prevent Jewish alcohol production and distribution, and the residential restrictions remained in force.[26] By the late 1820s, however, the contradictions of enlightened centralism were already deflating the promises of centralized, "energetic government." As the state's machinery failed to make headway on key priorities of social and economic reform, the optimistic progressivist vision of enlightened officials gradually succumbed to inertia, indecision, and impotence. Meanwhile, death carried off Alexander I, who had at least paid lip service to constitutionalism—as well as the generation of statesmen who had come of age politically during the final partitions and who felt a burning desire to correct the injustices of the Commonwealth through the medium of an "energetic government."

Their successors, in part because of the growing climate of reaction in Russia and Europe more generally, felt less eager for action and confrontation in defense of Enlightenment ideals. In this respect the "post-Enlightenment" in Poland mirrored the larger European conservative turn, as when Friedrich Wilhelm III rolled back the liberal reforms of the Napoleonic period.[27] In the Congress Kingdom, the unsuccessful November Insurrection, launched in 1830 against Russian control, brought more wide-ranging and dramatic consequences. Having pacified the revolt, Nicholas I abrogated the Polish constitution, sweeping away the parliament, dietines, and citizen councils. Ivan Paskevich, a general in charge of suppressing the insurrection, became the new viceroy and prince of Warsaw, remaining in his post until 1855. The administrative and legal systems, the precedents created in the autonomous period, as well as the predominant role of Poles in government remained in place. The organization of municipal government, too, persisted until Alexander II issued a new model in conjunction with the Great Reforms and a more muscular drive to incorporate the former Congress Kingdom into Russia proper.[28]

DISCIPLINE AND FINE

In March 1816 the newly appointed chairman of the Lublin provincial commission, Piotr Domański, discovered that the Lublin magistracy had not submitted a budget for approval since 1809. This period had coincided with Lublin's annexation into the Duchy as well as the Russian invasion, but Domański's chief concern was that, "the town coffers, remaining without a budget for eight years and depending on an arbitrary distribution of the town's property, have been exposed to the greatest possible damage." Domański levied a fine on Lublin mayor Benjamin Finke for tardiness, writing to his superiors, "I do not want to be responsible for the arbitrary expenditure of the town coffers, and the disorder which must arise in the records from this."[29]

Finke protested that the Napoleonic constitution had placed budgetary matters in the hands of the quasi-elected town council, over whom the mayor had no control. In fact, the mayor could not discipline or dismiss any subordinate official without the approval of provincial authorities, but Domański refused to waive the eight-zloty fine until the government had received a budget. The commission did fine the town council a year later for failing to include explanatory notes in its budgets, but Finke was not let off the hook. In May 1817 the provincial commission threatened the mayor with a further penalty if he did not promptly remit the previous fine.[30]

The Napoleonic system intended to ensure that no local magistrate would abuse power or misappropriate resources. Layers of oversight and accountancy would prevent subordinate, provincial officials from defrauding the state, while tables of precisely assigned functions meant that no municipal official could make decisions that were detrimental to the whole. Lublin, the largest city in the eastern part of the Duchy, employed significantly more civil servants than in any previous period. Not only the mayor but two aldermen, five chancellery officers, an archivist, a treasurer, a police chief, a schoolteacher, and numerous others drew salaries from the municipal budget. In theory each magistrate fulfilled precisely defined functions and was legally prohibited from taking any action outside these boundaries, and the state instituted processes to recruit and train officials, who would not act "arbitrarily." Each personnel appointment required the approval of a central or provincial superior, depending on the level of importance assigned. The king named the mayor, while the minister of the Interior confirmed councilors and aldermen, a process that required several months and multiple attestations on the part of local officials. The Napoleonic constitution did permit one element of local control for larger cities: elected councils, which convened to assemble the annual budget and distribute the tax burden among the citizens. Even in this case, the principle of supervision required the citizens to present sixty candidates for membership, from which the king selected thirty.[31] The Ministry of the Interior along with the provincial councils also supervised leases on city revenues to tax farmers as well as the composition of city budgets, which required extensive justifications for all projected revenues and expenditures. This vigilance intended to ensure that scarce resources would be available for good order and protected from waste or misappropriation, presumed to have been a major cause of the decline of cities in the eighteenth century.[32]

Such procedures proved difficult to follow, though, in light of the chaos and unanticipated expenditures arising from Napoleon's military campaigns, and officials such as Domański tended to translate "unanticipated expense" as incompetence or theft. In another example, a commissioner delegated by the new government in 1816 to Zamość, already effectively under complete state control (the state would purchase the town formally from Stanisław Zamoyski in 1821), reported numerous irregularities and abuses on the part of the magistracy.[33] In particular, the city coffers had been emptied "due to neglect, the incompetence of the mayor and treasurer, and discord in the city council, as testified by numerous orders and threats from higher authorities."[34] An investigation by the KRSW, though, showed that many of the unauthorized expenses had resulted from the Russian siege of the city in 1813, and the central government concluded that the mayor, "while not demonstrating criminal intent, collected and spent city funds without permission, emptied the coffers, and did not properly manage city records." In the end, the provincial commission concluded by reprimanding the mayor and advising his transfer to a less important town; the government meanwhile initiated a legal process against the treasurer for misappropriation of funds. The KRSW further instructed that the city council, which "is either lazy or incompetent" be dissolved and reconstituted with members chosen by the provincial commission.[35]

Over the next several years, the state made several modifications to the hierarchical system in order to prevent incidents such as these. In 1816 KRSW initiated a policy to secure urban revenues from rapacious officials by requiring newly appointed mayors to deposit a sum, equal to one-quarter of their annual salary, as a security to be held by the central government (with interest, admittedly) for the duration of the official's tenure in office.[36] In 1818 Zajączek promulgated a new configuration for town organization, which confirmed and enhanced the principle of hierarchical control. The new regulations ended the aberration of semi-elected city councils, transferring budgetary and tax authority to appointed magistrates with precisely defined functions.[37] To further stymie any potential for abuse or misappropriation, the municipal reorganization decreed additional layers of supervision and inspection. Each province was now divided into circuits and placed under the supervision of a circular commissar. Meanwhile, a dedicated town inspector toured each province with the authority to audit town finances and report on the implementation of regulations.

The KRSW also began collecting all the surplus revenues in excess of ordinary expenses from every municipality. In theory, this measure would provide sums for capital projects, infrastructure improvement, and good order. In reality, any sums in excess of basic personnel, chancellery, and petty maintenance funds fell under direct state control. Even the tiniest towns, such as Bychawa and Bełżyce sent money to the "disposal" of the KRSW. In 1819, a KRSW data table reported that 36.4 percent of all projected municipal revenues (620,005 of 1,704,229 zlotys) would accumulate to the KRSW's master treasury. This practice remained in place after 1830. New taxes and fees imposed in the Paskevich period for the benefit of city coffers in reality accrued to the KRSW.[38] Even these additional layers of control did not prevent financial misappropriation, at least from the perspective of the KRSW. In April 1829 the KRSW issued an order forbidding all towns from making any spending decisions without the provincial commissions' approval. In September, the order was reissued, apparently because of instances of improper spending.[39] Two decades of training had failed to recondition municipal officials away from autonomous financial decision-making. In fact, mayors and councilors became more adept at hiding and disguising unauthorized spending. In 1834 the KRSW discovered that the mayor of Tomaszów had diverted funds intended to pay state taxes to support revolutionaries in the 1830 November Insurrection.[40]

In theory, salaried professional administrators should have been more likely to fulfill directives, and the Napoleonic system exponentially increased the number of paid municipal positions. Regulations required that every urban settlement retain a salaried mayor, but larger cities swelled with new staff. Lublin projected an expenditure of 63 percent of its 62,062 zloty revenue on salaries in 1811, a figure that had decreased to 38 percent by 1819 only because of the major tax increases

TABLE 7. REVENUE AND EXPENDITURE FIGURES FOR SELECTED LUBLIN TOWNS, 1819

Town (p) = private	Population	Revenue in Zlotys	Revenue per Person	Revenue from Alcohol (%)	Expenditure on Salaries (%)
Bełżyce (p)	1,498	1,430	0.95	0%	55.94
Bychawa (p)	805	1,270	1.58	0%	83.78
Firlej (p)	615	650	1.06	0%	95.69
Lublin	10,603	113,371	10.69	65.80%	38.08
Kazimierz	2,157	16,623	7.71	76.56%	40.52
Szczebrzeszyn (p)	2,790	3,455	1.24	67.04%	82.84
Zamość	4,431	15,243	3.44	70.49%	39.34
Kraśnik (p)	2,723	3,052	1.12	2.85%	70.90
Urzędów	1,630	3,248	1.99	84.08%	55.05
Chełm	2,358	8,403	3.56	75.47%	55.59
Tomaszów (p)	2,562	4,755	1.86	56.80%	71.90

Sources: AGAD, KRSW 36, 64, 73; AGAD, KRSW 205, 21; Rożenowa, Produkcja wódki, 51–64.

(see table 7). Globally for the entire Kingdom, cities spent approximately 48 percent of their revenues on municipal officials in 1819, but significant variations existed between provinces, as well as among cities. Salaries and compensation consumed over 55 percent of the budgets of towns such as Chełm and Urzędów, while smaller private towns exhausted their entire revenue to pay for a single mayor and policeman. These figures held true after the insurrection, with smaller towns expending all but a few hundred zlotys on personnel, while larger cities budgeted around 45 percent of their revenue for salaries, pensions, and compensation.[41] Such budgeting reflected revenue projections that turned out to have been wildly optimistic. Even before the invasion of Russia in 1812, which required magistracies to quarter, feed, and supply both Napoleon's invasion force and the troops of the Russian counteroffensive, revenue streams failed to match projections. In 1811 the Lublin magistracy wrote to the minister of Internal Affairs complaining that officials had not been paid regularly for three years.[42]

After the war Lublin had incurred enormous debts and admitted to the KRSW that salaries projected in the 1811 budget had yet to be paid. In the budget submitted for 1816, the city modified all revenue projections downward, and all officials received a significant pay decrease.[43] Lublin town inspector Kazimierz Brandys claimed that undercollection and negligence were responsible for the shortfall. Following an audit of Lublin province in 1820, the town inspector argued that the undercollection of taxes had deprived Lublin of nine hundred thousand zlotys (about nine times the annual projected revenue) between 1809 and 1818, which, if true, would have accounted for nearly all of the city's funding. The KRSW expressed optimism that perhaps some of this money could still be collected, admitting, though, that the likelihood of success appeared low.[44] The state itself was one of the problems causing Lublin's budget projections to flounder. A notation on town income for 1815–1816 explained that the sum of 16,808 zlotys, which previously had been calculated into the budget, could not be considered revenue "because this amount includes rent from the town hall, which the state coffers regularly fail to pay."[45] Unmoved, Brandys claimed in an 1825 report that Lublin could collect twenty-five thousand zlotys more per annum than the current budget indicated and proposed that the state mandate additional expenses for the cities in order to motivate municipal administrators to collect funds more effectively. Other cities fared no better: throughout the 1830s, the magistracy of Chełm reported enormous arrears. As a result of low and uncertain salaries, municipal employment (as elsewhere in central and eastern Europe) recruited the poor and desperate, along with the zealous, as public servants.[46]

Unsurprisingly, the available officials failed to follow their precisely prescribed functions, and cities functioned because nonappointed citizens sometimes made up the difference. The traditions of municipal autonomy inherited from the Commonwealth meant that city citizens were accustomed to solving problems in a manner independent of higher authority, and institutions such as guilds and kahals typically disciplined their members without reference to higher authorities. These were precisely the habits that the Napoleonic system intended to break. For example, in an 1821 circular, the KRSW warned guild masters from "usurping executive power, which belongs exclusively to the magistracy."[47] In the same year, the KRSW warned in a memorandum to the provincial commissions that some private citizens, taking the false title of "town representatives" had been holding meetings on town finances without reference to the official municipal administration. The "town representatives" had been periodically corresponding with the provincial commissions in the name of the town, a practice that the KRSW claimed led to an increase in both paperwork and "disorder." In fact, though, only those with local knowledge and influence could provide the information necessary for budgeting and taxation. Town Inspector Brandys periodically relied on such clandestine "town representatives" to determine a given city's resources, presumably because of the magistracy's lack of knowledge in these matters. The informal role of nonprofessionals, in part to bypass cumbersome appointment procedures, continued after 1832. An 1836 inspection in Lublin determined that councilors failed to carry out assigned tasks and that "unauthorized" personnel had been working in the city chancellery.[48]

FROM GOOD POLICE TO POLICING

Enlightened officials in the Duchy and the Congress Kingdom inherited the eighteenth-century notion of police as the science of human happiness, and officials in the first third of the nineteenth century followed the tradition of the Good Order Commissions in viewing beautification, good order, and social engineering under the rubric of the state's obligation to realize "good police." In practice, good police in the Duchy/Congress Kingdom focused on three areas, all of which had been the concern of officials since the Commonwealth. In the first place, officials aimed to improve sanitation, cleanliness, and fire prevention through police regulations enforced by financial and criminal penalties. Second, the state continued the Department of Police's policy of weaning burghers from alcohol production in order to promote more useful trades. As an internal memo from 1821 observed, restrictions on alcohol production would encourage "greater aptitude for industry and other ways of making a living," whereas free trade in alcohol meant that merchants profited from drunkenness.[49] The state also viewed Jews as unfair and parasitic competitors to Christian burghers, and the multitude of Jewish taverns aroused particular indignation for allegedly swindling and indebting the peasantry. Until Jews assimilated and became proper Poles, government policy aimed to restrict the economic and residential opportunities of this community as much as possible.[50]

The possibility of imposing fines on disobedient citizens offered hope that the KRSW would have more success in correcting the unhygienic and "disorderly" behaviors of urban residents, but regulations issued in the nineteenth century proved no more effective than similar instructions from Good Order Commissions, Civil-Military Commissions, and Austrian authorities. In fact, rules issued by the KRSW in 1817, 1824, and 1828 often repeated verbatim the policies and wordings of their predecessors, and threats of fines failed to overcome indifference and disobedience. For example, the Lublin provincial commission threatened a six-zloty fine for throwing trash, feces, or animal corpses into the street, indicating that little headway had been achieved in the sixty-year battle to change residents' behaviors: "And because this type of disorder has crept into many of the residents of Lublin, the mayor should specifically pay attention to it and designate a place outside the town for dumping trash and waste."[51] The provincial commission also added rules for commerce on holidays, playing music at taverns (only twice a week), and writing numbers on houses. In 1824 the commission specifically reprimanded property owners for piling feces in their internal courtyards, which caused terrible disorder during rain. Townsmen were also reminded not to feed pigs inside their homes or while visiting taverns.[52] In 1828 the KRSW demanded a detailed report from municipal authorities, specifying how the regulations would be implemented and threatening fines for lax enforcement. Successive decrees only furthered the background static of unenforceable regulations, particularly since the state offered no incentives and little financing for improvement.

Good order regulations did provide a convenient pretext for city magistrates to harass the politically powerless Jewish community. In November 1830 the municipality of Lublin ordered that no more than one Jewish family could live in a single-room wooden house (*izba*); violators were granted forty-eight hours to depart. The Jewish community petitioned the government, citing both the short time frame and the approaching winter as mitigating factors. The KRSW ordered an investigation but observed that a government decree from 1822 did justify the city's actions, effectively siding with the magistracy. In other cases, the government authorized the demolition of houses in the Jewish quarter, offering—at least, according to the many complaints received by the government—woefully inadequate compensation. The pretext was always public health or urban planning, referencing images going back to the eighteenth century of the Jewish Town as unclean and disorderly. Some members of the Lublin Jewish community even petitioned Tsar Nicholas I directly to receive adequate compensation, though without result. The magistracy seems to have displayed none of this zeal when the time came to clean the streets in the "Christian city."[53]

When local citizens took an interest in hygienic and infrastructural improvement, the state undermined their suggestions and found excuses to withhold support. In October 1830 the citizen council of Lublin province wrote to the KRSW, complaining that many of Lublin's streets remained unpaved, while others were covered in filth and trash. The council observed that the new city consumption tax established by the viceroy, which netted twenty thousand zlotys annually, had been earmarked for good order and cleanliness. The KRSW responded in November 1830, regretfully admitting that Lublin's coffers were exhausted. The KRSW also rebuffed the citizens' suggestion for raising money by requiring government offices to pay for the buildings in Lublin, which they occupied, claiming once again that no money was available.[54] And Lublin was the provincial capital, which received the lion's share of the region's revenue. Lubowiecki, the chairman of the provincial commission from 1822 to 1831, boasted in his memoirs that more was built in Lublin during his nine-year tenure than anywhere else in the Kingdom. Unfortunately, the provincial commissioners' plans for construction—like those of the Department of Police—reflected a preference for grandiose state buildings over public use structures or even hygienic infrastructure, a fact about which parliamentary deputies regularly complained before the abrogation of constitutional rule.[55]

Smaller cities waited years for provincial officials to solve the most routine matters of good order. For example, in April 1833 the Lublin provincial commission notified the KRSW, that "certain stalls and butcher stands" in the city of Chełm, "have decayed from old-age . . . for which reason, the slaughtering and selling of meat takes place in private homes."[56] Contraband meat both reduced the government's consumption revenue and spread disease. Reporting on the matter, the magistracy elaborated that the stalls stood practically vacant, so covered in filth that one only approached them with difficulty. Throughout 1834 the provincial commission sent several reports to the KRSW on the issue, requesting repeatedly that approval for construction of the new stalls be "expedited." Finally, the city received approval, and in 1835 the KRSW instructed the state architect for the circuit to design plans, at which time it became apparent that the city lacked the estimated 22,393 zlotys apparently required for construction and would need to float a loan from the Polish Bank. Such a loan would naturally require a separate approval process, for which reason the old stalls remained in place for several years.[57] Even in Lublin, communications between local officials and the central government indicate enormous financial obstacles and delays, evidenced by numerous requests to expedite approval processes. Construction took place, of course, as attested by improvement reports submitted by provincial commissions to the KRSW on a regular basis, but the provincial capitals and projects with state backing benefited disproportionately. Lubowiecki complained in his memoirs that Zajączek's government lavished all the state's resources on Warsaw, "as though this one city were the entire country," but the residents of Lublin province could have made a similar complaint about their provincial commission chairman.[58]

Since financial limitations and the state's pet projects limited resources for sanitary infrastructure, government officials could only employ vigilance and discipline as methods for instituting cleanliness and order, while periodically promulgating the same good order rules with ever-increasing fines. The results of these efforts were underwhelming, particularly since the state immediately rejected any local proposal to institute good police. In 1837 the Lublin governor's office still confronted the problem of waste, ice, and filth on the streets of the provincial capital. When the governor's office proposed securing horse-drawn carts for removing refuse from the city, the KRSW rejected the proposal, citing the costs of feeding the horses and maintaining the equipment. Instead, the KRSW proposed subcontracting with "entrepreneurs" to clean the city. The governor's office reported in 1839 that this method "had brought no benefit" and exhausted the funds earmarked for cleaning the city.[59] Eventually, the governor's office obtained the horses desired, as well as the means to pave roads, construct sewer canals, and even build an open-air park, but autonomous self-governing municipal authorities had invested in similar infrastructure as early as the Renaissance. There is no indication that, as Raeff once argued, the continual repetition of these regulations played a role in improving the habits of the town citizens. Instead, eighty years of efforts on the part of multiple governments dating back to the 1780s align more closely with Eugene Avrutin's findings about the tsarist government's failures to compel Jews to adopt "modern" dress and customs.[60]

Similarly, efforts to wean burghers from alcohol production largely failed because of the state's inability to function without alcohol revenue. The explosion of officialdom—in a time of war and economic disruption—necessitated a ravenous all-out search for revenue streams, and this fact forced a compromise with "feudalism and misrule." Napoleonic officials authorized city magistrates to mine archives for royal privileges, allowing cities to draw any historic revenue for which a title existed. As in the Commonwealth, cities raised funds by collecting rents from residents, leasing out peasant villages, renting city-owned commercial space, and levying tolls on bridges, mills, and markets. In effect, the cities formed a system of internal tolls, set at historic rates and varying enormously one from another, just as in the Commonwealth. It was alcohol production that continued to prop up the finances of municipalities, and until 1823 cities collected revenue from alcohol in accordance with the 1776 propinacja law. Large cities taxed alcohol producers as sellers, while small towns (including some private towns in the Zamoyski entail) retained a city-controlled monopoly; in both cases such revenue accounted for over 50 percent of the municipality's total revenue.

In fact, the fiscal importance of alcohol exceeded the excise tax, as the municipalities collected a separate tax on imported wine, as well as a concession fee on alcohol producers. Alcohol-related revenue covered almost 66 percent of Lublin's budget in 1819, while Kazimierz Dolny, Chełm, and Zamość depended on alcohol for over 70 percent of their funding (see table 7). For the Kingdom as a whole, alcohol supplied almost 50 percent of municipal budgets; only in Kalisz province, one of the most industrialized, did a separate tax on industrial and entrepreneurial profits (*kanon od zarobków*) rival alcohol as a source of revenue. The state also took a share of the alcohol revenue, via the national consumption tax, as well as a separate concession fee for Jewish distillers. The obvious dependence of both state and municipal finances on this revenue undermined any plans, such as they were, to force citizens into more productive enterprises. When the KRSW proposed an interdiction on Jewish alcohol production in 1821, the magistracy of Kazimierz Dolny reported that the city's coffers would collapse without revenue from Jewish distillers, whose absence would also mean depopulation of the city's most prominent real estate addresses.[61]

Instead, the Kingdom's government opted to rationalize and monopolize alcohol revenue for the benefit of the state, hoping, as in the eighteenth century, that city monopolies would spur burghers to alternative industries. In October 1823 the Kingdom's minister of Finance, Franciszek Drucki-Lubecki, determined for the sake of both state and local finances to force all cities to accept an alcohol monopoly on the Russian model. One monopoly leaseholder per city would lease the right to sell alcoholic products, and producers could sell only to the monopolists at the latter's prices. Cities continued to levy excise taxes on this exchange. The government also raised the concession-fee for Jewish producers, while the law excluded Jews from the right to lease the state's alcohol monopoly or the city's excise tariff.[62] Producers resisted, protested, and even brought their grievances to Grand Duke Constantine, but Alexander backed Lubecki's reform, and the state disposed of soldiers, whom the Finance minister readily used to close down taverns, impound contraband, and enforce the monopoly. For the government, the reform proved a financial success: the consumption tax increased from 1.6 million zlotys to 3.0 million in the course of a year. For municipal finances (not to speak of producers), the reform proved less significant. The amount projected from Lublin's excise tax, wine tax, and concession fees in 1828, for example, roughly paralleled the sum produced in 1818, approximately 56 percent of the total revenue.[63] The profit structure of alcohol production changed, but consumption remained the same until 1844 restrictions combined with the potato blight reduced production levels. Even afterward, monopolists still relied upon local producers, for whom distilling vodka remained more viable than repairing shoes or selling cloth. For smaller cities alcohol production remained the dominant industry and the principal source of the municipality's revenue throughout the century.[64] The state had to accept abundant alcohol production as the price of administering the country and abandon (at least, in practice) some of the Enlightenment preoccupations with directing burghers to alternative industries.[65]

Moreover, despite the commercial and residential restrictions on Jewish residents, as well as the state's overtly anti-Jewish policies, Jewish leases and merchants shored up municipal finances. One of Lublin's principal non-alcohol funding sources, a lease of six stores in the municipal gates, was administered by Jewish families throughout the first third of the nineteenth century. In 1827 Judah Goldreich, who had unsuccessfully bid to lease the six stores, complained to the KRSW that the number of exempted Jews living in the Catholic city, leasing property and running stores, had led to the impoverishment of the Jewish Town. The KRSW rebuffed his request to end residential exclusion, though it did dispatch a separate letter to the provincial commission insisting that no further exemptions be allowed.[66] Such exemptions underwrote the solvency of the municipalities. In December 1831, writing to the KRSW, the Lublin provincial commission requested a dispensation from the law excluding Jews from holding the lease for alcohol excise taxes. As the commission explained, the city of Lublin had been economically ravaged by the November Insurrection, and no Christian had the capital to lease the alcohol tax upon which the city relied. Three members of the

Jewish community had come forward, though, potentially saving the city from default. The KRSW refused the request, even after a second auction failed. Finally, the tax farmer for the state's consumption tax "saved" the situation by offering an equal amount to the Jewish bidders. Had the bidder not come forward, there is little doubt that the KRSW would have been compelled to make yet another exception, as the government repeatedly did throughout the nineteenth century.[67]

In 1836 the KRSW circulated a memorandum, expressing hope that, with the extinguishing of the November Insurrection, the time was finally ripe to implement the numerous good order regulations in the cities. Observing that many regulations had lapsed during the "recent disorders," the KRSW circular reminded officials that good order depended on the hard work, diligence, and ability of all state officials, and that the happiness and prosperity of the urban residents rested upon their actions. Among the specific regulations reiterated, the KRSW returned to the issue of urban cleanliness, as well as the need to enforce residential restrictions on Jews.[68] Despite such pronouncements, in reality the ambitions of central state had declined even before 1830. After 1832 the Paskevich government increasingly emphasized the modern notion of policing over "good police," a fact revealed by comparing municipal regulations issued to the magistracy of Lublin in 1819 and 1836. In 1836, after an investigation had uncovered "improprieties" in the city administration, the KRSW issued new supplementary regulations to improve the clarity and precision of the old rules. In fact, the prior set of regulations had assigned exhaustively detailed functions to each municipal officer, placing special emphasis on police in its eighteenth-century meaning. Detailed portfolios for each councilor concerned matters such as statistics collection, urban planning, fire prevention, property maintenance, and economic stewardship. In the 1836 iteration, police in the sense of crime prevention and repression received a much more prominent role, and the goals of cleanliness, information gathering, and economic improvement had largely receded or moved to other echelons of government. Whereas the first schema presumed a more active and multifaceted government (one of the promises of centralization), the second modification, in 1836, simply viewed local government as an element of the state's security and taxation policies.[69] Enlightened centralism had, in the face of resistance and internal contradiction, devolved into centralized policing, which would remain the goal throughout the Nicholaevan era.

PROTECTION FROM THE POWERFUL?

The fiscal and bureaucratic limitations to enlightened reforms in state cities, in many cases self-imposed, paled in comparison to the difficulties faced when the centralized state attempted to tackle the issue of private towns. Since Napoleonic legislation had made private property sacrosanct, the state could not abolish these towns outright, but neither could the central government tolerate political entities outside of the state's control. The provisional Governing Commission, established in 1806, initially allowed private town owners to serve as mayors, but the state ultimately decided that town officials must be independent of owners and subordinate to Warsaw. The ability of a given community to support a salaried mayor proved the decisive point in determining whether a settlement would appear on the register of towns or lose its urban status. In the latter case, the commune mayor (*wójt gminny*), often the town's owner, could serve as a "temporary" government. Napoleonic officials considered every chartered town a link in the administrative chain necessitating a state presence, meaning that state officials proposed to prop up numerous towns that had degenerated into villages in all but name.[70] Lublin Prefect Jabłonowski, in his 1812 report to the Ministry of the Interior, strongly articulated a preference for protecting the residences of the towns from the rapacity of their owners by providing an independent state administration. Only in the most extreme cases, when town residents were simply too poor to afford an administration, would he consent to government by the owner. In response, Minister of the Interior Jan Łuszczewski concurred that burghers must be subject only to the laws of the state and enjoy a mayor "from their ranks" independent of the owner.[71]

Unfortunately, this drive for independence and legal equality, which state officials equated with the establishment of a salaried professional magistracy, collided with the French model of absolute property rights. The Code Napoléon abolished the mixed-possession arrangements associated with feudalism, including the distinction in private towns between the owner's *dominus directus* of the entire town and the residents' *dominus utile* of their individual possessions, in favor of absolute property rights. The possessions of private town residents now rested on shaky foundations and tradition, and evidence suggests that the courts favored the owner in property disputes (treating the burghers as mere tenants).[72] More significantly, the state's conception of property embraced all revenue-collection rights, labor obligations, and monopolies, to which a legal precedent from the Commonwealth existed. No new fees or dues could be added, but the law grandfathered in any obligation with historical foundation. In order to maintain an independent magistracy, the private towns would have to meet their obligations to the owner as well as contribute funds toward a magistracy. A municipal government also required administrative buildings, which could only be located on the territory of the town, thus requiring the state to lease property from the owner.[73]

Under the Commonwealth, private towns had enjoyed city governments backed by Magdeburg Law, but magistracies required few funds to operate, as most positions remained voluntary. The broad freedoms enjoyed by nobles in determining the structure of their towns incentivized owners to offer relatively attractive conditions for residents. Owners invested in their towns, particularly the showpiece capitals such as Zamość, for reasons of prestige. The Napoleonic state's push to establish independent administrations deprived owners of all nonfinancial benefits arising from the possession of towns, including the right to offer broad self-government and paternalistic protections. Divorced from these privileges, owners became rent collectors, viewing city governments on their territory with a mixture of hostility and suspicion, particularly as those magistracies consumed funds that would otherwise accrue to the owner. Many town residents, for their part, overestimated the state's conception of protection, believing that an independent administration would free them from dues or transfer the owners' revenues to the community. Prefects, town inspectors, and provincial authorities found themselves balancing between these poles, unable to please the former or protect the latter.

The Ministry of the Interior in the Duchy established the precedent that private town magistracies, like owners, could collect all revenues, for which a legal precedent (e.g., a privilege from a past owner) existed.

Some private towns enjoyed privileges to collect tolls or indirect taxes for communal benefit, and some cities, notably several settlements in the Zamoyski entail, even enjoyed the right to revenue from alcohol taxes, but the majority of smaller towns could claim no independent revenue stream whatsoever. In this case, the state required residents of private towns to conduct an annual levy (*składka*) in order to fund the minimal requirements of an administration, a mayor with a minimum salary set in 1818 at the paltry sum of six hundred zlotys per annum.[74] Towns that could not contribute the minimum requirements devised by the center found themselves converted into so-called free settlements under the administration of the commune wójt.

Landlords, who often owned all the villages and settlements in a given commune (an administrative division inherited from France), typically either served as wójt or appointed one, meaning that conversion to a settlement resulted in a return to administration by the owner. According to Mazurkiewicz, towns feared losing their urban status as such a conversion would further undermine property rights, end markets, and effectively convert the burghers into serfs. In addition, the citizens of Firlej complained of the inconvenience of relying on the wójt's jurisdiction, when that official was often based in another part of the commune.[75] The KRSW repeatedly expressed a preference for towns to retain independent administrations, if only for the sake of ensuring state control over the countryside. Official reports complained that state officials rarely ventured into rural communes when a single owner controlled all the property. Nonetheless, the government found itself occasionally rejecting, at least initially, petitions of downgraded towns for reconversion into cities. In 1815 the KRSW rebuffed such a request from the residents of Karol Sanguszko's Lubartów, one of the largest private towns in the Lublin region. In part the KRSW judged the amount offered by the citizens (383 zlotys) as insufficient, and in part the government frowned upon the residents' request that the provincial authorities present the eventual mayoral candidate for confirmation by the citizens, a violation of the vaunted hierarchical principle.[76]

In effect, the state's demands of private town residents placed cities in direct conflict with the owners. Particularly in poor, largely agricultural settlements, towns often had to choose between paying their rents to the owner and funding a municipal administration. The Duchy and the

Congress Kingdom tried to pressure owners into contributing funds to support the municipal administration, but most owners declared their preference that the towns in question be converted into villages. Karol Sanguszko, owner of the tiny town of Firlej, actively lobbied the state to convert his "town" into a village settlement, arguing in 1821: "The owner has the same income from Firlej as from a village, collecting only rents and propinacja, and the title of town would be an inconvenience both for the owner, as well as for the residents—due to the associated expenses. The current levy on the residents for maintaining a municipal administration has become too burdensome, and due to it many of them have not paid their rents to the owner. Therefore, the owner would happily see this little town converted into a village settlement."[77] For town owners, conversion into a settlement meant greater leverage over the officials. Stanisław Kossowski, owner of Bełżyce, informed Brandys outright that he preferred to pay six hundred zlotys to the wójt's deputy, whom he chose, than spend money on an official over whom he would have no control. The owner of Bychawa, Karol di Campio Scipio, similarly informed Brandys that he would not agree to pay for a mayor without the right to choose him. The Lublin prefect had already acknowledged in 1815 that most owners preferred having their small towns classified as villages for the simple reason that their influence over the settlements remained greater.[78]

In spite of the costs and lack of local control, private town residents almost universally preferred the maintenance of their urban status, and the state generally supported town residents over the protests of the owners. Firlej, a town of only 625 people, told Brandys in 1818 of its willingness to pay for a mayor, as long as that official would at least reside in the town. The record books for Firlej show that the town continued to conduct levies and pay the mayor's salary for several decades after Sanguszko's declaration of opposition. Bychawa, which fought numerous legal battles with its owner in the Congress Kingdom period, similarly declared its desire for a municipal administration, despite the high dues demanded by the owner. On his visit to Bychawa, Brandys also determined that Scipio's town could maintain its own administration and unilaterally composed a 2,577 zloty annual budget in 1820 based on projected market fees and bridge tolls.[79] The government was so determined to erect and maintain independent towns wherever possible that the state even chose to form municipal administrations in places where the residents had not requested it. The citizens of Bełżyce specifically appealed to Brandys in 1818 that they remain under the administration of the wójt for at least two more years, citing their lack of funds. Nonetheless, the record books show that the town collected 1,030 zlotys in 1819 to fund the administration, partially underwritten by the profits of the owner, Kossowski, in an agreement devised by Brandys.[80]

The Congress Kingdom's support for private town citizens rested in part on purely economic considerations deriving from the alcohol consumption tax. While most private towns remained subject to the owner's propinacja monopoly, the government still collected the alcohol consumption tax in these settlements, and urban settlements paid higher rates than rural ones. In reviewing the town of Rejowiec's 1829 request to remain under the administration of the owner, the KRSW flatly stated that the government would determine some means to pay for an administration so as not to lose the consumption income.[81] If the state's dependence on urban alcohol revenue argued for the maintenance of as many "cities" as possible, the owner's own dependence on alcohol revenue offered a vulnerability, which state agents exploited to pressure nobles into contributing funds for the maintenance of independent magistracies. Particularly, after the crushing of the November Insurrection, the ability of the state to hold propinacja revenue over the owners' heads ensured that most owners coughed up funds to support their cities.

In Bychawa, for example, city budgets from the 1830s and 1840s record that the new owner, Laniewski, provided six hundred zlotys per annum to compensate the mayor, to which sum the Christian and Jewish residents added two hundred zlotys. In 1838 Laniewski informed the government that he would no longer contribute money in view of the newly established canon tax on producers and artisans, authorized by Viceroy Paskevich in 1837. Convening a meeting on the subject, the Lublin governor's office rejected the owner's position, informing Laniewski that the governor's office had the exclusive right to set city budgets. Subsequent budgets showed Laniewski projected to contribute six hundred zlotys per annum toward the municipal administration—until 1847, after which time the city began to calculate its revenue in rubles.[82] Brzeziński, the owner of Bełżyce in the 1830s and 1840s, similarly paid eight hundred zlotys per annum toward the city government, while the towns of the Zamoyski entail benefited from either the owner's contribution or their own propinacja rights. Of the towns surveyed, only tiny Firlej maintained a municipal administration without support from the owner.[83]

On the other hand, attempts by owners to use their contributions as leverage on the state in order the maintain influence in their cities proved completely ineffective, as evidenced by the story of Stanisław Zamoyski's tussle with the government over his town of Kraśnik. Between 1811 and 1816, the Zamoyski entail's administration contributed 500 zlotys per annum to Kraśnik's coffers, a sum that covered the mayor's salary and supplemented the 1,259 zlotys paid by the town residents. In 1816, however, an entail official conveyed a note to the provincial commission to the effect that Stanisław Zamoyski would no longer provide the funds. The pretext, apparently, was the commission's decision to remove the town's mayor, Zienkowski, without consulting the owner. Domański, as head of the provincial commission, threatened to increase the resident's annual contribution (which would impact Zamoyski's revenue) and reduce the mayor's salary.[84] Following through, the 1819 budget drawn by Brandys projected the citizens' contributing 1,088 zlotys toward the city government, while the town inspector compensated for the remaining shortfall by establishing bridge, market, and fair tolls in the city. No sooner had the city magistracy leased these new tariffs than the entail administration contacted the provincial commission, protesting that the new tolls violated the owner's property rights. Further, "these tolls are currently not employed by the town, bring no benefit, harm trade, and raise the price of products, and thus are harmful to both the residents and the owner."[85] Following an exhaustive archival search by the newly appointed mayor, the government concluded in 1820 that the proposed tariffs indeed violated extant privileges as well as recent practice, and the KRSW annulled all the new tolls. Mollified, Zamoyski agreed to contribute 600 zlotys to support the mayor's salary for the next budgetary year.[86]

In April 1821 Zamoyski once again declared his unwillingness to pay the salaries of the mayors, not just for Kraśnik, but now for every town in his entail. In a detailed letter, Zamoyski explained that he had offered to supplement the budgets of his towns out of consideration for the poverty of the residents, in order to prevent them from having to pay costly taxes themselves. Further, he added, his offer was contingent upon the government keeping the revenue and expenses of the towns moderate and in proportion to the needs of the residents. Finally, Zamoyski had requested that the provincial commission confer on the composition of the towns' budgets with the administration of the entail, as the organization "having the closest and most complete knowledge about the status and wealth of the residents." Unfortunately, as Zamoyski recounted: "Despite such reasonable and, for the towns, beneficial requests, the town budgets were unilaterally composed according to the town inspector's opinion alone. In addition, the inspector established direct levies on the residents—in direct contradiction to the declaration of the owner. Therefore, the undersigned has no other choice but to refuse to make the contribution promised, as it is bringing no relief to the town residents."[87] Concluding, Zamoyski offered to support the municipal administration of any of his towns, so long as the budgets were made in collaboration with the entail administration, reserving the right to forgo payment if the town in question could manage without the money. Finally, Zamoyski informed the KRSW of his opinion that market and fair tolls could not be imposed without the appropriate privileges, and that Kraśnik specifically now had sufficient funds to do without either his contribution or a mandatory collection from the residents. In a response in May 1821, the KRSW rebuffed Zamoyski's points and explained that levies from residents of private towns could be decreased only insomuch as the owner would contribute. If Zamoyski refused to make a contribution, the KRSW explained, the government might have to convert his poorer towns into free settlements, an implicit threat to his urban revenue.[88]

State officials preferred to "emancipate" private towns completely from dependence on the owner's contributions, though. For this reason, officials such as Brandys encouraged municipalities to initiate legal proceedings against their owners, while assisting magistracy officials in the search for archaic privileges, which might assign funding rights currently benefiting the owner to the community. According to a list prepared by the KRSW in 1829, virtually every private town in Lublin province was engaged in some form of litigation against its owner, including the Zamoyski towns of Kraśnik and Turobin. Most court proceedings naturally resolved around the most lucrative prize, propinacja, which some owners had, at least in some of the residents' memory, shared with the citizenry.[89] As documentation was often missing or ambiguous, the court cases could easily devolve into wild goose chases. The magistracy of Kraśnik, one of the few Zamoyski cities without propinacja rights, requested support in gaining this revenue for the municipality in 1820, leading to a full review by the provincial commission and another archival search on the part of city authorities. Unfortunately, the process was delayed for several years, due to Zamoyski's unsurprising refusal to open the entail's own archive to state officials. The Lublin provincial commission reported in August 1822 and January 1823 that the administration continued to withhold the necessary documentation, having ignored repeated requests. The entail responded only in September 1824 with a note that no privileges existed to support Kraśnik's claim, prompting a renewed search in the city archives, which again turned up nothing. The 1829 summation simply stated that no privileges could yet be uncovered to support the claim. At least the process did not degrade the material position of the residents. In the case of a lawsuit initiated by Bychawa, the owner managed to win the right to collect even more rents from the residents.[90]

Lawsuits decreased in urgency after the November Insurrection, following which the Paskevich government more directly tied propinacja rights to owner contributions, as the eventual city "emancipation" ukaz of 1866 made evident. In effect, the contribution became a tax on the owner unmoored to any other commitment. Moreover, the state's imposition of canon revenue in private towns, as well as other fees, generated other funds for town magistracies.[91] Nonetheless, the limbo of dual subjugation to the owner and the state remained at least until the private town emancipation, a component of the larger peasant emancipation decreed in 1864. The state could block the owner from taking any independent action in the towns, but, as the following two examples illustrate, the increasingly dysfunctional, languid bureaucratic structure of the post-Enlightenment state could not protect private town residents in any meaningful way. In September 1841 the secretary of state in the Administrative Council (then the highest organ in the government) sent a note to the KRSW concerning the petition of Moshe Lewin to Viceroy Paskevich. Writing in the name of the Jews of Bełżyce, Lewin requested protection against the excessive and illegal demands of the town owner, Brzeziński. The complaint charged the owner with instituting a forced mill monopoly, charging two zlotys per barrel for milling Passover matzo flour (*na mąką świąteczną*), and levying unjust taxes on the community. A month later, the secretary forwarded a new complaint, this time against the Lublin governor's office, for allegedly delaying the investigation into Brzeziński's abuses. The governor's office answered the same month, asserting that the district captain (*naczelnik powiatu*) had already conducted an investigation, but his report contained "incomplete information" and "uncertainties," so a new one had to be undertaken. The governor's office assured the KRSW that the investigation would be completed "in the soonest period possible."[92]

The investigation, which took place between December 1843 and February 1844 included extensive interviews with the residents of the town, most of whom gave contradictory or incomplete answers about the chronology and size of the tolls. The owner, on the other hand, mustered documentation to prove his right to various fees and rents collected. Most recently, a court case between the residents and the owner had resulted in an 1828 verdict confirming the latter's rights. The owner further discredited Lewin by observing that he had been caught trying to smuggle flour into the city without paying the associated tariff. On a further complaint about unjust market fees on the sale of candles, the owner replied that the Jewish bailiff had traditionally leased this. The owner even claimed to have voluntarily renounced this revenue, "out of consideration for the poor" in exchange for a payment by the same bailiff to fund a hospital. Further, the owner argued that the state's appropriation of tobacco and salt monopolies, as well as other taxes, had reduced his revenue so that he barely profited from these fees. Finally, if taxes had been lighter in the past, that was in part because of the actions of the previous steward who had no legal right to adjust the underlying constitution of the city.[93]

The governor's office concluded that, while the charges and fees were indeed burdensome to the residents, the governor's office itself, as an administrative body, could only rule on the established practice (*używalność*) of the fees, which the owner had conclusively proved. Hence, the office ruled that Lewin's complaints were unfounded. Further, Lewin had "inappropriately taken on the title of city spokesman, to which he had no authority, and moreover, he dared to make unfounded complaints against the government in his letter to the viceroy." Although the tone of the report implied retribution against Lewin, he does not seem to have been punished by the state. In fact, Lewin reiterated and expounded upon his complaints in a new letter to the KRSW, dated September 1844, though this missive appears to have been unanswered. The failure on the part of Lewin to obtain a satisfactory settlement should not be taken as a reflection of the nobility's power and influence. The governor's office brusquely rebuffed Brzeziński's own efforts to secure tax relief for his alcohol contractors, yet the owner kept making his annual contribution to the town's coffers.[94]

At least Lewin's complaints eventually provoked a full inquiry, if unfavorable. An 1844 petition forwarded by the residents of Szczebrzeszyn, a town in the Zamoyski entail, led to an investigation that dragged on until the abolition of private town ownership in 1866. As before, the issue was the owner's right to levy taxes and fees on certain practices, in this case the felling of lumber from nearby forests. A personnel shuffle at the district level squashed the results of the initial inquiry, and in February 1845 the Lublin governor's office reported that the newly appointed district supervisor would investigate. No results of this investigation were forthcoming, and the secretary of state at the Administrative Council reported in December 1849 that the residents continued to complain of their lack of access to the forest and insufficient means to buy firewood. In January 1850 the KRSW demanded an investigation by the governor's office, noting the failure of three separate communications since 1843 to raise the officials to action. Meanwhile, one of the town residents wrote a separate letter to the viceroy, asking for assistance since none of the previous investigations had materialized.[95]

Finally, in February 1851 representatives of the KRSW, the procurator general, the Lublin governor's office, and the city held a meeting with Stanisław Zamoyski. In response to the residents' complaints about the violation of their felling rights, which had been in effect "since time immemorial," Zamoyski countered that the city owed him enormous arrears dating back to 1821 in unpaid rents, fees, and in-kind gifts amounting to 89,423 zlotys (13,413 rubles), suggesting that felling rights would be returned upon remittance of at least some of the monies owed. The matter seemed to remain unsettled, as the procurator general reported in August 1867 about the ongoing complaints of the residents of Szczebrzeszyn for not only wood-cutting rights but also propinacja and land-use rights. Zamoyski, for his part, continued to insist on payment of arrears as a starting point for negation. The KRSW responded in September 1867, charging the Lublin governor's office with investigating and pointing out the seemingly obvious fact that Tsar Alexander II's recent abolition of feudal dues and seigneurial rights in private cities had likely changed the dynamics of the case.[96]

Polish reformers welcomed the Duchy of Warsaw with the expectations that a centralized hierarchical government would enforce equality, revitalize the cities, and unleash entrepreneurial activity. Among these goals only centralization stands out as an obvious success story. The vertical power structure that was implemented by Napoleon and refined under Alexander I proved remarkably effective at rebuffing civic activism and quashing independent initiative, but the system proved much less capable when it came to the positive goals of social, economic, and sanitary improvement. Professionally trained career officials disposed only of punitive powers to engineer social and economic transformations, since no incentives existed for residents of cities to voluntarily change their behaviors or seek to improve their surroundings. The abolition of local control and the lack of funds to compensate salaried replacement also led to inefficiencies and bureaucratic improprieties, causing state officials to view appointed administrators much as the Permanent Council had imagined eighteenth-century urban elites: lazy, greedy, and negligent. Trapped by the logic of centralization, the government could only combat official malfeasance with further layers of bureaucracy and additional punitive measures. Outlays on additional supervisory officials crowded out investment in provincial towns, creating a vicious cycle in which alcohol production remained the most reliable occupation for townspeople as well as the only source of municipal revenue. The state's anti-Jewish legislation, though possibly popular with Christian townspeople, further undermined the goals of economic improvement. Municipalities survived as they did because of exemptions, petty violations, and concessions.

The government's policies in private towns serve as the most illustrative example of the contradictions resulting from policies rooted in abstract notions of urbanity and legality. Under the Commonwealth, owners faced market and monetary pressures to offer attractive deals to their town citizens, and the ability to offer privileges (as well as the prestige from building a splendid residential town) served as an inducement for owners to invest in their town and protect their citizens. Most of these nobles were also owners of serfs, and their treatment of towns owed nothing to any special love of mankind. Moreover, owners rarely endowed their towns with significant funding sources, as the universal expectation was pro bono municipal government. The Napoleonic state's demand that private towns possess salaried independent administration flowed from the centralist presumption that all urban centers must serve as links in the state hierarchy, which enabled control over the provinces. Once combined with a declaration in favor of the owner's property rights, including the historic fees and tariffs, this policy necessarily divided the interests of the owner from those of the town residents. In battles between town citizens and owners over revenue rights and obligations, incited by enlightened officials, the owners held most of the cards. Trapped by the contradictory impulses of the Napoleonic heritage, officials could only provide private cities with a municipal government, which increased the owner's hostility without offering any protections against his or her fiscal demands. After a while, it seems, most government officials abandoned any real hope of trying to improve the private towns, and the state lacked the means or incentive to purchase these properties, relegating most small private towns to an awkward limbo between state control and feudal overlordship.

6

The Persistence of the Old Commonwealth

CITIES, NOBLES, AND THE STATE IN THE WESTERN PROVINCES OF THE RUSSIAN EMPIRE

IN MAY 1810 PRINCE Dominik Radziwiłł's commissar for the city of Olyka wrote to the police chief of Dubno district in Volhynia *guberniia* to request assistance in handling the disobedient and disorderly residents of this private town. The commissar alleged that the city citizens enjoyed such generous privileges from the prince's ancestors that, "they pay nothing to the prince's treasury for the use of lands, meadows, urban plots, gardens, grazing fields, and forest rights, nor do they render any service beyond paying the monarch's taxes." Further, "when these provinces were incorporated under the rule of the Majestic Russian Empire, it pleased the guberniia office, with permission from the central government, to confirm the burghers' previous privileges and internal police powers. At the same time, the state did not diminish the owner's administrative rights on his urban property." Unfortunately, the letter continued, the citizens had neglected the responsibilities that justify their privileges, including the owner's explicit instructions to take fire-prevention measures. As a result, a recent fire had not only damaged the citizens' goods but also consumed the owner's capital stock. Further, "canals, bridges, stone gates, and even toll barriers have been abandoned and stand in ruins, while burghers make no effort to repair them; the Christians blame the Jews, and the Jews the Christians for the negligence." The commissar worried that the owner's authority was weakening, particularly since the local court protected the burghers, and he requested that the police chief visit the city for himself and compel the residents to obey their traditional superiors as required by imperial law.[1]

The citizens of Olyka, for their part, viewed the taxes and tributes recently collected by the Radziwiłł family as a violation of their ancient privileges. A meeting of the Christian magistracy and the Jewish kahal a few years prior had delegated a plenipotentiary to petition Governor-General A. G. Rozenberg with complaints that Radziwiłł's commissar in the city collected unjust dues and ordered those who could not pay beaten with clubs and lashed with whips.[2] As these dueling complaints attest, the Russian Empire's centralism proved remarkably hesitant, if not absent, when the state encountered such vestiges of the former Polish-Lithuanian Commonwealth as private towns. While Emperor Alexander I's Congress Kingdom of Poland raced energetically to construct a bureaucratic state and marshal resources in pursuit of enlightened reform, the Russian Empire appeared satisfied with limited goals of territorial control, initially tolerating pluralistic settlements and delegating broad powers to private town owners. S. A. Bershadskii once remarked that the early years of the nineteenth century were a kind of golden age for the great Polish landowners, who retained most of their prerogatives but now enjoyed an "energetic" and powerful state to enforce their writ.[3] As Daniel Beauvois has shown, this solicitous attitude toward the Polish nobility resulted from the state's need for partners in territorial control, a honeymoon period prolonged by the inconsistent and contradictory decisions of Russian civil servants, who struggled to apply the enlightened, Russocentric assumptions encoded into Catherine the Great's provincial and urban reforms on the multiethnic and corporate lands of Ukraine and Belarus.[4]

The regime's complications in absorbing the former Commonwealth's towns derived in part from one of the many contradictions inherent in the Russian Empire's approach to local government and social organization. As Alison Smith has recently explored, the Russian state's policy with regard to the *soslovie* system of estate divisions unsuccessfully balanced the desire to unleash economic mobility with the demand for stable tax revenue.[5] All experiments in devolving local power from Catherine the Great's reorganizations through the Great Reforms failed to overcome a similar dilemma. As a result of Russia's immense territorial scope and disproportionately meager bureaucracy, the state required cheap local government, but the empire's bureaucratic culture nurtured an impulse for hierarchical control mixed with suspicion toward initiative. Cities in the Russian empire found themselves in the crosshairs of these conflicting currents, and yet another duality encumbered official policy toward the western provinces. On the one hand, government rhetoric referred to the newly acquitted regions of Belarus and Ukraine as historic components of the core patrimony, which had been "reunited with Russia" after a long interlude; such provinces demanded speedy integration with the heartland. On the other hand, the reality on the ground, which included private towns, Magdeburg-Law traditions, and large Jewish populations, seemed to require a colonial policy, including concessions to local elites and modifications of "Russian" institutions.[6]

Catherine's legislation favored the latter approach, allowing regional diversity so long as the state's minimal requirements were satisfied, and her successors largely adhered to this policy, despite periodic pronouncements to the contrary. Such concessions rankled many of the empire's civil servants, who viewed exemptions from the standard administrative blueprint with suspicion and lobbied superiors in St. Petersburg for more centralized control over entities and organizations deemed inconvenient to uniform administration. The "enlightened bureaucrats" of the western provinces shared none of the reformist convictions of their counterparts in the Congress Kingdom, who actively combated the presumed exploitation of private town owners and dreamed of harnessing the state so as to unleash economic growth in the rural cities. Rather, governors and police inspectors, largely imported from the central provinces, devoted numerous pages in their reports to the pernicious consequences of particularism for administrative organization and territorial integration.[7] Nicholas I showed considerably more sympathy to this perspective than his predecessors, but, with the exception of minor modifications, no alternative policy appeared viable until the Great Reforms altered the regime's political calculus, leaving a persistent reminder of the Commonwealth's plurality and particularism in the lands "reunited with Russia."

In the face of the center's indifference, officials in the Nicholaevan era increasingly conceived of urban, socioeconomic problems in ethnic terms, as the result of poor discipline and bad character caused by the paucity of "Russian" townspeople.[8] Many of the small towns in the western provinces consisted largely of Jewish traders and artisans. In these "shtetls," the Polish and Ukrainian speaking "burghers" often earned a living from farming. Such conditions defied the neat enlightened assumptions encoded into Catherine's provincial and urban reforms, causing no end of difficulties for administrators attempting to register individuals into soslovie categories or to apply the provisions of the Charter to the Towns, which had been designed with St. Petersburg principally in mind. Encountering perceived disorder and insubordination in the cities as the imported model malfunctioned, Russian governors pleaded for the state to send more "Russians" to settle the cities and abolish remnants of particularism. If officials did not yet equate ethno-confessional status with loyalty, as was common after 1863, the presumption that Russian institutions required Russians (who were in short supply) reinforced the "colonial" approach to ruling the region by necessitating further compromises and modifications of the institutional arrangements imported from the core patrimony.[9] Meanwhile, the continued reliance on the nobility to fill the gap between the state's territorial aspirations and institutional weaknesses allowed not only nobles but also the Christian and Jewish residents of some private towns an unintended space for civic activity and self-government throughout the pre-reform era.

The ambiguity in imperial policy originated in Catherine's Provincial Reorganization (1775) and Charter to the Towns (1785), which had aimed to project state power into the countryside by establishing a network of district towns in each guberniia as the first point of contact between the Russian government and its subjects. Each district town, as well as the guberniia capital, fell under the jurisdiction of a magistracy, elected in accordance with the Charter's stipulations. Although a significant diminution of power in comparison with the prerogatives of cities under the Commonwealth, Catherine's reforms—in opposition to the Congress Kingdom's structure—retained an element of local control.

Town citizens could elect magistracies, subject to approval by the governor, and large cities also disposed of an additional body, a city duma, that managed urban finances and economic development. Taking the largest cities of the empire as the measure, the legislation intended the duma to represent the six supposed components of each town—town citizens, merchant corporations, artisans, foreign merchants, notable citizens, and taxpayers. The city could also elect a *gorodskaia golova* (town headsman), who served as the chief executive. In such a composition, the elected magistracy and mayors served primarily as a lower-level civil and criminal court, effectively a form of self-administration similar to that practiced in Austria before 1805.[10]

Catherine's legislation had specifically connected urbanity with state administration, and many peasant villages in Russia became "towns" overnight as the state struggled to locate suitable district capitals. Since cities served primarily as political loci, private towns had no formal existence in Russia prior to the partitions. As Catherine Evtuhov observes in her study of Nizhnii Novgorod province, many landowners in Russia did indeed erect commercial villages to provide peasants with a market for grain, and many of these "villages" were often more populous and better equipped than the official district towns of the region. These "villages" differed from the private towns of Poland-Lithuania not so much in function but, rather, by virtue of the fact that the state did not recognize the villagers as burghers with rights and privileges. The western provinces boasted a much larger urban network than Russia proper (in 1850, 35 percent of the Russian Empire's city citizens lived in the Ukrainian provinces alone), and over 70 percent of the cities belonged to nobles. The regime now had to designate a category for cities, which served no administrative function in the state hierarchy. Any town within a district not serving as a district capital became a "minor city" (*zashtatnyi gorod*), regardless of the center's economic role in the region.[11]

An appointed civil governor managed all the districts in a given guberniia under the authority of the Minister of Internal Affairs (MVD) or, in some cases, a military governor-general. The 1775 provincial reform granted enormous supervisory power to the governor. Among other prerogatives, the governor could select members of each urban magistracy from a pool of candidates presented by the citizens, with no obligation to choose candidates with the most votes. The governor also had the authority to invalidate city elections, though Alexander I issued an order in 1802 that attempted to limit the removal of urban officials without specific proof of illegal action. Urban governments had to present requests for extraordinary expenses for approval by the government. The governor also controlled two institutions intimately connected with everyday life in the towns: the police and the department of social welfare (*prikaz obshchestvennogo prizreniia*), which possessed jurisdiction over schools, hospitals, workhouses, and orphanages.[12] Particularly energetic governors would conduct inspection tours to evaluate the effectiveness of local government, but the power and ability of these officials to effect change was severely curtailed by the short tenure of their posts. Rarely did governors serve longer than three-year terms in a given province.[13]

Authority over the urban and rural police constituted the most significant attribute of the governor's authority and commensurate dependence of urban communities on the state. Officials in St. Petersburg chartered official police contingents in the provincial capitals and large district towns, and these officials answered directly to the governor. The minor towns, in conjunction with the district capitals, combined resources to pay the salary of the *gorodnichii*, a police chief-cum-mayor who patrolled an entire district. Usually a demobilized military official, the gorodnichii has often served as a symbol of petty bureaucratic corruption and local tyranny, an image immortalized by Skvoznik-Dmukhanovskii in Gogol's *The Government Inspector*. The memoirs of Roch Sikorski, a burgher from Bielsk in Grodno guberniia, also present a highly unflattering portrait of the local gorodnichii, who, having no connection to or dependence on the town, allegedly contented himself with extracting bribes from urban officials in exchange for keeping silent about bureaucratic irregularities.[14] Conversely, the territory of a single district, which in the western provinces often included multiple cities, represented an enormous police commitment for a single individual, so most cities compelled volunteers to serve as night watchmen, guards, and police assistants. By fulfilling their "police obligations," in this way, a practice dating back to the Commonwealth, the magistracy could assure itself of greater autonomy and independence, particularly when the gorodnichii had moved on to another city in the district.[15]

Upon concluding the second and third partitions, Catherine's government moved swiftly to integrate the new regions as far as possible into the standard administrative model. The Commonwealth's palatinates became provinces with no correspondence to their historic borders, a process that underwent several revisions.[16] For example, Volhynia guberniia, which encompassed much of the old Volhynia and Kijów palatinates, received its final formation in 1804 with Zhitomir as the administrative capital. Most of the old Nowogródek palatinate now entered Minsk guberniia, while Kamenets-Podol'skii remained the capital of Podolia, a province that now included the old Bracław palatinate (see maps 2 and 3).[17] The difficulty came in finding suitable capitals for the various districts; private towns frequently possessed better infrastructure and more robust economies than the old royal cities. Like rulers in the other partitioning powers, as well as Napoleon, the empress had promised to respect the private property of the owners and the rights of the residents, and Russia's concessions toward the Polish nobility far exceeded the privileges offered in Galicia and Prussia. In Russia, the designation of a private town as a district capital required guberniia authorities to lease property from owners for official buildings as well as to negotiate a settlement between the owners and the residents on issues such as compensating magistracies and police forces.[18]

The empire also encountered difficulties registering the inhabitants of the new provinces into the soslovie system. Soslovie classification determined a community's tax obligations, and Catherine's reforms had established two separate urban estates—townspeople (*meshchane*) and merchants (*kuptsy*)—differentiated by wealth and occupation. Enrollment in one of the merchant corporations granted exemption from corporal punishment, military service, and the poll tax, and the empire also created difficulties (notoriously, double taxation) for townspeople seeking to climb the social ladder. While burgher rights in the Commonwealth, as in central Europe in general, required only citizenship in a given city, Catherine's reforms reinforced the historic connection in Russia between status and service to the state. The presumption, derived again from taking St. Petersburg as a frame of reference, that urban government would rest in the hands of wealthy, Christian merchants contravened the reality that, in many of the small towns in Ukraine and Belarus, burghers earned their living from agriculture, and

Jews dominated commerce and industry.[19] The land surveyor Ekster wrote of Podolia in 1800 that the merchant soslovie consisted entirely of Jews, Armenians, and Greeks, and only a few dozen people in the entire province qualified for enrollment in the top merchant corporation. All industry and manufacturing, Ekster noted, occurred in the factories of private towns owned by noblemen and populated by Jewish burghers and Christian peasants.[20]

The predominant role of Jews in the urban economy would not have posed an administrative problem had imperial authorities proved willing to enroll Jewish urbanites as fully fledged townspeople, a preference indicated by Catherine herself. In 1795 the empress had proposed that Jews be classified as townspeople; she even indicated that, where possible, Jews living in villages should be resettled in towns, a policy enforced after 1823. The empress even authorized Jewish communities to participate in city elections, a provision that, from the perspective of the Christian townspeople, violated her promise to respect the privileges and prerogatives of the cities. Christian magistracies complained that such participation violated Magdeburg Law, which theoretically forbade Jews from exercising political power over Christians. Eventually, the Senate decreed that Jewish communities could elect one-third of the magistracy, even where Jews comprised the overwhelming majority of the population. This represented a significant concession in comparison with the Congress Kingdom, which had offered neither civil nor political rights to the Jewish community, but it signaled the end of any intention to treat Jewish urbanites as full-fledged meshchane. The 1804 Statute on the Jews further separated Jews from townspeople by confirming residential restrictions (the Pale of Settlement) and commercial limitations, as well as retaining a role for the kahal as a tax-collecting and self-governing body, despite many officials' disapproval of this "state within a state."[21] Although classified as townspeople to some extent, Jews and their communities remained legally distinct, forming their own semi-segregated estate.

If Jews could occupy only one-third of the magistracy posts and no other literate commercial people could be found, who would constitute the remainder of the magistracy and the dumas envisioned by the legislation? Governors were already grumbling about the lack of "qualified officials" in the first decade of the nineteenth century. In response, the imperial authorities modified the provisions of the Charter and forestalled the introduction of dumas. Larger cities, received an economic council with an appointed, rather than elected, chairman. The governor approved such an institution for Kamenets-Podol'skii in 1812, though Gur'ev along with other officials complained that this compromise undermined the administrative uniformity of the empire. The state was to a certain extent caught in a straightjacket, since the reality of the region did not correspond to the presumed requirements of the empire's legislation.[22]

The situation was more confused in private towns, where imperial authorities often classified the Christian burghers as the owner's serfs. At the same time, the Statute on the Jews placed the relationship of the Jewish population and the lord on a contractual basis, supposedly the free agreement of the two parties. In sum, imperial legislation created a bizarre situation in which many towns in Ukraine and Belarus lacked any officially ascribed townspeople. There was little consistency in this practice, and lawsuits arose from former burghers to win title back to meshchane status, much as Cossack military officers and landless *szlachta* fought imperial authorities for recognition of their claim to nobility. Success in this endeavor often depended upon the possession of written privileges, a fortuitous occurrence in a region of mostly wooden towns that was frequently the center of armed conflict.[23]

In other matters, the empire proved more willing to compromise with local tradition. For example, Catherine had permitted cities of the former Commonwealth to retain Magdeburg Law as a civil code for adjudicating litigation. Since the principal function of an urban government remained judicial, city governments could continue to employ their traditional procedures and precedents, which the state enforced. Polish remained the official administrative language for city records in the region until 1832.[24] Cities also retained revenue from their alcohol excise tax, a potential economic boon compared to the situation in Russia proper where the state monopolized the sale of alcohol and returned only 1 percent of the proceedings to fund urban government. In Ukraine and Belarus, referred as the "non-restricted" territories because of their alcohol privileges, the state appropriated the alcohol trade in the government cities, but paid the cities "in lieu of the excise tax" a far greater return.[25]

TABLE 8. REVENUE SOURCES AS A PERCENTAGE OF THE TOTAL IN SELECTED UKRAINIAN TOWNS, 1835

	Zhitomir	Kremenets	Lutsk	Vladimir	Kamenets—Podol'skii	Mogilev
Total revenue in rubles	26,761	6,833	6,178	5,447	52,157	15,303
1. State alcohol payment	49.8%	75.3%	70.4%	92.7%	64.2%	76.0%
2. Town tavern	2.1%	1.8%	2.9%	1.8%	3.9%	2.3%
3. Leasing of town property	11.8%	4.9%	13.1%		5.9%	
4. Leasing of town land					5.2%	10.9%
5. Levy on merchants	32.3%	17.6%	9.8%	5.5%	2.7%	10.8%
6. Rent payments from town serfs					10.4%	
7. Fees and fines	4%		3.7%			
8. Loan repayment					7.7%	
Reserve capital in rubles	11,924	5,061	3,301	618	21,389	
Back-due taxes and debts owed to the town	7,338	9,058	2,289		42,498	3,648

Source: TsDIAK, f. 442, o. 66, s. 496 (Budgets for state cities, 1835), 13–69.

Alcohol provided over 50 percent of every city's revenue, reaching up to 90 percent in some cases (see table 8), much as in the Congress Kingdom. Such funding still failed to generate adequate revenue for material improvement and sanitation. In 1804 Podolia Governor Vladimir Chevkin admitted that few towns had the resources to consider such projects as construction and hospital maintenance. In fact, the state implicitly acknowledged this problem, since the prefabricated rubrics provided to territorial officials for completing reports did not include categories for items such as sanitation and improvement.[26] Part of the reason for the difficulty in funding municipal improvement lay with the Charter itself, which strictly limited an urban government's ability for spending money to three categories: salaries for town officials and police, school construction, and town maintenance. Further, as the reports of the civil governors testify, provincial authorities established municipal salaries at set rates, often leaving city coffers empty for other expenditures. Town citizens also had to contribute to funding institutions of the central state, such as prisons, barracks, post offices, and customs houses. Any shortfall between the state's requirements and the city's revenue fell to the town residents, whose ability and willingness to pay appears doubtful given the significant arrears owed to each municipality.[27]

ALL DISTRICT TOWNS SHOULD BELONG TO THE STATE

Private cities, which became district capitals, received municipal magistracies modeled on the 1785 law and became subject to police supervision. Dubno was the largest town in Volhynia guberniia after the capital, Zhitomir, and was one of only three towns in the entire province with its own officially chartered police force. The remainder of private towns contributed funds toward the salary of the gorodnichii, unless the owner obtained an exemption. Cities with administrative functions had to conduct levies to pay magistracy and police salaries, just as in the Congress Kingdom, a process that involved negotiating a settlement between the owner and the residents. In 1806 the residents of Dubno contributed the entire 1,900 rubles allocated by the magistracy, while in neighboring Ostrog, the owner and the residents split the 230 rubles required to support the gorodnichii.[28] As a general rule, the owner's authority diminished in proportion to the importance assigned to the city by the state. The Radziwiłł family, for example, successfully prevented Nesvizh (Nieśwież) and Olyka from playing any role in the provincial structure—both entities were classified as minor cities with no administrative function, despite their comparatively large populations and diverse economies.[29] This does not mean that these burghers disposed of no revenue, though; the magistracy of Nesvizh continued to collect funds in accordance with its privileges, which allowed the city government to compensate chancellery officials and undertake repairs.[30] Simply, these accounts, as well as the officials controlling them, existed off the grid from the perspective of the empire. In such "off-the-grid" private cities, the owner could continue the traditional paternalistic and protective role of previous centuries, interacting with burghers much as under the Commonwealth, a reality brought to life by the experience of Nesvizh and Olyka in the first decades of the century.

In 1804, following fourteen years of infelicitous absentee caretaker government over the enormous Radziwiłł estates, Dominik Radziwiłł attained his majority and traveled to Lithuania to manage his properties. He soon named Antoni Rogoziński his commissar for the Nesvizh estates and dispatched this official to Minsk in order to negotiate a favorable settlement with the imperial government. As a result of Radziwiłł's successful lobbying, the Minsk governor's office issued a decree in April 1806 confirming all the owner's economic and regulatory powers in the city, as well as—most significantly—the right to control the police through the first mayor of the city, Karol Huryn. The decree even authorized the district police force to cooperate with Huryn in enforcing the owner's dispositions and regulations, while reminding the magistracy to focus solely on judicial matters—that is, to refrain from interfering in the police and economic powers of the owner. The governor's office indicated that these powers would allow Radziwiłł to improve the city, ensure the implementation of fire regulations, and combat disorder, strongly reminding town citizens to obey the instructions of the owner and the orders of his police. Radziwiłł received a similar concession for Olyka from the Volhynian authorities. In both "off-the-grid" cities, the state's presence appears to have been limited tax collection, the provision of a postal station, and the recruitment of soldiers.[31]

A few months later, an unfortunate tragedy in Nesvizh demonstrated the considerable power of the owner over his private town. In the evening of 24 September 1806, a fire engulfed much of the city, ultimately destroying about half the houses in the center, as well as merchant stalls and other infrastructure. Rogoziński reported that the fire consumed thirty houses in the first few minutes, leading to the destruction of twenty Christian and fifty Jewish domiciles. He requested financial assistance for the residents, many of whom had lost all their worldly possessions, while recommending that, in the future, town inhabitants not live so close together nor build their homes of wood.[32] The fire could not have come at a worse time for Dominik Radziwiłł, as the financial misadministration of the entail's caretakers going back to Karol Stanisław had saddled the young prince with enormous debts, claims, and lawsuits from various quarters. Dominik spent much of his short majority (1804–1813) settling with creditors and disaffected citizens, leaving him chronically short of cash. Nonetheless, Radziwiłł embraced his paternalistic role and established a fund of sixty thousand zlotys to provide rebuilding loans for the inhabitants of the city.[33] In order to prevent future fires, Radziwiłł charged his surveyor with drawing up a rebuilding plan for Nesvizh. Residents would be required to adhere to this plan in order to receive funds, and the records list numerous recipients signing pledges to this effect.

The surveyor, Nowicki, recorded a twenty-one-point list of notes and recommendations on how to proceed. The first principle to consider, he noted, were the privileges of the city dating back to the original founders. The second principle concerned the ukaz of the Minsk governor's office, "granting police and administration of the city completely to the owner," a generously self-serving interpretation of this decree. Nowicki then enumerated concrete suggestions. He proposed that houses on the principal streets should be built of stone, that residents employ bricks from the obsolete defensive walls as material for building sewer canals, that the disorderly side streets be regularized.[34] As in the eighteenth century, Nowicki blamed the Jewish population for causing the fire, since Jews continued to occupy houses on the market square and the main streets, in violation of the city's privileges and the good order measures of the late Karol Stanisław. Allegedly, such "disobedience" had forced the Christians to congregate in small tight spaces, susceptible to conflagration. Nowicki advised Dominik not only to forbid Jews from moving back to the main streets but also to rebuff any remonstrances about the plan "from those who dislike order, as well as the wellbeing of the residents and the owner," and the prince approved these suggestions in December 1806.[35] What is remarkable about this entire story is the complete absence of the Russian government, which appears to have played no role in any of the rebuilding considerations or paternalistic plans of the owner.

The presence of the Russian state could never be completely absent from the owner's consideration, though, particularly when the citizens themselves attempted to turn the state against their lord. On 5 May 1806, a few months before the fire, a faction of Nesvizh citizens recorded a complaint in the Novogrudok (Nowogródek) court, alleging that Dominik and Rogoziński had violated the privileges of the city and the protections of the Russian monarchy. Rogoziński was oppressing the residents with unreasonable demands, in particular forcing two former city councilors—Jan Bohdanowicz and Piotr Swiatłowicz—to perform physical labor and repair the embankment along the Slutsk (Słuck) gate. When the two citizens explained their unsuitability for the task, as well as their privileges and exemptions, Rogoziński allegedly invaded Bohdanowicz's house with armed Cossacks, who beat the "innocent" councilor, attacked him with a spade, and then descended upon all the onlookers who expressed pity, sparing neither young nor old. The complaint expressed hope that the Russian monarchy would intervene and bring a halt to the "rampant illegality" in the city.[36]

In fact, Radziwiłł and the Russian government were likely being drawn into an inter-urban quarrel. A week later, 18 May, the remainder of the citizens recorded a countercomplaint. The second record abjured the first as the "fantasy of some lowly lawyer, who operates in froth and idleness." The countercomplaint observed, in the first place, that as a city in Minsk guberniia, Nesvizh no longer had any connection with Novogrudok, formerly the capital of its palatinate. The letter praised Antoni Rogoziński for faithfully following orders and Dominik Radziwiłł for his beneficent care of the city, mentioning that the owner had donated money to repair the streets, build hospitals, and assist the poor.

Piotr Swiatłowicz specifically testified that the previous letter bearing his name was false, and that the "action of 10 April" (i.e., the forced labor) concerned only a few disobedient people, who "pretended not to know that government decrees, the privileges of the city, and the individual interest of the residents" require the repair of embankments. This letter bore the signatures of Karol Huryn, the entire city council, the aldermen, and a large cross-section of the Christian and Jewish citizens.[37]

Undaunted, the anti-owner faction signed a new petition in February 1807 (a few months after the fire), delegating "plenipotentiary powers" to Bohdanowicz for making remonstrances "at all judicial instances, and possibly to the very throne itself" against the violence and depredations of Rogoziński, "together with Karol Huryn, conspiring in various ways to oppress the citizenry."[38] Bohdanowicz, along with his brother, indeed presented a petition to the MVD, and initiated court cases against the owner at various judicial levels. In April 1807, Radziwiłł, "through his goodness, not wishing for [them] to incur further expenses," settled with the brothers out of court for an unspecified sum. The brothers signed an attestation before Rogoziński and Huryn renouncing their previous complaints and legal proceedings, claiming that they had no further grievances against the prince.[39] Most striking in this attestation is the reference to possible involvement by the Russian state. It appears that Dominik was willing to make significant financial sacrifices in order to preserve his city's independence from imperial oversight. There are other instances in the Nesvizh records of the prince settling with residents to forestall legal proceedings and intervention. Aron Ellowicz, whom Karol Stanisław had expelled from his house in the market square with inadequate compensation in the eighteenth century, received a more generous settlement from Dominik in 1807, again renouncing all intentions for further action at the state level. This did not prevent citizens from engaging in legal action, but the prince did appear to keep the special permission from the Minsk governor's office intact until his death in 1813. The Slutsk district court rebuffed a complaint by the Nesvizh Jewish community in 1811 concerning the owner's violation of their alcohol privileges, citing the authority granted the owner in 1806.[40]

Dominik Radziwiłł enjoyed perhaps extraordinary autonomy and authority over Nesvizh and Olyka in comparison with his other towns, as well as those of the other large landowners. Minor towns in Volhynia such as Zaslavl had no autonomy from the district police. Further, district towns, including Slutsk, had to contribute funds toward the gorodnichii, present magistracy elections for confirmation by the governor, and maintain administrative buildings.[41] The correspondence of Dominik Radziwiłł with his commissar for Slutsk, Stanisław Tomaszewski, shows a much greater level of state interference. Tomaszewski referred to his dealings with the local gorodnichii on a number of occasions, complaining in one letter that this official had confiscated fire-fighting equipment from the city treasury and requesting help to regain it. On another occasion, Tomaszewski informed an apparently nonplussed Dominik that he could not implement the prince's command to grant certain municipal real estate to a supporter because of the governor's designs on the same property. In several instances, Dominik also had to intervene personally with the governor's office, writing in 1810 to Minsk governor G. I. Roding with a request to confirm the recent elections to the Slutsk magistracy.[42] A district town was apparently a much greater inconvenience for the owner.

Russian officials also found district towns in private hands a significant inconvenience to themselves. Catherine II had evidently seen the administrative use of private towns as a temporary necessity, and an ukaz from 1795 had indicated that every effort should be made to convert district towns into state property, a sentiment reiterated in a joint report from the minister of Finance and the minister of Internal Affairs in 1806 to the Senate, which explained that, "as a general rule, district towns should belong to the state."[43] Governor Mikhail Komburlei of Volhynia, explained the difficulties caused by private towns for the rational administration of the countryside, particularly those serving as district capitals. In order to maintain a gorodnichii, the state needed to impose taxes on urban residents, but none of the officials in the governor's office could determine who should pay the contribution: the owner, the Christian peasants, or the Jews, who typically constituted the only registered townsmen. Moreover, if the town owner did not "appreciate" the value of paying for the district police, then "the town police chief encounters difficulties at every stage, both in establishing the amount of the contribution, and in collecting it. Equally [difficult] is hiring and supplying needed police servants." Podolia Governor Chevkin expressed a similar disquiet about the compromises necessary to institute police and government in private towns.[44]

The government also faced the problem of renting space for administration from town owners, which often placed the state on the defensive. As Komburlei explained: "If goodwill on the part of the owner is lacking, he could demand that property allotted for a particular government building be returned to him for his own enterprises, and since such property provides him income, the government cannot naturally deprive him of his rights in this case."[45] Komburlei most disliked the private town's incomplete connection to the chain of command, and his 1806 report to the MVD proposed the purchase of the largest and most valuable private towns, such as Dubno. Without irony, he argued that town citizens, once freed from the compulsion to pay rents and tolls to the owner, would then have the money to support the construction of soldiers' barracks and provide better salaries for the state police force. Further, the governor noted, the townsmen's earnings from trade generated such profits for the owner that the residents would easily repay the money employed by the state for their purchase after a few years.[46] Presumably for financial reasons, Komburlei was not granted his wish with regard to Dubno, but the principles he outlined were applied to the purchase of Mogilev in neighboring Podolia.

Mogilev, like Dubno, was a comparatively wealthy town integrated into an international commercial network, but Mogilev also possessed strategic significance as a frontier town on the border with Austria and the Ottoman empire. The state expended significant resources to lease buildings from Count Felix Potocki, the owner, in order to maintain a quarantine building and a customs house. The ministers of Finance and Interior cited these expenses in proposing the town's purchase, but they cautioned that the state should review the income and capacities of each town prior to considering such a transaction. Notably, the acquisition of Mogilev was structured in a remarkably similar fashion to the later emancipation of the serfs. In 1861 the state freed the peasants with land but required redemption payments from peasant communities as well as the continuation of labor obligations to the landlord for twenty years.[47] In Mogilev the government negotiated a purchase price of 580,760 rubles, or thirteen years of revenue (averaging 41,870 rubles per annum) plus 7 percent interest.[48] The town itself would finance this cost over the course of twenty-six years, using the remaining revenue now accruing to the magistracy to finance an administration and a police force. For twenty years the residents would also render payments to the owners from the rents and dues that the magistracy would no longer be entitled to collect once the "emancipation" had been completed. Mogilev had some Christian residents registered as townsmen and merchants, but the purchase specifically stated that all registered peasants living in the town would acquire townsperson status, meaning, in all likelihood, a return to the burgher state that had been lost after the partitions.[49]

Until the massive social changes unleashed by the peasant emancipations, none of the partitioning powers could find a solution to the private town paradox. In Prussia's Posen (Poznań) province, which contained the smallest number of private towns (sixty-nine in all), authorities effectively abolished seigneurial powers in 1831 and incorporated the cities into the state administration. Austria, with fewer resources and larger, more important private towns, followed a policy similar to Russia. The state purchased important border towns and commercial centers such as Brody and Rzeszów, while issuing regulations and restrictions to the rest, which remained private property but subject to state oversight. A final "emancipation" of private towns came in 1848, along with the complete abolition of serfdom in the Habsburg monarchy.[50] Similarly, Russia lacked the resources and the desire to compensate all owners on market terms before the peasant emancipations of 1861 and 1864; until then the empire had to compromise between private ownership and state regulation.

For the Radziwiłł towns, the occasion for greater state intervention came during Napoleon's invasion, when Dominik abandoned the empire to serve in the army of the Duchy of Warsaw, ignoring summons to return and defend Russia. Alexander placed a sequester on his property, which was only removed following Dominik's death in 1813 and the division of the immense (and immensely indebted) lands between Ludwig von Wittgenstein, Dominik's son-in-law, and Antoni Radziwiłł, an absentee figure who soon became Prussian King Friedrich Wilhelm III's ceremonial viceroy in the Grand Duchy of Posen. More significantly, in 1815 the emperor chartered a state-controlled police force in Nesvizh, erasing the 1806 concession of the Minsk governor, and Nesvizh further became the home of a permanent contingent of Russian soldiers.[51] Arguably, this decision was inevitable, as the Russian state was already beginning to exercise greater supervision over the administration and internal organization of even "minor" cities. An 1825 decree from the Minsk governor's office reminded the Radziwiłł estates to ensure that elections in the owner's cities proceeded in accordance with imperial regulations and decrees. The same ordinance, though, showed the considerable power still in the owner's hands. Among other prerogatives, Antoni Radziwiłł retained the right to choose the first mayor, or starosta, from candidates forwarded by the citizens.[52]

In fact, the relationship between the owner, the burghers, and the state remained very much in flux and subject to local interpretation for the first third of the nineteenth century. For example, the Senate and other authorities issued ambiguous and contradictory decisions with regard to the extremely urgent question of the private town residents' soslovie status. Lubomil in Volhynia and Olgopol in Podolia received favorable decisions for the townspeople, granting *meshchanstvo* status to the Christian burghers, but other private towns consisted entirely of serfs and not completely burgher Jews.[53] Another issue that lacked clarity for decades concerned the continued weight of the owner's past privileges to the town residents. In April 1816, following a decade of unresolved conflict between the Radziwiłł family and the burghers of Olyka, the Christians and Jews of the town brought the owner and his economic steward before the Dubno magistracy court for violating their ancient privileges, in particular for imposing market tolls on the sale of fish, salt, herring, and lumber and for levying extraordinary taxes on brewers and distillers. Unsurprisingly, the Dubno court, staffed by private town burghers, proved sympathetic to the plaintiffs. The decision noted that privileges dating back to 1633 had freed brewers from taxation, levying a payment only on vodka distillers, and imperial legislation had confirmed the residents' privileges. Moreover, two separate ukases from 1798 and 1809 had strictly forbidden owners from imposing tolls on victuals and locally produced handicrafts. The court found the steward in violation of the law, required the official to pay a fine, and ordered the entail to compensate burghers for their losses due to illegal taxes.[54]

Antoni Radziwiłł appealed the decision, and the matter meandered its way to the Senate, which finally issued a decision in August 1824. The Senate determined, first, that the imperial ukases confirming the rights and privileges of town citizens applied only to matters of public law—that is, legislation authorized by the Polish parliament. Privileges granted on the sole authority of the owner, by contrast, were not legally binding and could be altered by the owners at their discretion. In particular, the Senate noted that the relationship between the owner and the Jewish population, which had spearheaded the litigation, rested on a contractual basis in accordance with the 1804 Statute on the Jews. The protests of the burghers therefore had no merit and contravened the economic powers of the city owner. On the other hand, the Senate agreed with the Dubno magistracy that the imposition of tolls on victuals and locally produced goods did violate imperial law. Most significantly, the Senate ruled that, in accordance with ukases of 1801 and 1807, the residents of Olyka, "as free people," could leave Radziwiłł's land and move elsewhere if they disliked his terms.[55] The Senate's decision settled some of the imprecision with regard to the legal position of private town residents, indicating that the position of the owner remained strong but subject to imperial control. At the same time, this ruling did not conclude the disagreements between the owner and the residents, which continued for decades even after the city passed to Dominik's son-in-law, Ludwig von Wittgenstein, as part of the settlement of an imperial commission charged with sorting out the family's massive debts.[56]

THERE ARE PRACTICALLY NO RUSSIAN MERCHANTS IN THE PROVINCE

The November Insurrection in the Congress Kingdom spilled over into the Lithuanian, Belarusian, and Ukrainian provinces, dominated by Polish-speaking nobles and burghers. Facing insurrection on multiple fronts, Emperor Nicholas I ordered the civilian governors to marshal the resources of their provinces for the imperial counterattack, while perceived traitors, including city officials, found themselves in prison.[57] Following the pacification, Emperor Nicholas I made a number of changes to the administration of the region. In Ukraine a military governor-general now presided over the civilian administrations of Kiev, Volhynia, and Podolia, and the civil governors answered to this official with regular reports. As evidenced by these documents, governors now felt a much greater need to highlight their vigilance and mastery of the territory, particularly by conducting regular inspection tours of their provinces. A. Rimskii-Korsakov, governor of Volhynia, prefaced his 1832 inspection tour report by explaining that his primary goal was to "become better acquainted with the local situation and most of all to ensure that . . . there is no evidence of any temptation to destroy the general peace."[58] Two years later, G. S. Lashkarev wrote of his tour in Podolia that "although in this province, thank God, all is well, no doubt minds still wander . . . and possibly . . . certain conditions feed an antagonistic spirit."[59]

Faced with treachery in the reunited provinces, imperial authorities moved to eliminate concessions to the demographic realities of the region in favor of more integration and police supervision. Paradoxically, the new assimilationist approach designed to restore the region's "Russianness" did not overturn the institutional modifications justified by the western provinces' distinctiveness. Instead, the empire found itself in a vicious cycle, in which each new reactionary measure served to highlight the region's separateness from Russia, a fact that in turn demanded further modifications from the standard model. Linguistic changes came immediately; in 1832 Nicholas I issued a decree requiring Russian to become the sole language for official business, and officials now had to speak and write in Russian in order to preserve their positions. Previously, records had been conducted in Polish and Russian, and evidence suggests that monolingual speakers of Polish constituted sizable portions of the cities' populations. Even in 1832, a failed candidate for the Zhitomir magistracy's Jewish cohort had complained that he knew "Russian and Polish better than the other candidates elected as Jewish councilors, and especially better than Gershko Fishlang," whom the governor had confirmed.[60] Now, though, governors had to police the language usage of city officials, which was completely unnecessary in the core provinces. Conducting an inspection tour in 1836, Governor N. V. Zhukovskii observed that the mayor of Kremenets kept his records in Polish because, as the official admitted, he did not know how to write in Russian. After returning to Zhitomir, Zhukovskii fired the mayor and called for new elections, ordering the town to choose only officials proficient in Russian.[61]

In addition to changes in the administrative language, the state also insisted on a greater police presence in the towns. No more would the Russian state allow a voluntary police force in combination with the supervision of the gorodnichii, particularly in the larger state and private towns. In 1828 the governor of Podolia had already complained about the reliance on voluntary policing in most of the towns in the region, writing: "In general, it would be desirable to establish a police force composed of discharged soldiers [in all the cities], similar to the practice in Kamenets-Podol'skii. Their aptitude for military discipline and strict implementation [of orders] corresponds better to this type of service."[62] By 1835 the government had ordered all towns to support full complements of state-appointed police inspectors, patrolmen, and firefighters. These requirements placed an enormous strain on the finances of smaller, district towns, which now had to dedicate about 40 percent of their revenue to police control, and upward of 90 percent on salaries in total (see table 9). Mogilev, converted into a state town, stands out as the only district capital to gain resources for meeting these obligations; other

TABLE 9. COMPARATIVE EXPENDITURES ON MAGISTRACY AND POLICE SALARIES AS A PERCENTAGE OF REVENUE

City	1804/1806		1835	
	Rubles	Percentage (%)	Rubles	Percentage (%)
Zhitomir	6,945	47.5	13,750	50.6
Kremenets	2,004	60.2	6,348	92.7
Lutsk	1,036	17	4,848	79.7
Kamenets-Podol'skii	8,905	60.2	9,050	19.5
Mogilev	2,720	90.2	8,294	56.3

Sources: TsDIAK, f. KMF 11, o. 1, s. 94, 17; TsDIAK, f. KMF 11, o. 1, s. 91, 81–84; TsDIAK, f. 442, o. 66, s. 496, 13–17, 26–31, 36–40, 57–61, 68–69.

provincial cities now saw their entire revenue stream diverted to meet police obligations since no new sources of funding were forthcoming.[63]

As in the Congress Kingdom, towns in Russia received resources and funding allotments in accordance with their perceived importance. Zhitomir and Kamenets-Podol'skii had additional funding sources to dedicate to urban improvement and cleanliness projects. District cities, on the other hand, could afford only the salary requirements, particularly as municipal revenue remained static in the face of additional budgetary demands. In this environment there could be little room for construction or improvement projects. Indeed, the Kremenets magistracy faced a choice in 1835 between drawing upon its capital reserve fund and collecting back taxes in order to satisfy ordinary expenditures, to speak nothing of beautification and improvement projects. The presence of large arrears in every town's budget suggests that the option of collecting back taxes was tenuous at best. Even the lucrative alcohol revenue barely covered necessary expenses, as Governor Lubianovskii observed in 1833. The Ministry of the Interior effectively acknowledged this problem, since—as already observed—no space on the prefabricated form for governors' reports was allotted to the topic of town cleanliness and construction.[64]

Unsurprisingly, complaints about the poor material conditions of the majority of towns surfaced repeatedly in the governors' reports. In 1832 Governor Rimskii-Korsakov observed that most administrative buildings in the towns of Volhynia were wooden and of poor condition, while the roads were both irregular and uneven.[65] His successor, Zhukovskii, echoed this assessment in reports from 1835 and 1836, when his inspection tour revealed that no new government buildings had been erected in several years, cleanliness was lacking, and construction often deviated from official standards. While material conditions bothered Rimskii-Korsakov and Zhukovskii, the governors devoted significantly more space in their reports to procedure and *deloproizvodstvo* (efficient record keeping). During Zhukovskii's 1836 inspection tour of Volhynia, the governor concerned himself most of all with the efficiency of the municipal courts and the record-keeping procedures. His report contained comments about each city in the region, many of them unfavorable:

> Lutsk: Although the activity of the town magistracy is relatively successful, I noticed some incompetence and a slight sluggishness in composing court case summaries. . . . The financial books are not kept properly, nor are the sums recorded on the page in the correct manner.
>
> Vladimir: In town business one observes sluggishness; laws, directives, and orders are not implemented successfully. Moreover, I found that although the sums in the town treasury were intact, several expenditures had not been recorded in the record books, and some inscriptions in the town journal were not signed, as all members of the magistracy were personally instructed to do. In general, this town magistracy requires improvement.[66]

Only Zhitomir, site of the governor's residence as well as beneficiary of far greater revenue streams satisfied Zhukovskii's criteria in terms of *deloproizvodstvo*.

Private towns fared no better in terms of the criteria established by the state. Zhukovskii reproached the magistracy of Dubno, "and particularly its secretary" for failing to record instances of fulfilling government directives and for handling state business slowly.[67] A similar preoccupation appeared in an 1832 inspection tour of Zaslavl, a private town and district capital, by Sublieutentant Vol'ianskii, a gorodnichii. Vol'ianskii noted the poor condition of state buildings, which had to be located in private homes rented by the state. Further, the magistracy's limited resources, in part because of the owner's exactions, confined municipal expenditures to the gorodnichii's salary and subsidies for the billeting commission. Vol'ianskii noted that the town hospital was in a poor location, but the owner had refused to move it. Further, the owner's lack of cooperation meant that the police had to store their fire-fighting equipment outside in the open air. Vol'ianskii's only proposal, though, consisted of a suggestion to convert the less-populated of the two local Catholic monasteries into a state building for housing administrative offices, courts, and even a prison. As a result the government would no longer have to rent private homes from the owner.[68] Again, state officials worried more about securing convenient conditions for Russian administration than about the lack of material well-being or funding for urban development.

Although provincial authorities complained of the sluggishness and disorder in local administration, governors categorically disapproved of any hint of civic initiative to combat these problems. Zhukovskii's 1836 report emphatically stated that gubernatorial authorities needed to increase their vigilance to prevent magistracies from authorizing new taxes or fees without state approval. He also complained that town magistracies in Volhynia frequently usurped police functions, sending out their own members to collect back taxes. No one denied that magistracies remained chronically underfunded or that tax arrears presented one of the regions' most pressing problems. Repeated declarations to this effect circulated, but the state insisted that only governors could authorize taxes and only police could collect arrears.[69] On the other hand, provincial officials did not evaluate the work of the state police much higher. Rimskii-Korsakov had written in 1832 that, "In general, one cannot expect intelligent and honest work from the majority of [police] employed in Volhynia guberniia."[70]

Instead, governors followed the path of the KRSW in the Congress Kingdom and placed their confidence in vigilance and discipline, particularly in their power to fire and fine officials. In some cases, authorities took this authority to legalistic extremes. In 1834 the Kremenets magistracy wrote to Governor-General Levashov to appeal a fine of 180 rubles levied by the treasury chamber on the members of the town government. The treasury chamber had issued this punishment because the magistracy had failed to submit its financial records for the year 1830 on time. According to the magistracy, the mayor could not present these documents punctually, as the records in question were located in the home of the magistracy secretary, Semetskii, who, along with the mayor, had been imprisoned following the November Insurrection. Russian authorities had also confiscated the municipal books from the secretary's home. Neither the secretary nor the mayor was released until May 1831, and the military authorities did not allow other members of the magistracy to receive Semetskii's books from prison.[71] In response to Levashov's inquiry about this matter, Rimskii-Korsakov supported the treasury chamber, citing an obscure law from 1727, in which Emperor Peter II had required all provincial authorities to maintain their records in one central location. On the basis of this law, Rimskii-Korsakov observed, the town's books should have been located at the magistracy office, not with the secretary, making the magistracy culpable for the tardiness. Levashov apparently accepted the governor's reasoning as one month later Rimskii-Korsakov wrote to the town magistracy, explaining that he could not excuse them from their obligation to pay the treasury chamber's fine.[72]

On the other hand, the lack of "qualified" officials and committed administrators limited the efficacy of such threats, as the state had to rely on someone to staff these municipal posts. An 1838 police report filed with the governor-general's office charged that members of the Kremenets magistracy frequently played truant from their jobs; city officials frequently arrived late to the office or not at all, creating an artificial backlog of court cases. Further, the inspector noted that he had issued several written and oral warnings to three particularly truant members, who nonetheless failed to appear for work during the three days of the inspector's most recent tour. The vice-governor of Volhynia responded that strict measures would be taken to avoid such irresponsibility and disorder, including not only the removal of these officials from office but also possible summons to court.[73] There is no record of such a summons, but the low number of merchants combined with the poor incentives to serve in a largely powerless municipal post suggest that the empire essentially had to tolerate substandard administration in its borderlands.

For governors, the apparent lack of qualified urban officials, the sluggishness of municipal business, and even the economic underdevelopment of the region increasingly merged into symptoms of a deeper malady: the lack of "Russian" inhabitants in the cities. The ethnic composition of the region provided a comforting explanation for the political and economic shortcomings of the towns, as Podolia Vice-governor Gur'ev explained in an 1832 report: "In [almost all] towns of the province there are practically no Russian merchants. The best merchants here are only Jews, and although there are enough meshchane, the greater part are poor. . . . Moreover, they are either completely illiterate or due to their low level of literacy are incapable of service. As a result of this lack of merchants and capable meshchane, elections to even the town magistracies occasionally present difficulties. The guberniia government is frequently forced to [annul and] redo the elections until at least a few capable people are found to occupy these posts."[74] Podolia governor Lubianovskii confirmed the concern about the lack of qualified people in 1833; Rimskii-Korsakov complained in 1832 that the magistracy secretaries conducted town business in Volhynia, since most ordinary members were meshchane and Jews.[75]

Despite the complications caused by the restricted Jewish franchise for urban government, governors such as Rimskii-Korsakov saw even this concession as a detriment to the well-being of urban government. His 1832 report noted that most magistracies in Volhynia contained Jewish members, as per the law, "and the cunningness particular to them manifests itself in the course of [the magistracy's court] business."[76] Echoing Świniarski's pamphlet from 1789, the governor of Podolia complained in 1834 that Jews, because of their alleged habit of low profit margins and willingness to stock their stalls with substandard merchandise, frequently undersold their "Russian" competitors. In the governor's view, this led to anemic trade and forced the "Russians" to practice agriculture in order to make a living.[77] In reality, the primary problem posed by Jewish communities for tsarist authorities was their preservation of an autonomous institution, the kahal, which the central government had excluded from external supervision and management. As is well known, the tsarist government exploited the kahal as a recruiting instrument, delegating to the Jewish elders the unpleasant task of furnishing soldiers, often with the aid of hired kidnappers. When the kahal was abolished in 1844, this institution had lost most of its remaining legitimacy and Jewish society had suffered enormous internal divisions and crises as a result of the state's policies.[78] For governors such as Zhukovskii, though, the kahal was objectionable primarily because of its autonomy from civil administration: "Jewish kahals are too unconstrained in their expenditures and are not subject to any kind of accountability. They spend money according to their whim without any kind of principles or confirmed budgets. They exploit . . . the trust of society, which very often leads to abuse. From this complaints arise, the resolution of which causes serious difficulties for the authorities."[79] For Zhukovskii, the solution was to subject the kahal, "like every tax-paying society" to standard accounting practices, in particular the submission of revenue and expenditure records to the treasury chamber. In this way, the government could determine how much each kahal member contributed and ensure that each expense would be grounded in a legitimate need. As is evident from the purchase of Mogilev, a rationalized picture of the kahal's budget would also allow the state to determine whether individual Jews could afford higher taxes (for which reason kahals had fought for autonomy in fiscal matters since the period of the Commonwealth).[80]

The autonomous outsider status of Jewish institutions and social organizations, a reality reinforced by imperial law, created a nationality problem for Russian administrators and justified municipal restrictions on Jews, which then created an administrative problem for governors. Faced with the difficulties of applying Russian law to the non-Russian borderlands, Lashkarev proposed a classic colonial solution: settle the region with Great Russian colonists. In his 1834 report, the governor proposed that the state could offer inducements such as a seven-year exemption from merchant corporation payments and contributions in lieu of military service. He further proposed that the settlement of Russians would produce the following benefits:

a. The Russian language, Russian customs, and morals will take root in the towns.
b. Cathedrals [will be constructed and maintained] with the necessary magnificence.
c. Russian merchants will intermarry with the local population, which contains no small number of Catholics. This will bring the Orthodox faith to the population.
d. Industry will flourish, towns will improve, and the poor class of townsmen will obtain work and more reliable sources of income.
e. The Jews themselves will be invigorated by competition and will begin to practice more honest trade in better [quality goods].[81]

Lashkarev's solution does not seem to have become policy, but his ideas echoed Bismarck's later Germanification policy in Polish Prussia, and Prussian provincial authorities also complained about the lack of "qualified officials" in the Polish regions. Evidently, the Russian state was not the only regime to discover the intertwining of seemingly neutral administrative questions with nationality problems.[82]

National differences served as a pretext to stall the creation of institutions, which would have rendered the region more administratively similar to the Russian heartland. In 1837, for example, the provinces of Volhynia and Podolia contained only one town duma, in the city of

Novograd-Volynskii, a settlement that had received urban status only after the partitions. In 1836 the emperor promulgated a decree mandating that the establishment of town dumas in the western territories required approval by the governor and the MVD.[83] Lashkarev explained the hesitancy in part by noting that in Podolia, for example, there were "no Russian merchants" to fulfill these positions.[84] Only in 1837 did some of the provincial capitals, notably Zhitomir and Kamenets-Podol'skii, receive dumas. The extra procedures and restrictions governing these institutions seem more peculiar, given the arguments of Eroshkin and Kupriianov that dumas commanded little prestige or respect in towns where they did exist. Unlike service as a mayor, judge, or town council member, membership on the duma did not confer a place in the table of ranks. Further, Kupriianov argues that townsmen indicated the importance of a given position by the order in which they conducted elections, and members of the duma were often elected second-to-last, ahead of deputies to the Quartering Commission.[85] Nonetheless, provincial officials devoted significant energy to the question of town dumas, under the presumption that the Charter could not operate without them. The same concerns played out in 1836, when the state decided to establish civil and criminal appeals courts for the western provinces on the model of the 1775 reform. The original design of the courts called for the nobility and the merchant corporations to elect two members apiece for each court. In the western guberniia, where the "merchants are generally Jews," the nobility continued to elect two representatives, but the state decided to appoint someone to represent the merchants on the court.[86]

The presence of private towns also separated the western provinces from Russia throughout the reign of Nicholas I, who retained the status quo that developed in the second half of Alexander I's government with only minor modifications. The state would take charge of police matters in one way or another, but the owner remained free in all economic matters not forbidden by law. By 1848, both Austria and Prussia had "emancipated" their private towns, but Nicholas—as was his wont—preferred to tinker around the edges. In 1836 the emperor approved the decision of a committee of ministers declaring that private town residents should refuse all illegal tolls in private towns, as well as dues not consistent with explicit privileges or free contracts. Decades later, in 1855, imperial authorities began making plans for a new round of purchases, naming the Radziwiłł town of Slutsk as one of the candidates.[87] Otherwise, the relationship of private town residents to their owners does not appear to have undergone significant modifications.

A report on the status of Olyka, authored in 1859 for the benefit of Wilhelm Radziwiłł, described a familiar situation: The new owner, Wittgenstein, had sought to increase his revenue by again instituting tolls on victuals, but the residents had protested to state authorities, leading the owner to withdraw the duties. Meanwhile, a legal battle continued between owners and burghers over permissible dues and residential rights. The report doubted whether the owner would be able to increase his revenue from the city, since, as in Nesvizh, city property remained exempt from any rents or dues. The owner's legal prerogatives were confined to restricting the burghers from selling their property to nobles or clerics, who enjoyed additional privileges and exemptions. In fact, a lawsuit between the town owner and a noble widow, who had received a certain plot of urban land from Dominik Radziwiłł, stretched back to 1818. Exploiting her noble status, the widow had begun distilling vodka in collusion with the citizens of Olyka and in violation of the owner's alcohol monopoly. As the report concluded, the only outcome of the decades-old legal battle was that the widow continuously raised her price for vacating the land.[88] Far from buttressing all-powerful feudal control, Russian privileges to the private towns had cemented the lord's dependence on the cooperation and goodwill of the residents. This problem does not seem to have bothered Russian officials, presumably because the affairs of "minor" towns had no bearing on the schematized administration of the province.

Catherine the Great's enlightened regulations for urban government proved too rigid even for Russia proper, and the "reunited" western provinces defied almost every assumption encoded into the reforms. Having defined qualified applicants for municipal posts in a manner that excluded most Ukrainian and Belarusian urbanites, the Russian state struggled to implement the basic provisions of the Charter. Official worries about the large presence of "cunning" Jews and "disloyal" Poles, while testifying to well-known prejudices and to the postrevolutionary climate of reaction, also reflect a deep-seated distrust of local government on the part of imperial administrators. At best, the delegation of power represented a risky endeavor, not to be employed except under the proper conditions; even then, superior authorities had to be vigilant in order to prevent excessive initiative. Even after the Great Reforms, the same tension colored the governors' relations with zemstvos and city dumas; not every governor was hostile or confrontational, but many continued to police the initiatives of these institutions with suspicion.[89] In the western provinces after 1830, the natural reserve toward local control conspired with ethnic stereotypes to limit local authority to such an extent that officials judged the risk too great of introducing even such comically insignificant institutions as dumas. Unsurprisingly, the resulting caliber of local government dwindled, as apathy, inertia, and malfeasance increasingly characterized officials in city chancelleries.

On the other hand, imperial concessions to owners such as the Radziwiłłs unintentionally sheltered residents in towns like Nesvizh and Olyka from imperial interference and regulation. Emancipation meant a transfer of subordination from a distant owner with relatively narrow options to a much more potent administrative state. Protests of violence and injustice, expressed by the Christian and Jewish residents of the "minor" private cities, fulfilled the same role as under the Commonwealth: masking the owner's inability to extract funds or enforce discipline and testifying to the citizens' collective action in defense of perceived rights and privileges. Prince Dominik's preference to manage the "disobedient" citizens in his minor towns for himself elided with the narrow concerns of Russian administrators, who appeared satisfied with classifying residents and enforcing administrative uniformity at the district level. Even as the empire under Nicholas I tightened state supervision and police control, owners and citizens preserved a political arena at least faintly reminiscent of the old Commonwealth.

Conclusion

Emancipating Citizens into Subjects

IN 1880 THE POLISH positivist Julian Łapicki published an article in *Ateneum* that was harshly critical of the peasant community (*gmina*) assemblies in the Congress Kingdom of Poland. Alexander II's 1864 emancipation decree had abolished estate distinctions in the Congress Kingdom and established peasant community assemblies with the right to tax all residents—including their former landlords—for local improvement and maintenance projects. Private town owners, too, lost their remaining feudal prerogatives, and a decree of 1867 reclassified most such entities as villages, a transition that encompassed the former private towns of Bełżyce, Firlej, Bychawa, as well as the state cities of Kazimierz Dolny and Urzędów. In opposition to earlier periods, the loss of municipal status now conferred positive benefits; the former burghers gained the right to participate in "peasant" self-government, the only form of local self-government allowed in the kingdom after the January Insurrection. For Łapicki, though, the new institution offered too much autonomy to rural society; he noted that no community assembly in the country had established a single hospital, nor did the communities adequately fund schools. In fact, community assemblies regularly voted down requests for school construction, while villages consistently failed to stock equipment for fire prevention or to fulfill their responsibility to maintain roads. Echoing Kazimierz Brandys in the constitutional period, Łapicki proposed that the Russian government should impose mandatory expenditures on the communities in order to force the peasant assemblies to support such essential measures. Stanisław Schultz, himself a former community mayor, concurred with Łapicki's negative assessment but proposed as a solution that the intelligentsia somehow make a greater effort to enlighten the peasants as to their genuine needs.[1] As these complaints attest, the tendency toward devolution and self-government in nineteenth-century Europe did not spell the end of enlightened centralism. Rather, the consensus of opinion in favor of uniformity, rationality, and enlightened leadership simply migrated from the royal council to the bourgeois salon.

Following the emancipation of the peasants in Prussia (1831), Austria (1848), and the Russian Empire (1861–1864), monarchs increasingly favored devolution and local self-administration as remedies to the high cost of administering diverse regions and to the danger of excluding educated society from civic life. In the Muscovite heartland of Russia, Alexander II's government acted to correct the shortcomings that had plagued local self-government since 1785, in particular the limited competencies of locally chosen officials. After 1864 zemstvos managed provincial and rural affairs in conjunction with governors, and elected town dumas became the principal organs of municipal government in 1870. In the cities and provinces of Russia, locally chosen officials now disposed of extensive tax-collecting powers as well as broader authority over education, sanitation, and infrastructure.[2] In Austria Crown-land diets received substantial autonomy after the compromise of 1867, a fact that allowed the *szlachta*-dominated diet in Lemberg the ability to rule Galicia in the name of Franz Josef. It would be a mistake, though, to view these concessions as analogous to the political rights enjoyed by urban citizens before the Enlightenment. The state always remained a looming presence, with officials standing ready to annul locally taken decisions and to prod elected officials to sponsor the "correct" priorities. In Russia the counterreforms of Alexander III gave significant supervisory power to appointed governors, and in Austrian Galicia conflict between Poles and Ukrainians provided no shortage of opportunities for imperial intervention.[3]

Even such limited decentralization as the state might offer never reached the Congress Kingdom, and in fact the pendulum swung in the opposite direction toward the final abrogation of autonomy. The January Insurrection had convinced the tsar of the impracticality of relying on the nobility for political stability, and prominent Russian administrators concluded that the autonomy of the Congress Kingdom had served only to buttress Polish revolutionary movements. To punish the noble landlords, the emancipation of 1864 granted to Polish peasants more generous allotments of land with fewer redemption obligations than their Russian counterparts had received. Outside the granting of peasant self-government, the tsar tightened the supervisory structure of urban and provincial government with imported Russian officials. In a territory now officially, but inconsistently, called "Vistula Land," no zemstvos or municipal dumas would appear before the fall of the Romanov dynasty.[4] Russia's western territories also benefitted less from the new tendency of decentralization. Private towns were equally abolished, and their residents became renters of urban property, much as in the baronial burghs in Scotland or lordly towns in Ireland, but the emperor hesitated to grant any self-governing powers to a region still thought to be dominated by Poles.[5] As a result, the urban reform came to the Ukrainian and Belarusian regions only in 1875, and the modified concession gave the Minister of Internal Affairs significant power to approve and remove municipal officials at will. An analogous process applied to the 1911 introduction of zemstvos in Ukraine, where the government chose to rely on appointed members in order to prevent the Polish nobility from exercising "disproportionate" influence over these bodies.[6]

While the chambers of power debated the limits of decentralization, the liberal opposition dreamed of harnessing the centralized state in order to continue the work of eighteenth-century monarchs. As Pieter Judson has recently argued, liberals in Austria continued to favor a centralized state that would pursue "the victory of enlightened progress at all costs." Heirs to the enlightened tradition faulted the state for the meekness of its social program while criticizing decentralization as a remnant of feudal, oligarchic rule. Richard Evans and Andrzej Kamiński have argued that the Polish, Hungarian, and German liberals who rose up against autocratic power in 1830, 1848, and 1863 aimed not so much to restore ancient liberties as to seize the machinery of the state in order to re-create the ideals of either Josephinism or Napoleonic progress after decades of conservative reaction.[7] Once these liberals came to power in Austria, their aim was to arrest devolution in favor of a centralized state. Polish positivists, though deprived of any political power, hoped that their policy of *ugoda* (conciliation) with the Russian state would inspire tsarist officials to pursue policies that contributed to their idea of socio-economic progress. Henryk Konic was relatively alone in placing his hope on peasant self-government as a "school of civics" that would spontaneously raise the people to democratic maturity. Among opposition figures, only a few socialist dreamers imagined a future utopia of communal living not unlike an idealized Magdeburg Law city; the leaders of the ill-fated Paris Commune in 1871 described their would-be revolution as a return to the "communal freedoms" of the Middle Ages, but the bureaucratic state triumphed over them quickly and functioned without interruption under the Third Republic.[8]

Since the nineteenth century, European states have alternated between centralizing and devolutionary tendencies. Centralism returned with a vengeance after the First World War, when the newly created nation-states of east central Europe collectively adopted centralized, hierarchical structures as means of overcoming "backwardness." Their socialist successors replicated the same state machinery, if in the service of much more radical aims. Since the 1970s the pendulum has swung back toward devolution, with experiments in local self-government taking place in France, Italy, and as of this writing, Ukraine. As the recent crisis in Catalonia has shown, though, all such experiments with devolution and autonomy have been granted by the *bon plaisir* of the state, and what the state has bestowed can also be rescinded.[9] At the level of the European Union, the fiercest critics of bureaucratic overreach have emerged from east central Europe, where governments are increasingly transferring decision-making powers to the central government in order to harness the presumptive will of the nation. Although the political maneuvers of Poland and Hungary have aroused controversy, the machinery allowing the governments to pursue their controversial policies broadly matches the European norm. When Vladimir Putin's government abolished gubernatorial and mayor elections for the Russian Federation in 2004 (a decision partially reversed in 2012), the state could argue, with some justification, that many countries in the European Union appoint, rather than elect, their intermediary officials.[10] For some, succession from the state offers the only chance to return to genuine self-government, but even had referendums in Scotland or Catalonia succeeded, there is little likelihood that a new system of *Kleinstaaterei* will return power to locals any more than devolution, since the miniature states will simply replicate the political structure of their parents, and local governments even in these smaller states will remain a creature of state administration, not an alternative to it.

Urban self-government in the medieval and early modern world, at least in the former Polish-Lithuanian Commonwealth, differed qualitatively and functionally from modern decentralization, though certain similarities might be found with city corporations in the United States before the mid-twentieth century.[11] Rather than a vertical power structure, the relationship of each member of the urban community to all other political authorities resembled a constellation. City liberties originated with royal charters and privileges, but the mechanisms of subsequent royal influence remained indirect while authority and repressive power accrued to multiple, imprecisely delineated officeholders. The city mayor reported neither to the starosta nor to the king, while magistracies shared territorial control over urban space with kahals, jurydyki, and nobles until 1791. Hence the constellation metaphor; some lights shone brighter and enjoyed greater primacy of place, but the relationship of one star to another was contingent and much more tentative than an orderly chain of command. Precisely because there was no bureaucratic hierarchy, no overpowering state to compel all to obedience, precisely as well because of the messy tangle of competing and contradictory jurisdictions, cities became centers of civic space. Even if the rhetoric of republican self-government did not necessarily match the ideal, citizens in the Commonwealth could participate in collective decision-making and negotiating modi vivendi with other groups and authorities.

Following Quentin Skinner, I have argued that the rhetoric of republicanism, no matter how closely it hewed to the reality of urban politics, established boundaries between acceptable and unacceptable behavior, provided resources for evaluating claims, and limited the possibilities that could be imagined.[12] Civic republicanism, in other words, was a worldview. In making this claim, I am not implying any necessary equation between the conceptions of "citizens" and "morally good people," nor between "republican self-government" and "democracy." Cities were hierarchical places where some groups enjoyed greater liberties and protections than others, and every privileged individual fought to preserve ethically indefensible prerogatives, including rights that discriminated against others or brought undeserved gain. Sinecures, residential and political restrictions on minorities, economically self-defeating concessions, all comprised the sacred guarantees of the king's ancestors and the inviolable private property of an estate. Defending these privileges was simply part of the broader mental universe of civic republicanism, for the adherents of which the accumulated liberties of the estate collectively guaranteed "liberty." This mental universe saw no contradiction between liberty and the rule of wealthy elites. Tumults and protests against magistracy officials did not imply that tanners and waste-carriers should enter the magistracy but, rather, that city elites operate in a consultative manner.[13] Rhetoric about equality, the common good, and local self-government no doubt masked the pecuniary benefits and perks claimed by the elite, but the ideal nonetheless shaped local reactions to the policies of the center and influenced how individuals evaluated and explained the actions of their town neighbors.

Republican citizenship meant in part conceiving of the city as the principle frame of reference, the center of a universe that radiated out to the larger republic. Petitions and remonstrances to central officials had aimed to attract outside attention, but the point of reference always remained the local quarrel. The burghers of Łęczyca sabotaged a reform designed to improve their own material circumstance because their quarrel with the starosta over rights and privileges took precedence. Dastkiewicz authored two separate petitions to lustration officials not from any interest in the royal audit but because he hoped for assistance in his own partisan battle in Lutsk. The Christian and Jewish antagonists in Kremenets did not let the complete destruction of their country at foreign hands interfere in their continuing legal battle about taxation authority. In fact, both parties assumed that the Russian authorities would uphold decisions of the Assessor Court because neither could imagine an alternative. The Bohdanowicz brothers threatened Dominik Radziwiłł with a Russian investigation that could have abolished their city's autonomy as part of political maneuvers against the commissar and his allied citizens. Republicanism frequently diverged from wise decision-making, but this did not make city citizens backward. From their perspective, citizens had a right to follow through on their own poor choices, and all available evidence suggests that civic republicanism at the most basic level shaped the assumptions of all urban residents. The Black Procession and the Humble Petition both took unprecedented measures to preserve a way of life idealized by this conception, which all urban groupings understood to be threatened by the innovations of enlightened rulers.

Just as the civic republican mentality generated its own values and limited citizens' ability to imagine future possibilities, the Enlightenment vision of reform through centralization and rationalization brought its own package of assumptions and expectations that guided and limited political choices. Eighteenth-century thinkers proposed that new scientific knowledge and economic theories offered rulers a bird's-eye view of the entire country and therefore the prerogative to make decisions affecting the whole. Slogans such as "indivisible sovereignty," "the common good," and "rationality" served as weapons against particularistic privileges, laws, and jurisdictions that benefited specific groups at the expense of the imagined whole. Whereas earlier monarchs had experimented with economic development on a case-by-case basis, following the logic that the king was "father of the kingdom," the new model saw the rulers as operators of the machine of state. In a neat, rationally schematized state, professional officials could, in the words of Hegel, "carry out state functions not on account of their particular wills, but [from] the unity of the state."[14] Since only those operating the machine understood how all the components worked and the needs of the whole edifice, the decisions of statesmen became by definition the embodiment of reason and rationality, for how could a mere valve judge its proper function?

Statesmen in eighteenth-century Poland-Lithuania confronted genuine material and economic crises in the cities, in part resulting from broader structural factors over which the country had limited control. Poverty, dilapidated infrastructure, nonexistent sanitation, and stagnation characterized all small towns, and many burghers sincerely hoped for assistance from the central government. The succession of solutions attempted after 1764 never came close to realizing the ambitions of reformers, however, even after the triumph of the unitary state in the nineteenth century. True, the former Commonwealth was a peripheral, underdeveloped territory, but the failures of enlightened centralism in the region rest more squarely on problems inherent to the idea itself. Claiming a monopoly on rationality and reason, enlightened reformers fell victim to their own unempirical assumptions and irrational prejudices. Most glaringly, every political actor from Stanisław August Poniatowski to Nikolai Rimskii-Korsakov approached the question of urban reform with an abstract, idealized conception of what a city should be and what burghers should do. Cities, in virtually every vision, should contain sober, economically productive, property-owning Christian burghers, whose professional magistracy would fulfill the plans of higher authorities. In this schematization, the defining features of cities in the Commonwealth—the prominence of Jews in trade, the reliance on agriculture as a means of making a living, the preponderance of the alcohol business, the rule of nonprofessional magistrates, the multiplicity of jurisdictions, and the prominence of private towns—appeared as aberrations in need of correction. In fact, though, each of these so-called problems fulfilled vital functions that could not easily be replicated.

From the 1760s forward, every regime viewed the solution to bridging the gap between the reality of urban life in the Commonwealth and the idealized city of the imagination in much the same way. A hierarchy of professional officials appointed from above would replace self-serving city oligarchs and introduce rational budgeting procedures; the state would allocate money for urban improvement to prevent abuse and misappropriation; laws would restrict alcohol production and the ostensibly parasitical role of Jews in the economy, the absence of which would stimulate industry and commerce; a single law and a single scheme of property rights would replace the jurisdictions and feudal relationships of the old regime to create a more orderly, simple environment conducive to entrepreneurship and development. Each of these abstracted plans failed because of the realities on the ground. The much vaunted bureaucratic hierarchy, for example, had to be built of the same human material as the old magistracy oligarchies, often employing the same people. The municipal roster of Lublin in the Congress Kingdom's constitutional period, for example, featured a litany of faces familiar since the Commonwealth. Benjamin Finke, mayor from 1809 to 1817, had served as mayor under Austrian rule, a commissioner on the Civil-Military Commission, and a city councilor in the pre-partition magistracy. Similar stories could be told about every member of Lublin's magistracy, as well as the people serving in other cities such as Zamość.[15] Conversely, the Russian Empire's requirements for municipal service disqualified all competent locals, necessitating a continual meddling in local elections or the acceptance of unqualified magistrates. In neither case did these local elites become the compliant vessels of the state's will, and higher-placed administrators were left continually seeking explanations and culprits to explain away abuse and incompetence. Austrian authorities blamed the electoral principle for returning unqualified elites, the KRSW in the Congress Kingdom placed its hope on ever-increasing restrictions and penalties for local officials, while Russian governors gradually became convinced that the fault lay in the ethnic composition of the human material and lobbied for greater internal colonization.

Enlightened centralism produced uneven results because of the one-size-fits-all mentality of legislators, who set uniform targets for administrative and policing costs regardless of need or condition. The provincial capitals, where representatives of central power lived, could afford these expenditures, since high-placed authorities took care that these centers received priority for investment decisions, while townspeople in the capitals profited from their role as service providers to state bureaucrats, much as private towns had enriched themselves by provisioning the lord's court. Lublin prospered most out of all of the Congress Kingdom's southeastern centers, receiving the lion's share of improvement and reconstruction funding for the region. Much more dramatic was the case of Zhitomir, described by the Civil-Military Commission in 1791 as "a collection of huts with residents who barely know they are burghers," which became one of southwestern Russia's major towns as a result of its designation as the capital of Volhynia guberniia.[16] Rulers in capital cities located funds and surmounted bureaucratic obstacles to finance road and bridge construction, building repair, and eventually, sanitary infrastructure, but the results did not lead to an economic miracle or a noticeable improvement in either personal hygiene or entrepreneurship.

The minimal personnel requirements established by the state proved too much for other cities, draining money away from infrastructure and investment in the small towns. Faced with mandatory expenses for municipal salaries and centrally limited revenue streams, small towns essentially had to beg for money from the state to support improvement projects. In those places where the state had neither the ability nor inclination to find additional revenues—and locals had no say in the matter—police regulations served as the only tool for introducing good order. The Good Order Commissions, the Austrian authorities, the provincial commissions, and even private town owners like Andrzej Zamoyski, apparently believed that precise rules and policies could engineer good order on the cheap. Without the means to encourage local compliance, though, the state's only tool for social engineering became the stick, applied irregularly and inconsistently in accordance with the disposition of any given official. The stream of regulations emanating from each regime's chancellery failed to improve behaviors until administrators located funds for building sewer canals, water pipes, and the infrastructure of good order. In the meantime, the periodic reissuing of rules over a hundred-year period against a backdrop of filth and disrepair only signaled the failure of each new authority to alter behaviors. The impulse to sanitize and beautify the city was itself commendable, but magistracy oligarchs and private town owners had themselves sponsored good order regulations and funded sanitary infrastructure in more prosperous times without any external prodding.

While clean streets and fireproof buildings seem unquestionable goods, each regime also approached the problem of city improvement with abstract assumptions about the proper ethnic composition of cities, and these ideas rarely coincided with the actual nature of cities in the former Commonwealth. For example, Polish officials and private town owners considered "good order" to include residential separation between Jews and Christians, in which the former were confined to extramural suburbs or side streets. Andrzej Zamoyski and Karol Stanisław Radziwiłł, both of whom depended extensively on Jewish intermediaries for revenue, pursued similar policies. Although anti-Jewish prejudices and restrictions existed from the earliest period of Jewish settlement in the region, the bird's-eye view of Enlightenment thinking combined popular biases with pseudo-economic explanations condemning Jewish communities as a whole to produce policies that systematically targeted Jewish livelihoods. At the same time, the obvious dependence of cities and states on Jewish services, including alcohol production, limited legislative possibilities, which from the assimilationist perspective of many enlighteners resulted in the worst of both worlds. Restrictions divided Jews from Christian society, encouraging communal solidarity and allegedly reactionary trends such as Hasidism, but the economic dominance of Jews in the small towns and in the alcohol trade endured.[17] Ironically, the unenlightened, more particularistic kings of the seventeenth century had appreciated the crucial role of Jews in the Commonwealth's economy much better than Stanisław August's advisors or successors.

Similarly, efforts to curtail the alcohol trade as a means of reviving commerce and productivity achieved neither goal. No one seems to have considered why this industry had become so dominant, and officials vastly underestimated the attachment of urban residents to their propinacja privilege. Taxing alcohol at the local level either as a monopoly or as an individual excise did provide a windfall for municipal improvement projects, which continued to buttress urban finances from 1776 through the 1860s, but the dominant position of this revenue in all city budgets from the whole period only confirmed the lack of alternative enterprises. What rational burgher would abandon a stable and lucrative trade in order to produce goods for which demand was weak and capricious? Government-enforced monopolies in Russia and Congress Poland, as in the private cities, reduced the incomes but not the number of alcohol producers. Leaseholders subcontracted production and distribution to a network of private contractors, and no one seems to have lacked willing suppliers. Only in the more industrialized western stretches of the Congress Kingdom, where an economic revival had begun under the Commonwealth, did opportunities for trade with Prussia and Austria displace alcohol as the primary industrial product. For the remainder, no viable alternative to alcohol production existed, because of weak demand for other products, abundant grain, and the state's own financial requirements. Despite regulations and reforms, the overall trade remained largely unchanged until the Great Reforms temporarily abolished alcohol monopolies in favor of individual excise taxes, a concession to the realities of the region.[18]

The most unfortunate outcome from the conflict between reality and the vision of would-be reformers concerns the case of private towns. Private towns violated every assumption that enlightened officials cherished about the proper relationship between state and society. While the eighteenth-century owners had possessed a share of the state's sovereignty, they had divided their property and political rights with the town residents. Burghers and Christians conducted urban business in the name of the lord but paid taxes to the king on property granted by the owner. In centralized states, though, private property served as the primary basis of the social contract between the government and the elite, particularly in areas governed by the Napoleonic Code. Legislators had to accept, if begrudgingly, a nobleman's right to collect tolls, fees, and labor dues from urban residents, but no ruler could tolerate an autonomous source of privilege and political power. Trapped in the liberal assumptions of the Napoleonic Code or the social contract of the Russian Empire, the state could not conceive, as later Soviet politicians easily could, of simply confiscating the private property of nobles without cause. Instead, policies in the Congress Kingdom, Russia, and Austria systematically deprived owners of "the power to do good," in Theodore von Faber's phrase, permitting only their rent-seeking prerogatives. The paternalistic impulses of Dominik Radziwiłł and Stanisław Zamoyski had to yield to a profit-seeking motive, to the "cold, calculating selfishness" that J. Toulmin Smith claims was the ultimate aim of the centralized state.[19]

Private towns thus lost their attractiveness to potential settlers and owners, who could neither lure new residents with generous promises nor impose additional burdens to compensate for the shortfall. Centralization also undermined the prestige and pageantry of private town ownership, particularly where the state came into conflict with the owners over urban space. As power accrued to the provincial capitals and St. Petersburg, nobles abandoned their residential capitals in favor of the centers of power or their still autonomous country estates. The Niasvizh of 1784, which welcomed King Stanisław August with a multiday festival, a specially staged play, and a legendary feast, passed into memory. In the face of flatlining revenue, increased state oversight, and difficulties from residents, the Radziwiłłs, absentee landlords following Antoni's inheritance, allowed their cities to become a species of peasant village. In reminiscences about his childhood in the Minsk region, Władysław Syrokomla reported that the administration of Ludwig von Wittgenstein had briefly operated out of Niasvizh in the 1840s, but the heir to one part of the Radziwiłł fortune soon moved to Vilnius, closer to the corridors of power in the western provinces. Upon his visit in 1853, Syrokomla wrote of Niasvizh, which had suffered two additional conflagrations in the first half of the nineteenth century: "this small city, famous of old, hardly deserves any notice in its current state." The Christian residents earned their living from farming, while the much larger Jewish population lived from petty trade and leaseholding, a situation reminiscent of many provincial towns. Józef Ignacy Kraszewski, writing in 1840, described Olyka in similarly negative terms as a provincial backwater with few artisans, markets, or economic power. The *Geographical Dictionary of the Polish Kingdom*, assembled between 1880 and 1895, corroborates these descriptions, emphatically contrasting the contemporary poverty and decay with the legendary splendor of these two cities.[20]

Throughout Congress Poland and the Russian Empire, the private town story in the nineteenth century was one of stagnation and decline. In the eighteenth century, almost every other burgher lived in a private town, and the wealthiest private towns overshadowed the palatinate capitals under the king's authority. Six of the ten largest cities treated in this book (and five of the largest cities overall [see chapter 4]) belonged to private owners (see appendix 1), and these towns comprised the largest urban settlements in their region. In the Chełm land of the Ruthenian palatinate, Zamość not Chełm presented the most populous and prosperous city, Mogilev and Dubno were much more important commercial centers than Kam'ianets-Podils'kyi and Lutsk in their respective Podolian and Volhynian palatinates, and Slutsk and Niasvizh attracted much more business than the ruins of Navahrudak. Only Lublin stood above the rest as a major center of trade and commerce, and the nearest competition belonged to the Zamoyskis and the owners of Lubartów, the Sanguszko family. The infrastructure, fortifications, and even education institutions of the largest private towns also surpassed the offerings of most royal cities.

By the end of the nineteenth century, only those private towns purchased by the state—Zamość, Mogilev, and Rzeszów in Austria—remained viable commercial centers. The demographic boom of the nineteenth century caused by decreasing mortality and, later, industrialization brought population growth to every city, but the private towns failed to keep pace. By the end of the nineteenth century, the recently emancipated private towns no longer rivaled the state centers, particularly the provincial capitals. Of the cities surveyed, the private towns grew by 139 percent over the course of the nineteenth century, while the state towns grew by almost 800 percent. In 1897 less than one in five urban residents lived in a former private town. More people resided in Lublin and Zhitomir than in all the private towns of the two districts combined. Long-term structural factors likely played a role in this decline. Nonetheless, one cannot but be struck by the fact that not a single private town managed to retain a position of commercial significance in the nineteenth century, a fact that held true for the Prussian and Austrian partitions as well. The states' policies of political subordination proved the decisive factor in engineering the decline of private cities, which, in the Congress Kingdom at least, officials had assiduously worked to protect. The en masse conversion of most small towns to villages in 1867 signified acknowledgment that the state's efforts to shore up these urban centers had produced the opposite effect.[21]

If the centralized state of the nineteenth century showed a languid appetite for social improvement, administrators proved much more effective in undermining civic activism. Beginning with the Department of Police, state officials consistently disciplined or undermined local efforts to participate in decision-making, whether by "correcting" budget requests, imposing inapplicable rules, or rejecting the advice of citizen commissions. Attempts to make use of local knowledge and experience represented temporary exceptions. At the same time, the simplification of the power structure from a constellation to a hierarchy reduced the possible resources for locals to defend themselves against arbitrary decisions. Enlightened centralism proved especially detrimental to the Jewish community in the Congress Kingdom, which after 1791 lost powerful allies and the ability to evade restrictions, but the municipal government's monopoly on local government hardly benefited the Christian citizens either. Lacking the potential to appeal to starostas or escape to the jurydykas, burghers could only protest misadministration to provincial or national bureaucrats. The willingness of state officials in the Congress Kingdom or Russian Empire to address local concerns reflected only individual dedication to duty or perseverance in the face of bureaucratic inertia.

One concrete manifestation of the loss of political rights can be found in language. At the beginning of the nineteenth century, Christian and Jewish petitioners described themselves as "citizens" (*obywatele*) of their particular city, and state agencies applied the same description. In the late eighteenth century, Russian officials even borrowed this term (*obyvatel'*) for use in legislation on cities in the western provinces, and "citizen" in both its Polish and Russian form remained in use for the first two decades of the nineteenth century. Private town residents, in particular, continued to employ this terminology when corresponding with the state, and Jewish communities, who were second-class citizens in the best-case scenario, never ceased to refer to themselves as "citizens" of their chosen city. By the 1820s, however, both Polish and Russian officials increasingly employed the term "resident" (*mieszkaniec* or *zhitel'*) for internal and external correspondence. Etymologically, the three words convey similar meaning connected with inhabitance, but there is no escaping the long association of the term *obywatel* with Roman citizenship and republican political theory. Magistracy officials, no less than noble republicans, read legal treatises and histories in both Polish and Latin, a fact evidenced by the testaments of burghers such as the long-standing mayor of Niasvizh, Karol Klawzowski. Such people must have appreciated the significance of this reclassification as a downgrade in status—a "resident," after all, is defined only by an ascription to a particular place, not by a collection of rights.[22] When the word "citizen" returned to prominence in the twentieth century, the republican associations had largely disappeared and all that remained was a synonym of "resident," a person with the right to enter and reside within a given space indefinitely. The Soviet Union, after all, had citizens no less than the United States.[23]

Having lost power and resources, provincial and urban officials eventually lapsed into indifference and helplessness. Legalism—once used as a means of defending one's rights through continuous litigation—became an excuse for inaction, which both defended individual bureaucrats against charges of malfeasance from above and served to reinforce the impotence of local residents. The stagnant, ignorant world of petty corruption captured by Gogol in *The Government Inspector* owed its kernel of truth to the transfer of power, ambition, and talent to the capitals as a result of centralization. Those who remained in small stagnant cities often did so from incapacity or the inability to advance; the provincial cities, once the center of the world, became "provincial." Not coincidentally, the population of Jews, who could not leave the Pale or pursue government careers, increased as a proportion of the small town population, bequeathing the myth of the sleepy insular shtetl, almost completely devoid of gentile presence.[24]

It may be true, as Stefan Rohdewald has shown in the case of Polotsk, that the nineteenth century saw new community activism under the rubric of civil society, meaning the proliferation of social clubs, religious fraternities, and professional associations with agendas unthreatening to the central power. As in Russia, the intellectual interest in *kraevedenie* (the study of local knowledge and history) may also have offered an antidote to provincialism, but neither of these tendencies returned local control over budgets, police, and justice.[25] Instead, the void left by the destruction of civic identification and local patriotism was increasingly occupied by nationalist discourse, which gradually divided the former Polish-Lithuanian Commonwealth into hostile Polish, Lithuanian, Ukrainian, and Belarusian pieces, none of which had any room for the Jewish population. As Eugene Weber demonstrated a generation ago, nationalism and centralism fed into one another, conspiring to eradicate local attachments and generalize the bird's-eye view of the enlightened centralists onto the whole population. Writers such as Łapicki could now demand that the state intervene in the functioning of peasant self-government, precisely because those peasants were now part of his people and their successes and failures reflected on his personal national identity. Less "enlightened" nationalists could also appropriate the bird's-eye view inherited from the decay of local citizenship in their quest to organize and mobilize a future homogenous society.[26]

Perhaps I am simply citing well-known features in the inevitable process of modernization. After all, similar stories could be told about each corner of Europe. Every country, after all, did ultimately abolish serfdom and private town ownership, and the state model of Europe now exists across the world, with the differences only concerning the date of adoption.[27] The enlightened centralizers in the former Polish-Lithuanian Commonwealth borrowed their ideas, plans, and assumptions from states that subsequently achieved political hegemony over the entire globe. The fact that those subscribing to a particular vision presided over powerful and militarily successful states, though, does not mean that their particular vision was responsible for these achievements. In this book I have attempted to demonstrate a broad disconnect between Enlightenment assumptions and the results of particular polices. I contend that scholars are only recently coming to appreciate this disconnect because of the dominance of the progressive narrative of history, which the heirs of enlightened centralism successfully alchemized from propaganda into "common sense." The shortcomings of enlightened centralism may only hold true for the peripheral, perpetually backward East, but I propose that similar outcomes might appear if one examines all of European history without associating the state with progress or with modernity. The case of enlightened centralism in Poland-Lithuania, at the very least, suggests that such assumptions lack universal applicability and may indeed mask the real reasons for the success of European states.

If one casts aside assumptions about progress and modernity, then the story of city citizens and citizenship in the Polish-Lithuanian Commonwealth between 1764 and 1867 becomes a tale of antiprogress, a decline in political possibilities and self-government with little compensation or improvement. After 1809, having tamed and subordinated the particularisms and complex jurisdictions that provided space for civic activism in royal cities, centralization moved to eliminate the political and economic benefits of private towns for both residents and owners. Manifestations of a civic character, although appearing periodically in the first decades of the nineteenth century, gradually declined. I realize that this claim confronts the philosophical problem of "absence of evidence," but the fact that evidence of the old civic republican mentality can be found only in the smallest private towns most remote from the state's presence does suggest an inverse relationship between centralization and citizenship. The conflict between citizens and their owners showed a faint echo of citizens exploiting the multiplication of authorities that had once existed in the Commonweatlh. The emancipation of private towns ended this conflict only by completing the subordination of city residents to the state, thus removing the opportunity of citizens to play the state authorities and the owners against one another. Indeed, if we approach the issue of emancipation without any expectations about the progressive direction of historical change, then we may conclude that the abolition of private towns represented the final act in the century-long transition of town residents from citizens to subjects.

Appendix 1
Principal Towns Discussed in This Book, Ranked by Their Size in the Late Eighteenth Century

Town	1772 Status	Location 1772	Location Today	Pop. ca. 1780	Pop. ca. 1820	Pop. ca. 1880	Pop. in 1897	Rank in 1897
1. Lublin	Royal	Lublin palatinate	Poland	8,550	10,603	29,771	50,152	2 (–1)
2. Mohyłów	Private	Podolia	Ukraine	6,400	3,222	20,000	22,093	4 (–2)
3. Dubno	Private	Volhynia	Ukraine	6,200	5,603	12,000	13,785	9 (–6)
4. Słuck	Private	Nowogródek palatinate	Belarus	5,300	3,672	20,000	14,180	8 (–4)
5. Kamieniec-Podolski	Royal	Podolia	Ukraine	5,100	1,723	19,157	34,483	3 (+2)
6. Zamość	Private	Galicia (formerly Chełm land)	Poland	4,000	4,491	7,620	12,400	11 (–5)
7. Kraśnik	Private	Lublin palatinate	Poland	3,781	2,733	4,621	8,028	14 (–7)
8. Zasław	Private	Volhynia	Ukraine	3,376	4,608	10,229	12,688	10 (–2)
9. Krzemieniec	Royal	Volhynia	Ukraine	3,300	3,915	12,617	17,618	7 (+2)

10. Łuck	Royal	Volhynia	Ukraine	3,200	2,650	11,000	18,525	6 (+4)
11. Ołyka	Private	Volhynia	Ukraine	3,200	n/a	1,073	4,210	17 (–6)
12. Nieśwież	Private	Nowogródek palatinate	Belarus	2,900	n/a	8,177	8,446	13 (–1)
13. Włodzimierz	Royal	Volhynia	Ukraine	2,800	2,510	8,336	9,695	12 (+1)
14. Urzędów	Royal	Lublin palatinate	Poland	1,704	1,049	2,596	<2,000	21 (–7)
15. Żytomierz	Royal	Kijów palatinate	Ukraine	1,700	6,472	54,935	64,452	1 (+14)
16. Lubartów	Private	Lublin palatinate	Poland	1,625	3,011	4,869	5,249	16 (0)
17. Chełm	Royal	Chełm land	Poland	1,608	2,358	7,152	19,236	5 (+12)
18. Nowogródek	Royal	Nowogródek palatinate	Belarus	n/a	1,571	8,000	7,770	15 (+3)
19. Bełżyce	Private	Lublin palatinate	Poland	1,380	1,498	2,496	3,182	19 (0)
20. Kazimierz Dolny	Royal	Lublin palatinate	Poland	1,093	2,157	3,297	3,402	18 (+2)
21. Bychawa	Private	Lublin palatinate	Poland	606	805	1,595	2,034	20 (+1)
22. Firlej	Private	Lublin palatinate	Poland	425	615	1,092	<2,000	22 (0)

Sources: AGAD, AR XXV.3839a, 1–55; AGAD, AR XXV.2690, part 2, 1–20; AGAD, KRSW 205, 21; BC, rrs. 1093, 589–627; Kleczyński, "Spis ludności"; TsDIAK, f. KMF 11, o. 1, s. 94, 19, 131–32; TsDIAK, f. KMF 11, o. 1, s. 91, 81–84; SGKP, vols. 1–15; Teller, Money, Power, and Influence, 30–35; Pervaia vseobshchaia perepis' naselenii Rossiiskoi Imperii 1897 g., vols. 2, 11.

Appendix 2
A Note on Demographic Methodology

POPULATION FIGURES IN THE Commonwealth are notoriously difficult to determine since raw population data with no indication of capacity to pay taxes had absolutely no utility for government agents or private town owners. The chief unit of taxation in the eighteenth century was the hearth (*dym*), a term that seems to have varied locally in meaning. For some surveyors, a "hearth" referred to a physical chimney, while others defined the term as a household. The situation becomes more complex when considering private towns, where owners employed their own idiosyncratic measures. On the Radziwiłł properties, surveyors used a measure of urban space called a *plac*, which recorded the size of the dwelling (the Radziwiłł family palace in Niasvizh, for example, constituted 4.5 *place*). In addition, urban farmers were taxed according to rural units of land called *włoky*, so records list information about two different land types without any clear reference to the number of people. Since Jews were subject to a capitation tax, the Radziwiłłs also recorded the names of Jewish householders, but such limited information offers little value for capturing the full demographic picture. A full population survey of the Kraków diocese in 1787, including the Lublin palatinate, offers an important point of comparison, though historians doubt its accuracy.[1] As a result, one must make gross estimations to arrive at eighteenth-century population counts. Rostworowski uses the general multiplier of 6.5 people per hearth, but I think this fails to account for differences among cities, small towns, and villages. I equate one hearth to 5.5 people, except in towns under 300 hearths, which by the Commonwealth's own definition were "agricultural towns." In this latter case, I employ 6.5 as a multiplier to reflect the rural character of the settlement. Nineteenth-century governments more assiduously recorded population statistics, though one must always consider the figures as tenuous at best.

1. Cezary Kuklo, *Demografia Rzeczypospolitej przedrozbiorowej*, 60–89; Rostworowski, "Miasta i mieszczanie," 141–42.

Notes

INTRODUCTION: PROGRESS OR BACKWARDNESS?

1. "List Władysława Gomułki z 27 III 1971 do członków KC PZPR," in *Gomułka i inni: Dokumenty z archiwum KC, 1948–1982*, 225 (first quotation), 226–27; see also 196–237. Translations here and elsewhere are my own unless noted otherwise.
2. John Lind, *Letters Concerning the Present State of Poland, Together with an Appendix Containing the Manifestos of the Courts of Vienna, Petersburgh, and Berlin, and Other Authentic Papers*, 54, 73; Montesquieu, *De L'Esprit des lois*, 248; *Documents of Catherine the Great: The Correspondence with Voltaire and the Instruction of 1767*, 118–19, 162–63. On the divergent development of the Commonwealth and other European states, see Władysław Konopczyński, *Geneza i ustanowienia Rady Nieustającej*, 39–55; Richard Butterwick, *Poland's Last King and English Culture: Stanisław August Poniatowski, 1732–1798*, 1–40.
3. See Hans-Jürgen Bömelburg, "Inklusion und Exklusion nach der Ersten Teilung Polen-Litauens: Die österreichische, preussiche und russländlische Regierungspraxis in Galizien, Westpreussen und den weissrussi-

schen Gouvernements Polack und Mahilëŭ im Vergleich (1772–1806/07)," 174–77; Iryna Vushko, *The Politics of Cultural Retreat: Imperial Bureaucracy in Austrian Galicia, 1772–1867*, 29–44. See also Larry Wolff, *Inventing Eastern Europe: The Map of Civilization on the Mind of the Enlightenment*, 236–79.

4. Alexander Hamilton and James Madison invoked the specter of Poland's partition as one of the calamities that could result if the United States retained its decentralized and weak Articles of Confederation. Alexander Hamilton, John Jay, and James Madison, *The Federalist Papers*, 96, 187.
5. Frank Thackeray, *Antecedents of Revolution: Alexander I and the Polish Kingdom, 1815–1825*, 54–60. For a nineteenth-century Russian view of Poland, see Fedor Smitt, *Istoriia pol'skago vozstaniia i voiny 1830 i 1831 godov*, 1:13–38. The current Russian textbook curriculum calls for textbooks to emphasis the "positive significance of integration into the Russian Empire for the various peoples, including: security from external enemies, the end of internal disorders and strife, [and] economic development." See "Obshchestvennoe obsuzhdenie proekta istoriko-kul'turnogo standarta," online at http://минобрнауки.рф/документы/3483/.
6. Marian Henryk Serejski, *Europa a rozbiory Polski: Studium historiograficzne*, 230. For an example of the Kraków School, see Michał Bobrzyński, *Dzieje Polski w zarysie*, 43–59. See also Joseph Rothschild, *East Central Europe between the Two World Wars*, 27–72.
7. On Jarosław Kaczyński's views, see "L. Kaczyński: Decentralizacja osłabia państwo," *Wprost*, May 27, 2008, online at http://www.wprost.pl/ar/130537/L-Kaczynski-decentralizacja-oslabia-panstwo/; Andrzej Ajnenkiel, "The Influence of the Constitution of 3 May on Constitutional Life of the Second Republic (1919–1939): Reality and Myth," 519–26. For the current constitution of the Republic of Poland, see *Dziennik Ustaw Rzeczypospolitej polskiej* 78 (1997): 483. See also Jennifer A. Yoder, "Decentralization and Regionalism after Communism: Administrative and Territorial Reform in Poland and the Czech Republic."
8. Claude Rulhière, *Histoire de l'anarchie de Pologne et du démembrement de cette république*, 1:127.
9. See, for example, H. M. Scott, "Reform in the Habsburg Monarchy, 1740–90"; Éva H. Balázs, *Hungary and the Habsburgs 1765–1800: An Experiment in Enlightened Absolutism*, 7–42; Helmut Reinalter, "Der Josephinismus als Variante des Aufgeklärten Absolutismus und seine Reform Komplexe."

10. James B. Collins, "Le pouvoir municipal et l'écroulement de l'Ancien Régime: question sociale ou question politique?"

11. Jan de Vries, *The Industrious Revolution: Consumer Behavior and the Household Economy, 1650 to the Present*, 2–15, 52–71. On Cameralism, see Andre Wakefield, *The Disordered Police State: German Cameralism as Science and Practice*, 6–23; Marc Raeff, *The Well-Ordered Police State: Social and Institutional Change through Law in the Germanies and Russia, 1600–1800*; Mack Walker, *German Home Towns: Community, State, and General Estate, 1648–1871*, 145–84; Keith Tribe, "Cameralism and the Science of Government."

12. Adam Smith, *An Inquiry into the Nature and Causes of the Wealth of Nations*, 422–30; G. W. F. Hegel, *Outlines of the Philosophy of Right*, 265.

13. Max Weber, *Economy and Society: An Outline of Interpretive Sociology*, 971–74, 1351–62; Gerald Frug, "The City as a Legal Concept," 1092–100; Otto von Gierke, *Community in Historical Perspective: A Translation of Selections from Das deutsche Genossenschaftrecht (The German Law of Fellowship)*, 108–21. See also Anthony Black, *Guild and State: European Political Thought from the Twelfth Century to the Present*, xvi–xxi, 153–61.

14. Raeff, *Well-Ordered Police State*. See also H. M. Scott, "Reform in the Habsburg Monarchy"; T. C. W. Blanning, *Joseph II and Enlightened Despotism*, 73–82.

15. C. B. A. Behrens, *Society, Government and the Enlightenment: The Experiences of Eighteenth-Century France and Prussia*, 68–88; Brian M. Downing, *The Military Revolution and Political Change: Origins of Democracy and Autocracy in Early Modern Europe*, 86–145; Christopher Clark, *Iron Kingdom: The Rise and Downfall of Prussia, 1600–1947*, 247–83.

16. S. R. Epstein, *Freedom and Growth: The Rise of States and Markets in Europe, 1300–1750*, 8–19, 36, 159–74; Martin van Creveld, *The Rise and Decline of the State*, 59–125; Robert von Friedeburg, *Luther's Legacy: The Thirty Years War and the Modern Notion of "State" in the Empire, 1530s to 1790s*, 13–28, 385–86.

17. James B. Collins, *Classes, Estates, and Order in Early Modern Brittany*, 187–229; J. Russell Major, *Representative Government in Early Modern France*, 514–664; Karin Friedrich, *The Other Prussia: Royal Prussia, Poland, and Liberty, 1569–1772*, 150–59; Frug, "The City as a Legal Concept," 1092–100; Gierke, *Community in Historical Perspective*, 108–21.

18. See M. S. Anderson, "The Italian Reformers"; Claude Nières, *Les Villes de Bretagne au XVIIIe siècle*, 418–39, 507–24; Pavel Bělina, *Česká města v 18.*

století a osvícenské reformy, 7–20; Jaroslav Miller, *Urban Societies in East-Central Europe, 1500–1700*, 156–65; Irmgard Plattner, "Josephinismus und Bürokratie."

19. François Guizot, *Histoire de la Civilisation en Europe depuis la chute de l'empire romain jusqu'a la révolution français*, 310–11.
20. Serejski, Europa a rozbiory Polski, 230–38.
21. Scott, "Reform in the Habsburg Monarchy," 153; Friedeburg, *Luther's Legacy*, 13–28.
22. Quentin Skinner, *Liberty before Liberalism*, 17–60; J. G. A. Pocock, *The Machiavellian Moment: Florentine Political Thought and the Atlantic Republican Tradition*, 54–76.
23. Isaiah Berlin, "Two Concepts of Liberty," in *The Proper Study of Mankind: An Anthology of Essays*, 191–242. See also Peter Blickle, *From the Communal Reformation to the Revolution of the Common Man*, 1–13, 178–88. On the constitutional theory of republicanism, see Anna Grześkowiak-Krwawicz, *Queen Liberty: The Concept of Freedom in the Polish-Lithuanian Commonwealth*. See also Hannah Arendt, *The Human Condition*, 175–241; Maurizio Viroli, *From Politics to Reason of State: The Acquisition and Transformation of the Language of Politics*, 11–125.
24. Reinhart Koselleck, *Critique and Crisis: Enlightenment and the Pathogenesis of Modern Society*, 98–136.
25. Pierre Bourdieu, *The Logic of Practice*. For another example of conflicts between the "rational" center and "irrational" locals, see David Warren Sabean, *Power in the Blood: Popular Culture and Village Discourse in Early Modern Germany*, 174–98.
26. Arendt, *The Human Condition*, 179–221.
27. Heinz Schilling, *Religion, Political Culture and the Emergence of Early Modern Society: Essays in German and Dutch History*, 3–56; Andrzej S. Kamiński, *Historia Rzeczypospolitej wielu narodów 1505–1795*, 8–22.
28. See Emmanuel Rostworowski, "Miasta i mieszczanie w ustroju Trzeciego Maja."
29. See Butterwick, *Poland's Last King*, 147–70; Józef Andrzej Gierowski, *The Polish-Lithuanian Commonwealth in the XVIIIth Century: From Anarchy to Well-Organized State*, 247–61; Emanuel Rostworowski, *Ostatni król Rzeczypospolitej: Geneza i upadek Konstytucji 3 maja*, 26–50.
30. For the constitution and its related laws, see *Volumina legum: Przedruk zbioru praw staraniem XX. pijarów w Warszawie od roku 1732 do roku 1793*

wydanego (hereafter referred to as *VL*), 9:215–19, 277–82. See also Krystyna Zienkowska, "Reforms relating to the Third Estate"; Taduesz Korzon, *Wewnętrzne dzieje Polski za Stanisława Augusta (1764–1794)*, 2:282–405.

31. On the Duchy and Congress Kingdom, see John Stanley, "The Adaptation of the Napoleonic Political Structure in the Duchy of Warsaw (1807–1813)"; Andrzej Nieuważny, "The Polish Kingdom (1815–1830): Continuity or Change?"

32. Kamiński, *Historia Rzeczypospolitej*, 8–22; Berlin, "Two Concepts of Liberty," in *The Proper Study of Mankind*, 191–242. See also Skinner, *Liberty before Liberalism*.

33. Walker, *German Home Towns*, 185–215; Nières, *Les Villes de Bretagne*, 431–39; Arthur Hertzberg, *The French Enlightenment and the Jews*, 62–80; George Munro, "The Charter to the Towns Reconsidered: The St. Petersburg Connection."

34. Wakefield, *Disordered Police State*, 6–23, 137–42; Vushko, *Politics of Cultural Retreat*; Hans-Jürgen Bömelburg, *Zwischen Polnischer Ständegesellschaft und Preussischem Obrigkeitsstaat: Von Königlichen Preußen zu Westpreußen (1756–1806)*, 399–420; Bömelburg, "Inklusion und Exklusion," 171–200; Glenn Dynner, *Yankel's Tavern: Jews, Liquor, and Life in the Kingdom of Poland*, 4–10, 174.

35. Stanisław Staszic, "Przestrogi dla Polski (1790)," in *Wybór pism*, 82–83.

36. Hugo Kołłątaj, *Uwagi nad teraźnieyszym położeniem tey części ziemi polskiey*, którą od pokoiu tylżyckiego zaczęto zwać Xięstwem Warszawskim, 200.

37. Kajetan Koźmian, *Pamiętniki*, 3:46–47.

38. Joachim Lelewel, "Uwagi nad dziejami Polski i ludu je"; Stanisław Kutrzeba, *Historya ustroju polski w zarysie*, vol. 1; Konopczyński, *Geneza i ustanowienia*, 19–44.

39. Tadeusz Korzon, *Odrodzenie w upadku: Wybór pism historycznych*, 12–26, 298–326; Rostworowski, *Ostatni król Rzeczypospolitej*, 291–318; Gierowski, *Polish-Lithuanian Commonwealth*, 248–61.

40. Downing, *The Military Revolution*, 130–45; Jerzy Lukowski, *Disorderly Liberty: The Political Culture of the Polish-Lithuanian Commonwealth in the Eighteenth Century*. See also Butterwick, *Poland's Last King*, 236–313; Jerzy Lukowski, *Liberty's Folly: The Polish-Lithuanian Commonwealth in the Eighteenth Century, 1697–1795*.

41. Historians who make use of the term "progressive" include Arthur

Eisenbach, *The Emancipation of the Jews in Poland, 1780–1870*, 13–15, 23–24; Aleksander Czaja, *Między tronem, buławą a dworem petersburskim: Z dziejów Rady Nieustającej, 1786–1789*, 359–66. Paweł Cichoń makes the case that centralization was "modern" without using the term. See Paweł Cichoń, *Rozwój myśli administracyjnej w Księstwie Warszawskim, 1807–1815*, 142–48.

42. On the Confederacy and its detractors, see Andrzej Walicki, *The Enlightenment and the Birth of Modern Nationhood: Polish Political Thought from Noble Republicanism to Tadeusz Kościuszko*, 8–26; Kamiński, Historia Rzeczypospolitej, 211–15. For a more standard treatment, see Jerzy Lukowski, *The Partitions of Poland, 1772, 1793, 1795*, 44–51.

43. Andrzej Zahorski, *Centralne instytucje policyjne w Polsce w dobie rozbiorów*, 26–29, 50–58; Czaja, *Między tronem*, 171–211.

44. Korzon, *Wewnętrzne dzieje Polski*, 2:380–405; Krystyna Zienkowska, *Sławetni i urodzeni: Ruch polityczny mieszczaństwa w dobie Sejmu Czteroletniego*, 186–267; Krystyna Zienkowska, "Reforms relating to the Third Estate"; Józef Kermisz, *Lublin i lubelskie w ostatnich latach Rzeczypospolitej (1788–1794). Vol. I: W czasie Sejmu Wielkiego i wojny Polsko-Rosyskiej 1792 r. oraz pod rządami Targowo-Grodzieńskimi*, 72.

45. Cichoń, *Rozwój myśli administracyjnej*, 67–162; Marian Kallas, "Koncepcje organizacji nowoczesnej administracji terytorialnej w Księstwie Warszawskim"; Marian Kallas, *Organy administracji terytorialnej w Księstwie Warszawskim; Józef Mazurkiewicz and Władysław Ćwik, "Własność w miastach prywatnych Lubelszczyzny doby Księstwa Warszawskiego i Królestwa Kongresowego (1809–1866)."*

46. Jean-Jacques Rousseau, *The Government of Poland*, 27.

47. See Grześkowiak-Krwawicz, *Queen Liberty*; Lukowski, *Disorderly Liberty*.

48. Butterwick, *Poland's Last King*, 313; Maria Bogucka and Henryk Samsonowicz, *Dzieje miast i mieszczaństwa w Polsce przedrozbiorowej*, 562–73; Jacek Kochanowicz, "The Polish Economy and the Origins of Dependency."

49. Gershon David Hundert, *Jews in Poland-Lithuania in the Eighteenth Century: A Genealogy of Modernity*, 11. See also Daniel Stone, "Jews and the Urban Question in Late Eighteenth Century Poland," 533; Butterwick, *Poland's Last King*, 313.

50. Czaja, *Między tronem*, 171–91; Zienkowska, *Sławetni i urodzeni*, 11–31;

Zahorski, *Centralne instytucje policyjne*, 30–60; Bogna Tyszkiewicz, *Komisja Dobrego Porządku w Poznaniu, 1780–1784*, 9–12, 78–102; Władysław Ćwik, *Miasta królewskie lubelszczyzny w drugiej połowie XVIII wieku*, 50–63; Marian Surdacki, *Urzędów w XVII i XVIII wieku: Miasto—Społeczeństwo—Życie codzienne*, 266–99.

51. Two notable exceptions to this principle focus on the history of the Jews in Poland: Eisenbach, *Emancipation of the Jews*; Marcin Wodziński, "'Wilkiem orać': Polskie projekty kolonizacji rolnej żydów, 1775–1823."

52. See appendix 1 for a list of the twenty-two towns most prominently discussed with their approximate population figures.

53. Paul R. Hanson, *Provincial Politics in the French Revolution: Caen and Limoges, 1789–1794*, 186–246; Stuart Woolf, *Napoleon's Integration of Europe*, 84–137. On the impact of Napoleonic conquests, see Walker, *German Home Towns*, 185–215; Michael Broers, "Centre and Periphery in Napoleonic Italy: The Nature of French Rule in the *départements réunis*, 1800–1814," 55–72; Andreas Fahrmeir, "Centralisation versus Particularism in the 'Third Germany,'" 107–20; Monika Senkowska-Głuck, "Les institutions napoléoniennes dans l'histoire de la nation polonaise."

54. Marcin Wodziński, *Władze Królestwa Polskiego wobec chasydyzmu*, 150–59.

55. Tsentralnyi Derzhavnyi Istorychnyi Arkhiv Ukraini m. Kyiv [TsDIAK], fond (f). 442, opys (o). 1, sprava (s). 1519 (Reports to the Kiev, Volhynia and Podolia General-Governor, 1834), 42.

56. Quoted in Stanisław Smolka, *Polityka Lubeckiego przed powstaniem listopadowem*, 1:185–86.

57. Alexis de Tocqueville, *The Old Regime and the French Revolution*, 209.

58. J. Toulmin Smith, *Local Self-Government and Centralisation: The Characteristics of Each, and its Practical Tendencies, as Affecting Social, Moral, and Political Welfare and Progress, Including Comprehensive Outlines of the English Constitution*, 180–81; see also 27–29, 62–66.

CHAPTER 1: WE BUILT THIS CITY ON MAGDEBURG LAW

1. "Relacja delegatow Kamienca Podolskiego 17 November, 1789–3 January, 1790," in *Materiały do dziejów Sejmu Czteroletniego* (hereafter cited as *MDSC*), 2:229–40.

2. "Stanisław August do Antoniego Dembolego (5 December, 1789)," *MDSC* 2:367. See also William Doyle, *The Oxford History of the French Revolution*, 90–133.
3. "Memoriał miast (pierwsza redakcja)" and "Memoriał miast (druga i trzecia redakcja)," *MDSC*, 2:259–68, 339–57. See also Zienkowska, *Sławetni i urodzeni*, 32–90.
4. William Coxe, *Travels in Poland and Russia*, 110.
5. Tocqueville, *Old Regime*, 101–31; also Guizot, *Histoire de la Civilisation en Europe*, 190–95; Christine Lamarre, *Petites villes et fait urbain en France au XVIIIème siècle: Le cas bourguignon*, 104–9, 403–16.
6. Wawrzyniec Surowiecki, *O upadku przemysłu y miast w Polszcze*, 156–57. This was also the view of Soviet historians; see Juozas Jurginis, "Sud'ba magdeburgskogo prava w litovskikh gorodakh."
7. "Prawa miast polskich do władzy prawodawczej, wykonywającej i sądowniczej," *MDSC*, 2:270.
8. Kamiński, *Historia Rzeczypospolitej*, 8–22; David Frick, *Kith, Kin, and Neighbors: Community and Coexistence in Seventeenth-Century Wilno*, 274–89; Yvonne Kleinmann, "Rechtsinstrumente in einer ethnisch-religiös gemischten Stadtgesellschaft des frühneuzeitlichen Polen. Der Fall Rzeszów."
9. For the term "continuous litigation," see Edward Muir, "Was There Republicanism in the Renaissance Republics? Venice after Agnadello". See also Kamiński, *Historia Rzeczypospolitej*, 8–22.
10. Schilling, *Essays in German and Dutch History*, 3–59.
11. Quentin Skinner, *The Foundations of Modern Political Thought*, 1:3–22; Adam Smith, *Wealth of Nations*, 422–30; Weber, *Economy and Society*, 971–74, 1351–62.
12. J. Michael Hittle, *The Service City: State and Townsmen in Russia, 1600–1800*, 22–28, 40–55; B. N. Mironov, *Sotsial'naia istoriia Rossii perioda imperii (XVIII–nachalo XX v.): Geneza lichnosti, demokraticheskoi sem'i, grazhdanskogo obshchestva i pravovogo gosudarstva*, 1:282–85, 291–93; A. A. Kizevetter, *Istoricheskie ocherki*, 219–22. On the Ottoman city, see Mark Mazower, *Salonica, City of Ghosts: Christians, Muslims and Jews*, 1430–1950.
13. Guicciardini quoted in Karin Tilmans, "Republican Citizenship and Civic Humanism in the Burgundian-Habsburg Netherlands (1477–1566)," 110. See also Niccolò Machiavelli, *The Prince and the Discourses*, 39–41; Xavier

Gil, "Republican Politics in Early Modern Spain: The Castilian and Catalono-Aragonese Traditions."

14. "Prawa miast poliskich," *MDSC*, 2:271. On Althusius, see Black, *Guild and State*, 129–40.

15. Frug, "The City as a Legal Concept," 1093–94; Robert A. Schneider, *Public Life in Toulouse, 1463–1789: From Municipal Republic to Cosmopolitan City*, 59–75; Robert von Friedeburg, "Civic Humanism and Republican Citizenship in Early Modern Germany."

16. Originally, residents in Polish towns directed judicial appeals to the town of Magdeburg as the recognized authority in urban government, but in 1356 Kazimierz established an appellate court for urban residents as a means of integrating cities into the political structure of the kingdom. For the model of Magdeburg Law, see Bartłomej Groicki, *Porządek sądów miejskich prawa majdeburskiego w Koronie Polskiej*, 21–40. See also Juliusz Bardach, *Historia państwa i prawa Polski do połowy XV wieku*, 379–80, 404–22; Bogucka and Samsonowicz, *Dzieje miast*, 46–82.

17. Groicki, Porządek sądów miejskich, 24.

18. Pocock, *Machiavellian Moment*, 466–67. On "gifts" and other perks, see Józef Mazurkiewicz, "Lublin w okresie reform (1764–1795)," 177–78; Jan Riabinin, *Rada miejska lubelska w XVIII wieku*, 7–11, 15–25.

19. Viroli, From Politics to Reason of State, 11–30; Pocock, Machiavellian Moment, 54–79; Schilling, Essays in German and Dutch History, 26–31.

20. The wójt thus became the chief judge of the criminal and small claims court, while the council served as a civil court and heard appeals from the wójt's bench. Bardach, *Historia państwa i prawa Polski*, 404–12; Bogucka and Samsonowicz, *Dzieje miast*, 63–76.

21. Jan Ptaśnik, "Walki o demokratyzację Lwowa od XVI do XVIII wieku," 228–48; Bogucka and Samsonowicz, *Dzieje miast*, 460–62.

22. Bardach, Historia państwa i prawa Polski, 423–29; Harry E. Dembkowski, The Union of Lublin Polish Federalism in the Golden Age, 30–46, 61–67. On Jadwiga as king, see Oscar Halecki, Jadwiga of Anjou and the Rise of East Central Europe, 39–78.

23. See Robert I. Frost, The Oxford History of Poland-Lithuania. Volume I: The Making of the Polish-Lithuanian Union, 1385–1569, 477–94.

24. Bogucka and Samsonowicz, *Dzieje miast*, 455–61; Grześkowiak-Krwawicz, *Queen Liberty*, 14–15.

25. Michał Świniarski, *Wiadomość o pierwiastokowey miast zasadzie w Polszcze*,

ich szczegulnych przywileiach i wolnościach oraz o przyczynach upadku tychże miast, 21–22.

26. "Jan Kaspary do Franciszka Żeleńskiego," *MDSC*, 2:222–24, 379; Friedrich, *The Other Prussia*, 16–47; Bobrzyński, *Dzieje Polski*, 243–44. See also Grześkowiak-Krwawicz, *Queen Liberty*, 12–13.
27. Adam Mędrzecki and Fredryck Barssa, *Zbiór praw, dowodów i uwag dla obiaśnienia zaszczytów stanowi mieyskiemu ex juribus municipalibus służących*, part 1, 6.
28. Bogucka and Samsonowicz, *Dzieje miast*, 516–17; Stanisław Tworek, "Rozkwit miasta. Renesans," 80–88.
29. Lublin, for example, was occupied by Muscovite, Polish, Swedish, and Hungarian forces over the span of a few years, each time suffering exactions, forced payments, and billeting duties. See Maria Stankowa, "Zmierzch znaczenia Lublina. Upadek (1648–1764)."
30. Robert I. Frost, *The Northern Wars: War, State and Society in Northeastern Europe, 1558–1721*, 156–87, 310–27.
31. Józef Andrzej Gierowski, *Między saskim absolutyzmem a złotą wolnością: z dziejów wewnętrznych Rzeczypospolitej w latach 1712–1715*, 32–89; Jerzy Topolski, *Polska w czasach nowożytnych od środkowoeuropejskiej potęgi do utraty niepodległości (1501–1795)*, 503–19, 669–87.
32. On medieval starostas, see Marcin Kromer, *Polska, czyli o położeniu, ludności, obyczyajach, urzędach, i sprawach publicznych Królestwa Polskiego Księgi Dwie*, 117–55; Aleksander Wejnert, *O starostwach w Polsce do końca XVIII wieku z dołączeniem wykazu ich miejscowości*, 5–39.
33. Kromer, *Polska*, 120–35; Medrzecki and Barssa, *Zbiór praw*, part 5, 20–25.
34. Mędrzecki and Barssa, *Zbiór praw*, part 5, 1–25; Wejnert, *O starostwach*, 73–79.
35. Riabinin, *Rada miejska lubelska*, 6–25.
36. Surdacki, *Urzędów*, 209–20; Ćwik, *Miasta królewskie lubelszczyzny*, 78–107. For examples of such confrontations, see Archiwum Główne Akt Dawnych (hereafter cited as AGAD), Tak zwana Metryka Litewska (hereafter ML) VII.79 (Minutes of the Permanent Council [hereafter PC Minutes], 1777), 122–27, 150–55; AGAD, ML VII.78 (PC Minutes, 1777), 425–28.
37. Antony Polonsky, *The Jews in Poland and Russia*, 1:17–110; Anna Michałowska-Mycielska, *The Jewish Community: Authority and Social Control in Poznań and Swarzędz, 1650–1793*, 13–80. For examples of the privileges, see *Jewish*

Privileges in the Polish Commonwealth: Charters of Rights Granted to Jewish Communities in the Sixteenth to Eighteenth Centuries.

38. Majer Bałaban, *Die Judenstadt von Lublin,* 7–13; Polonsky, *The Jews in Poland and Russia,* 70–83.

39. Jürgen Heyde, "Ewolucja zwierzchności królewskiej nad ludnością żydowską w XVI wieku"; Stanisław Grodziski, "The Kraków Voivode's Jurisdiction over Jews: A Study of the Historical Records of the Krakow Voivode's Administration of Justice to Jews"; Frick, *Kith, Kin, and Neighbors,* 6–19, 274–89; Adam Teller, "Przedmowa."

40. Adam Teller, *Money, Power, and Influence in Eighteenth-Century Lithuania: The Jews on the Radziwiłł Estates,* 151–71, 188–99. In this reading, Teller argues against earlier claims that Jews were simply better capitalists. See John Doyle Klier, *Russia Gathers Her Jews: The Origins of the "Jewish Question" in Russia, 1772–1825,* 7–12; Gershon David Hundert, *The Jews in a Polish Private Town: The Case of Opatów in the Eighteenth Century,* 14–68.

41. AGAD, ML VII.78, 253–54, 375–76; AGAD, ML VII.79, 111–21; Polonsky, *Jews in Poland and Russia,* 1:70–83; Hundert, *Jews in Poland-Lithuania,* 21–45; *Jewish Privileges in the Polish Commonwealth,* 119–20, 151–55.

42. Zenon Guldon and Jacek Wijaczka, *Procesy o mordy rytualne w Polsce w XVI–XVIII wieku,* 5–140; Janusz Tazbir, "Anti-Jewish Trials in Old Poland." See also Paweł Maciejko, *The Mixed Multitude: Jakub Frank and the Frankist Movement, 1755–1816,* 92–126.

43. A petition to the central government in 1794 emphasized that "both Christian and Jews" lived in Podzamcze. AGAD, Archiwum Królestwa Polskiego (hereafter AGAD, AKP), 88, no. 18 (Reports to the Council of Ministers, 1794), 101–2.

44. The classic study of jurydykas is Józef Mazurkiewicz, *Jurydyki lubelskie.* On jurydykas as individual houses, see Frick, *Kith, Kin, and Neighbors,* 20–58.

45. On private towns outside of Poland-Lithuania, see Finn-Einar Eliassen, "The Urbanization of the Periphery: Landowners and Small Towns in Early Modern Norway and Northern Europe"; Ian D. Whyte, "The Function and Social Structure of Scottish Burghs of Barony in the Seventeenth and Eighteenth Centuries," 11–24; Balázs Szelényi, "The Dynamics of Urban Development: Towns in Sixteenth and Seventeenth Century Hungary"; Tomasz Opas, "Der Emanzipationsprozess der Privatgrundherrschaftlichen Städte im Königreich Galizien und Londomerein als Forschungsproblem."

46. On the lack of capital outlets in the premodern world, see Kenneth Pomeranz, *The Great Divergence: China, Europe, and the Making of the Modern World Economy*, 167, 193. See also Andrzej Wyrobisz, "Rola miast prywatnych w Polsce w XVI i XVII.wieku."
47. Anzelm Gostomski, *Gospordarstwo*, 100–104.
48. In Ireland, for example, the lord owned each lot of land and leased it out to tenants, making property rights in towns and villages equal. See Lindsay J. Proudfoot, *Urban Patronage and Social Authority: The Management of the Duke of Devonshire's Towns in Ireland, 1764–1891*, 11–117. In Poland-Lithuania, according to Tomasz Opas, burghers in private towns had the right of *dominus utile* over their property, and the town owner was considered to be *dominus direcutus*, much like the king in relation to royal towns. Tomasz Opas, "Wolność osobista mieszczan miast szlacheckich województwa lubelskiego w drugiej połowie XVII i w XVIII wieku"; Tomasz Opas, "Własność w miastach szlacheckich województwa lubelskiego w XVIII wieku."
49. Tomasz Opas, "Miasta prywatne a Rzeczpospolita."
50. Hundert, *Jews in a Polish Private Town*, 14–45; Kleinmann, "Rechtsinstrumente," 183–93; Stefan Gąsiorowski, *Chrześcianie i żydzi w Żółkwi w XVII i XVIII wieku*, 158–64; Maurycy Horn, "The Chronology and Distribution of Jewish Craft Guilds in Old Poland, 1613–1795"; Tadeusz Mencel, *Galicja Zachodnia 1795–1809: Studium z dziejów ziem polskich zaboru austriackiego po III rozbiorze*, 177–79.
51. Teller, *Money, Power, and Influence*, 74–171; Moshe Rosman, *The Lord's Jews: Magnate-Jewish Relations in the Polish-Lithuanian Commonwealth in the Eighteenth Century*, 62, 110–140. See also Dynner, *Yankel's Tavern*, 16–46.
52. Malby quoted in Hertzberg, *French Enlightenment and the Jews*, 76. See also Moshe Rosman, *Founder of Hasidism: A Quest for the Historical Ba'al Shem Tov*, 63–77; Guldon and Wijaczka, *Procesy*, 54–57.
53. On good order regulations in Lublin, see Archiwum Państwowe w Lublinie (hereafter APL), Akta Luźne Miasta Lublina 55 (1771–1791), 4–5. For private towns, see Bazyli Rudomicz, *Efemeros czyli diariusz prywatny pisany w Zamościu w latach 1656–1672*, 2:172–222; Stankowa, "Zmierzch znaczenia Lublina," 137–48.
54. Gąsiorowski, *Chrześcianie i żydzi*, 76–89, 172–79; Frick, *Kith, Kin, and Neighbors*, 274–89; Teller, "Przedmowa," 23–24.

55. See Irena Grochowska, *Stanisław Antoni Szczuka—Jego działność w ziemi wiskiej, 1682–1710*, 56–94; Gąsiorowski, *Chrześcianie i żydzi*, 179–95; Kleinmann, "Rechtsinstrumente," 176–87.
56. Lukowski, *Liberty's Folly*, 68–243; Stankowa, "Zmierzch znaczenia Lublina," 128–37; Bogucka and Samsonowicz, *Dzieje miast*, 455–56, 461–68, 516–17; Wejnert, *O starostwach*, 45–46.
57. For a thirteenth-century critique of urban autonomy, see Philippe de Rémi, sire de Beaumanoir, *Coutumes de Beauvaisis*, 2:266–69.
58. Schilling, *Essays in German and Dutch History*, 36–49; Skinner, *Foundations of Modern Political Thought*, 2:284–301. See also Friedeburg, *Luther's Legacy*, 177–94, 284–300.
59. Jean Domat, *The Civil Law in its Natural Order Together with the Public Law*, 473, 483; also 349–58, 478–88. Black, *Guild and State*, 129–40.
60. Collins, *Classes, Estates, and Order*, 187–229; Lamarre, *Petites villes*, 104–9.
61. Thomas Hobbes, *Leviathan*, 218. Frug also makes use of this quotation. Frug, "The City as a Legal Concept," 1092.
62. Johann von Justi quoted in Walker, *German Home Towns*, 166. On "police" in its eighteenth-century meaning, see Nicolas de la Mare, *Traité de la Police, où l'on trouvera l'histoire de son établissement, les fonctions et les prérogatives de ses magistrats; toutes les loix et tous les règlements qui la concernent*, vol. 1.
63. De la Mare, *Traité de la Police*, 1:145–84; Black, *Guild and State*, 153–61; Behrens, *Society, Government and the Enlightenment*, 52–66; Herztberg, *French Enlightenment and the Jews*, 50–137; Mencel, *Galicja Zachodnia*, 33–66; Koselleck, *Critique and Crisis*, 128–54.
64. Justus Möser, "Deutsche Geschichte." See also Isaiah Berlin, "The Counter-Enlightenment," in *The Proper Study of Mankind*, 256–60; Voltaire, *Philosophical Dictionary*, 2:359–63.
65. James C. Scott, *Seeing like a State: How Certain Schemes to Improve the Human Condition Have Failed*, 25–52; Nières, *Les Villes de Bretagne*, 509–24; Benoît Garnot, "Administrer une ville au XVIIIème siècle: Chartres"; Wojciech Trzebiński, "Nadzór budowlany i przepisy policyjno-budowlane w Polsce oświecenia jako środki naprawy miast królewskich."
66. Raeff, *Well-Ordered Police State*, 190–240; Hittle, *Service City*, 77–83; A. I. Kupriianov, "Gorodskaia demokratiia: vybory v russkoi provintsii (vtoraia polovina 1780-kh–nachalo 1860-kh gg.)," 31–33.

67. *Polnoe sobranie zakonov Rossiiskoi Imperii* (hereafter cited as *PSZRI*), ser. 1, vol. 20, no. 14392, 234–35, 256–58, 271–72; Munro, "Charter to the Towns," 18–32; Isabel de Madriaga, *Russia in the Age of Catherine the Great*, 277–304; A. A. Kizevetter, *Gorodovoe polozhenie Ekateriny II 1785 g. Opyt istoricheskago kommentariia*, 322–40, 288–301.
68. On the political stalemate in Poland before Stanisław August, see Jędrzej Kitowicz, *Pamiętniki, czyli Historia polska*, 46–126; Topolski, *Polska*, 669–87.
69. Stanisław Leszczyński, *Głos wolny wolność ubezpieczający*, 95–98; Stanisław Poniatowski, *List ziemianina do pewnego przyjaciela z inszego województwa* (1744); Stanisław Konarski, *O skutecznym rad sposobie albo o utrzymywaniu ordynaryinych Seymów*, 1:8–10. On Poniatowski the Younger's plans, see Rostworowski, *Ostatni król Rzeczypospolitej*, 41–43.
70. Jerzy Michalski, "Plan Czartoryskich naprawy Rzeczypospolitej"; Rostworowski, *Ostatni król Rzeczypospolitej*, 26–50; Butterwick, *Poland's Last King*, 147–70.
71. In the title-obsessed Commonwealth, where every noble of standing could claim some honorific appellation, the future king's only designation was "Pantler of Lithuania," a meaningless position that did not confer admission to the Senate. Kamiński, *Historia Rzeczypospolitej*, 199–240; Gierowski, *Polish-Lithuanian Commonwealth*, 247–61; Rostworowski, *Ostatni król Rzeczypospolitej*, 26–50; Kitowicz, *Pamiętniki*, 160–74.
72. See Kitowicz, *Pamiętniki*, 160–74; Rostworowski, *Ostatni król Rzeczypospolitej*, 54–80; Lukowski, *Partitions of Poland*, 30–99; Butterwick, *Poland's Last King*, 147–70.
73. *VL*, 7:242–43.
74. *VL*, 7:351–52. An anonymous justification for ending burghers' right of direct appeal appears in Biblioteka Książąt Czartoryskich (hereafter cited as BC), ms. 817 (Internal Politics and the Affairs of Courland), 277.
75. Stanisław Lubomirski, *Pamiętniki*, 29–32, 143–50; Władysław Konopczyński, *Konfederacja barska*, 1:90–95.
76. Kitowicz, *Pamiętniki*, 46–126; Lukowski, *Partitions of Poland*, 30–81.
77. Czaja, *Między tronem*, 101–14; Konopczyński, *Geneza i ustanowienia*, 125–98, 227–36; Rostworowski, *Ostatni król Rzeczypospolitej*, 69–77.
78. The acting chairman always signed the resolutions of the department. All were either members of the Permanent Council or ministers of the king. The acting chairmen of the department from 1777 to 1778 include Bazyli

Walicki, Jan Kicki, Antoni Giełgud, Bishop Ignacy Massalski, Bazyli Grochowski, and Franciszek Rzewuski. Of these, Massalski and Grochowski specifically fought against the king's plans at the 1773–1775 partition Sejm. See Konopczyński, *Geneza i ustanowienie*, 200–236. For a list of members of the Permanent Council, see AGAD, ML VII.84 (PC Minutes, 1778), 265.

CHAPTER 2: IF ONLY OUR COMMISSION HAD MORE POWER

1. Sections of this chapter have previously appeared in Curtis G. Murphy, "Burghers vs. Bureaucrats: Enlightened Centralism, the Royal Towns and the Case of the *Propinacja* Law in Poland-Lithuania, 1776–1793," *Slavic Review* 71, no. 2 (Summer 2012): 385–409 and reproduced here with permission.
2. AGAD, ML VII.84, 263.
3. Tyszkiewicz, *Komisja Dobrego Porządku w Poznaniu*, 9–80; Ignacy Baranowski, *Komisye porządkowe (1765–1788)*, 21–28; Mazurkiewicz, "Lublin w okresie reform," 170–72. For a more recent treatment, which essentially restates earlier conclusions, see Dariusz Złotkowski, *Miasta departamentu kaliskiego w okresie Księstwa Warsawskiego (Studium gospodarcze)*, 27–30.
4. Czaja, *Między tronem*, 172–73, also 174–91. See also Lukowski, *Liberty's Folly*, 243; Zahorski, *Centralne instytucje policyjne*, 35–50; Zienkowska, *Sławetni i urodzeni*, 32–90.
5. On the rationality of Enlightenment-era assumptions, see Berlin, "Two Concepts of Liberty," in *The Proper Study of Mankind*, 204–14.
6. On Enlightenment-era stereotypes of Jews, see Eisenbach, *Emancipation of the Jews*, 23–110; Wodziński, "Wilkiem orać'," 105–29; Dynner, *Yankel's Tavern*, 16–46.
7. In all, the department answered at least 527 petitions between 1777 and 1788 from 167 of the 224 royal towns that remained within the Polish Crown's 1772 borders. In addition to cities from the Lublin, Chełm, Volhynian, and Podolian regions, I also follow cities from the western regions of the Commonwealth, including Łęczyca, Płock, Piotrków (all three in Great Poland), and Warka (Mazowia palatinate). When I refer to additional towns in the footnotes, I will make note of the palatinate or region in which they were located, as indicated on Map 1.
8. For examples of this imagery from the burghers themselves, see AGAD,

Archiwum Zamoyskich (hereafter cited as AGAD, AZ) 73 (Supplications of various cities to Crown Chancellor Andrzej Zamoyski, 1765), 106, 113–15, 147–50; Konarski, *O skutecznym rad sposobie*, 1:8–10; Wolff, *Inventing Eastern Europe*, 243–60.

9. Mazurkiewicz, "Lublin w okresie reform," 177–88; Rostworowski, "Miasta i mieszczanie," 144–49.
10. AGAD, ML IX.105 (Documents concerning Lublin, eighteenth century), 9–10. See also APL, Księgi Komisji Boni Ordinis w Lublinie (hereafter APL, KBO) 5 (Papers, 1780–1790), 11–18.
11. See, for example, AGAD, ML VII.83 (PC Minutes, 1778), 282, 286, 298.
12. AGAD, ML IX.105, 334.
13. AGAD, ML VII.78, 18.
14. AGAD, ML VII.84, 264.
15. AGAD, ML VII.78, 23, see also 18, 24–29.
16. Mazurkiewicz, *Jurydyki lubelskie*, 24–29.
17. BC, ms. 2619 (Miscellaneous letters and publications, 1774–1782), 237.
18. Surdacki derives the origin of the term *czopowe* from the word *czop*, a keg or barrel of spirits. Surdacki, *Urzędów*, 274. On the Commonwealth's revenue in the eighteenth century, see BC, ms. 804 (Cities, townships, and villages, as well as taxation), 621–47; Korzon, *Wewnętrzne dzieje Polski*, 3:174–75.
19. *VL*, 7:352. Most royal charters after 1776 required the assent of the Permanent Council, but the Good Order Commissions were issued in the name of the king alone. For examples of the charters, see AGAD, Księgi kanclerskie 58, 129–34; AGAD, Księgi kanclerskie 60, 40–11.
20. These regulations were published by order of the king in 1780 and have been reprinted in Tyszkiewicz, *Komisja Dobrego Porządku w Poznaniu*, 108–86. See also Baranowski, *Komisye porządkowe*, 11–14.
21. AGAD, ML VII.75 (PC Minutes, 1776), 180–81, 211–12; AGAD, ML VII.77 (PC Minutes, 1777), 60–73. Zahorski has shown, for example, that the library of Stanisław Lubomirski contained Nicholas de la Mare's *Traité de la Police*. Zahorski, *Centralne instytucje policyjne*, 24–25. On abolishing guilds, see Jerzy Michalski, "Zagadnienie polityki antycechowej w czasach Stanisława Augusta."
22. *VL*, 8:533. Hryniewiecki himself worried that the new law would enable the Department of Police to interfere in private towns. Lubormirski, the titular minister of the Department of Police, complained that the government was seizing authority from the starostas. *Dyaryusz seymu ordynary-*

inego pod związkiem konfederacyi generalney oboyga narodów agituiącego się, 122, 182; *Zbiór mów rożnych w czasie dwóch ostatnich seymów roku 1775 y 1776 mianych*, 3:19, 40. On the 1776 parliament, see Andrzej Stroynowski, *Opozycja sejmowa w dobie rządów Rady Nieustającej: studium z dziejów kultury politycznej*, 35–75.

23. *VL*, 8:562.
24. AGAD, ML VII.78, 17, see also 18–29.
25. For the final decree, see AGAD, ML VII.19 (Public decrees of the Permanent Council, 1777), 289.
26. A glance at the members of the Permanent Council shows that even the lower-ranking members (that is, those possessing no official title such as chancellor, bishop, palatine, castellan, etc.) were listed as starostas. Mędrzecki and Barssa, *Zbiór praw*, part 5, 20–22; *Dyaryusz seymu ordynaryinego*, 458–59. On the king's power to distribute positions, see Konopczyński, *Geneza i ustanowienie*, 227–36.
27. *VL*, 8:567. Korzon claimed that this dramatic change led to a mass migration from Lithuania to Russia, but no scholarly treatment of this topic has come to my attention. See Korzon, *Wewnętrzne dzieje Polski*, 2:298; Zienkowska, *Sławetni i urodzeni*, 54.
28. AGAD, ML VII.78, 314.
29. AGAD, ML VII.78, 315–16.
30. Płock, Sandomierz, and Łęczyca, all three capitals of palatinates, failed to achieve exemptions as a result of their size. AGAD, ML VII.78, 22–23; *VL*, 8:88.
31. AGAD, ML VII.79, 64–70; AGAD, ML VII.78, 249–52.
32. *VL*, 8:562. The Jews of Chełm referenced the favorable resolution for their bretheren in Kazimierz Dolny in their own petition. Similarly, once the department had granted a temporary exception to the propinacja monopoly, other towns requested similar dispensations. See AGAD, ML VII.78, 375–76; AGAD, ML VII.83, 88–89.
33. The rival petitions are often so widely contradictory that one cannot tell what actually happened. For examples of this particular problem, see AGAD, ML VII.79, 187–88, 622–33.
34. In 1777 four starostas claimed to have bid higher or to have been absent from the auction, though the towns managed to convince the department otherwise. In Łuków (Lublin palatinate), Janów (Ruthenia palatinate), and Tuszyn (Great Poland), the starosta charged that the magistracy had

awarded the contract to a burgher without sufficient property. AGAD, ML VII.78, 310–11, 314–15, 316–19; AGAD, ML VII.79, 9–14, 263–72, 238–41, 488–95, 542–48.

35. A similar case occurred in 1777 in Szydłow (Great Poland). AGAD, ML VII.79, 24–29, 219–37, 622–33.

36. Burgher contractors in Ryczwoł and Zwoleń (both Sandomierz palatinate) wrote to the department in 1777 to complain that the starosta was blocking their Jewish contractors' operations under the pretense of enforcing the law denying Jews propinacja rights, an example of the confusion caused by these new regulations. AGAD, ML VII.79, 744–48; AGAD, ML VII.80, 126–28.

37. AGAD ML VII.78, 310–11, 314–15; AGAD, ML VII.79, 9–14; AGAD, ML VII.82 (PC Minutes, 1777–1778), 292–94.

38. AGAD, ML VII.84, 87–88, 196–98.

39. AGAD, ML VII.79, 470–71, see also 331–34. On dietines, see Wojciech Kriegseisen, *Sejmiki rzeczypospolitej szlacheckiej w XVII i XVIII wieku*, 9–60.

40. AGAD, ML VII.79, 331–34; AGAD, ML VII.80, 130–33; AGAD, ML VII.87 (PC Minutes, 1780), 177–79.

41. AGAD, ML VII.86 (PC Minutes, 1779), 40.

42. AGAD, ML VII.86, 39–41. Other examples of starostas complaining that burghers were not obeying them occurred in Chełm, Gostynin (Mazovia palatinate), and Rypin (Great Poland). AGAD, ML VII.82, 351–53; AGAD, ML VII.83, 217–18; AGAD, ML VII.84, 5–7.

43. See Surdacki, *Urzędów*, 203–33, Ćwik, *Miasta królewskie lubelszczyzny*, 78–107; Bogucka and Samsonowicz, *Dzieje miast*, 324–25.

44. AGAD, ML VII.78, 377–78.

45. "Proshenie malorossiiskago shliakhetstva i starshin vmeste s getmanom o vozstanovlenii raznykh starshinnykh prav Malorossii, podannoe Ekaterine II v 1764 godu." See also Zenon E. Kohut, *Russian Centralism and Ukrainian Autonomy: Imperial Absorption of the Hetmanate, 1760s–1830s*, 277–85.

46. AGAD, ML VII.78, 316–17; AGAD, ML VII.79, 263–72, 338–41, 488–95.

47. For example, the government usually accepted the attestation of the burgher community in lieu of collateral, but the department denied such a petition in the case of Włodzimierz in 1778 and demanded that a new auction be conducted. In another instance, the department awarded the contract to the starosta despite the fact that neither he nor the town had presented the documentation typically necessary for the government to

back one or the other claim. AGAD, ML VII.82, 294–95; AGAD, ML VII.79, 288–94. See Michel Crozier, *The Bureaucratic Phenomenon*, 196–207.

48. AGAD, ML VII.79, 481–87; AGAD, ML VII.84, 152–54, 172–73.
49. The towns of Tuszyn, Dubienka (Bełz palatinate, south of Chełm), and Włodzimierz used stalling tactics two years in a row. AGAD, ML VII.83, 363–68; AGAD, ML VII.79, 738–42; AGAD, ML VII.82, 292–94; AGAD, ML VII.78, 377–79; AGAD, ML VII.86, 7–8.
50. The department approved a similar compromise for Chełm, Koło, and Brdów (both of the latter, Great Poland). AGAD, ML VII.82, 351–53; AGAD, ML VII.83, 29–30, 33–34, 88–89.
51. AGAD, ML VII.84, 263.
52. AGAD, ML VII.90 (PC Minutes, 1782), 401–2.
53. In a separate decree, issued conterminously with the propinacja instructions, the government instructed both town magistracies and their starostas to submit reports detailing the income sources, expenses, and debts of the town. According to the department's records, 67 percent of the towns surveyed (140 of 207) provided the requested information, but only 51 percent (107 of 209) of the starostas did likewise. AGAD, ML VII.84, 277.
54. AGAD, ML VII.79, 738–42; AGAD, ML VII.88 (PC Minutes, 1780–1781), 398–401.
55. For example, Hryniewiecki complained to the king about Jews luring customers from the intramural city into "Jewish Town" by hawking goods at the city gates. AGAD, ML IX.105, 9–10.
56. Until the end of its existence, the Commonwealth functioned on a kind of "pay-to-play" system of justice. Commissions dispatched by the Royal Assessor Court, as well as the Good Order Commissions, operated on funds provided by the towns in which they worked.
57. Kazimierz Dolny, Płock, Piotrków, and Urzędów also requested permission to fund these commissions with propinacja revenue. See AGAD, ML VII.92 (PC Minutes, 1784–1785), 288; AGAD, ML VII.96 (PC Minutes, 1785), 265–67; Surdacki, *Urzędów*, 267–87.
58. AGAD, ML IX.105, 10.
59. APL, Księgi miejskie Lublina (hereafter APL, KML] 145 (Decrees and regulations of the Good Order Commission, 1782–1787), 108–17.
60. APL, KBO 5, 61–62.
61. APL, KBO 5, 64–69, 72–74; Mazurkiewicz, "Lublin w okresie reform," 171–72.

62. APL, KBO 5, 11–18.
63. AGAD, ML IX.105, 112, 159, 334. To give some perspective, Tadeusz Korzon explains that in the late eighteenth century one could rent a room in Lublin for 30 zlotys a year, and 280 zlotys would provide for an absolutely minimal existence. Korzon, *Wewnętrzne dzieje Polski*, 2:92, 103. See also Władysław Adamczyk, *Ceny w Lublinie od XVI do końca XVIII wieku*.
64. AGAD, ML IX.105, 90, see also 91–92, 159–62, 311–13; APL, KBO 5, 11–18; APL, KML 145, 131–33.
65. AGAD, ML IX.105, 9 (letter). See also AGAD, ML VII.89 (PC Minutes, 1782), 351–52; AGAD, ML VII.91 (PC Minutes, 1782–1783), 413–16.
66. AGAD, ML IX.105, 99.
67. APL, KBO 5, 155–58; APL, KML 145, 132–33; APL, KML 197e (Register of receipts and expenses, 1796–1798), 2–16.
68. AGAD, ML IX.105, 112, 90–92, 159–62, 311–13.
69. AGAD, ML IX.105, 334.
70. APL, KBO 4 (Further decrees of the Good Order Commission's court, 1788), 121.
71. APL, KBO 4, 121, 125; Adamczyk, *Ceny w Lublinie*, 79–81; Korzon, *Wewnętrzne dzieje Polski*, 2:92, 103. On town executioners, see Hanna Zaremska, *Niegodne rzemiosło: Kat w społeczeństwie Polski, XIV–XVI w.*, 33–82.
72. AGAD, ML VII.88, 19–20; AGAD, ML VII.91, 453; TsDIAK, f. 13, o. 1, s. 1 (Zhytomyr municipal records, 1782–1787), 188–211.
73. The decree of March 1777 did not make these conditions explicit, but they were applied in practice. AGAD, ML VII.83, 90–91, 187–88, 215–16, 280–81.
74. AGAD, ML VII.95 (PC Minutes, 1784), 30–31.
75. AGAD, ML VII.95 (PC Minutes, 1784), 30–31.
76. Kazimierz Dolny and Płock presented such a request, as did at least four other towns. AGAD, ML VII.83, 280–82; AGAD, ML VII.84, 25, 112–13, 132–35, 146–47.
77. AGAD, ML VII.83, 296, 298–99, 369–70, 375; AGAD, ML VII.84, 17–20.
78. This happened with the requests of Urzędów in 1779, Bielsk in 1780, and Łęczyca in 1781. AGAD, ML VII.86, 87–88; AGAD, ML VII.87, 81–82; AGAD, ML VII.88, 525–26. For this wording, see *Dziennik Handlowy i Ekonomiczny* (October 1788): 693 (quotation); AGAD, ML VII.95, 31.

79. Warka's request to rebuild the town hall had to be followed with additional requests for money, as was Bielsk's project to build a parish church. In these cases the cooperation of the starosta was a key element in obtaining further money. AGAD, ML VII.87, 198–200; AGAD, ML VII.85 (PC Minutes, 1785–1786), 245.
80. Of the towns surveyed, only Urzędów and Krzemieniec experienced conflict with the starosta over spending requests. Both towns remained in dispute with their starostas over propinacja auctions, and in both cases the department overruled the starosta and accepted the validity of the towns' requests. AGAD, ML VII.79, 21–23; AGAD, ML VII.84, 9–10; AGAD, ML VII.86, 81–82,155–56; AGAD, ML VII.87, 144–47.
81. AGAD, ML VII.85, 342–44; AGAD, ML VII.93 (PC Minutes, 1784), 357–62.
82. AGAD, ML VII.156 (PC Minutes, 1786), 390.
83. AGAD, ML VII.156, 387; AGAD, ML VII.101 (PC Minutes, 1788), 55–62.
84. In the handwritten version of the report, the number is thirty-three. *Dziennik Handlowy i Ekonomiczny* (October 1788): 694; AGAD, ML VII.155 (PC Minutes, 1788), 166; AGAD, ML VII.101 (PC Minutes, September 1787–February 1788), 55–56.
85. AGAD, ML VII.101, 382. See also *Dziennik Handlowy i Ekonomiczny* (October 1788): 694.
86. AGAD, ML VII.93, 357–62.
87. *VL*, 9:64, 146.
88. AGAD, ML VII.90, 400.
89. AGAD, ML IX.105, 334.
90. AGAD, ML VII.84, 263.
91. AGAD, ML VII.142 (PC Minutes, 1778–1779), 335.
92. AGAD, ML VII.90, 400–401.
93. In the Ukrainian palatinates specifically, private towns vastly outnumbered royal towns, so the total number of towns was much higher. BC, ms. 1093 (City taxation, eighteenth century), 589–627.
94. AGAD, ML VII.84, 263; AGAD, ML VII.90, 389–90. On auctioning revenues in Napoleonic Poland, see AGAD, Komisja Rządowa Spraw Wewnętrznych (hereafter cited as AGAD, KRSW) 3634 ("Lublin, 1811"), 7–15.
95. *Dziennik Handlowy i Ekonomiczny* (October 1788): 697–99.

96. "Memoriał miast," *MDSC*, 2:347.
97. Staszic, "Przestrogi dla Polski," in *Wybór pism*, 105.

CHAPTER 3: WEAPONIZING GOOD ORDER

1. AGAD, Archiwum Skaru Koronnego (hereafter cited as AGAD, ASK) XLVI.20 (Lustration of Łuck, Włodzimierz, and Krzemieniec starosties, 1789), 316.
2. AGAD, ASK XLVI.20, 327.
3. Bömelburg, *Zwischen Polnischer Ständegesellschaft*, 223–33, 398–409; Bömelburg, "Inklusion und Exklusion," 171–200; Vushko, *Politics of Cultural Retreat*, 29–67. See also Henryk Mościcki, *Dzieje porozbiorowe Litwy i Rusi*, 1:24–25.
4. Hugo Kołłątaj, *Listy anonima i prawo polityczne narodu polskiego*, 80, 205–21; Staszic, "Przestrogi dla Polski," 67–75.
5. Rostworowski, *Ostatni król Rzeczypospolitej*, 120–80; Gierowski, *Polish-Lithuanian Commonwealth*, 247–61.
6. See Zahorski, *Centralne instytucje policyjne*, 62–63.
7. "Akt zjednoczenia miast," *MDSC*, 2:305; "Memoriał miast: druga i trzecia redakcja," *MDSC*, 2:350. For Warsaw's predominant role in the Black Procession, see Władysław Smoleński, *Jan Dekert Prezydent Starej Warszawy i sprawa miejska podczas Sejmu Czterletniego*, 17–50; Krystyna Zienkowska, *Jan Dekert*, 131–95.
8. *VL*, 9:215–19.
9. Korzon, Wewnętrzne dzieje Polski, 2:400–405; Zienkowska, Sławetni i urodzeni, 198–215. For a recent celebratory account, see Richard Butterwick, The Polish Revolution and the Catholic Church, 1788–1792: A Political History, 241–48.
10. Eisenbach, Emancipation of the Jews, 72.
11. *Pokorna Prośba od Żydów Warszawskich i Prowincyi Koronnych do Nayjaśnieyszych Seymuiących Stanów*, 2. On civic duties transcending religious differences, see TsDIAK f. 13, o. 2, s. 6 (Circulars of the Kyiv [Kijów] Civil-Military Commission, 1790), 7.
12. Eisenbach, *Emancipation of the Jews*, 83–91; Hundert, *Jews in Poland-Lithuania*, 227–30; Zienkowska, "Reforms relating to the Third Estate," 330–51.
13. On continuous litigation, see Muir, "Was There Republicanism?" 138–39; Ćwik, *Miasta królewskie lubelszczyzny*, 106–7; Zienkowska, *Sławetni i urodzeni*, 11–27.

14. *VL*, 9:215–19; Eisenbach, *Emancipation of the Jews*, 83–91; Hundert, *Jews in Poland-Lithuania*, 227–30; Zienkowska, "Reforms relating to the Third Estate," 330–51.
15. See Walicki, *Enlightenment and the Birth of Modern Nationhood*, 1–26; Stanisław Cynarski, "The Ideology of Sarmatism in Poland (16th–18th centuries)"; Grześkowiak-Krwawicz, *Queen Liberty*, 12–20.
16. "Prośba Krakowa w sprawach skarbowych," *MSDC*, 2:106.
17. Andrzej Maksymilian Fredro, "W obronie liberum veto," in *Filozofia i myśl społeczna XVII wieku*, 307.
18. "Odpowiedź od stanu szlacheckiego miastom żądającym posiadania dóbr ziemskich," *MDSC*, 2:64.
19. Aleksander Fredo, "Zemsta," 67–70. The term "background static of violence" comes from David Nirenberg, *Communities of Violence: Persecution of Minorities in the Middle Ages*, 127. See also Frick, *Kith, Kin, and Neighbors*, 274–89.
20. Jerzy Michalski, "The Jewish Question in Polish Public Opinion during the First Two Decades of Stanisław August Poniatowski's Reign"; Stone, "Jews and the Urban Question," 531–41.
21. On unsuccessful efforts to enforce rabbinical jurisdiction, see Teller, "Przedmowa," 23–35; Michałowska-Mycielska, *The Jewish Community*, 243–49.
22. AGAD, ASK XLVI.20, 26, 28.
23. AGAD, ASK XLVI.20, 28–29 . See also Ćwik, *Miasta królewskie lubelszczyzny*, 106–7.
24. AGAD, ASK XLVI.20, 30–39, 63–73.
25. AGAD, ASK XLVI.20, 78. Notably, the eventual delegate from Łuck, Józef Brzeziński, had signed Dastkiewicz's petition. See "Akt zjednoczenia miast," *MDSC*, 2:318.
26. Ćwik, *Miasta królewskie lubelszczyzny*, 106–7. See also Zienkowska, *Sławetni i urodzeni*, 11–27.
27. AGAD, ML VII.79, 269, 270.
28. "Odpowiedź," *MDSC*, 2:64–65. For other examples of nobles "oppressed" by the burghers, see BC, ms. 817, 277; BC, ms. 897 (Proposals for introducing good order into the cities, eighteenth century), 22.
29. A similar split between the magistracy and starosta against the burgher community occurred in Radom and Łuków in 1777. AGAD, ML VII.78, 318–19; AGAD, ML VII.79, 9–14.

30. AGAD, ML VII.83, 364, also 365–68. AGAD, ML VII.79, 9–14, 288–94; AGAD, ML VII.84, 128–31.
31. Such excuses were quite common to avoid the alcohol law (see chapter 2).
32. AGAD, ASK XLIV.129 (Lustration of the Lublin starosty), 56. See also "List do przyjaciela w okolicznościach miast tyczących się z Warszawy pisanego z dodatkami druga edycja," *MDSC*, 2:458.
33. AGAD, ASK XLIV.132 (Lustration of Chełm land, 1789), 70–71, 75.
34. *VL*, 9:146–47.
35. For an example of a dispute between Christians and Jews in a private town over billeting, see APL, Akta miasta Tomaszowa (hereafter cited as APL, Tomaszów) 11 (Records of the city of Tomaszów, 1762–1789), 20.
36. TsDIAK, f. 13, o. 2, s. 6, 7–8; APL, Księgi Komisji Cywilno-Wojskowskiej ziemi lubelskiej (hereafter cited as APL, KCW Lublin) 1 (Diary, 1790–1791), 4–27.
37. TsDIAK, f. 8, o. 1, s. 15 (Protocol of the Kyiv Civil-Military Commission, 1791), 454–55.
38. APL, KCW Lublin 3 (Protocol of the Civil-Military Commission, 1790–1792), 21, 76.
39. The town government, for its part, claimed that the paving treasury had been depleted. APL, KCW Lublin 3, 24.
40. APL, Księgi Komisji Cywilno-Wojskowej ziemi chełmskiej (hereafter cited as APL, KCW Chełm) 1, 1.
41. KCW Chełm 1, 28.
42. Lukowski, *Liberty's Folly*, 243.
43. APL, KCW Lublin 1, 162. See also TsDIAK, f. 41, o. 1, s. 2 (Regulations of the Kremenets' [Krzemieniec] Commission, 1790), 12–23.
44. *Dyaryusz seymu ordynaryinego*, 265; Staszic, "Przestrogi dla Polski," 67–75.
45. *Dziennik Handlowy i Ekonomiczny* (October, 1788), 697.
46. Kołłątaj, *Listy anonima*, 221, 355.
47. Kołłątaj, *Listy anonima*, 80.
48. AGAD, ML VII.83, 100, 102.
49. "Wiadomość," *MDSC*, 2:41.
50. "Głos miast i miasteczek litewskich do Najjaśniejszych Sejmujących Stanów," *MDSC*, 2:111.
51. Mędrzecki and Barssa, *Zbiór praw*, part 2, 2–3. See also Smoleński, *Jan Dekert*, 31–41.
52. AGAD, ASK XLIV.20, 75–76.

53. *VL*, 9:215–19, 280, also 215–19, 277–79. See also Zienkowska, "Reforms relating to the Third Estate," 348–52; Eisenbach, *Emancipation of the Jews in Poland*, 103–11.
54. Juliusz Bardach, "Le principe fédéraliste et le principe unitaire dans la législation de la Diète polono-lithuanienne de Quatre Ans (1788–1792)"; Rostworowski, *Ostatni król Rzeczypospolitej*, 263–300; Kamiński, *Historia Rzeczypospolitej*, 229–38.
55. AGAD, AKP 86, no. 1 (Petitions to the Police Commission of Both Nations), 31. See also APL, KML 253 (Municipal records, 1792), 14, 17.
56. AGAD, ML VII.173 (Council of Ministers, 1792), 216.
57. AGAD, AKP 86, no. 1, 17–18.
58. AGAD, AKP 88, no. 18, 35–36.
59. AGAD, ML VII.173, 183–84.
60. TsDIAK, f. 13, o. 2, s. 6, 7–8. On the difficulty of collecting statistical information from Jewish communities, see Eugene M. Avrutin, "The Politics of Jewish Legibility: Documentation Practices and Reform during the Reign of Nicholas I."
61. Heyde, "Ewolucja zwierzchoności królewskiej," 35–48; Michałowska-Mycielska, *The Jewish Community*, 244–49.
62. According to Jerzy Michalski, the 1768 law was never enforced. Michalski, "The Jewish Question," 130. On the relationship between noble town owners and Jews, see Rosman, *The Lord's Jews*, 39–73.
63. Eisenbach, *Emancipation of the Jews*, 72. For a challenge to this argument, see Adam Teller, "The Shtetl as an Arena for Polish-Jewish Integration in the Eighteenth Century."
64. "Wiadomść o pierwiastkowej miast zasadzie," *MDSC*, 2:46–47.
65. On the conflict between Jews and Christians in Warsaw, see Smoleński, *Jan Dekert*, 74–83; also Gąsiorowski, *Chrześcianie i żydzi*, 173–79.
66. APL, KCW Chełm 1, 2.
67. APL, KCW Chełm 1, 2. See also Hundert, *Jews in Poland-Lithuania*, 79; Michałowska-Mycielska, *The Jewish Community*, 243–49.
68. AGAD, ASK XLVI.20, 27–28.
69. AGAD, ASK XLVI.20, 26.
70. AGAD, ASK XLVI.20, 36.
71. AGAD, ML VII.79, 111–19. In 1777 the Warta kahal did cosign a petition authored by the starosta to protest the activities of the magistracy, suggesting a kind of patron-client relationship. For additional accusations that

starostas were shielding Jewish communities from taxation, see AGAD, ML VII.78, 282–83; AGAD, ML VII.79, 481–85; AGAD, ML VII.82, 292–94.

72. "Wiadomość," *MDSC*, 2:40–41.

73. Świniarski, *Wiadmość o pierwiastkowey miast zasadzie*, 29–30. See also Schilling, *Essays in German and Dutch History*, 39–40.

74. Admittedly, this occurred in a private town immediately after the final partition. See AGAD, Archiwum Radziwiłłów (hereafter cited as AGAD, AR) V.10430 (Letters from Nieśwież citizens, 1702–1808), 40–41; also AGAD, ML VII.79, 111–19.

75. *VL*, 9:146.

76. APL, KCW Lublin 1, 83. Rostworowski notes that Jewish homes were much more densely populated than Christian households, so this attempt was not quite as unjust as it might appear. Rostworowski, "Miasta i mieszczanie," 144–45.

77. Kołłątaj, *Listy anonima*, 330–33; "Głos miast i miasteczek litewskich do Najjaśniejszych Sejmujących Stanów," *MDSC*, 2:109–13.

78. Pokorna Prośba, 2.

79. Pokorna Prośba, 2–3.

80. AGAD, ML VII.173, 124.

81. AGAD, AKP 86, no. 1, 52–53; AGAD, AKP 86, no. 2 (Reports of cities to the Police Commission, 1791–1792), 9–10.

82. AGAD, AKP 88, no. 18, 13–14.

83. TSDIAK, f. 20, o. 1, s. 44 (Records of the city of Kremenets', 1794–1796), 114.

84. TSDIAK, f. 20, o. 1. s. 44, 114.

85. TSDIAK, f. 20, o. 1. s. 44, 179, also 180–81, 220–301.

86. On the Targowica Confederacy, see Łukasz Kądziela, *Od konstytucji do insurekcji: Studia nad dziejami Rzeczypospolitej w latach 1791–1794*, 143–54, 181–96.

87. Mazurkiewicz, *Jurydyki lubelskie*, 34–80; Bałaban, *Die Judenstadt*, 10–13.

88. Both Lublin and Włodzimierz used this language. AGAD, ML VII.88, 398–401; AGAD, ML VII.92, 46–47.

89. AGAD, ASK XLVI.18 (Lustration of Volhynia palatinate, 1765), 24, also 25–32.

90. AGAD, ML VII.91, 223–25; AGAD, ML VII.95, 198.

91. "Wiadomość," *MDSC*, 2:43; "Prośba z przełożeniem miasta Kamieńca Podolskiego," *MDSC*, 2:256.

92. APL, KCW Lublin 3, 33–34, 70.

93. See Zahorski, *Centralne instytucje policyjne*, 148–60.
94. AGAD, AKP 88, no. 18, 114, 181.
95. AGAD, AKP 88, no. 18, 101, 104.
96. APL, KML 320 (Resolutions of the magistracy, 1799–1798), 38–39, 43, 82, 106, 113, 135, 162; Akta miasta Chelma 18 [APL, KCW Chełm 18] (Records of laws and regulations, 1789–1801), 33–36, 39; Wacław Tokarz, *Galicya w początkach ery józefińskiej w świetle ankiety urzędowej z roku 1783*, 17–37; Mencel, *Galicja Zachodnia*, 21–53.
97. APL, KML 320, 32, 43, 61, 86, 162.
98. APL, KCW Chełm 18, 32–33.
99. Mencel, *Galicja Zachodnia*, 145; Mazurkiewicz, "Lublin w okresie reform," 179–84; Wiesław Śladkowski, "W epoce zaborów," 12–13.
100. APL, KML 320, 113, 162; APL, KCW Chełm 18, 41; Vushko, *Politics of Cultural Retreat*, 127–53.
101. Machiavelli, *The Prince and the Discourses*, 118–20. See also Skinner, *Foundations of Modern Political Thought*, 1:157–70.

CHAPTER 4: ENLIGHTENED PROFIT-SEEKING

1. Ryszard Orłowski, *Między obowiązkiem obywatelskim a interesem własnym: Andrzej Zamoyski, 1717–1792*, 64–190; Ewa Borkowska-Bagieńska, *Zbiór praw sądowych Andrzeja Zamoyskiego*, 19–50.
2. For negative views of Karol Stanisław Radziwiłł, see Solomon Maimon, *Solomon Maimon: An Autobiography*, 81–88; Jerzy Michalski, "Wokół powrotu Karola Radziwiłła z emigracji pobarskiej"; Konopczyński, *Konfederacja barska*, 1:90–99.
3. BC, ms. 1093, 589–627; Józef Kleczyński, "Spis ludności dyecezyi krakowskiej z r. 1787."
4. Kołłątaj, *Listy anonima*, 280. For examples of this tradition, see Bogucka and Samsonowicz, *Dzieje miast*, 325; Wyrobisz, "Rola miast prywatnych," 33; Józef Mazurkiewicz, Jerzy Reder, and Jerzy Markiewicz, "Miasta prywatne powiatu lubelskiego a ich dziedzice w XIX.w.," 122–34; Opas, "Wolność osobista," 610–25; also Wojciech Trzebiński, *Działalność urbanistyczna magnatów i szlachty w Polsce XVIII wieku*, 86–89.
5. Hundert, *Jews in a Polish Private Town*, 135. Yvonne Kleinmann makes a similar argument, though she describes a process of gradually diminishing prerogatives. Kleinmann, "Rechtsinstrumente," 185–93.

6. Tomasz Opas, "Der Emanzipationsprozess," 358. See also Tomasz Opas, "Powinności na rzecz dziedziców w miastach szlacheckich województwa lubelskiego w drugiej połowie XVII i XVIII wieku"; Tomasz Opas, "Z badań nad przywracaniem miastom prawo apelacji do asesorii i innych sądów państwowych w XVIII wieku." See also Henryk Gmiterek, "Dzieje miasta w XVII–XVIII wieku"; Wyrobisz, "Rola miast prywatnych," 19–45.
7. Rosman, *The Lord's Jews*, 49–62; Teller, *Money, Power and Influence*; Grochowska, *Stanisław Antoni Szczuka*, 56–94.
8. The parliament of 1768 specifically forbade private owners from erecting new towns closer than two Polish miles (approximately fifteen kilometers) from a royal town. *VL*, 7:352. The Austrian authorities believed there were too many small towns in the Polish territories and sought to abolish the majority of them. Mencel, *Galicja Zachodnia*, 148–50. For land measurement conversions, see Horace Doursther, *Dictionnaire universel des poids et mesures anciens et modernes, contenant des tables des monnaies de tous les pays*, 585.
9. Proudfoot's study of the duke of Devonshire's towns demonstrates the lord's continuous negotiation with the tenants in order to accomplish political and economic goals. Szelényi's study argues that landlords and burghers worked together when their interests aligned. See Proudfoot, *Urban Patronage and Social Authority*, 110–17; Szelényi, "Dynamics of Urban Development," 361–76.
10. Kleinmann, "Rechtsinstrumente," 159–200; Adam Kaźmierczyk, *Żydzi w dobrach prywatnych w świetle sądownych i administracyjnych praktyki dóbr magnackich w wiekach XVI–XVIII*, 22–54, 160–77; Gąsiorowski, *Chrześcianie i żydzi*, 158–95. See also Hundert, *Jews in a Polish Private Town*, 85–113; Rosman, *Founder of Hasidism*, 65–90.
11. Walker, *German Home Towns*, 12, also 13–24.
12. Weber, *Economy and Society*, 1351–62.
13. Gąsiorowski, *Chrześcianie i żydzi*, 158–95.
14. See Appendix 1 for full population data. AGAD, AR XXV.3839a (Survey of Słuck, 1765), 1–55; AGAD, AR XXV.2690, part 2 (Survey of Nieśwież, eighteenth century), 1–20.
15. The Memoirs of Ber of Bolechow (1723–1805), 132–40.
16. AGAD, AR XXIX.18 (Dispositions made during Dominik's minority, 1791–1792), 141–66, 197–200; Michalski, "Wokół powrotu Karola Radziwiłła."

17. Orłowski, *Między obowiązkiem*, 49–54, 196–206, 220–26; Ryszard Szczygieł, "Zamość w czasach staropolskich"; Władysław Ćwik, "Zamość pod zaborami," 129–30.
18. *Słównik Geograficzny Królestwa Polskiego i innych krajów słowiańskich* (hereafter cited as *SGKP*), 7:118–22; Szczygieł, "Zamość w czasach staropolskich."
19. See Henryk Mierzwiński, "Kock w czasach Anny Jabłonowskiej."
20. Teller, *Money, Power, and Influence*, 5–21; Gąsiorowski, *Chrześcianie i żydzi*, 71–101; Zbigniew Anusik and Andrzej Stroynowski, "Problemy majątkowe Radziwiłłów w XVIII w."
21. AGAD, AR XV.5, no. 2 (Privileges of Nieśwież), 13; *SGKP*, 7:118–22.
22. AGAD, AR XXIX.12 (Economic and legal regulations of Karol Radziwiłł, 1769–1773), 23–25, 81.
23. AGAD, AR XV.5, no. 2, 99–100.
24. AGAD, AR XV.5, no. 2, 133–34.
25. AGAD, AR XXIX.5 (Economic and legal instructions of Michał Radziwiłł, 1745–1748), 610.
26. The Grand Duchy of Lithuania had its own currency, the kopa, which was equal to 2.5 zlotys, according to a calculation made by Radziwiłł in the early eighteenth century. Unlike the zloty, which was divisible into thirty groszy, the kopa was divisible into sixty. Each urban property unit paid thirty Lithuanian groszy to the town treasury, while each market garden paid one kopa. See AGAD, AR XXV.2690, part 1 (Survey of Nieśwież, eighteenth century), 25–26; AGAD, AR XXV.2666 (Survey of the Nieśwież principality, 1628–1629), 5–6.
27. AGAD, AR XXV.2690, part 1, 25–26.
28. Urzędów collected about 3.5 zlotys per hearth. AGAD, AR XV.7, no. 1 (Documents about Nieśwież), 126–27; AGAD, ML IX.105, 112; AGAD, ML VII.84, 25; AGAD, ML VII.86, 87–88.
29. AGAD, AR XXIX.19 (Instructions of Maciej Radziwiłł, 1791–1793), 25. See also AGAD, AR XV.5, no. 2, 89.
30. AGAD, AR XV.5, no. 2, 126–27. See also Gąsiorowski, *Chrześcianie i żydzi*, 158–95.
31. AGAD, AR XXIX.12, 81, 90.
32. AGAD, AR XXIX.13 (Regulations of Karoł Radziwiłł, 1778–1779), 172.
33. AGAD, AR V.10845 (Letters from Ołyka, 1751–1779), 2–5.
34. AR XXIX.15 (Regulations of Karol Radziwiłł, 1780–1783), 179, see also

303. For further examples of judicial practice, see: AGAD, AR XXIX.5, 608–12; AGAD, AR XXIX.12, 68; AGAD, XXIX. Ritual murder accusations against Jewish communities for allegedly murdering Christians appeared with increasing frequency in the seventeenth and eighteenth centuries. See Guldon and Wijaczka, *Procesy*, 130–41. On ritual murder in private towns, see Rudomicz, *Efemeros*, 2:73; Kaźmierczyk, *Żydzi w dobrach prywatnych*, 206.

35. AGAD, AR V.11370, part 2 (Letters from Jerzy Paszkowski, wójt of Nieśwież, 1750–1755), 3–4, 9–11, 111.

36. *Cudzoziemcy o Polsce: Relacje i opinie*, 1:345–47. In 1789, the Civil-Military Commission of Volhynia complained that General Lubomirski, who was in charge of military forces there, preferred to keep his soldiers garrisoned in his personal town of Dubno, since it was much better fortified than the palatinate capital of Łuck. BC, ms. 953 (Papers of the Civil-Military Commissions in Kijów, Podolia, and Volhynia, 1789), 157–58. See also Bogucka and Samsonowicz, *Dzieje miasta*, 407; Wyrobisz, "Rola miast prywatnych," 36.

37. AGAD, AR XXV.2690, part 2, 1.

38. AGAD, AR V.11370, part 2, 3–4, 9–11; AGAD, AR V.11370, part 4 (Letters from Jerzy Paszkowski, 1765–1774), 111; AGAD, AR XXIX.15, 113.

39. Rosman, *Lord's Jews*, 62, 110; AGAD, AR XXIX.5, 611.

40. AGAD, AR XXIX.12, 52, 68.

41. "Prośby miast litewskich," *MDSC*, 2:94–95.

42. AGAD, AR V.10430, 4–5, 10.

43. AGAD, AR V.10843 (Letters from the Ołyla kahal, 1774), 8. See also AGAD, AR V.10845, 2–5.

44. AGAD, AR V 10845, 6–7; AGAD, AR XV.7, no. 1, 274–76.

45. AGAD, AR V.10845, 8. See also AGAD, AR XV.7, no. 1, 65–66, 117–20.

46. AGAD, AR XXV.2666, 6.

47. AGAD, AR XXV.2690, part 1, 25–26; AGAD, AR XXV.2658, part 1 (Survey of Nieśwież, seventeenth century), 13–26; AGAD, AR XXV.2669, part 1 (Survey of the principality of Nieśwież, seventeenth century), 16–17.

48. AGAD, AR XXIX.13, 34–40; AGAD, AR XXIX.15, 14–20. On leaseholding, see Teller, *Money, Power, and Influence*, 110–41.

49. AGAD, AR XXIX.13, 34–40.

50. Bogucka and Samsonowicz, *Dzieje miast*, 402–7. On the origins of Zamość, see Wojciecj Kalinowski, "Miasto idealne i jego przemiany," 87–93; Szczygieł, "Zamość w czasach staropolskich." On the Zamość Academy, see Bogdan Szyszka, ed., *Akademia Zamoyska i jej tradycyje*.

51. APL, Akta Ordynacji Zamoyskiej (hereafter cited as APL, AOZ) 1547 (Entail budget, 1767–1771), 3–33, 130–90; APL, AOZ 1550 (Entail budget, 1773–1774), 198–311; Władysław Ćwik, "Jurysdykcja Rady Ekonomicznej Ordynacji Zamoyskiej."

52. AGAD, AZ 2494a (Decrees of Andrzej Zamoyski to the cities of the entail), 1–2; APL, Akta miasta Kraśnika (hereafter APL, Kraśnik) 40 (City records, 1761–1788), 2–4, 22–25, 44–47; Akta Trybunału Zamoyskiego 14 (Tribunal records, 1760–1778), 5–24, 246–99.

53. Rudomicz, *Efemeros*, 2:68, also 47–59.

54. APL, Kraśnik 40, 2.

55. APL, Kraśnik 40, 3–5, 8–10, 15–17, 27–28, 33–34, 40–47, 67–69, 110–12, 116–18; AGAD, AZ 2579 (Tax payments and military contributions of the Zamoyski family treasury), 33; APL, Akta miasta Zamościa (hereafter APL, Zamość) 73 (Tax collecting in Zamość, 1696), 2–38; APL, Zamość 18 (Zamość city minutes, 1780–1786), 182.

56. APL, Kraśnik 40, 22–25, 116–18.

57. APL, Tomaszów 11, 43–55, 84–91.

58. APL, AOZ 1547, 3–33, 130–90.

59. APL, AOZ 1550, 198–311; APL, AOZ 1553 (Entail budget, 1781–1782), 1–84.

60. APL, AOZ 1550, 154; APL, AOZ 1553, 74.

61. APL, Akta Trybunału Zamoyskiego, 14, 260–63.

62. APL, AOZ 1586 (Record of supplications and resolutions, 1770–1771), 24–25.

63. Rudomicz, *Efemeros*, 147–48.

64. APL, Kraśnik 40, 46; Frick, *Kith, Kin, and Neighbors*, 6–9.

65. APL, AOZ 1586, 21.

66. AGAD, AZ 2521 (Records related to the status, revenue, and expenditures of the Zamoyski coffers, 1601–1840), 15, 45, 53, 72.

67. APL, AOZ 1547, 130–90; APL, AOZ 1550, 198–311.

68. *Dyaryusz seymu ordynaryinego*, 265; Staszic, "Przestrogi dla Polski," 71–72.

69. AGAD, AR XV.5, no. 2, 94–95; Rudomicz, *Efemeros*, 191–92, 199–200.

70. APL, Akta luźne miasta Lublina 55, 173; APL, Tomaszów 11, 44–49; APL, Kraśnik 40, 8–10; AGAD, AR XXIX.5, 608–12; Andrzej Komoniecki, *Chronografia albo dziejopis żywiecki*, 272–73.

71. AGAD, AR XXIX.5, 608–12; AGAD, AR XXIX.12, 68. On humanist thinking, see Gerhard Oestreich, *Neostoicism and the Early Modern State*, 126–35.

72. APL, Tomaszów 11, 6.

73. APL, Kraśnik 40, 22–23; AGAD, AR XXIX.12, 68, 73–74, 81. See also Groicki, *Porządek sądów miejskich*, 28–30.

74. AGAD, AR V.10845, 2. See also Orłowski, *Między obowiązkiem*, 192–93.

75. AGAD, AZ 615 (Correspondence of Andrzej Zamoyski, 1726–1786), 131–33.

76. AGAD, AZ 1771 (Letter from Heinrich von Auersperg), 1–2; APL, Tomaszów 11, 43–55, 84–87; APL, Zamość 18, 20, 35, 72; Ćwik, "Zamość pod zaborami," 129–30.

77. Mencel, *Galicja zachodnia*, 139–45.

78. APL, Zamość 18, 206, also 182, 202–5.

79. APL, Kraśnik 40, 23, 23, 24, also 25–34.

80. APL, Tomaszów 11, 5–6, 10–13.

81. APL, Kraśnik 40, 24.

82. APL, Zamość 18, 204–5.

83. Orłowski, *Między obowiązkiem*, 41–44, 49–54, 68, 155; Trzebiński, *Działność urbanistyczna*, 54.

84. APL, Kraśnik 40, 45–46.

85. APL, Kraśnik 40, 45–46, 72–74; APL, Tomaszów 11, 24–28; AGAD, ML IX.105, 90–92.

86. APL, Kraśnik 40, 38, 109–14.

87. APL, KCW Lublin 3, 37–39, 65–67, 81.

88. APL, Akta miasta Firleja 3 (City records, 1789–1809), 3–4.

89. APL, Akta miasta Modliborzyce 4 (City records, 1788–1799), 6, 23; APL, Akta miasta Żółkiewki (hereafter APL, Żółkiewka) 1 (City records, 1775–1810), 1, 25; APL, Akta miasta Lubartowa (hereafter APL, Lubartów) 6 (City records, 1762–1808), 142.

90. APL, Lubartów 6, 161; APL, Żółkiewka 1, 72–73; Mencel, *Galicja zachodnia*, 147–48.

91. AGAD, AR XXIX.13, 71–73, 172; AGAD, AR XXIX.15, 167–68, 312.

92. AGAD, AR V.11370, part 4, 9–14; AGAD, AR XV.7, no. 1, 117–31.

93. AGAD, AR XV.7, no, 1, 117–20; AGAD, AR XV.18, no. 3 (Nieśwież city documents), 20.
94. AGAD, AR XXIX.15, 167–68, 207.
95. AGAD, AR XXIX.13, 179. See also AGAD, AR XXIX.15, 312–13.
96. AGAD, AR XV.7, no. 1, 126–27.
97. AGAD, AR XV.7, no. 1, 139; AGAD, AR XXIX.18, 161, 165–66.
98. AGAD, AR XXIX.19, 5, 28.
99. AGAD, AR XXIX.17 (Dispositions of Michał Hieronim Radziwiłł, 1791–1802), 145–46, 267–70.
100. AGAD, AR V.10430, 42–43.
101. Adam Naruszewicz, *Dyjaryjusz podroży Jego Królewskiej Mości na sejm grodzieński*, 344. For examples of the duties imposed on Radziwiłł family's peasants, see AGAD AR XXV.2669, 5–33.
102. See Friedeburg, *Luther's Legacy*, 238–352.

CHAPTER 5: THE APOGEE OF ENLIGHTENED CENTRALISM

1. Jarosław Czubaty, *The Duchy of Warsaw: A Napoleonic Outpost in Central Europe*, 13–36. See also Woolf, *Napoleon's Integration of Europe*, 96–102; Broers, "Centre and Periphery," 55–73; Senkowska-Głuck, "Les institutions napoléoniennes," 541–47.
2. AGAD, KRSW 33 (Reports on cities, 1809–1812), 188–89.
3. Kołłątaj, *Uwagi nad teraźnieyszym położeniem*, 168–69, 182, 200; Koźmian, *Pamiętniki*, 2:65–77, 183–89. On other thinkers in the period, see Cichoń, *Rozwój myśli administracyjnej*, 56–65, 142–60. On parallels between France and Austria, see Woolf, *Napoleon's Integration of Europe*, 12–30, 97–124; R. J. W. Evans, "Josephinism, 'Austrianness,' and the Revolution of 1848," 145–56.
4. "Ignacy Stawiarski to Józef Szaniawski," in *Korrespondencya w materyach obraz kraiu i narodu polskiego rozniaśniaiących*, 97–99; Surowiecki, *O upadku przemysłu i miast*, 157.
5. For use of these terms, see Złotkowski, Miasta departamentu kaliskiego, 250; Cichoń, *Rozwój myśli administracyjnej*, 141–45. See also Kallas, *Organy administracji terytorialnej*.
6. Vushko, *Politics of Cultural Retreat*, 127–53, 182–205. On the "Post-

Enlightenment," see also Wodziński, *Władze Królestwa Polskiego*, 121–45. See also Jan Wąsicki, *Ziemie polskie pod zaborem pruskim: Wielkie Księstwo Poznańskie 1815–1848*, 148–72.

7. Ignacy Lubowiecki, *Pamiętniki*, 79–96; Jacek Arkadiusz Goclon, *Polska na królu pruskim zdobyta: Ustrój, administracja, i sądownictwo doby Komisji Rządzącej w 1807 roku*, 20–39; Woolf, *Napoleon's Integration of Europe*, 125–48.
8. For the Napoleonic constitution, see *Dziennik Praw Księstwa Warszawskiego* (hereafter cited as *DPKW*) 1, no. 1 (1810): 2–4, 29–32. On the Napoleonic system, see Woolf, *Napoleon's Integration of Europe*, 96–102; Fahrmeir, "Centralisation versus Particularism"; Kallas, *Organy administracji terytorialnej*, 45–64. For urban government under Napoleon in France, see Theodor von Faber, *Sketches of the Internal State of France*, 34–35; Igor Moullier, "Police et politique de la ville sous Napoléon."
9. *DPKW* 1, no. 1 (1810): 32. Kallas, *Organy administracji terytorialnej*, 142–45.
10. See AGAD, KRSW 33, 183–94; APL, Akta miasta Lublina (hereafter cited as APL, AML) 2740 (City budgets, 1809–1818, 1822–1828), 236–41; Kallas, *Organy administracji terytorialnej*, 15–108.
11. "Uwagi Stanisława Węgrzeckiego z 20 III 1813 o konstytucji Księstwa Warszawskiego," in *Wybór tekstów źródłowych z historii Polski w latach 1795—1864*, 188. See also BC, ms. 2620 (Letters and prints, 1807–1815), 43–44.
12. Critics of the regime, such as Domnik Krysinski, complained about the extraneous number of officials, a fact admitted even by government sympathizers. BC, ms. 2620, 43–44, 179; Koźmian, *Pamiętniki*, 2:156; Joachim Owidzki, *Spostrzeżenia, uwagi, i myśli obywatela w zaciszu domowem przyszłemu seymowi podane*, 25–38, 51; Cichoń, *Rozwój myśli adminstracyjnej*, 147–50.
13. Czubaty, *Duchy of Warsaw*, 139–67.
14. AGAD, KRSW 3010 (Solec, 1811–1818), 11–12, 14.
15. AGAD, KRSW 4145 (Zamość, 1816–1819), 21.
16. Originally, the proposal for suspending civil rights was meant to last ten years. In the meantime, the state levied a massive contribution from the Jewish community at large in lieu of military service. See John Stanley, "The Politics of the Jewish Question in the Duchy of Warsaw, 1807–1813," 50–51.
17. In official reports, administrators placed Jewish settlement outside of the

rewir in the same category as other symptoms of disorder. See AGAD, KRSW 167 (Organizing cities, 1832–1862), 6–8. See also Eisenbach, *Emancipation of the Jews*, 129–44; Wodziński, "'Wilkiem orać'."

18. *Dziennik Praw Królestwa Polskiego* (hereafter cited as *DPKP*) 1, no. 1 (1815): 26. Previous tsars had rejected any notion of a contractual monarchy. In 1654 the Pereiaslav negotiations between the Cossacks and representatives of Tsar Aleksei Mikhailovich almost broke down over the tsar's refusal to swear an oath to uphold the agreement. See *Vossoedinenie Ukrainy s Rossiei: Dokumenty i materialy v 3-kh tomakh*, 3:465.
19. On Poles attempting to use the British model of loyal opposition, see Thackeray, Antecedents of Revolution, 70–72. See also Alicja Kulecka, Wapno i alabaster: Biurokratyczna wizija rzeczywistości w raportach urzędowych Królestwa Polskiego (1815–1867), 55–86.
20. Angela T. Pienkos, *The Imperfect Autocrat: Grand Duke Constantine Pavlovich and the Polish Congress Kingdom*, 40–65; Jerzy Skowronek, "Eksperyment liberalizmu parlamentarnego w Królestwie Polskim."
21. Maciej Mycielski, *Rząd Królestwa Polskiego wobec sejmików i zgromadzeń gminnych*, 81–85; see Thackeray, *Antecedents of Revolution*, 17–34, 54–77. On France, see David Laven and Lucy Riall, "Restoration Government and the Legacy of Napoleon."
22. After 1832 the KRSW was renamed the Governing Commission for Internal Affairs, Clergy, and Public Education, which would be KRSWDOP. I will retain the acronym KRSW for clarity's sake.
23. *DPKP* 6, no. 22 (1818): 25–32; Tadeusz Mencel, "Organizacja i działność administracji miejskiej w Lublinie w latach 1809–1866," 68–69, 78.
24. *Dyaryusz Seymu Królestwa Polskiego r. 1818*, 12–13.
25. Lubowiecki, *Pamiętniki*, 169. See APL, Akta miasta Bełżyc (hereafter APL, Bełżyce) 15 (City organization, 1815–1860), 12.
26. Eisenbach, *Emancipation of the Jews*, 155–80; Dynner, *Yankel's Tavern*, 52–102.
27. Wodziński, *Władze Królestwa Polskiego*, 121–45. See also Wąsicki, *Ziemie polskie pod zaborem pruskim*, 148–72.
28. "Statut Organiczny Królestwa Polskiego"; Mencel, "Organizacja i działność," 80; Śladkowski, "W epoce zaborów," 111–15.
29. APL, AML 2739 (City budgets, 1811–1817), 98, 110. See also AGAD, KRSW 3634, 2–4, 12.
30. APL, AML 2739, 6–9, 27, 40, 66, 83, 110–11.

31. The Napoleonic Constitution established that a city's population determined the number and type of officials employed. *DPKW* 1, no. 1 (1810): 35–36, 187; AGAD, KRSW 3634 (Lublin, 1811), 2–4, 8; APL, AML 2740, 236–41.
32. For example, Lublin's mayor spent several months attempting to have Alexander Fiedorowicz selected as councilor, a process that required testimony from officials at every layer of government. AGAD, KRSW 3634, 7–8, 16; AGAD, KRSW 3688 (Lublin, 1840), 209–14. See also APL, AML 2740, 236–41.
33. The government paid 3.4 million zlotys (568,561 rubles) and transferred government land in other parts of the Kingdom to the Zamoyskis in compensation. *DPKP* 7, no. 29 (1820): 111; Ćwik, "Zamość pod zaborami," 136–37.
34. AGAD, KRSW 4145, 121.
35. AGAD, KRSW 4145, 124, 125.
36. AGAD, KRSW 36 (KRSW reports, 1820), 41–44; AGAD, KRSW 7033 (Provincial commission reports, 1826), 170–71.
37. *DPKP* 1, no. 1 (1815): 25–26, 50; *DPKP* 6, no. 22 (1818), 25–28. See also APL, AML 6 (Magistracy organization, 1819–1867), 21–26.
38. AGAD, KRSW 36, 73; AGAD, KRSW 3234 (Bychawa, 1833–1849), 124–26; AGAD, KRSW 3252 (Bełżyce, 1829–1849), 238–41; APL, AML 2741 (City budgets, 1828–1829), 7–9.
39. AGAD, KRSW 41 (Reports on cities, 1829–1833), 245.
40. AGAD, KRSW 4042 (Tomaszów, 1833–1842), 12–19.
41. APL, AML 2040, 178–84; AGAD, KRSW 4042, 92–95.
42. APL, AML 2739, 1–2.
43. APL, AML 2740, 236–41.
44. AGAD, KRSW 36, 41–44; Owidzki, *Spostrzeżenia*, 9–11.
45. APL, AML 2740, 183.
46. Mencel, "Organizacja i działność," 68–69. See also AGAD, KRSW 3673 (Lublin, 1830–1832), 193–94; AGAD, KRSW 3283 (Chełm, 1832–1836), 40–60; Vushko, *Politics of Cultural Retreat*, 143–53.
47. APL, KML 1302 (Guild regulations, 1817–1866), 11–12.
48. APL, AML 6, 12; AGAD, KRSW 38 (Reports on cities, 1821–1824), 83–85; AGAD, KRSW 3418 (Firlej, 1811–1835) 5–6; APL, Bełżyce 15, 9–10; APL, AML 6, 12–19, 21–26.
49. AGAD, KRSW 205 (Propinacja changes, 1820–1837), 84.

50. See Dynner, *Yankel's Tavern*, 52–79.
51. APL, AML 999 (Police regulations, 1824–1861), 16.
52. APL, AML 999, 3–24.
53. AGAD, KRSW 3673, 153–54; AGAD, KRSW 3734 (Jewish residence in Lublin, 1811–1830), 210–16, 301–8, 326–28.
54. AGAD, KRSW 3673, 176–81.
55. Lubowiecki, *Pamiętniki,* 171–73; Kulecka, *Wapno i alabaster*, 77–85.
56. AGAD, KRSW 3283, 88.
57. AGAD, KRSW 3283, 171–72, also 197–99, 248. See also AGAD, KRSW 3673, 10–20.
58. Lubowiecki, *Pamiętniki,* 173. See also AGAD, KRSW 3673, 10–20; AGAD, KRSW 39 (Reports on cities, 1824–1826), 7–13.
59. AGAD, KRSW 3688, 4, 5.
60. Raeff, *Well-Ordered Police State*, 85–150. Avrutin shows that the Jewish community did accommodate themselves to certain practices, such as self-documentation for statistical purposes, but other state policies failed to change behaviors. Eugene M. Avrutin, *Jews and the Imperial State: Identification Politics in Tsarist Russia*, 53–85. See also Śladkowski, "W epoce zaborów," 53–58.
61. AGAD, KRSW 205, 91–96. Prohibition on rural, Jewish distillers was enforced. See Dynner, *Yankel's Tavern*, 52–79.
62. Halina Rożenowa, *Produkcja wódki i sprawa pijaństwa w Królestwie Polskim, 1815–1863*, 60–80; Jan Rutkowski, *Historia gospodarcza Polski (do 1864)*, 451–53; Smolka, *Polityka Lubeckiego*, 1:117–28.
63. APL, AML 2741, 7–9; Rutkowski, *Historia gospodarcza*, 451.
64. AGAD, KRSW 3283, 59–63; AGAD, KRSW 3234, 98–116.
65. Rożenowa, *Produkcja wódki*, 75–94, 140–87; Śladkowski, "W epoce zaborów," 64–68.
66. AGAD, KRSW 3734, 301–8.
67. AGAD, KRSW 3673, 274–89; Dynner, *Yankel's Tavern*, 155–74.
68. AGAD, KRSW 167, 6–24.
69. APL, AML 6, 12–19, 21–26.
70. *DPKW* 1, no. 1 (1810): 35–37, 203–6.
71. AGAD, KRSW 33, 189.
72. Karol de Campo Scipio, the owner of Bychawa, claimed that the new law had turned his town into a serf village and demanded corvée labor from his burghers, but this appears to have been an extreme case. See Senkowska-

Głuck, "Les institutions napoléoniennes," 541–47; Taduesz Mencel, "Od III rozbioru Polski do powstania styczniowego"; Mazurkiewicz et al., "Miasta prywatne powiatu lubelskiego," 106–7, 138–47.

73. Marian Kallas, "Le système administratif du Duché de Varsovie, 1806–15."

74. AGAD, KRSW 3581 (Kraśnik, 1811–1820), 9–10; APL, Bełżyce 15, 18–22; Mazurkiewicz et al., "Miasta prywatne powiatu lubelskiego," 148–49; *DPKP* 6, no. 22 (1818): 25–28.

75. AGAD, KRSW 3418, 5–6; Józef Mazurkiewicz, "Likwidacja ustroju miejskiego mniejszych miast w Księstwie Warszawskim i Królestwie Polskim w okresie przed masową zmianą miast na osadę (1807–1864)."

76. AGAD, KRSW 35 (City reports, 1813–1819), 208–11.

77. AGAD, KRSW 3418, 80.

78. APL, Bełżyce 15, 9–10; APL, Akta miasta Bychawy (hereafter cited as APL, Bychawa) 4 (Description by town inspector Brandys, 1820), 1–9; AGAD, KRSW 35, 208–11.

79. AGAD, KRSW 3418, 5–6, 80, 142–52; APL, Bychawa 4, 1–9.

80. APL, Bełżyce 15, 18–22.

81. AGAD, KRSW 7033, 169–72. See also Rożenowa, *Produkcja wódki*, 68–86.

82. AGAD, KRSW 3234, 8–12, 63–65, 98–116, 124–26, 325–27.

83. The owner of Bełżyce received some of his contribution back, as the town had to lease a chancellery building from him for one hundred zlotys a year. AGAD, KRSW 3252, 77–80, 238–41; AGAD, KRSW 3419 (Firlej, 1836–1865), 7–9, 58–60, 211–13; AGAD, KRSW 4042, 92–95.

84. AGAD, KRSW 3581, 9–17, 25.

85. AGAD, KRSW 3581, 89–90.

86. AGAD, KRSW 3581, 33–40, 84–107, 150–54.

87. AGAD, KRSW 38, 15–16.

88. AGAD, KRSW 38, 16–17, 19–21.

89. AGAD, KRSW 7033, 172–79; AGAD, KRSW 3418, 80; APL, Bełżyce 15, 9–10; APL, Bychawa 4, 1–9.

90. AGAD, KRSW 3588 (Lawsuit between Kraśnik and the Zamoyski entail), 5–15, 41–62; AGAD, KRSW 7033, 169–79; Smolka, *Polityka Lubeckiego*, 1:122–28.

91. AGAD, KRSW 172 (Information about the legislation of 1866), 6–16.

92. AGAD, KRSW 3252, 326, 327.

93. AGAD, KRSW 3252, 362.

94. AGAD, KRSW 3252, 366–67, also 224–26.
95. AGAD, KRSW 3943 (Case between Szczebrzeszyn and the Zamoyski entail), 1–18.
96. AGAD, KRSW 3943, 16, also 19–22, 71–75.

CHAPTER 6: THE PERSISTENCE OF THE OLD COMMONWEALTH

1. AGAD, AR XV.20, no. 10 (Lawsuit with Olyka burghers, 1804–1859), 4.
2. AGAD, AR XV.20, no. 10, 1–2, 5–6.
3. S. A. Bershadskii, "Polozhenie o evreiakh 1804 goda," *Voskhod* 15, no. 1 (January 1895), 86. See also Kohut, *Russian Centralism*, 125–236. Koźmian refers to the early years of Alexander's reign as a "good time for Poles, particularly in Ukraine and Lithuania." See Koźmian, *Pamiętniki*, 1:272. On the survival of old institutions and practices more generally, see Arno J. Mayer, *The Persistence of the Old Regime: Europe to the Great War*.
4. Daniel Beauvois, *Pouvoir russe et noblesse polonaise en Ukraine, 1793–1830*, 122–55. See also Daniel Beauvois, *The Noble, the Serf, and the Revizor: The Polish Nobility between Tsarist Imperialism and the Ukrainian Masses (1831–1863)*, 20–44.
5. Alison K. Smith, *For the Common Good and Their Own Well-Being: Social Estates in Imperial Russia*, 48–65.
6. Nineteenth-century historiography referred to the partitions as the "Reunification of Rus'," an interpretation that continued into the Soviet period. See P. V. Stegnii, *Razdely Pol'shi i diplomatiia Ekateriny II: 1772, 1793, 1795*, 25–28, 64; "Theses on the Three-Hundredth Anniversary of the Reunion of the Ukraine with Russia," in John Basarab, *Pereiaslav 1654: A Historiographic Study*, 270–88.
7. On enlightened bureaucrats, see W. Bruce Lincoln, *In the Vanguard of Reform: Russia's Enlightened Bureaucrats*, 1–40.
8. Officials used the term *russkie*, which would encompass any Orthodox eastern Slav, including people who would later identify as Ukrainians. Russians considered future Ukrainians as "Little Russians," part of the national family. See Alexei Miller, *The Ukrainian Question: The Russian Empire and Nationalism in the Nineteenth Century*, 3–62.
9. Faith Hillis, *Children of Rus: Right-Bank Ukraine and the Invention of a Russian Nation*, 1–21, 117–49; Munro, "Charter to the Towns," 17–35.

10. *Polnoe sobranie zakonov Rossiiskoi Imperii* (hereafter cited as *PSZRI*), ser. 1, vol. 22, no. 16187, 382–83.
11. Catherine Evtuhov, *Portrait of a Russian Province: Economy, Society, and Civilization in Nineteenth-Century Nizhnii Novgorod*, 53–56; Madriaga, *Russia in the Age of Catherine the Great*, 277–304; P. G. Ryndziunskii, *Gorodskoe grazhdanstvo doreformennoi Rossii*, 290–310.
12. TsDIAK, f. KMF 11, o. 1, s 94 (Reports of the Podolia civil governor, 1804–1809), 19, 131–32; TsDIAK, f. KMF 11, o. 1, s. 91 (Reports of the Volhynia civil governor, 1806–1811), 81–84; *PSZRI*, ser. 1, vol. 20, no. 14392, 234–35, 256–58, 271–72; Kupriianov, "Gorodskaia demokratiia," 35–38.
13. On governors, see Richard Robbins, Jr., *The Tsar's Viceroys: Russian Provincial Governors in the Last Years of the Empire*, 95–174. In the provinces of Volhynia and Podolia, no governor served longer than four years during the 1830s. Some of the governors discussed in this chapter include the Volhynian governors A. Rimskii-Korsakov (1831–1835) and Nikolai Vasil'evich Zhukovskii (1835–1837) and the Podolian governors Fedor Petrovich Lubianovskii (1831–1833) and Grigorii Sergeevich Lashkarev (1833–1834, 1835–1836). See Fedor Petrovich Lubianovskii, *Vospominaniia, 1777—1834*, 307–15; A. A. Polovtsov, ed., *Russkii biograficheskii slovar,'* vol. 10 (St. Petersburg, 1914), 119, and vol. 13 (St. Petersburg, 1902), 96; O. V. Moriakova, *Sistema mestnogo upravleniia v Rossii pri Nikolae I*, 40–54.
14. Nikolai Gogol, "Revizor: Komedia v piati deistviiakh," 6–7; Roch Sikorski, *"Łyki" i "kołtuny": Pamiętnik mieszszanina podlaskiego (1790–1816)*, 82–86.
15. In 1806, in a report to his superiors, the Volhynia governor Mikhail Komburlei even felt compelled to justify the diverging amounts spent on police protection in his province with the excuse that "in certain towns police duties are carried out by the residents themselves, which sometimes costs more money." TsDIAK, f. KMF 11, o. 1, s. 91, 145. See also TsDIAK, f. KMF 11, o. 1, s. 94, 18–19.
16. *PSZRI*, ser. 1, vol. 23, no. 17323, 691–92. Approximately 4.5 million people lived in these territories, including a much greater percentage of nobles and burghers than in Russia proper. Lukowski, *Partitions of Poland*, 44–51.
17. *PSZRI*, ser. 1, vol. 28, no. 21364, 403.
18. *PSZRI*, ser. 1, vol. 23, no. 17327, 694–95; *PSZRI*, ser. 1, vol. 23, no. 17354, 728.
19. *PSZRI*, ser. 1, vol. 22, no. 16187, 366–70; Alison K. Smith, *Social Estates*

in Imperial Russia, 73–83; Kupriianov, "Gorodskaia demokratiia," 35–44; Ryndziunskii, *Gorodskoe grazhdanstvo*, 44–51; N. P. Eroshkin, *Istoriia gosudarstvennykh uchrezhdenii dorevoliutsionnoi Rossii*, 192–98; Mironov, *Sotsial'naia istoriia Rossii*, 494–95; Hittle, *Service City*, 233–36.

20. Opysy podil's'koi hybernii (1800 ta 1819 rr.), 33–34.

21. Bershadskii, "Polozhenie o evreiakh," *Voskhod* 15, no. 6 (June 1895), 45–55; Klier, *Russia Gathers Her Jews*, 116–43.

22. On the lack of qualified officials, see TsDIAK, f. 442, o. 1, s. 1519, 62. See also TsDIAK, f. KMF 11, o. 1, s. 94, 51–64.

23. Serhii Plokhy, *The Cossack Myth: History and Nationhood in the Age of Empires*, 163–68; Oksana Karlina, "Konflikt mizh tradishchiami mis'koho samovriadubannia i systemoiu mistsevoho upravlinnia na Volyni naprykintsi XVIII pershykh desiatylittiakh XIX st.," 280–84.

24. *PSZRI*, ser. 2, vol. 7, no. 5407, 346.

25. *PSZRI*, ser. 1, vol. 29, no. 22028, 56.

26. TsDIAK, f. KMF 11, o. 1, s. 94, 18–19; f. 442, o. 1, s. 1196 (Reports on municipal governments, 1832), 56.

27. *PSZRI*, ser. 1, vol. 22, no. 16187, 381–83; Eroshkin, *Istoriia gosudarstvennykh uchrezhdenii*, 141–43.

28. TsDIAK, f. KMF 11, o. 1, s. 91, 31–32, 145; TsDIAK, f. 2227, o. 1, s. 177, 255–56.

29. TsDIAK, f. KMF 11, o. 1, s. 94, 17; Karlina, "Konflikt mizh tradishchiami," 281–84; Madriaga, *Russia in the Age of Catherine the Great*, 284–87.

30. AGAD, AR XXIX.175 (Regulations of the Minsk civil governor, 1806), 10–15.

31. AGAD, AR XXIX.175, 1–2, 10–15; AGAD, AR XV.20, no. 10, 4; AGAD, AR V.13176 (Letters from Nieśwież commissar Antoni Rogoziński, 1806–1817), 3–4.

32. AGAD, AR V.13176, 7–8.

33. AGAD, AR XV.18, no. 3, 68–69; AGAD, AR XXIX.20 (Regulations of Dominik Radziwiłł, 1809–1810), 20, 23–24.

34. AGAD, AR XV.7, no. 1, 190.

35. AGAD, AR XV.7, no. 1, 191, 193, see also 185–86, 212–15. Authorities also viewed the comparatively greater number of books and papers in Jewish homes as a fire hazard. See Gąsiorowski, *Chrześcianie i żydzi*, 88–90.

36. AGAD, AR XV.6, no. 31 (Dispute between the burghers of Nieśwież and Dominik Radziwiłł, 1806), 4, 5.

37. AGAD, AR XV.6, no. 3, 12, also 1314.
38. AGAD, AR XV.6, no. 31, 16.
39. AGAD, AR XV.8, no. 3 (General Documents on Nieśwież), 17, 18. The original complaint refers to "Jan Bohdanowicz," while the latter two documents name "Piotr Bohdanowicz" and his brother, "Jakub." However, the dating of their case from April 1806 makes clear that this is the same person.
40. AGAD, AR XV.18, no. 4 (Miscellaneous Nieśwież documents), 15; AGAD, AR XV.18, no. 3, 85–87.
41. Karlina, "Konflikt mizh tradishchiami," 280–85; TsDIAK, f. 442, o.1, s. 1196, 13–15.
42. AGAD, AR V.16136 (Letters from Słuck commissar Stanisław Tomaszewski, 1804–1810), 35–37, 80–81; AGAD, AR XXIX.20, 27.
43. *PSZRI*, ser. 1, vol. 29, no. 21988, 20. See also *PSZRI*, ser. 1, vol. 23, no. 17327, 694–95.
44. TsDIAK, f. KMF 11, o. 1, s. 91, 31 (Komburlei); TsDIAK, f. KMF 11, o. 1, s. 94, 18–20 (Chevkin). See also AGAD, AR V.7035 (Letters from Volhynia governor Mikhail Komburlei, 1806–1809), 11.
45. TsDIAK, f. KMF 11, o. 1, s. 91, 39–40.
46. TsDIAK, f. KMF 11, o. 1, s. 91, 41–42.
47. On the emancipation of the serfs, see *PSZRI*, ser. 2, vol. 39, no. 36650, 129–34; Petr Zaionchkovskii, *Provedenie v zhizn' krest'ianskoi reformy 1861 g.*
48. By comparison, the province's capital, Kamenets-Podol'skii, collected 22,311 rubles from its tolls and taxes.
49. *PSZRI*, ser. 1, vol. 29, no. 21988, 20–23.
50. Opas, "Der Emanzipationsprozess"; Eisenbach, *Emancipation of the Jews*, 274–300.
51. *PSZRI*, ser. 1, vol. 32, no. 25539, 749–50; AGAD, AR XV.7, no. 1, 278–81. On the participation of Ukrainian and Lithuanian nobles in the Napoleonic campaign, see Beauvois, *Pouvoir russe*, 140–55.
52. AGAD, AR XV.18, no. 3, 92–94.
53. *PSZRI*, ser. 1, vol. 40, no. 30557, 569; Karlina, "Konflikt mizh tradishchiami," 283–84.
54. AGAD, AR XV.20, no. 10, 7–19.
55. AGAD, AR XV.20, no. 10, 45.
56. AGAD, AR XV.20, no. 10, 61–68.
57. Lubianovskii, who began his tenure as governor of Podolia during the

uprising, spent his first several months in Kamenets-Podol'skii working feverishly to supply the local troops "or answer for their hunger with [his] head." Lubianovskii, *Vospominaniia*, 312.

58. TsDIAK, f. 442, o. 1, s. 1196, 20. See also Beauvois, *The Noble*, 16–44.
59. TsDIAK, f. 442, o. 1, s. 1519, 24.
60. The magistracy Kamenets-Poldol'skii, for example, continued to employ a secretary for Polish-language business through 1835. TsDIAK, f. 442, o. 1, s. 1269 (Controversy about elections to the Zhitomyr magistracy, 1832), 2. See also TsDIAK, f. 442, o. 66, s. 496, 57–61.
61. TsDIAK, f. 442, o. 1, s. 2324 (Case of firing a Kremenets' magistracy official, 1837), 1–4.
62. TsDIAK, f. KMF 11, o. 1, s. 96 (Report of the Podolia civil governor, 1828), 9–10.
63. TsDIAK, f. KMF 11, o. 1, s. 91, 81–84; TsDIAK, f. KMF 11, o. 1, s. 94, 17; TsDIAK, f. 442, o. 66, s. 496, 13–69.
64. TsDIAK, f. 442, o. 1, s. 1196, 56; TsDIAK, f. 442, o. 1, s. 1519, 42.
65. TsDIAK, f. 442, o. 1, s. 1196, 20.
66. TsDIAK, f. 442, o. 1, s. 1804 (Surveys of gubernii by civil governors, 1835–1836), 69.
67. TsDIAK, f. 442, o. 1, s. 1804, 68.
68. TsDIAK, f. 442, op. 1, s. 1196, 13–16.
69. TsDIAK, f. 442, o. 1, s. 1804, 67–73; AGAD, AR XXIX.21 (Government ukases, 1820–1827), 26–35.
70. TsDIAK, f. 442, o. 1, s. 1196, 20.
71. TsDIAK, f. 442, o. 140, s. 503 (Case about the fine levied on the Kremenets' magistracy, 1835), 1–5.
72. TsDIAK, f. 442, o. 140, s. 503, 5, 10.
73. TsDIAK, f. 442, o. 147, s. 747 (Report of the Kremenets' city inspector, 1838), 1–4. Moriakova reports that governors themselves often failed to submit their own reports on time, leading the Ministry of Internal Affairs to threaten its subordinates repeatedly with removal and court prosecution. Moriakova, *Sistema mestnogo upravleniia*, 12–14.
74. TsDIAK, f. 442, o. 1, s. 1519, 62.
75. TsDIAK, f. 442, o. 1, s. 1196, 20–25, 56; Kupriianov, "Gorodskaia demokratiia,"44–45.
76. TsDIAK, f. 442, o. 1, s. 1196, 23.
77. TsDIAK, f. 442, o. 1, s. 1519, 30–31; *Opysy podils'koi hubernii*, 9.

78. Michael Stanislawski, *Tsar Nicholas I and the Jews: The Transformation of Jewish Society, 1825–1855*, 13–48; Arnold Springer, "Gavriil Derzhavin's Jewish Reform Project of 1800," 4–16; Michael F. Hamm, *Kiev: A Portait, 1800–1917*, 119.
79. TsDIAK, f. 442, o.1, s. 1804, 71.
80. TsDIAK, f. 442, o.1, s. 1804, 71.
81. TsDIAK, f. 442, o. 1, s. 1519, 30–31.
82. Wąsicki, *Ziemie polskie pod zaborem pruskim*, 156–57. See also William Hagen, *Germans, Poles, and Jews: The Nationality Conflict in the Prussian East, 1772–1914*, 146–56.
83. TsDIAK, f. 442, o. 1, s. 1196, 20; *PSZRI*, ser. 2, vol. 11, no. 9226, 609; *PSZRI*, ser. 2, vol. 12, no. 10574, 796.
84. TsDIAK, f, 442, o. 1, s. 1519, 30.
85. Kupriianov, "Gorodskaia demokratiia," 33–35; Eroshkin, *Istoriia gosudarstvennykh uchrezhdenii*, 198.
86. *PSZRI*, ser. 2, vol. 11, no. 9226, 607.
87. *PSZRI*, ser. 2, vol. 29, no. 28521, 752–53.
88. AGAD, AR XV.20, no. 10, 61–68.
89. Robbins, *Tsar's Viceroys*, 147–74; Boris N. Chicherin, *Vospominaniia: Zemstvo i moskovskaia duma*, 206–34; Alessandro Stanziani, "Statisticiens, zemstva, et état dans la Russie des anneés 1880."

CONCLUSION: EMANCIPATING CITIZENS INTO SUBJECTS

1. Julian Łapicki, "Stosunki gmine," 290–310; Stanisław Schultz, "O administracji gminnej w Królestwie Polskim," 400–405. See also Ryszard Kołodziejczyk, "Zamiana miast na osady w Królestwie Polskim."
2. *PSZRI*, ser. 2, vol. 45, no. 48498, 821–23; *PSZRI*, ser. 2, vol. 50, no. 54640, 460–61; Valeriia A. Nardova, "Municipal Government after the 1870 Reform"; Frederick Starr, *Decentralization and Self-Government in Russia, 1830–1870*, 304–34.
3. Larry Wolff, *The Idea of Galicia: History and Fantasy in Habsburg Political Culture*, 231–79, 308–50; Stanziani, "Statisticiens, zemstva, et état," 445–68.
4. Śladkowski, "W epoce zaborów," 111–15; J. Kukulski, "Realizacja reformy gminnej w 1864 roku w Królestwie Polskim."
5. *PSZRI*, ser. 2, vol. 45, no. 48498, 821–23; *PSZRI*, ser. 2, vol. 50, no.

54640, 460–61; Proudfoot, *Urban Patronage and Social Authority*, 3–12, 220–37.

6. Kimitaka Matsuzato, "The Issue of Zemstvos in Right-Bank Ukraine, 1864–1905: Russian Anti-Polonism under the Challenges of Modernization," 235. See also *PSZRI*, ser. 3, vol. 12, no. 8707, 430; Theodore R. Weeks, *Nation and State in Late Imperial Russia: Nationalism and Russification on the Western Frontier, 1863–1914*, 199–241.
7. Pieter M. Judson, *The Habsburg Empire: A New History*, 278, also 279–309, 370–76. See also Evans, "Josephinism," 145–56; Andrzej S. Kamiński, "Polish-Lithuanian Commonwealth and Its Citizens (Was the Commonwealth a Stepmother for Cossacks and Ruthenians?)," 47–48.
8. Henryk Konic, *Samorząd gminny w Królestwie Polskim w porównaniu z innemi krajami europejskimi*, 19, also 42, 67, 113. On "communal freedoms," see Black, *Guild and State*, 190.
9. See Rothschild, *East Central Europe*; Robert Putnam, *Making Democracy Work: Civic Traditions in Modern Italy*; Daniel Treisman, *The Architecture of Government: Rethinking Political Decentralization*; Daniel Ziblatt, *Structuring the State: The Formation of Italy and Germany and the Puzzle of Federalism*, 80–108.
10. Bryon J. Moraski and William M. Reisinger, "Eroding Democracy: Federal Intervention in Russia's Gubernatorial Elections"; J. Paul Goode, "The Puzzle of Putin's Gubernatorial Appointments."
11. On cities in the United States before the twentieth century, see Robert A. Dahl, *Who Governs? Democracy and Power in an American City*. For subsequent changes, see Ruth P. Morgan, *Governance by Decree: The Impact of the Voting Rights Act in Dallas* .
12. Skinner, *Foundations of Modern Political Thought*, 1:ix–xvi.
13. Ptaśnik, "Walki o demokratyzację Lwowa," 228–48; Schilling, *Essays in German and Dutch History*, 1–49.
14. Hegel, *Philosophy of Right*, 265–66.
15. AGAD, KRSW 3644, 43–50; Mazurkiewicz, "Lublin w okresie reform," 179–84; Śladkowski, "W epoce zaborów," 12, 18–24.
16. TsDIAK, f. 13, o. 1, s. 1, 211.
17. Wodziński, *Władze Królestwa Polskiego*, 121–50; Dynner, *Yankel's Tavern*, 1–46.
18. David Christian, "A Neglected Great Reform: The Abolition of Tax Farming in Russia," 102–14.

19. Faber, *Sketches*, 35; J. Toulmin Smith, *Local Self-Government and Centralisation*, 64–65.
20. Władysław Syrokomla, *Wędrówki po moich niegdyś okolicach: Wspomnienia, studja hisoryczne i obyczajowe*, 180–81. See also Józef Ignacy Kraszewski, *Wspomnienia Wołynia, Polesia i Litwy*, 213–15; *SGKP*, vol. 5 (Warsaw, 1884), 421–36; *SGKP*, vol. 7, 528–29.
21. Kołodziejczyk, "Zamiana miast na osady," 190–200.
22. AGAD, AR XV t. 7, no. 1, 234–35; Riabinin, *Rada miejska lubelska*, 15–25.
23. See Eric Lohr, *Russian Citizenship: From Empire to Soviet Union*.
24. See Antony Polonsky, "Introduction: The Shtetl, Myth and Reality."
25. Stefan Rohdewald, *"Vom Polocker Venedig." Kollektives Handeln sozialer Gruppen in einer Stadt zwischen Ost- und Mitteleuropa (Mittelalter, Frühe Neuzeit, 19. Jh. bis 1914)*, 419–71. See also Evtuhov, *Portrait of a Russian Province*, 206–50.
26. Łapicki, "Stosunki gminne," 290–310; Eugene Weber, *Peasants into Frenchmen: The Modernization of Rural France, 1870–1914*, 95–114. See also Timothy Snyder, *The Reconstruction of Nations: Poland, Ukraine, Lithuania, Belarus, 1569–1999*; Bernard Yack, "The Myth of the Civic Nation"; Brian Porter, *When Nationalism Began to Hate: Imagining Modern Politics in Nineteenth-Century Poland*, 136–231.
27. See, for example, Jerome Blum, *The End of the Old Order in Rural Europe.*

Bibliography

ARCHIVAL SOURCES AND MANUSCRIPTS

Archiwum Główne Akt Dawnych w Warszawie (AGAD)

Archiwum Królestwa Polskiego (AKP) 85–86, 88.

Archiwum Radziwiłłów (AR) V.7035, 10430, 10843, 10845, 11370, 13176, 16136; XV.5, no. 2; XV.6, no. 30; XV.7, no. 1; XV.18, nos. 3–4; XV.20, no. 10; XXV.2658/1, 2666, 2684/2, 2689, 2690/2, 2690/3, 2691, 2691/1; 3839a; XXIX.5, 12–13, 15, 18–21.

Archiwum Skarbu Koronnego (ASK) XLVI.18, 20, 129, 132.

Archiwum Zamoyskich (AZ) 73, 615, 1888, 1996, 2494a, 2521, 2579.

Komisja Rządowa Spraw Wewnętrznych (KRSW) 33, 35–41, 167, 172, 205, 3010, 3234, 3252, 3277, 3283, 3418–19, 3581, 3588, 3598, 3634, 3673, 3688, 3734, 3943, 4042, 4145, 7021, 7024, 7030, 7033.

Księgi Kancellerskie, 58/4.

Tak zwana Metryka Litewska (ML) IVB.49; VII.18–19, 75–101, 142, 155–56, 173; IX.105.

Archiwum Państwowe w Lublinie (APL)

Akta luźne miasta Lublina 55

Akta miasta Bełżyc (Bełżyce) 15, 17, 36–37.

Akta miasta Bychawy (Bychawa) 4.

Akta miasta Chełma (Chełm) 14.

Akta miasta Firleja (Firlej) 3.
Akta miasta Kazimierza Dolnego (Kazimierz Dolny) 205.
Akta miasta Kraśnika (Kraśnik) 40.
Akta miasta Łęcznej (Lęczna) 24.
Akta miasta Lubartowa (Lubartów) 6.
Akta miasta Lublina (AML) 6, 11a, 73, 78, 593, 923, 999, 1013–14, 1302, 2739, 2740, 2741.
Akta miasta Modliborzyc (Modliborzyce) 4, 6.
Akta miasta Tomaszowa (Tomaszów) 11.
Akta miasta Zamościa (Zamość) 18, 73, 76.
Akta miasta Żółkiewki (Żółkiewka) 1.
Akta Ordynacji Zamoyskiej (AOZ) 1513, 1547–53, 1586.
Księgi Komisji Boni Ordinis w Lublinie (KBO) 4–5.
Księgi Komisji Cywilno-Wojskowej Chełmskiej (KCW Chełm) 1.
Księgi Komisji Cywilno-Wojskowej Lubelskiej (KCW Lublin) 1, 3.
Księgi miejskie Lublina (KML) 55, 126, 145, 178, 187, 197e, 253, 261, 283, 285, 320.
Trybunał Zamoyski 14.

Biblioteka Książąt Czartoryskich (BC)
Manuscripts 804, 817, 897, 953, 1093, 2619–20.

Tsentral'nyi Derzhavnyi Istorychnyi Arkhiv m. Kyiv (TsDIAK)
Fond 8: Tsyviln'no-viis'kova poriadkova komisiia Kyivs'koho voevodstva, opys 1, sprava 15
Fond 13: Magistrat m. Zhytomyr, opys 1, sprava 1; opys 2, sprava 2.
Fond 21: Krements'kii grods'kyi sud, opys 1, sprava 44.
Fond 41: Tsyvil'no-viis'kova poriadkova komisiia Kremenets'koho povitu, opys 1, sprava 2.
Fond 442: Kantseliariia kyivs'koho, podil's'koho i volyns'koho general-gubernatora, opys 1, sprava 1196, 1269, 1519, 1804, 2324; opys 66, sprava 496; opys 67, sprava 507; opys 140, sprava 503; opys 141, sprava 609; opys 147, sprava 747.
Fond KMF (Kollektsia mikrofilmov) 11, opys 1, sprava 91, 94, 96.

PUBLISHED SOURCES

Beaumanoir, Philippe de Rémi, sire de. *Coutumes de Beauvaisis*. Edited by Amédée Salmon. Vol. 2. Paris, 1900.

Coxe, William. *Travels in Poland and Russia*. New York, 1970.

Chicherin, Boris N. *Vospominaniia: Zemstvo i moskovskaia duma*. Moscow, 1934.

Cudzoziemcy o Polsce: Relacje i opinie. Edited by Jan Gintel. Vol. 1. Krakow, 1971.

De la Mare, Nicolas. *Traité de la Police, où l'on trouvera l'histoire de son établissement, les fonctions et les prérogatives de ses magistrats; toutes les loix et tous les règlements qui la concernent*. 2 vols. Paris, 1722.

Documents of Catherine the Great: The Correspondence with Voltaire and the Instruction of 1767. Edited by W. F. Reddaway. Cambridge, UK, 1931.

Domat, Jean. *The Civil Law in Its Natural Order Together with the Public Law*. Translated by William Strahan. London, 1722.

Dyaryusz Seymu Królestwa Polskiego r. 1818. Warsaw, 1818.

Dyaryusz seymu ordynaryinego pod związkiem konfederacyi generalney oboyga narodów agituiącego się. Warsaw, 1777.

Dziennik Handlowy y Ekonomiczny. 1788.

Dziennik Praw Królestwa Polskiego. 1815–1820.

Dziennik Praw Księstwa Warszawskiego. 1807–1811.

Faber, Theodor von. *Sketches of the Internal State of France*. Philadelphia, PA, 1812.

Fredo, Aleksander. "Zemsta." Edited by Barbara Włodarczyk. Krakow, 2008.

Fredro, Andrzej Maksymilian. "W obronie liberum veto." In *Filozofia i myśl społeczna XVII wieku*, edited by Zbigniew Ogonowski, 301–48. Warsaw, 1979.

Gogol, Nikolai. "Revizor: Komedia v piati deistviiakh." St. Petersburg, 2007.

Gostomski, Anzelm. *Gospodarstwo*. Edited by Stefan Inglot. Wrocław, 1951.

Groicki, *Bartołomej. Porządek sądów miejskich prawa majdeburskiego w Koronie Polskiej*. Edited by Karol Koranyi. Warsaw, 1953.

Hamilton, Alexander, John Jay, and James Madison. *The Federalist Papers*. New York, 2008.

Hobbes, Thomas. *Leviathan*. Edited by Edwin Curley. Indianapolis, 1994.

Jewish Privileges in the Polish Commonwealth: Charters of Rights Granted to Jewish Communities in the Sixteenth to Eighteenth Centuries. Edited by Jacob Goldberg. 3 vols. Jerusalem, 1985.

Kitowicz, Jędrzej. *Pamiętniki, czyli Historia polska*. Edited by Przemysława Matuszewska. Warsaw, 2005.

Kleczyński, Józef. "Spis ludności dyecezyi krakowskiej z r. 1787." *Archiwum Komisji Historycznej Akademii Umiejętności w Krakowie* 7 (1894): 265–453.

Kołłątaj, Hugo. *Listy anonima i prawo polityczne narodu polskiego*. Edited by B. Leśnodorski and Helena Wereszycka. Warsaw, 1954.

Kołłątaj, Hugo. *Uwagi nad teraźnieyszym położeniem tey części ziemi polskiey, którą od pokoiu tylżyckiego zaczęto zwać Xięstwem Warszawskim*. Leipzig, 1808.

Komoniecki, Andrzej. *Chronografia albo dziejopis żywiecki*. Edited by Stanisław Grodziski and Irena Dwornicka. Żywiec, 1987.

Konarski, Stanisław. *O skutecznym rad sposobie albo o utrzymywaniu ordynaryinych Seymów*. 4 vols. Warsaw, 1923.

Korrespondencya w materyach obraz kraiu i narodu polskiego rozniaśniaiących. Warsaw, 1807.

Koźmian, Kajetan. *Pamiętniki*. 3 vols. Wrocław, 1972.

Kraszewski, Józef Ignacy. *Wspomnienia Wołynia, Polesia i Litwy*. Vilnius, 1840.

Kromer, Marcin. *Polska, czyli o położeniu, ludności, obyczyajach, urzędach, i sprawach publicznych Królestwa Polskiego Księgi Dwie*. Edited by Roman Marchwiński. Olsztyn, 1977.

Łapicki, Julian. "Stosunki gmine." *Ateneum* (1880): 268–437.

Leszczyński, Stanisław. Głos wolny wolność ubezpieczający, edited by Stanisław Jedynak. Lublin, 1987.

Lind, John. *Letters Concerning the Present State of Poland, Together with an Appendix Containing the Manifestos of the Courts of Vienna, Petersburgh, and Berlin, and Other Authentic Papers*. London, 1773.

Lubianovskii, Fedor Petrovich. *Vospominaniia, 1777–1834*. Moscow, 1872.

Lubomirski, Stanisław. *Pamiętniki*. Edited by Władysław Konopczyński. L'viv, 1925.

Lubowiecki, Ignacy. *Pamiętniki*. Edited by Norbert Kasparek. Lublin, 1997.

Machiavelli, Niccolò. *The Prince and the Discourses*. Edited by Max Lerner. New York, 1950.

Maimon, Solomon. *Solomon Maimon: An Autobiography*. Translated by J. Clark Murray. Chicago, 2001.

Materiały do dziejów Sejmu Czteroletniego. Edited by Janusz Woliński, Jerzy Michalski, and Emanuel Rostworowski. 6 vols. Wrocław, 1955-1961. Cited in notes as *MDSC*.

Mędrzecki, Adam, and Frydrych Barssa. *Zbiór praw, dowodów i uwag dla obiaśnienia zaszczytów stanowi mieyskiemu ex juribus municipalibus służących*. Warsaw, 1790.

The Memoirs of Ber of Bolechow (1723–1805). Translated by M. Vishnitzer. New York, 1973.

Montesquieu. *De L'Esprit des lois*. Edited by Paul Janet. Paris, 1892.

Möser, Justus. "Deutsche Geschichte." In *Von Deutsche Art und Kunst*, edited by Edna Purdie, 154–58. London, 1924.

Naruszewicz, Adam. *Dyjaryjusz podroży Jego Królewskiej Mości na sejm grodzieński*. Edited by Magdalena Bober-Jankowska. Warsaw, 2008.

Opysy podil's'koi hubernii (1800 ta 1819 rr.). Edited by Iurii Serhiiovych Zems'kyi and Valerii Vasil'ovych Diachok. Khmel'nyts'kyi, Ukraine, 2005.

Owidzki, Joachim. *Spostrzeżenia, uwagi, i myśli obywatela w zaciszu domowem przyszłemu seymowi podane*. Lublin, 1811.

Pervaia vseobshchaia perepis' naselenii Rossiiskoi Imperii 1897 g. Edited by N. A. Troinitskii. 89 vols. St Petersburg, 1899.

Pokorna Prośba od Żydów Warszawskich i Prowincyi Koronnych do Nayjaśnieyszych Seymuiących Stanów. Warsaw, n.d.

Polnoe sobranie zakonov Rossiiskoi Imperii. Ser. 1–3. 1775–1890.

Poniatowski, Stanisław (the elder). *List ziemianina do pewnego przyjaciela z inszego woiewództwa*. [Warsaw?], 1744.

"Proshenie malorossiiskago shliakhetstva i starshin vmeste s getmanom o vozstanovlenii raznykh starshinnykh prav Malorossii, podannoe Ekaterine II v 1764 godu." *Kievskaia Starina* 2, no. 6 (May 1883): 317–43.

Rousseau, Jean Jacques. *The Government of Poland*. Translated by Willmoore Kenall. Indianapolis, 1972.

Rudomicz, Bazyli. *Efemeros czyli diariusz prywatny pisany w Zamościu w latach 1656–1672*. 2 vols. Lublin, 2002.

Rulhière, Claude. *Histoire de l'anarchie de Pologne et du démembrement de cette république*. 4 vols. Paris, 1807.

Schultz, Stanisław. "O administracji gminnej w Królestwie Polskim." *Niwa* 12 (1880): 397–417.

Sikorski, Roch. *"Łyki" i "kołtuny": Pamiętnik mieszszanina podlaskiego (1790–1816)*. Edited by Kazimierz Bartoszewicz. Białystock, 2008.

Słównik Geograficzny Królestwa Polskiego i innych krajów słowiańskich. Edited by Filip Sulimierski, Bronisław Chlebowski, and Władyslaw Walewski. 15 vols. Warsaw, 1880–1914.

Smith, Adam. *An Inquiry into the Nature and Causes of the Wealth of Nations*. Edited by Edwin Cannan. Chicago, 1976.

Staszic, Stanisław. "Przestrogi dla Polski (1790)." In *Wybór pism*, edited by Celina Bobińska, 40–109. Warsaw, 1948.

"Statut Organiczny Królestwa Polskiego." In *Królestwo Polskie: Dokumenty historyczne dotyczące prawno-politycznego stosunku Królestwa Polskiego do Cesarstwa Rosyjskiego*, edited by Maciej Radziwiłł and Bohdan Winiarski, 123–34. Warsaw, 1915.

Surowiecki, Wawrzyniec. *O upadku przemysłu y miast w Polszcze*. Warsaw, 1810.

Świniarski, Michał. *Wiadomość o pierwiastkowey miast zasadzie w Polszcze, ich szczegulnych przywileiach i wolnościach oraz o przyczynach upadku tychże miast*. Warsaw, 1789.

Syrokomla, Władysław. *Wędrówki po moich niegdyś okolicach: Wspomnienia, studja hisoryczne i obyczajowe*. Wilno, 1853.

Voltaire. *Philosophical Dictionary*. Translated by Peter Gay. 2 vols. New York, 1962.

Volumina Legum: Przedruk zbioru praw staraniem XX. pijarów w Warszawie od roku 1732 do roku 1793. Vols. 7–8. St. Petersburg, 1860.

Volumina Legum: Przedruk zbioru praw staraniem XX. pijarów w Warszawie od roku 1732 do roku 1793. Vol. 9. Krakow, 1889.

Vossoedinenie Ukrainy s Rossiei: Dokumenty i materialy v 3-kh tomakh. Edited by P. P. Gudzenko. 3 vols. Moscow, 1954.

Wybór tekstów źródłowych z historii Polski w latach 1795–1864. Edited by Stefan Kieniewicz, Tadeusz Mencel, and Władysław Rostocki. Warsaw, 1956.

Zbiór mów różnych w czasie dwóch ostatnich seymów roku 1775 y 1776 mianych. 3 vols. Poznań, 1777.

SECONDARY WORKS

Adamczyk, Władysław. *Ceny w Lublinie od XVI do końca XVIII wieku*. Lwów, 1935.

Ajnenkiel, Andrzej. "The Influence of the Constitution of 3 May on Constitutional Life of the Second Republic (1919–1939): Reality and Myth." In *Constitution and Reform in Eighteenth Century Poland: The Constitution of 3 May 1791*, edited by Samuel Fiszman, 519–26. Bloomington, IN, 1997.

Anderson, M. S. "The Italian Reformers." In *Enlightened Absolutism: Reform and Reformers in Later Eighteenth-Century Europe*, edited by H. M. Scott, 55–74. Ann Arbor, MI, 1989.

Anusik, Zbigniew, and Andrzej Stroynowski. "Problemy majątkowe Radziwiłłów w XVIII w." *Roczniki dziejów społecznych i gospodarczych* 48 (1987): 79–112.

Arendt, Hannah. *The Human Condition*. 2nd ed. Chicago, 1998.

Avrutin, Eugene M. *Jews and the Imperial State: Identification Politics in Tsarist Russia*. Ithaca, 2010.

Avrutin, Eugene M. "The Politics of Jewish Legibility: Documentation Practices and Reform during the Reign of Nicholas I." *Jewish Social Studies* 11, no. 2 (Winter 2005): 136–69.

Bałaban, Majer. *Die Judenstadt von Lublin*. Berlin, 1919.

Balázs, Éva H. *Hungary and the Habsburgs, 1765–1800: An Experiment in Enlightened Absolutism*. Translated by Tim Wilkinson. Budapest, 1997.

Baranowski, Ignacy. *Komisye porządkowe (1765–1788)*. Krakow, 1907.

Bardach, Juliusz. *Historia państwa i prawa Polski do połowy XV wieku*. Warsaw, 1957.

Bardach, Juliusz. "Le principe fédéraliste et le principe unitaire dans la législation de la Diète polono-lithuanienne de Quatre Ans (1788–1792)." *Acta Poloniae Historica* 70 (1994): 75–86.

Basarab, John. *Pereiaslav 1654: A Historiographic Study*. Edmonton, 1982.

Beauvois, Daniel. *The Noble, the Serf, and the Revizor: The Polish Nobility between Tsarist Imperialism and the Ukrainian Masses (1831–1863)*. Translated by Barbara Reising. New York, 1991.

Beauvois, Daniel. *Pouvoir russe et noblesse polonaise en Ukraine, 1793–1830*. Paris, 2003.

Behrens, C. B. A. *Society, Government and the Enlightenment: The Experiences of Eighteenth-Century France and Prussia*. London, 1985.

Bělina, Pavel. *Česká města v 18. století a osvícenské reformy*. Prague, 1985.

Berlin, Isaiah. *The Proper Study of Mankind: An Anthology of Essays*. Edited by Henry Hardy and Roger Hausheer. New York, 1998.

Bershadskii, S. A. "Polozhenie o evreiakh 1804 goda." *Voskhod* 15, no. 1 (January 1895): 82–103; *Voskhod* 15, no. 6 (June 1895): 33–63.

Black, Anthony. *Guild and State: European Political Thought from the Twelfth Century to the Present*. 2nd ed. New Brunswick, 2005.

Blanning, T. C. W. *Joseph II and Enlightened Despotism*. London, 1970.

Blickle, Peter. *From the Communal Reformation to the Revolution of the Common Man*. Translated by Beat Kümin. Leiden, 1998.

Blum, Jerome. *The End of the Old Order in Rural Europe*. Princeton, NJ, 1978.

Bobrzyński, Michał. *Dzieje Polski w zarysie*. Edited by M. H. Serejski and A. F. Grabski. Warsaw, 1974.

Bogucka, Maria, and Henryk Samsonowicz. *Dzieje miast i mieszczaństwa w Polsce przedrozbiorowej*. Wrocław, 1986.

Bömelburg, Hans-Jürgen. "Inklusion und Exklusion nach der Ersten Teilung Polen-Litauens: Die österreichische, preussiche und russländlische Regierungspraxis in Galizien, Westpreussen und den weissrussischen Gouvernements Polack und Mahilëŭ im Vergleich (1772–1806/07)." In *Die Tielungen Polen-Litauens: Inklusions- und Exklusionsmechanismen—*

Traditionsbildung—Vergleichsebenen, edited by Hans-Jürgen Bömelburg, Andreas Gestrich, and Helga Schnabel-Schüle, 171–200. Osnabrück, 2013.

Bömelburg, Hans-Jürgen. *Zwischen Polnischer Ständegesellschaft und Preussischem Obrigkeitsstaat: Von Königlichen Preußen zu Westpreußen (1756–1806)*. Munich, 1995.

Borkowska-Bagieńska, Ewa. *Zbiór praw sądowych Andrzeja Zamoyskiego*. Poznań, 1986.

Bourdieu, Pierre. *The Logic of Practice*. Translated by Richard Nice. Stanford, CA, 1990.

Broers, Michael. "Centre and Periphery in Napoleonic Italy: The Nature of French Rule in the *départements réunis*, 1800–1814." In *Collaboration and Resistance in Napoleonic Europe: State Formation in an Age of Upheaval, c. 1800–1815*, edited by Michael Rowe, 55–72. New York, 2003.

Butterwick, Richard. *Poland's Last King and English Culture: Stanisław August Poniatowski, 1732–1798*. Oxford, 1998.

Butterwick, Richard. *The Polish Revolution and the Catholic Church, 1788–1792: A Political History*. Oxford, 2011.

Christian, David. "A Neglected Great Reform: The Abolition of Tax Farming in Russia." In *Russia's Great Reforms, 1855–1881*, edited by Ben Eklof, John Bushnell and Larissa Zakharova, 102–14. Bloomington, IN, 1994.

Cichoń, Paweł. *Rozwój myśli administracyjnej w Księstwie Warszawskim, 1807–1815*. Krakow, 2006.

Clark, Christopher. *Iron Kingdom: The Rise and Downfall of Prussia, 1600–1947*. Cambridge, MA, 2006.

Collins, James B. *Classes, Estates and Order in Early Modern Brittany*. Cambridge, UK, 1994.

Collins, James B. "Le pouvoir municipal et l'écroulement de l'Ancien Régime: question sociale ou question politique?" In *L'exercice du pouvoir municipal en France de la fin du Moyen Age à 1789*, edited by Philippe Hannon and Catherine Laurent, 333–48. Rennes, 2012.

Creveld, Marin van. *The Rise and Decline of the State*. 10th ed. Cambridge, UK, 2009.

Crozier, Michel. *The Bureaucratic Phenomenon*. Chicago, 1964.

Ćwik, Władysław. "Jurysdykcja Rady Ekonomicznej Ordynacji Zamoyskiej." *Annales Universitatis Mariae Curie-Skłodowska, Sectio G: Ius* 18, no. 2 (1971): 147–69.

Ćwik, Władysław. *Miasta królewskie lubelszczyzny w drugiej połowie XVIII wieku.* Lublin, 1968.

Ćwik, Władysław. "Zamość pod zaborami." In *Czterysta lat Zamościa,* edited by Jerzy Kowalczyk, 129–43. Wrocław, 1983.

Cynarski, Stanisław. "The Ideology of Sarmatism in Poland (16th–18th centuries)." *Polish Western Affairs* 33, no. 2 (1992): 25–43.

Czaja, Aleksander. *Między tronem, buławą a dworem petersburskim: Z dziejów Rady Nieustającej, 1786–1789.* Warsaw, 1988.

Czubaty, Jarosław. "The Attitude of the Polish Political Elite towards the State in the Period of the Duchy of Warsaw, 1807–1815." In *Collaboration and Resistance in Napoleonic Europe: State Formation in an Age of Upheaval, c. 1800–1815,* edited by Michael Rowe, 169–85. New York, 2003.

Czubaty, Jarosław. *The Duchy of Warsaw: A Napoleonic Outpost in Central Europe.* London, 2015.

Dahl, Robert A. *Who Governs? Democracy and Power in an American City.* New Haven, CT, 1961.

Dembkowski, Harry E. *The Union of Lublin: Polish Federalism in the Golden Age.* Boulder, CO, 1982.

De Vries, Jan. *The Industrious Revolution: Consumer Behavior and the Household Economy, 1650 to the Present.* Cambridge, UK, 2008.

Doursther, Horace. *Dictionnaire universel des poids et mesures anciens et modernes, contenant des tables des monnaies de tous les pays.* Amsterdam, 1965.

Downing, Brian M. *The Military Revolution and Political Change: Origins of Democracy and Autocracy in Early Modern Europe.* Princeton, NJ, 1992.

Doyle, William. *The Oxford History of the French Revolution.* Oxford, 1989.

Dynner, Glenn. *Yankel's Tavern: Jews, Liquor, and Life in the Kingdom of Poland.* Oxford, 2014.

Eisenbach, Arthur. *The Emancipation of the Jews in Poland, 1780–1870.* Translated by Janina Dorosz. Cambridge, MA, 1991.

Eliassen, Finn-Einar. "The Urbanization of the Periphery: Landowners and Small Towns in Early Modern Norway and Northern Europe." *Acta Poloniae Historica* 70 (1994): 49–74.

Epstein, S. R. *Freedom and Growth: The Rise of States and Markets in Europe, 1300–1750.* New York, 2000.

Eroshkin, N. P. *Istoriia gosudarstvennykh uchrezhdenii dorevoliutsionnoi Rossii.* Edited by A. E. Ivanov and A. D. Stepanskii. Moscow, 2008.

Evans, R. J. W. "Josephinism, 'Austrianness,' and the Revolution of 1848." In

The Austrian Enlightenment and Its Aftermath, edited by Ritchie Robertson and Edward Timms, 145–60. Edinburgh, 1991.

Evtuhov, Catherine. *Portrait of a Russian Province: Economy, Society, and Civilization in Nineteenth-Century Nizhnii Novgorod*. Pittsburgh, PA, 2011.

Fahrmeir, Andreas. "Centralisation versus Particularism in the 'Third Germany.'" In *Collaboration and Resistance in Napoleonic Europe: State Formation in an Age of Upheaval, c. 1800–1815*, edited by Michael Rowe, 107–20. New York, 2003.

Frick, David. *Kith, Kin, and Neighbors: Community and Coexistence in Seventeenth-Century Wilno*. Ithaca, NY, 2013.

Friedeburg, Robert von. "Civic Humanism and Republican Citizenship in Early Modern Germany." In *Republicanism: A Shared European Tradition*, edited by Martin van Gelderen and Quentin Skinner, 1:127–45. New York, 2002.

Friedeburg, Robert von. *Luther's Legacy: The Thirty Years War and the Modern Notion of "State" in the Empire, 1530s to 1790s*. Cambridge, UK, 2016.

Friedrich, Karin. *The Other Prussia: Royal Prussia, Poland, and Liberty, 1569–1772*. Cambridge, UK, 2000.

Frost, Robert I. *The Northern Wars: War, State and Society in Northeastern Europe, 1558–1721*. Harlow, UK, 2000.

Frost, Robert I. *The Oxford History of Poland-Lithuania. Volume I: The Making of the Polish-Lithuanian Union, 1385–1569*. Oxford, 2015.

Frug, Gerald E. "The City as a Legal Concept." *Harvard Law Review* 93, no. 6 (1980): 1057–154.

Garnot, Benoît. "Administrer une ville au XVIIIème siècle: Chartres." *Histoire, Economie, et Société* 7, no. 2 (1988): 169–86.

Gąsiorowski, Stefan. *Chrześcianie i żydzi w Żółkwi w XVII i XVIII wieku*. Krakow, 2001.

Gierke, Otto von. *Community in Historical Perspective: A Translation of Selections from Das deutsche Genossenschaftrecht (The German Law of Fellowship)*. Translated by Mary Fischer. Cambridge, UK, 1990.

Gierowski, Józef Andrzej. *Między saskim absolutyzmem a złotą wolnością; z dziejów wewnętrznych Rzeczypospolitej w latach 1712–1715*. Wrocław, 1953.

Gierowski, Józef Andrzej. *The Polish-Lithuanian Commonwealth in the XVIIIth Century: From Anarchy to Well-Organized State*. Translated by Henry Leeming. Krakow, 1996.

Gieysztorowa, Irena. *Wstęp do demografii staropolskiej*. Warsaw, 1976.

Gil, Xavier. "Republican Politics in Early Modern Spain: The Castilian and Catalono-Aragonese Traditions." In *Republicanism: A Shared European Tradition*, edited by Martin van Gelderen and Quentin Skinner, 1:263–88. New York, 2002.

Gmiterek, Henryk. "Dzieje miasta w XVII–XVIII wieku." In *Dzieje Bychawy*, edited by Ryszard Szczygieł, 55–72. Lublin, 1994.

Goclon, Jacek Arkadiusz. *Polska na królu pruskim zdobyta: Ustrój, administracja, i sądownictwo doby Komisji Rządzącej w 1807 roku*. Wrocław, 2002.

Goode, J. Paul. "The Puzzle of Putin's Gubernatorial Appointments." *Europe-Asia Studies* 59, no. 3 (2007): 365–99.

Grochowska, Irena. *Stanisław Antoni Szczuka—Jego działność w ziemi wiskiej, 1682–1710*. Warsaw, 1989.

Grodziski, Stanisław. "The Krakow Voivode's Jurisdiction over Jews: A Study of the Historical Records of the Krakow Voivode's Administration of Justice to Jews." In *The Jews in Old Poland 1000–1795*, edited by Antony Polonsky, Jakub Basista, and Andrzej Link-Lenczkowski, 199–217. London, 1993.

Gruder, Vivian R. *The Royal Provincial Intendants: A Governing Elite in Eighteenth-Century France*. Ithaca, NY, 1968.

Grześkowiak-Krwawicz, Anna. *Queen Liberty: The Concept of Freedom in the Polish-Lithuanian Commonwealth*. Translated by Daniel Sax. Leiden, 2012.

Guizot, François. *Histoire de la civilisation en Europe depuis la chute de l'empire romain jusqu'a la révolution français*. Paris, 1868.

Guldon, Zenon, and Jacek Wijaczka. *Procesy o mordy rytualne w Polsce w XVI–XVIII wieku*. Kielce, 1995.

Hagen, William. *Germans, Poles, and Jews: The Nationality Conflict in the Prussian East, 1772–1914*. Chicago, 1980.

Halecki, Oscar. *Jadwiga of Anjou and the Rise of East Central Europe*. Boulder, CO, 1991.

Hamm, Michael F. *Kiev: A Portait, 1800–1917*. Princeton, NJ, 1993.

Hanson, Paul R. *Provincial Politics in the French Revolution: Caen and Limoges, 1789–1794*. Baton Rouge, LA, 1989.

Hegel, G. W. F. *Outlines of the Philosophy of Right*. Translated by T. M. Knox. Oxford, 2008.

Hertzberg, Arthur. *The French Enlightenment and the Jews*. New York, 1968.

Heyde, Jürgen. "Ewolucja zwierzchności królewskiej nad ludnością żydowską w XVI wieku." In *Małżeństwo z rozsądku? Żydzi w społeczeństwie dawnej Rzeczypospolitej*, edited by Marcin Wodziński and Anna Michałowska-Mycielska, 35–48. Wrocław, 2007.

Hillis, Faith. *Children of Rus: Right-Bank Ukraine and the Invention of a Russian Nation*. Ithaca, NY, 2013.

Hittle, J. Michael. *The Service City: State and Townsmen in Russia, 1600–1800*. Cambridge, MA, 1979.

Horn, Maurycy. "The Chronology and Distribution of Jewish Craft Guilds in Old Poland, 1613–1795." In *The Jews in Old Poland 1000–1795*, edited by Antony Polonsky, Jakub Basista, and Andrzej Link-Lenczkowski, 249–65. London, 1993.

Hundert, Gershon David. *The Jews in a Polish Private Town: The Case of Opatów in the Eighteenth Century*. Baltimore, MD, 1992.

Hundert, Gershon David. *Jews in Poland-Lithuania in the Eighteenth Century: A Genealogy of Modernity*. Berkeley, CA, 2004.

Judson, Pieter M. *The Habsburg Empire: A New History*. Cambridge, MA, 2016.

Jurginis, Juozas. "Sud'ba magdeburgskogo prava w litovskikh gorodakh." *Istoriia SSSR* 4 (1975): 145–55.

Kądziela, Łukasz. *Od konstytucji do insurekcji: Studia nad dziejami Rzeczypospolitej w latach 1791–1794*. Warsaw, 2011.

Kalinowski, Wojciech. "Miasto idealne i jego przemiany." In *Czterysta lat Zamościa*, edited by Jerzy Kowalczyk, 87–93. Wrocław, 1983.

Kallas, Marian. "Koncepcje organizacji nowoczesnej administracji terytorialnej w Księstwie Warszawskim." *Annales Universitatis Mariae Curie-Skłodowska, Sectio F: Historia* 37, no. 10 (1982): 189–210.

Kallas, Marian. *Organy administracji terytorialnej w Księstwie Warszawskim*. Toruń, 1975.

Kallas, Marian. "Le système administratif du Duché de Varsovie, 1806–15." *Canadian Slavonic Papers* 19, no. 3 (September 1977): 259–80.

Kamiński, Andrzej S. *Historia Rzeczypospolitej wielu narodów*. Lublin, 2000.

Kamiński, Andrzej S. "Polish-Lithuanian Commonwealth and Its Citizens (Was the Commonwealth a Stepmother for Cossacks and Ruthenians?)." In *Poland and Ukraine: Past and Present*, edited by Peter J. Potichnyj, 32–57. Edmonton, 1980.

Karlina, Oksana. "Konflikt mizh tradishchiami mis'koho samovriadubannia i systemoiu mistsevoho upravlinnia na Volyni naprykintsi XVIII pershykh desiatylittiakh XIX st." *Sotsium* 7 (2007): 280–89.

Kaźmierczyk, Adam. *Żydzi w dobrach prywatnych w świetle sądownych i administracyjnych praktyki dóbr magnackich w wiekach XVI–XVIII*. Krakow, 2002.

Kermisz, Józef. *Lublin i lubelskie w ostatnich latach Rzeczypospolitej (1788–1794)*.

Vol. 1, *W czasie Sejmu Wielkiego i wojny Polsko-Rosyjskiej 1792 r. oraz pod rządami Targowo-Grodzieńskimi*. Lublin, 1939.

Kizevetter, A. A. *Gorodovoe polozhenie Ekateriny II 1785 g. Opyt istoricheskago kommentariia*. Moscow, 1909.

Kizevetter, A. A. *Istoricheskie ocherki*. Moscow, 1912.

Kleinmann, Yvonne. "Rechtsinstrumente in einer ethnisch-religiös gemischten Stadtgesellschaft des frühneuzeitlichen Polen. Der Fall Rzeszów." *Konkurrierende Ordnungen: Verschränkungen von Religion, Staat und Nation in Ostmitteleuropa vom 16. bis zum 20. Jahrhundert* (2015): 159–200.

Klier, John Doyle. *Russia Gathers Her Jews: The Origins of the "Jewish Question" in Russia, 1772–1825*. Dekalb, IL, 1986.

Kochanowicz, Jacek. "The Polish Economy and the Origins of Dependency." In *The Origins of Backwardness in Eastern Europe: Economics and Politics from the Middle Ages until the Early Twentieth Century*, edited by Daniel Chirot, 92–130. Berkeley, CA, 1989.

Kohut, Zenon E. *Russian Centralism and Ukrainian Autonomy: Imperial Absorption of the Hetmanate, 1760s–1830s*. Cambridge, MA, 1988.

Kołodziejczyk, Ryszard. "Zamiana miast na osady w Królestwie Polskim." *Kwartalnik Historyczny* 68, no. 1 (1961): 191–200.

Konic, Henryk. *Samorząd gminny w Królestwie Polskim w porównaniu z innemi krajami europejskimi*. Warsaw, 1906.

Konopczyński, Władysław. *Geneza i ustanowienia Rady Nieustającej*. Krakow, 1919.

Konopczyński, Władysław. *Konfederacja barska*. 2 vols. Reprint ed. Warsaw, 1999.

Korzon, Tadeusz. *Odrodzenie w upadku: Wybór pism historycznych*. Edited by A. F. Grabski and M. H. Serejski , 298–326. Warsaw, 1975.

Korzon, Tadeusz. *Wewnętrzne dzieje Polski za Stanisława Augusta (1764–1794)*. 6 vols. Warsaw, 1897.

Koselleck, Reinhart. *Critique and Crisis: Enlightenment and the Pathogenesis of Modern Society*. Oxford, 1988.

Kriegseisen, Wojciech. *Sejmiki rzeczypospolitej szlacheckiej w XVII i XVIII wieku*. Warsaw, 1991.

Kuklo, Cezary. *Demografia Rzeczypospolitej przedrozbiorowej*. Warsaw, 2009.

Kukulski, J. "Realizacja reformy gminnej w 1864 roku w Królestwie Polskim." In *Gmina wiejska i jej samorząd: praca zbiorowa*, edited by Helena Brodowska, 151–92. Warsaw, 1989.

Kula, Witold. *An Economic Theory of the Feudal System: Towards a Model of the Polish Economy, 1500–1800*. Translated by Lawrence Garner. London, 1976.

Kulecka, Alicja. *Wapno i alabaster: Biurokratyczna wizija rzeczywistości w raportach urzędowych Królestwa Polskiego (1815–1867)*. Warsaw, 2005.

Kupriianov, A. I. "Gorodskaia demokratiia: vybory v russkoi provintsii (vtoraia polovina 1780-kh–nachalo 1860-kh gg.)." *Otechestvennaia istoriia* 5 (2007): 31–49.

Kutrzeba, Stanisław. *Historya ustroju polski w zarysie*. 4 vols. Lwów, 1917.

Lamarre, Christine. *Petites villes et fait urbain en France au XVIIIème siècle: Le cas bourguignon*. Dijon, 1993.

Laven, David, and Lucy Riall. "Restoration Government and the Legacy of Napoleon." In *Napoleon's Legacy: Problems of Government in Restoration Europe*, edited by David Laven and Lucy Riall, 1–19. New York, 2000.

Lelewel, Joachim. *Polska: Dzieje i rzeczy jej*. Poznań, 1859.

Lelewel, Joachim. "Uwagi nad dziejami Polski i ludu je." In *Wybór pism historycznych*, edited by Helena Więckowska, 145–82. Wroclaw, 1949.

Lincoln, W. Bruce. *In the Vanguard of Reform: Russia's Enlightened Bureaucrats*. Dekalb, IL, 1986.

Lincoln, W. Bruce. *Nicholas I: Emperor and Autocrat of All the Russias*. Bloomington, IN, 1978.

"List Władysława Gomułki z 27 III 1971 do członków KC PZPR." In *Gomułka i inni: Dokumenty z archiwum KC, 1948–1982*, edited by Jakub Andrzejewski, 196–237. London, 1987.

Lohr, Eric. *Russian Citizenship: From Empire to Soviet Union*. Cambridge, MA, 2012.

Lukowski, Jerzy. *Disorderly Liberty: The Political Culture of the Polish-Lithuanian Commonwealth in the Eighteenth Century*. London, 2010.

Lukowski, Jerzy. *Liberty's Folly: The Polish-Lithuanian Commonwealth in the Eighteenth Century, 1697–1795*. London, 1991.

Lukowski, Jerzy. *The Partitions of Poland, 1772, 1793, 1795*. New York, 1999.

Maciejko, Paweł. *The Mixed Multitude: Jakub Frank and the Frankist Movement, 1755–1816*. Philadelphia, PA, 2011.

Madriaga, Isabel de. *Russia in the Age of Catherine the Great*. New Haven, CT, 1981.

Major, J. Russell. *Representative Government in Early Modern France*. New Haven, CT, 1980.

Matsuzato, Kimitaka. "The Issue of Zemstvos in Right-Bank Ukraine, 1864–

1905: Russian Anti-Polonism under the Challenges of Modernization." *Jahrbücher für Geschichte Osteuropas* 51, no. 2 (2003): 218–35.

Mayer, Arno J. *The Persistence of the Old Regime: Europe to the Great War*. New York, 1981.

Mazower, Mark. *Salonica, City of Ghosts: Christians, Muslims and Jews, 1430–1950*. New York, 2005.

Mazurkiewicz, Józef. *Jurydyki lubelskie*. Wrocław, 1956.

Mazurkiewicz, Józef. "Likwidacja ustroju miejskiego mniejszych miast w Księstwie Warszawskim i Królestwie Polskim w okresie przed masową zmianą miast na osadę (1807–1864)." *Rocznik lubelski* 10 (1967): 211–28.

Mazurkiewicz, Józef. "Lublin w okresie reform (1764–1795)." In *Dzieje Lublina: Próba syntezy*, vol. 1, edited by Józef Mazurkiewicz, Jan Dobrzański, and Jerzy Kłoczowski, 174–84. Lublin, 1965.

Mazurkiewicz, Józef, and Władysław Ćwik. "Własność w miastach prywatnych Lubelszczyzny doby Księstwa Warszawskiego i Królestwa Kongresowego (1809–1866)." *Annales Universitatis Mariae Curie-Skłodowska, Sectio G: Ius* 4 (1957): 1–116.

Mazurkiewicz, Józef, Jerzy Reder, and Jerzy Markiewicz. "Miasta prywatne powiatu lubelskiego a ich dziedzice w XIX w." *Annales Universitatis Mariae Curie-Skłodowska, Sectio G: Ius* 1 (1954): 103–97.

Mencel, Tadeusz. *Galicja Zachodnia, 1795–1809: Studium z dziejów ziem polskich zaboru austriackiego po III rozbiorze*. Lublin, 1976.

Mencel, Tadeusz. "Lublin przedkapitalistyczny." In *Dzieje Lublina: Próba syntezy*, edited by Józef Mazurkiewicz, Jan Dobrzański and Jerzy Kłoczowski, 170–84. Lublin, 1965.

Mencel, Tadeusz. "Od III rozbioru Polski do powstania styczniowego." In *Dzieje Bychawy*, edited by Ryszard Szczygieł, 73–80. Lublin, 1994.

Mencel, Tadeusz. "Organizacja i działność administracji miejskiej w Lublinie w latach, 1809–1866." *Rocznik lubelski* 4 (1962): 45–112.

Michałowska-Mycielska, Anna. *The Jewish Community: Authority and Social Control in Poznań and Swarzędz, 1650–1793*. Translated by Alicja Adamowicz. Wrocław, 2008.

Michalski, Jerzy. "The Jewish Question in Polish Public Opinion during the First Two Decades of Stanisław August Poniatowski's Reign." In *Studies in the History of the Jews in Old Poland: In Honor of Jacob Goldberg*, edited by Adam Teller, 123–46. Jerusalem, 1998.

Michalski, Jerzy. "Plan Czartoryskich naprawy Rzeczypospolitej." *Kwartalnik Historyczny* 63, no. 4–5 (1956): 29–43.

Michalski, Jerzy. "Wokół powrotu Karola Radziwiłła z emigracji pobarskiej." *Kwartalnik Historyczny* 106, no. 4 (1999): 21–72.

Michalski, Jerzy. "Zagadnienie polityki antycechowej w czasach Stanisława Augusta." *Przegląd Historzyczny* 45, no. 4 (1954): 635–51.

Mierzwiński, Henryk. "Kock w czasach Anny Jabłonowskiej." *Rocznik lubelski* 27–28 (1985–1986): 61–84.

Mikhailyna, P. V. "Z istorii sotsial'no-ekonomichnoho zhittia Ukrains'kikh mist (Kinets' XVI–persha polovyna XVII st.)." *Ukrains'kyi Istorychnyi Zhurnal* 11 (1969): 66–72.

Miller, Alexei. *The Ukrainian Question: The Russian Empire and Nationalism in the Nineteenth Century*. Budapest, 2003.

Miller, Jaroslav. *Urban Societies in East-Central Europe, 1500–1700*. Burlington, VT, 2008.

Mironov, B. N. *Sotsial'naia istoriia Rossii perioda imperii (XVIII–nachalo XX v.): Geneza lichnosti, demokraticheskoi sem'i, grazhdanskogo obshchestva i pravovogo gosudarstva*. 2 vols. St. Petersburg, 1999.

Moraski, Bryon J., and William M. Reisinger. "Eroding Democracy: Federal Intervention in Russia's Gubernatorial Elections." *Democratization* 14, no. 4 (2007): 603–19.

Morgan, Ruth P. *Governance by Decree: The Impact of the Voting Rights Act in Dallas*. Lawrence, KS, 2004.

Moriakova, O. V. *Sistema mestnogo upravleniia v Rossii pri Nikolae I*. Moscow, 1998.

Mościcki, Henryk. *Dzieje porozbiorowe Litwy i Rusi. Vol. 1: 1772–1800*. Vilnius, 1913.

Moullier, Igor. "Police et politique de la ville sous Napoléon." *Revue d'histoire moderne et contemporaine* 54, no. 2 (2007): 117–39.

Muir, Edward. "Was There Republicanism in the Renaissance Republics? Venice after Agnadello." In *Venice Reconsidered: The History and Civilization of an Italian City-State, 1297–1797*, edited by John Martin and Dennis Romano, 138–67. Baltimore, MD, 2000.

Munro, George. "The Charter to the Towns Reconsidered: The St. Petersburg Connection." *Canadian-American Slavic Studies* 23, no. 1 (1989): 17–35.

Mycielski, Maciej. *Rząd Królestwa Polskeigo wobec sejmików i zgromadzeń gminnych*. Warsaw, 2010.

Nardova, Valeriia A. "Municipal Government after the 1870 Reform." In *Russia's Great Reforms, 1855–1881*, edited by Ben Eklof, John Bushnell, and Larissa Zakharova, 181–96. Bloomington, IN, 1994.

Nières, Claude. *Les Villes de Bretagne au XVIIIe siècle*. Rennes, 2004.

Nieuważny, Andrzej. "The Polish Kingdom (1815–1830): Continuity or Change?" In *Napoleon's Legacy: Problems of Government in Restoration Europe*, edited by David Laven and Lucy Riall, 116–24. New York, 2000.

Nirenberg, David. *Communities of Violence: Persecution of Minorities in the Middle Ages*. Princeton, NJ, 1996.

"Obshchestvennoe obsuzhdenie proekta istoriko-kul'turnogo standarta." Online at http://минобрнауки.рф/документы/3483/.

Oestreich, Gerhard. *Neostoicism and the Early Modern State*. Translated by David McLintock. Cambridge, UK, 1982.

Opas, Tomasz. "Der Emanzipationsprozess der Privatgrundherrschaftlichen Städte im Königreich Galizien und Londomerein als Forschungsproblem." *Österreichische Osthefte* 32, no. 2 (1990): 358–75.

Opas, Tomasz. "Miasta prywatne a Rzeczpospolita." *Kwartalnik Historyczny* 78, no. 1 (1971): 28–47.

Opas, Tomasz. "Miasta prywatne w świetle ustawy 'Miasta nasze królewskie wolne w państwach Rzeczypospolitej' z 1791 r." *Czasopismo Prawno-Historyczne* 25, no. 2 (1973): 221–29.

Opas, Tomasz. "Powinności na rzecz dziedziców w miastach szlacheckich województwa lubelskiego w drugiej połowie XVII i w XVIII wieku." *Rocznik lubelski* XIV (1971): 121–43.

Opas, Tomasz. "Własność w miastach szlacheckich województwa lubelskiego w XVIII wieku." *Czasopismo Prawno-Historyczne* 22, no. 1 (1970): 21–54.

Opas, Tomasz. "Wolność osobista mieszczan miast szlacheckich województwa lubelskiego w drugiej połowie XVII i w XVIII wieku." *Przegląd Historzyczny* 61, no. 4 (1970): 609–27.

Opas, Tomasz. "Z badań nad przywracaniem miastom prawo apelacji do asesorii i innych sądów państwowych w XVIII wieku." *Czasopismo Prawno-Historyczne* 41, no. 1 (1989): 153–73.

Opas, Tomasz. "Z badań nad zagadnieniem wolności osobistej mieszczan miast prywatnych w Polsce XVII i XVIII wieku." *Czasopismo Prawno-Historyczne* 35, no. 1 (1983): 59–93.

Orłowski, Ryszard. *Między obowiązkiem obywatelskim a interesem własnym: Andrzej Zamoyski, 1717–1792*. Lublin, 1974.

Pienkos, Angela T. *The Imperfect Autocrat: Grand Duke Constantine Pavlovich and the Polish Congress Kingdom*. Boulder, CO, 1987.

Plattner, Irmgard. "Josephinismus und Bürokratie." In *Josephinismus als Aufgeklärter Absolutismus*, edited by Helmut Reinalter, 53–69. Vienna, 2008.

Plokhy, Serhii. *The Cossack Myth: History and Nationhood in the Age of Empires*. Oxford, 2012.

Pocock, J. G. A. *The Machiavellian Moment: Florentine Political Thought and the Atlantic Republican Tradition*. Princeton, NJ, 2003.

Polonsky, Anthony. "Introduction: The Shtetl, Myth and Reality." *Polin: Studies in Polish Jewry* 17 (2004): 3–24.

Polonsky, Anthony. *The Jews in Poland and Russia. Vol I: 1350–1881*. Portland, OR, 2010.

Polovtsov, A. A., ed. *Russkii biograficheskii slovar.'* 25 vols. St. Petersburg, 1896–1918.

Pomeranz, Kenneth. *The Great Divergence: China, Europe, and the Making of the Modern World Economy*. Princeton, NJ, 2000.

Porter, Brian. *When Nationalism Began to Hate: Imagining Modern Politics in Nineteenth-Century Poland*. Oxford, 2000.

Proudfoot, Lindsay J. *Urban Patronage and Social Authority: The Management of the Duke of Devonshire's Towns in Ireland, 1764–1891*. Washington, DC, 1995.

Ptaśnik, Jan. "Walki o demokratyzację Lwowa od XVI do XVIII wieku." *Kwartalnik Historyczny* 39, no. 2 (1925): 228–57.

Putnam, Robert. *Making Democracy Work: Civic Traditions in Modern Italy*. Princeton, NJ, 1993.

Raeff, Marc. *The Well-Ordered Police State: Social and Institutional Change through Law in the Germanies and Russia, 1600–1800*. New Haven, CT, 1983.

Reinalter, Helmut. "Der Josephinismus als Variante des Aufgeklärten Absolutismus und seine Reform Komplexe." In *Josephinismus als Aufgeklärter Absolutismus*, edited by Helmut Reinalter, 9–16. Vienna, 2008.

Riabinin, Jan. *Rada miejska lubelska w XVIII wieku*. Lublin, 1933.

Robbins, Richard, Jr. *The Tsar's Viceroys: Russian Provincial Governors in the Last Years of the Empire*. Ithaca, NY, 1987.

Rohdewald, Stefan. *"Vom Polocker Venedig." Kollektives Handeln sozialer Gruppen in einer Stadt zwischen Ost- und Mitteleuropa (Mittelalter, Frühe Neuzeit, 19. Jh. bis 1914)*. Stuttgart, 2005.

Rosman, Moshe. *Founder of Hasidism: A Quest for the Historical Ba'al Shem Tov*. Berkeley, CA, 1996.

Rosman, Moshe. *The Lords' Jews: Magnate-Jewish Relations in the Polish-Lithuanian Commonwealth in the Eighteenth Century*. Cambridge, MA, 1990.

Rostworowski, Emanuel. "Miasta i mieszczanie w ustroju Trzeciego Maja." In *Sejm Czteroletni i jego tradycje*, edited by Jerzy Kowecki, 138–51. Warsaw, 1991.

Rostworowski, Emanuel. *Ostatni król Rzeczypospolitej: Geneza i upadek Konstytucji 3 maja*. Warsaw, 1966.

Rothschild, Joseph. *East Central Europe between the Two World Wars*. Seattle, 1974.

Rożenowa, Halina. *Produkcja wódki i sprawa pijaństwa w Królestwie Polskim, 1815–1863*. Warsaw, 1961.

Rutkowski, Jan. *Historia gospodarcza Polski (do 1864)*. Warsaw, 1953.

Ryndziunskii, P. G. *Gorodskoe grazhdanstvo doreformennoi Rossii*. Moscow, 1958.

Sabean, David Warren. *Power in the Blood: Popular Culture and Village Discourse in Early Modern Germany*. Cambridge, UK, 1983.

Schilling, Heinz. *Religion, Political Culture and the Emergence of Early Modern Society: Essays in German and Dutch History*. Leiden, 1992.

Schneider, Robert Alan. *Public Life in Toulouse, 1463–1789: From Municipal Republic to Cosmopolitan City*. Ithaca, NY, 1989.

Scott, H. M. "Reform in the Habsburg Monarchy, 1740–90." In *Enlightened Absolutism: Reform and Reformers in Later Eighteenth-Century Europe*, edited by H. M. Scott, 145–87. Ann Arbor, MI, 1989.

Scott, James C. *Seeing like a State: How Certain Schemes to Improve the Human Condition Have Failed*. New Haven, CT, 1998.

Senkowska-Głuck, Monika. "Les institutions napoléoniennes dans l'histoire de la nation polonaise." *Annales Historiques de la Révolution Française* 53, no. 4 (1981): 541–47.

Serejski, Marian Henryk. *Europa a rozbiory Polski: Studium historiograficzne*. Warsaw, 1970.

Skinner, Quentin. *The Foundations of Modern Political Thought*. 2 vols. Cambridge, UK, 1978.

Skinner, Quentin. *Liberty before Liberalism*. Cambridge, 1998.

Skowronek, Jerzy. "Eksperyment liberalizmu parlamentarnego w Królestwie Polskim." *Przegląd Humanistyczny* 3, no. 330 (1995): 1–14.

Śladkowski, Wiesław. "Pod zaborem austriackim, w księstwie warszawskim i królewstwie polskim 1795–1831." In *Dzieje lubelszczyzny*, edited by Tadeusz Mencel, 485–541. Warsaw, 1974.

Śladkowski, Wiesław. "W epoce zaborów." In *Lublin: Dzieje miasta Vol. II: XIX i XX wiek*, edited by Tadeusz Radzik, Wiesław Śladkowski, Grzegorz Wójcikowski, and Włodzimierz Wójcikowski, 11–148. Lublin, 2000.

Smith, Alison K. *For the Common Good and Their Own Well-Being: Social Estates in Imperial Russia*. Oxford, 2014.

Smith, J. Toulmin. *Local Self-Government and Centralisation: The Characteristics of Each, And Its Practical Tendencies as Affecting Social, Moral, and Political Welfare and Progress, Including Comprehensive Outlines of the English Constitution*. London, 1851.

Smitt, Fedor. *Istoriia pol'skago vozstaniia i voiny 1830 i 1831 godov*. 3 vols. St. Petersburg, 1863.

Smoleński, Władysław. *Jan Dekert Prezydent Starej Warszawy i sprawa miejska podczas Sejmu Czterletniego*. Warsaw, 1912.

Smolka, Stanisław. *Polityka Lubeckiego przed powstaniem listopadowym*. 2 vols. Krakow, 1907.

Snyder, Timothy. *The Reconstruction of Nations: Poland, Ukraine, Lithuania, Belarus, 1569–1999*. New Haven, CT, 2003.

Springer, Arnold. "Gavriil Derzhavin's Jewish Reform Project of 1800." *Canadian-American Slavic Studies* 10, no. 1 (1976): 1–24.

Stanislawski, Michael. *Tsar Nicholas I and the Jews: The Transformation of Jewish Society, 1825–1855*. Philadelphia, PA, 1983.

Stankowa, Maria. "Zmierzch znaczenia Lublina. Upadek (1648–1764)." In *Dzieje Lublina: Próba syntezy*, vol. 1, edited by Józef Mazurkiewicz, Jan Dobrzański, and Jerzy Kłoczowski, 123–48. Lublin, 1965.

Stanley, John. "The Adaptation of the Napoleonic Political Structure in the Duchy of Warsaw (1807–1813)." *Canadian Slavonic Papers* 31, no. 2 (June 1989): 128–45.

Stanley, John. "The Politics of the Jewish Question in the Duchy of Warsaw, 1807–1813." *Jewish Social Studies* 44, no. 1 (Winter 1982): 47–62.

Stanziani, Alessandro. "Statisticiens, zemstva, et état dans la Russie des anneés 1880." *Cahiers du Monde Russe et Soviétique* 32, no. 4. (1991): 445–68.

Starr, Frederick. *Decentralization and Self-Government in Russia, 1830–1870*. Princeton, NJ, 1972.

Stegnii, P. V. *Razdely Pol'shi i diplomatiia Ekateriny II: 1772, 1793, 1795*. Moscow, 2002.

Stone, Daniel. "Jews and the Urban Question in Late Eighteenth Century Poland." *Slavic Review* 50, no. 3 (Autumn 1991): 531–41.

Stroynowski, Andrzej. *Opozycja sejmowa w dobie rządów Rady Nieustającej: studium z dziejów kultury politycznej*. Łódź, 2005.

Surdacki, Marian. *Urzędów w XVII i XVIII wieku: Miasto—Społeczeństwo—Życie codzienne*. Lublin, 2007.

Szczygieł, Ryszard. "Zamość w czasach staropolskich." In *Czterysta lat Zamościa*, edited by Jerzy Kowalczyk, 95–116. Wrocław, 1983.

Szelényi, Balázs. "The Dynamics of Urban Development: Towns in Sixteenth and Seventeenth Century Hungary." *American Historical Review* 102, no. 2 (April 2004): 360–86.

Szyszka, Bogdan, ed. *Akademia Zamoyska i jej tradycyje*. Zamość, 1994.

Tazbir, Janusz. "Anti-Jewish Trials in Old Poland." In *Studies in the History of the Jews in Old Poland: In Honor of Jacob Goldberg*, edited by Adam Teller, 233–45. Jerusalem, 1998.

Teller, Adam. *Money, Power, and Influence in Eighteenth-Century Lithuania: The Jews on the Radziwiłł Estates*. Stanford, CA, 2016.

Teller, Adam. "Przedmowa." In *Materiały źródłowe do dziejów żydów w księgach grodzkich lubelskich z doby panowania Augusta II Sasa 1697–1733*, edited by Henryk Gmiterek, 19–34. Lublin, 2001.

Teller, Adam. "The Shtetl as an Arena for Polish-Jewish Integration in the Eighteenth Century." *Polin* 17 (2004): 25–40.

Thackeray, Frank W. *Antecedents of Revolution: Alexander I and the Polish Kingdom, 1815–1825*. Boulder, CO, 1980.

Tilmans, Karin. "Republican Citizenship and Civic Humanism in the Burgundian-Habsburg Netherlands (1477–1566)." In *Republicanism: A Shared European Tradition*, edited by Martin van Gelderen and Quentin Skinner, 1:109–25. New York, 2002.

Tocqueville, Alexis de. *The Old Regime and the French Revolution*. Translated by Stuart Gilbert. Gloucester, MA, 1978.

Tokarz, Wacław. *Galicya w początkach ery józefińskiej w świetle ankiety urzędowej z roku 1783*. Krakow, 1909.

Topolski, Jerzy. *Polska w czasach nowożytnych od środkowoeuropejskiej potęgi do utraty niepodległości (1501–1795)*. Poznań, 1994.

Treisman, Daniel. *The Architecture of Government: Rethinking Political Decentralization*. Cambridge, UK, 2007.

Tribe, Keith. "Cameralism and the Science of Government." *Journal of Modern History* 56, no. 2 (June 1984): 263–84.

Trzebiński, Wojciech. *Działalność urbanistyczna magnatów i szlachty w Polsce XVIII wieku*. Warsaw, 1962.

Trzebiński, Wojciech. "Nadzór budowlany i przepisy policyjno-budowlane w Polsce oświecenia jako środki naprawy miast królewskich." In *Miasta doby feudalnej w Europie środkowo-wschodniej: Przemiany społeczne a układy przestrzenne*, edited by Aleksander Gieysztor and Tadeusz Rosłanowski, 253–73. Warsaw, 1976.

Tworek, Stanisław. "Rozkwit miasta. Renesans." In *Dzieje Lublina: Próba syntezy*, vol. 1, edited by Józef Mazurkiewicz, Jan Dobrzański, and Jerzy Kłoczowski, 80–112. Lublin, 1965.

Tyszkiewicz, Bogna. *Komisja Dobrego Porządku w Poznaniu, 1780–1784*. Poznań, 2005.

Viroli, Maurizio. *From Politics to Reason of State: The Acquisition and Transformation of the Language of Politics*. Cambridge, UK, 1992.

Vushko, Iryna. *The Politics of Cultural Retreat: Imperial Bureaucracy in Austrian Galicia, 1772–1867*. New Haven, CT, 2015.

Wakefield, R. Andre. *The Disordered Police State: German Cameralism as Science and Practice*. Chicago, 2009.

Walicki, Andrzej. *The Enlightenment and the Birth of Modern Nationhood: Polish Political Thought from Noble Republicanism to Tadeusz Kościuszko*. Translated by Emma Harris. Notre Dame, IN, 1989.

Walker, Mack. *German Home Towns: Community, State, and General Estate, 1648–1871*. Ithaca, NY, 1971.

Wąsicki, Jan. *Ziemie polskie pod zaborem pruskim: Wielkie Księstwo Poznańskie, 1815–1848*. Poznań, 1980.

Weber, Eugene. *Peasants into Frenchmen: The Modernization of Rural France, 1870–1914*. Stanford, CA, 1976.

Weber, Max. *Economy and Society: An Outline of Interpretive Sociology*. Edited by Guenther Roth and Claus Wittich. New York, 1968.

Weeks, Theodore R. *Nation and State in Late Imperial Russia: Nationalism and Russification on the Western Frontier, 1863–1914*. Dekalb, IL, 1996.

Wejnert, Aleksander. *O starostwach w Polsce do końca XVIII wieku z dołączeniem wykazu ich miejscowości*. Warsaw, 1877.

Whyte, Ian D. "The Function and Social Structure of Scottish Burghs of Barony in the Seventeenth and Eighteenth Centuries." In *Gründung und Bedeutung kleinerer Städte in nördlichen Europa der frühen Neuzeit*, edited by Antoni Mączak and Christopher Smout, 11–24. Hanover, 1991.

Wodziński, Marcin."'Wilkiem orać': Polskie projekty kolonizacji rolnej żydów 1775–1823." In *Małżeństwo z rozsądku? Żydzi w społeczeństwie dawnej Rzeczypospolitej*, edited by Marcin Wodziński and Anna Michałowska-Mycielska, 105–29. Wrocław, 2007.

Wodziński, Marcin. *Władze Królestwa Polskiego wobec chasydyzmu*. Wrocław, 2008.

Wojtowicz, Jerzy. "The Town in the Social Thought of the Enlightenment." *Acta Poloniae Historica* 67 (1993): 101–17.

Wolff, Larry. *The Idea of Galicia: History and Fantasy in Habsburg Political Culture*. Stanford, CA, 2010.

Wolff, Larry. *Inventing Eastern Europe: The Map of Civilization on the Mind of the Enlightenment*. Stanford, CA, 1994.

Woolf, Stuart. *Napoleon's Integration of Europe*. New York, 1991.

Wyrobisz, Andrzej. "Rola miast prywatnych w Polsce w XVI i XVII wieku." *Przegląd Historzyczny* 65, no. 1 (1974): 19–45.

Yack, Bernard. "The Myth of the Civic Nation." In *Theorizing Nationalism*, edited by Ronald Beinger, 103–18. Albany, NY, 1999.

Yoder, Jennifer A. "Decentralization and Regionalism after Communism: Administrative and Territorial Reform in Poland and the Czech Republic." *Europe-Asia Studies* 55, no. 2 (March 2003): 263–86.

Zahorski, Andrzej. *Centralne instytucje policyjne w Polsce w dobie rozbiorów*. Warsaw, 1959.

Zaionchkovskii, Petr. *Provedenie v zhizn' krest'ianskoi reformy 1861 g*. Moscow, 1958.

Zakrzewska-Dubasowa, Mirosława. "Polityka handlowa Jana Zamoyskiego i jego następców." *Annales Universitatis Mariae Curie-Skłodowska, Sectio F: Historia* 38, no. 6 (1983): 93–113.

Zaremska, Hanna. *Niegodne rzemiosło: Kat w społeczeństwie Polski, XIV–XVI w*. Warsaw, 1986.

Ziblatt, Daniel. *Structuring the State: The Formation of Italy and Germany and the Puzzle of Federalism*. Princeton, NJ, 2006.

Zienkowska, Krystyna. *Jan Dekert*. Warsaw, 1982.

Zienkowska, Krystyna. "Reforms relating to the Third Estate." In *Constitu-*

tion and Reform in Eighteenth Century Poland: The Constitution of 3 May 1791, edited by Samuel Fiszman, 330–51. Bloomington, IN, 1997.

Zienkowska, Krystyna. *Sławetni i urodzeni: Ruch polityczny mieszczaństwa w dobie Sejmu Czteroletniego*. Warsaw, 1976.

Złotkowski, Dariusz. *Miasta departamentu kaliskiego w okresie Księstwa Warsawskiego (Studium gospodarcze)*. Częstochowa, 2001.

Index